D1826483

You Can
Become
Pure In Heart

You Can Become Pure In Heart

Don M and Arda Jean Christensen
Mary Christensen Latimer

Salt Lake City, Utah
1996

Blessed are all the pure in heart,
for they shall see God.

3 Nephi 12: 8

Acknowledgments

The authors thank all those who assisted in the preparation of this book. So many hours of research, typing, editing, and proofreading, plus myriad other errands required for the many quotations and scriptural references were done by many people. We mention Stacey Jensen, Don's secretaries Linda Mano and Jeri Stevens; our daughter-in-law Angela Christensen; our granddaughter Lexia Dew; and particularly our daughter Ruth Hocker for fearless editing.

We are grateful to the following people who read the manuscript and made helpful suggestions: Einar Anderson, Jackie Davey, James Day, Jeffery Jones, Kenneth Mattheson, Diane Phillips, Billie Telford, and Robert Warnock. Thanks to Cindy Ruybal for inspiration and for the gift of time.

Thanks also to our family: Rolf D. and Jean Larie Dixon, William S. and Jolene Dew, Kyle D. Latimer, Martin D. and Sherri Christensen, Evan W. and Sonja Christensen, Rachel and Jeremiah K Clark, Glenn L. and Angela Christensen, and Jeffrey C. and Ruth Angela Hocker, for reading the manuscript and making comments. The many years of paying tuition have been well rewarded.

Special thanks to Mary's children: Emily Jean, Andrew Kyle, and Eliza Ruth, for "donating" their mother for the writing of this book over the several years it was in process. They stood next to the word processor for eons, patiently waiting for mom to "finish just one more page."

All the chapters were a cooperative effort, and separate authorship is not established.

We give our gratitude, admiration, and sincere appreciation for the beautiful cover, original artwork by Jean Dixon, M.A.

Please note that source citations within the text refer to author, book title, and page numbers. Full publishing information is available in the bibliography.

Contents

SECTION II HOW TO DO IT

The Divine Commission

This is number two in the companion volumes, *You Can Control Your Thoughts* and *You Can Become Pure in Heart*. In exploring the influence of our thoughts in relation to our actions, we learn from the scriptures and the prophets that we can control the outcome of our lives by controlling our thoughts. This knowledge enables us to control our actions and affect the results of those actions.

In this way we can accomplish our earthly missions, fulfill our divine destinies and receive the happiness that results therefrom, both in this life and in the eternity to come. The majestic truth is that we can become pure in heart. This is our destiny, our goal, and our challenge. This is the test we came here to pass. Becoming pure in heart not only is possible, but is a divine commission from our Heavenly Father who sent us here. It is our purpose and mission in mortality.

Sometimes we look at our own humble situations, and feel that the scriptures are above us. We feel that the stories therein are about unique or unusual people who were somehow better than we are, more important than we are—that they were somehow more worthy, more able, or more blessed than we, and there is no hope for ordinary persons like us. A prayerful consideration of the whole gospel will reassure us that we are indeed all children of God, and that He is no respecter of persons. The arms of His love are stretched out to each of us, and His gospel of hope is for all of us without regard to status.

The Message of the Ages

This book will explore the principles of purification one by one in simple language. It will be shown that through an understanding of these principles, ordinary members of the Church can become pure in heart. The research draws heavily upon the words of the prophets. The message of the ages, the proclamation of the good news of the gospel, is repeated throughout the scriptures, and repeated over and over again by the prophets of this dispensation. Quotations from many prophets, ancient as well as modern, show the admonitions re-echoing through time. The problems are universal, and the solutions are timeless. The quoted writers received their direction and inspiration from the Lord Himself.

A theme is carried through the ages: *Keep the commandments.* Commandments are given for a purpose. By them we learn, by them we are empowered to do good, by them we show reverence and gratitude to God, by them we make ourselves worthy, by them we are enabled to save ourselves and help our families and others. As we learn, the key is to keep this question at the forefront: "What change will this knowledge make in my life?" Knowledge is power. Faith in God is power. Purity is power. Our purpose in life is to deliver that power to the accomplishment of good. With God's help we can succeed.

By His own word, any of His children who love (fear) the Lord are entitled to His unfathomable blessings. We are to begin with love, proceed on through obedience, repentance, service, baptismal and temple covenants, and enduring faith; then by the Holy Spirit the "hidden mysteries" of eternity will be unfolded, in our minds and hearts, and in our lives here and hereafter. Those who have simple faith and are educated by the Spirit of the Lord will receive more blessings than those who are educated and wise only in the ways of the world.

> For thus saith the Lord—I, the Lord, am merciful and gracious unto those who fear me, and delight to honor those who serve me in righteousness and in truth unto the end.
>
> Great shall be their reward and eternal shall be their glory.
>
> And to them will I reveal all mysteries, yea, all the hidden mysteries of my kingdom from days of old, and for ages to come, will I make known unto them the good pleasure of my will concerning all things pertaining to my kingdom.
>
> Yea, even the wonders of eternity shall they know, and things to come will I show them, even the things of many generations.
>
> And their wisdom shall be great, and their understanding reach to heaven; and before them the wisdom of the wise shall perish, and the understanding of the prudent shall come to naught.
>
> For by my Spirit will I enlighten them, and by my power will I make known unto them the secrets of my will—yea, even those things which eye has not seen, nor ear heard, nor yet entered into the heart of man. (D&C 76:5-10.)

Our Consecrated Journey

This is our commission, the quest the Lord has conferred upon us: to overcome all obstacles and become pure in heart, with the help of the Lord. We have the journey and the goal outlined for us. He who appointed us to this expedition has provided for us the map, the Guide, instructions, directions, provisions, roadsigns, filling stations along the way, safe havens for rest and refreshment, continual protection, and a clear picture of the glorious destination. He has also endowed us with the power to do it.

Once we shouted for joy when we knew we would be allowed to undertake this pursuit. Now we are here, in the midst of the challenge, surrounded by hazards and demands we have forgotten that we accepted. Let us once again review our plan and map, and put our goal firmly before us. On both sides of the veil are fellow journeymen who urge and inspire us forward. Prophets, Church leaders, friends, and family offer encouraging words and support. Unseen beings assist us. Our leader, our Elder Brother, does not ask us to walk anywhere He has not already trod. He pleads, "Come, follow me."

The Full Armor of God

The Apostle Paul urged this course upon the former-day Saints in Ephesus. He tells them (Ephesians, chapter 6) that God is no respecter of persons (v. 9). He prompts them to put on the protective armor God their Father has provided, and reminds them of the real adversaries they face: "For we wrestle not against flesh and blood, but against principalities, against powers, against the rulers of the darkness of this world, against spiritual wickedness in high places" (v. 12).

He enumerates the protections and powers of the full armor of God. We can choose these to help us on our journey (verses 13-17). They are:

1. The girdle of truth.
2. The breastplate of righteousness.
3. The shoes, hiking boots, if you will, of the gospel of peace.
4. The shield of faith.
5. The helmet of salvation.
6. The sword of the Spirit, which is the word of God.

We have applied this analogy to the principles of purification found in the Articles of Faith. These are the tools, the protection, and the equipment we need for our journey. Paul states the need to keep in constant communication with the Lord by "Praying always, with all prayer and supplication in the Spirit" (v. 18). Let us use our tools, communicate steadily with home base, and enjoy the expedition. Part of the reward is the excitement of the search. We will find much to cherish as we go along.

Section I

Principles of Purification

---- 1 ----

You Can Become Pure in Heart

Purity of Heart

What does it mean to be pure in heart? Elder Bruce McConkie said, "Those who love the Lord, and who seek to do his will, have as their objective the cleansing, *purifying*, and sanctifying of their own souls. The *pure in heart* are those who are free from moral defilement or guilt; who have bridled their passions, put off the natural man and become saints through the atonement; who have been born again, becoming the sons and daughters of Christ; who are walking in paths of uprightness and virtue and seeking to do all things that further the interests of the Lord's earthly kingdom." (*Mormon Doctrine*, p. 612.)

This sounds like a lofty goal, doesn't it? When we look at our lives we may feel overcome at the thought of trying to "put off the natural man and become saints," since this means bridling our passions, and "walking in paths of uprightness and virtue." Sometimes we may feel that it is all we can do to get through the day. But we need to always remember that this life is more than just the activities we engage in each day. It is an eternal struggle against selfishness and the evil one. An oft-stated truism is that we are not mortals seeking a spiritual experience, we are spiritual beings in the midst of a mortal experience.

The Prophet Joseph Smith spoke of his own life as being purified by the experiences he went through, not all of them pleasant: "I am like a huge, rough stone rolling down from a high mountain; and the only polishing I get is when some corner gets rubbed off by coming in contact with something else, . . . knocking off a corner here and a corner there. Thus I will become a smooth and polished shaft in the quiver of the Almighty." (*Teachings*, p. 304.)

Pure Hearts and Pure Motives

Elder Dallin H. Oaks describes purity of heart using these scriptures:

"Who shall ascend into the hill of the Lord?" the Psalmist asked, "or who shall stand in his holy place? He that hath clean hands, and a pure heart" (Psalms 24:3-4). "I say unto you," Alma declared to his people, "can ye look up to God at that day with a pure heart and clean hands?" (Alma 5:19).

If we do righteous acts and refrain from evil acts, we have clean hands.

If we act for the right motives and if we refrain from forbidden desires and attitudes, we have pure hearts. Those who would "look up to God," those who would ascend and stand in the ultimate "holy place," must have "clean hands, and a pure heart." (*Pure in Heart*, p. 1.)

The ultimate goal of our efforts is to stand before God with clean hands and a pure heart. Be assured that it is possible to become pure in heart—and in this life. This does not mean to be perfect. If our hearts are right before the Lord, and our motives are pure, it is accounted unto us for righteousness, even though at times we may make a misstep. Perfection must be understood as different from purity of heart.

Elder Oaks continues, "The Savior also taught the importance of our desires. 'Blessed are they which do hunger and thirst after righteousness,' he taught in the Sermon on the Mount (Matthew 5:6; 3 Nephi 12:6). The scriptures say that when we desire righteousness our 'heart is right' with God." (*Pure in Heart*, p. 4.)

So, as Elder Oaks says, when we *desire* righteousness, our hearts are right with God. If we have done all in our power to accomplish a righteous act, Elder Oaks explains that the Lord will count it as though we had accomplished it. This idea is beautifully illustrated in the Book of Mormon. King Benjamin was speaking to the poor of his people who nevertheless desired to give of their substance to others, but were unable because of their poverty. He said, "I say unto the poor, ye who have not and yet have sufficient, that ye remain from day to day; I mean all you who deny the beggar, because ye have not; I would that ye say in your hearts that: I give not because I have not, but if I had I would give. And now, if ye say this in your hearts ye remain guiltless, otherwise ye are condemned." (Mosiah 4:24-25)

Elder Oaks quotes President Brigham Young's words on the importance of our motives:

> No matter what the outward appearance is—if . . . the hearts of the people are fully set to do the will of their Father in heaven, though they may falter and do a great many things through the weaknesses of human nature, yet, they will be saved. . . .
>
> If their motives are pure, . . . their acts will be discerned by the Spirit of the Lord, and will be appreciated for what they were intended. If people act from pure motives, though their outward movements may not always be so pleasant as our traditions would prefer, yet God will make those acts result in the best good to the people. [*Journal of Discourses* 5:256.] (Quoted in *Pure in Heart*, p. 60.)

The manifestation of pure motives is integrity—no pretense or hypocrisy, complete honesty before God and man. President Spencer W. Kimball uses these synonyms for integrity: "quality or state of being complete, undivided, unbroken, unimpaired; purity, moral soundness, unadulterated genuineness, deep sincerity, courage, honesty, uprightness, and righteousness." (*Teachings of Spencer W. Kimball*, p. 192.) This honesty will display itself in the everyday actions of an individual who is seeking to become pure in heart. Commonplace dishonesties such as lying, cheating, pretentiousness, thievery, trickery will find no place in pure lives. Seeking the good of others like unto our own good replaces impulses to get gain by deceit. Our Father in Heaven, who looks upon the heart, knows what our true motives are—there is no deceiving Him. Integrity is achieved when we truly submit our will to His, desiring what He desires because we have lost our selves in His service. When His love is in our hearts, our selfish desires tend to disappear.

How Can We Become Pure in Heart?

We must become pure in heart in order to gain our exaltation. As Elder Bruce R. McConkie states, "In the final analysis, men are not saved unless they have struggled and labored through repentance and the attainment of forgiveness to the point that they stand clean and spotless before the judgment bar, for 'no unclean thing can inherit the kingdom of heaven.' (Alma 11:27.)" (*Mormon Doctrine*, p. 298.) This includes cleanliness of mind, which is a basic step toward cleanliness of heart. Other important aspects follow.

How can we become pure in heart? We love our Savior, and draw closer to Him, because "Christ is the *Purifier*." Elder McConkie writes: "It is in and through him and his atoning sacrifice that the righteous become pure, clean, spotless, and qualified to dwell in his presence. It is by his power and command that the Holy Ghost operates. He is also the embodiment of the attribute of purity, and the very plan of salvation itself consists in purifying oneself even as he is pure." (*Mormon Doctrine*, p. 611.)

Jesus Christ made it possible for us to repent of all our sins and become pure in heart. He gave His life for us and redeemed us, giving the glory to His Father in Heaven; never with a thought of gain for himself, but out of pure love for us. Then He told us to "Love one another as I have loved you." (John 13:34.) We are to lose our will, as He did, in the will of our Father, and to act from pure love one toward another, as He did. He taught His disciples plainly this doctrine of love just before His crucifixion, preparing them to carry on after He left them. "By this," He said, "shall all men know that ye are my disciples, if you have love one to another." (John 13:35.) Then He promised them that the Comforter would come and stand by them. The Comforter is the Holy Ghost, which we receive upon baptism. If we live worthy lives, the Holy Ghost will be our companion. He will teach, guide, and direct our lives (see John 14:26; 16:13-15). He will cleanse, sanctify, and purify our souls and prepare us to dwell with our Father in Heaven.

Elder McConkie goes on to explain the purifying power of the Holy Ghost in these words: "The Holy Ghost is also a *Purifier* in that, because of Christ and the atonement, this Spirit member of the Godhead has power given him to cleanse, sanctify, and purify the human soul." (*Mormon Doctrine*, p. 612.)

He then refers to the Book of Mormon where the Savior tells us that receiving the Holy Ghost sanctifies us: "Repent, all ye ends of the earth, and come unto me and be baptized in my name, that ye may be sanctified by the reception of the Holy Ghost, that ye may stand spotless before me at the last day." (3 Nephi 27:20.)

A change is necessitated from the carnal state to a pure state in which one has been forgiven of his sins, that is, purified through the atoning blood of Christ. Elder McConkie writes, "The very process of working out one's salvation consists in the cleansing and purifying of the human soul. Men must change from their 'carnal state' to a pure state in which they have been forgiven of their sins, that is, 'purified' through 'the atoning blood of Christ.' (Mosiah 4:2.) The pure in heart shall see God, be saved in his kingdom, enter into the rest of the Lord, possess all things, be one in Christ, and have exaltation." (*Mormon Doctrine*, p. 613.)

We were sent here to be tested and proven. We must keep this uppermost in our minds. Our Father in Heaven wants us to be strict in keeping His commandments. He expects us to magnify our callings in His Church, build the kingdom, and help prepare the world for the coming of the Savior and the starting of the millennium. Each of us is to do this in our own way, according to the talents with which we are endowed.

President George Q. Cannon, formerly Counselor in the First Presidency, said:

> It should be the aim of every Latter-day Saint to be godly, to understand godliness, and to carry out godliness in his or her life, so that we all shall be like our Father in Heaven as near as we possibly can be. Jesus has given us to understand that it is possible for His disciples to be perfect; for He says: "Be ye therefore perfect, even as your Father which is in heaven is perfect." (Matthew 5:48.) He did not mean by that that we should attain to the fullness of godhood in this life, but that we should carry out in our lives and exemplify in our conduct those laws and principles which God has revealed and which are the principles of perfection and godliness. (*Gospel Truth*, p. 19.)

The Prophet Joseph Smith said, "The nearer man approaches perfection, the clearer are his views, and the greater his enjoyments, till he has overcome the evils of his life and lost every desire for sin; and like the ancients, arrives at that point of faith where he is wrapped in the power and glory of his Maker, and is caught up to dwell with Him." (*History of the Church*, 2:8.)

Let's have clean hands and a pure heart. Let's do whatever it takes to bring this about. We have a dual goal, happiness in this life and eternal life in the world to come. There is no greater prize that we can receive. It is truly the pearl of great price. The Lord Jesus Christ tells us through the Prophet Joseph Smith that this is possible:

"But learn that he who doeth the works of righteousness shall receive his reward, even peace in this world, and eternal life in the world to come. I, the Lord, have spoken it, and the Spirit beareth record." (D&C 59:23-24.)

President Cannon assured us that this is the mission and purpose of the gospel: "There was a period when we, with Jesus and others, basked in the light of the presence of God and enjoyed His smiles. We are the children of God, and as His children there is no attribute we ascribe to Him that we do not possess, though they may be dormant or in embryo. The mission of the Gospel is to develop these powers and make us like our Heavenly Parent. I know this is true, and such knowledge makes me feel happy." (*Gospel Truth*, p. 3.)

This knowledge makes us feel happy too!

You Can Become Pure in Heart in This Life

Did you know that it is possible to become pure in heart in this life? Elder McConkie writes, "Many of the present day saints and many in former days...attained the status of the pure in heart." (*Mormon Doctrine*, p. 612.) So it is true! If we want to become pure in heart, if we love the Lord with all our hearts and want to become Christlike, we can achieve this goal while in this life. *Many* will attain the status of pure in heart!

Elder McConkie gives some examples of those who became pure in heart in this life: "Those who dwelt in Enoch's Zion attained such a high degree of purity and perfection that the Lord himself dwelt with them, they all in due course being translated and taken up into heaven. (Moses 7:16-21, 67-69.) Many of the Nephite saints yielded themselves to the Lord 'even to the purifying and the sanctification of their hearts.' (Helaman 3:35.) Alma says that among the ancients 'there were many, exceedingly great many, who were made pure and entered into the rest of the Lord.' (Alma 13:11-12.) Peter said that the hearts of some of the Gentiles were purified by faith (Acts 15:9)." (*Mormon Doctrine*, p. 612.)

So how do we become pure in heart? Part of this is cleansing our thoughts. Elder Theodore M. Burton said, "I admit that except for the Savior no person alone can completely harness his appetites and passions. I do say, however, that with the help of God we can all learn to control those appetites and passions. As we practice righteousness and approach ever closer to God, the easier it becomes to resist temptation and to live in accordance with that light and truth which emanates from Jesus Christ." (CR, *Ensign*, May 1981, p. 30.)

Beyond this, remember that part of becoming pure in heart is learning to know and understand our Father in Heaven. Elder Royden G. Derrick explains how purity of heart leads to understanding God: "The Savior said, 'Blessed are the pure in heart: for they shall see God.' (Matthew 5:8.) The dictionary has twenty-two different definitions for the word *see*, one of which is 'to understand.' When one develops purity of heart, he will come to understand God. As one develops an understanding of God, he comes to know Him. The Savior said, addressing the Father, 'And this is life eternal, that they might know thee the only true God, and Jesus Christ, whom thou hast sent.' (John 17:3.)" (CR, *Ensign*, May 1989 p. 77.)

S. Michael Wilcox, Instructor at the LDS Institute of Religion, adjacent to the University of Utah, collected scriptural incidents to show that the pure in heart will not only *understand* God, they will see him:

"Blessed are all the pure in heart, for they shall see God." (3 Nephi 12:8.) Several verses in scripture speak of seeing God: Moses "sought diligently to sanctify his people that they might behold the face of God." (D&C 84:23.) The Savior promised that "every soul who forsaketh his sins and cometh unto me, and calleth on my name, and obeyeth my voice, and keepeth my commandments, shall see my face and know that I am." (D&C 93:1.) Likewise, we are told to have an eye "single to [God's] glory" and to "sanctify yourselves that your minds become single to God, and the days will come that you shall see him." (D&C 88:67-68.) The purity needed to see God involves obedience, sanctification, and having an eye single to God's glory.

The scriptures contain numerous examples of people who reached the necessary purity of heart and were able to see God or his messengers and converse with them. The attitude they exhibited as they did so gives a beautiful picture of purity:

On the road to Damascus, Paul said, "What wilt thou have me to do?" (Acts 9:6.) The boy Samuel, as instructed by Eli, said, "Speak; for thy servant heareth." (1 Samuel 3:10.) Nephi said, "I will go and do" (1 Ne. 3:7) and "I must obey" (2 Ne. 33:15). And Mary said, "Behold the handmaid of the Lord; be it unto me according to thy word." (Luke 1:38.)

A common thread runs through each of these statements—an attitude of obedience, a purity of motive, and a desire to do the Lord's will. The eye is single to the Lord's will and glory. ("The Beatitudes, Pathway to the Savior," Ensign, January 1991, p. 19.)

As we are becoming pure in heart, we are developing an obedient attitude and pure motives. We are making our eyes single to the things of God.

Zion, the Pure in Heart

Imagine a society filled with people who are pure in heart! Elder Bruce R. McConkie affirms that some day this will be the case: "Eventually, *in this life, the hearts of the saints generally will be pure,* for Zion is to be redeemed by the pure in heart. (D&C 101:18.) Indeed, 'this is Zion—the pure in heart.' (D&C 97:21.)" (*Mormon Doctrine*, p. 612. Emphasis added.)

Among the goals of the Latter-day Saints are to become a people pure in heart, redeem Zion, build a city and a temple there, and prepare for the second coming of the Lord. President Kimball explains: "For many years we have been taught that one important end result of our labors, hopes, and aspirations in this work is the building of a Latter-day Zion, a Zion characterized by love, harmony, and peace—a Zion, in which the Lord's children are as one. . . . Zion can be built up only among those who are the pure in heart, not a people torn by covetousness or greed, but a pure and selfless people. Not a people who are pure in appearance, rather a people who are pure in heart." (*Teachings of Spencer W. Kimball*, pp. 362-363.)

The Saints of Joseph Smith's day had this goal: "A great and marvelous work is about to come forth unto the children of men. . . . Seek to bring forth and establish my Zion. Keep my commandments in all things." (D&C 14:1-6.) But it was not realized. They had to leave their Zion, Jackson County, Missouri, forced out by unrelenting persecution. We are told that there were additional reasons:

> Behold, I say unto you, were it not for the transgressions of my people, speaking concerning the church and not individuals, they might have been redeemed even now.
>
> But behold, they have not learned to be obedient to the things which I required at their hands, but are full of all manner of evil, and do not impart of their substance, as becometh saints, to the poor and afflicted among them;
>
> And are not united according to the union required by the law of the celestial kingdom. (D&C 105:2-4.)

They were unable to sufficiently purify their hearts and become united in their feelings of love of the Lord and their fellowmen. But this goal has never been rescinded by the Lord: "And now I give unto you a word concerning Zion. Zion shall be redeemed, although she is chastened for a little season. . . . Therefore, let your hearts be comforted; for all things shall work together for good to them that walk uprightly, and to the sanctification of the church. For I will raise up unto myself a pure people, that will serve me in righteousness." (D&C 100:13, 15-16.)

When the time comes again to establish Zion, the gathering of the pure in heart, will we be ready? We have been chastened for a season, for the purpose of becoming a pure-in-heart people. Let's consider the qualifications of those who will redeem Zion.

Jesus Himself gave the key to turning our hearts to purity. He said the "first and great commandment is to "Love the Lord thy God with all thy heart, and with all thy soul, and with all thy mind. . . . And the second is like unto it, Thou shalt love thy neighbour as thyself." (Matthew 22:37-40.) If we can give all our heart, soul, and mind to the love of God, losing our own will in His, He can purify us. The attitude toward those around us is likewise to be that of love, esteeming them as ourselves. In this way, our motives become pure as we seek their welfare as inspired and directed by the will of God. "On these two commandments," Jesus continued, "hang all the law and the prophets." (v. 40.)

Zion will be characterized by love, harmony, peace, and oneness, a people who are pure in heart, a people who are free from covetousness and greed, with "every man seeking the interest of his neighbor and doing all things with an eye single to the glory of God." (D&C 82:19.)

President Kimball suggested three things that we can to do "bring again Zion":

> First, we must eliminate the individual tendency to selfishness that snares the soul, shrinks the heart, and darkens the mind. . . .
>
> It is incumbent upon us to put away selfishness in our families, our business and professional pursuits, and our Church affairs. . . .
>
> Second, we must cooperate completely and work in harmony one with another. There must be unanimity in our decisions and unity in our actions. After pleading with the Saints to "let every man esteem his brother as himself" (D&C 38:24), the Lord concludes. . . . "If ye are not one ye are not mine." (D&C 38:27.)
>
> If the Spirit of the Lord is to magnify our labors, then this spirit of oneness and cooperation must be the prevailing spirit in all that we do. . . .

Third, we must lay on the altar and sacrifice whatever is required by the Lord. We begin by offering a "broken heart and a contrite spirit." We follow this by giving our best effort in our assigned fields of labor and callings. We learn our duty and execute it fully. Finally we consecrate our time, talents, and means as called upon by our file leaders and as prompted by the whisperings of the Spirit. In the Church . . . we can give expression to every ability, every righteous desire, every thoughtful impulse....and in the end, we learn it was no sacrifice at all. (*The Teachings of Spencer W. Kimball*, pp. 363-64.)

The law of consecration is the embodiment of the law of love. It should be the ruling power in the hearts of those who love the Lord. Of it, President Marion G. Romney said,

When we reach the state of having the "pure love of Christ," our desire to serve one another will have grown to the point where we will be living fully the law of consecration. Living the law of consecration exalts the poor and humbles the rich. In the process, both are sanctified. The poor, released from the bondage and humiliating limitations of poverty, are enabled as free men to rise to their full potential, both temporally and spiritually. The rich, by consecration and the imparting of their surplus for the benefit of the poor, *not by constraint, but willingly as an act of free will*, evidence that charity for their fellowmen characterized by Mormon as "the pure love of Christ." (Moroni 7:47.) "This will bring both the giver and the receiver to the common ground on which the Spirit of God can meet them." (CR, *Ensign*, November 1981, p. 93, emphasis included.)

Service develops compassion. It rids us of selfishness, greed and pride. We learn to esteem our neighbor as ourself.

Elder Bruce McConkie said, "And as we seek to build up Zion we are brought back to the Lord's definition of Zion. Our revelation says: 'This is Zion—THE PURE IN HEART.' (D&C 97:21.) Again the message comes through loud and clear. Zion is people. Zion is those whose sins are washed away in the waters of baptism. Zion is those out of whose souls dross and evil have been burned as though by fire. Zion is those who have received the baptism of fire so as to stand pure and clean before the Lord. Zion is those who keep the commandments of God." (*The Millennial Messiah*, p. 286.)

He further explained, "Wherever the saints build an old or a new Jerusalem, wherever they establish cities of holiness, wherever they create stakes of Zion, there is Zion." (p. 293.)

In a place, in a time, in a condition where all the people are committed and prepared to live pure lives, the Lord will come and dwell with His people. It is the millennial hope.

At this time let us commit ourselves to become a Zion people. Let's love our Father in Heaven and His Son Jesus Christ. Let's be obedient to all of their commandments. Love is basic. If we love our neighbors as ourselves, we will be found looking out for our neighbor's interests. We will be rid of covetousness, selfishness and greed. We will be honest and cooperative, in harmony with our fellow men. Peace, accord, and contentment are attributes of a Zion people.

The law of consecration is really the law of immeasurable love. When we have given our hearts to our Savior and our Father in Heaven, we will love all their children fullheartedly, and freely expend our time, talents, and means as needed for their uplift and good. Those who truly love have no problem with the requirements of becoming pure in heart.

As God is, Man May Be

President Lorenzo Snow brought forth a lovely and powerful statement of truth. This was a sweet revelation to him, a trust he carried for years before he was allowed to teach it openly to the Saints. President Snow tells it in his own words:

I remember an incident which occurred in Kirtland when I received my first patriarchal blessing from Father Smith. A better man never existed, nor was there a man better-loved than he. I was introduced by my sister Eliza R., though at that time I was not a Latter-day Saint and had no idea of becoming one. He said to me: "Don't worry, take it calmly and the Lord will show you, and you will want to be baptized." He told me another thing that greatly surprised me. He said, "You will be great, and as great as you want to be, as great as God Himself, and you will not wish to be greater." I could not understand this, but years after in Nauvoo while talking upon a principle of the gospel, the Spirit of God rested powerfully upon me and showed me more clearly than I can now see your faces a certain principle and its glory, and it came to me summarized in this brief sentence: "As man is now, God once was; as God is now man may be." The Spirit of God was on me in a marvelous manner all that day, and I stored that great truth away in my mind. . . .

This principle, in substance, is found also in the scriptures. The Lord said to John, as recorded in the third chapter of his Revelation: "To him that overcometh will I grant to sit with me in my throne, even as I also overcame, and am set down with my Father in his throne." . . . As John said, "Every man that hath this hope in him purifieth himself, even as [God] is pure" (1 John 3:3).

Now how is it that God proposes to confer this mighty honor upon us and to raise us to this condition of glory and exaltation? Who are we that God should do all this for us? Why, we are just beginning to find out that we are the offspring of God, born with the same faculties and powers as He possesses, capable of enlargement through the experience that we are now passing through in our second estate.

We are God's offspring. We . . . possess in our spiritual organizations the same capabilities, powers, and faculties that our Father possesses—although in an infantile state—requiring [us] to pass through a certain course of ordeal by which they will be developed and improved according to the heed we give to the principles we have received. (*Teachings of Lorenzo Snow*, pp. 1,2,6.)

The Book of Mormon closes with this ringing invitation to do just as President Snow has told us—to become perfect in Christ, as we have the power to do, being the offspring of our Heavenly Father:

Yea, come unto Christ, and be perfected in him, and deny yourselves of all ungodliness; and if ye shall deny yourselves of all ungodliness, and love God with all your might, mind, and strength, then is his grace sufficient for you, that by his grace ye may be perfect in Christ; and if by the grace of God ye are perfect in Christ, ye can in nowise deny the power of God.

And again, if ye by the grace of God are perfect in Christ, and deny not his power, then are ye sanctified in Christ by the grace of God, through the shedding of the blood of Christ, which is in the covenant of the Father unto the remission of your sins, that ye become holy, without spot. (Moroni 10:32-33.)

2

We Believe in God the Eternal Father, and in His Son Jesus Christ, and in the Holy Ghost

The Journey Begins

All who begin this journey, that is, all who are born into this world, receive the divine gift of the light of Christ to illuminate the dark way. He did not leave us alone or unattended. In the travel pack we received His light, the Spirit of Christ, which we recognize as our conscience, a compass to help us know right from wrong. "That was the true Light, which lighteth every man that cometh into the world." (John 1:9, D&C 93:2.)

"Wherefore, I beseech of you, brethren, that ye should search diligently in the light of Christ that ye may know good from evil; and if ye will lay hold upon every good thing, and condemn it not, ye certainly will be a child of Christ." (Moroni 7:19.)

This light emanates from Jesus Christ, or Jehovah, who stood with our Father in Heaven as Creator of the world, even the universe in which we reside. The purpose of this entire creation is *us*, you and me, his children—for our development and progress to eternal life! We are, as it were, the center of the universe.

> And behold, the glory of the Lord was upon Moses, so that Moses stood in the presence of God, and talked with him face to face. And

the Lord God said unto Moses: For mine own purpose have I made these things. Here is wisdom and it remaineth in me.

And by the word of my power, have I created them, which is mine Only begotten Son, who is full of grace and truth.

And worlds without number have I created; and I also created them for mine own purpose; and by the Son I created them, which is mine Only Begotten. . . .

For behold, this is my work and my glory—to bring to pass the immortality and eternal life of man. (Moses 1:31-33, 39.)

We Believe

The first Article of Faith expresses this precept: "We believe in God, the Eternal Father, and in His Son, Jesus Christ, and in the Holy Ghost." Faith in God and His Son is the starting point for building our testimonies as we take our journey of faith into the unfamiliar territory of our second estate. We put on our shoes, our hiking boots, perhaps, which is our preparation in the gospel of peace (Ephesians 6:14).

The beginning, the basis for our quest is a belief in our Father in Heaven and His Son, Jesus Christ; that they live, that they love us, and that they have infinite power. "For my thoughts are not your thoughts, neither are your ways my ways, saith the Lord. For as the heavens are higher than the earth, so are my ways higher than your ways, and my thoughts than your thoughts." (Isaiah 55:8-9.)

King Benjamin explained this when he exhorted us to "believe in God; believe that he is, and that he created all things, both in heaven and in earth; believe that he has all wisdom, and all power, both in heaven and in earth; believe that man doth not comprehend all things which the Lord can comprehend." (Mosiah 4:9.)

We cannot think of our God and creator in finite terms. His ways are not the ways of men on earth. President Brigham Young described Him thus: "He is our Heavenly Father; he is also our God, and the Maker and upholder of all things in heaven and on earth. . . . He is the Supreme Controller of the universe." (*Discourses of Brigham Young*, p. 19.)

Of God's power, Elder James E. Talmage wrote: "There is no part of creation, however remote, into which God cannot penetrate; through the medium of the Spirit the Godhead is in communication with all things at all times." (*Articles of Faith*, p. 42.)

Alma gives a strong statement for belief in the existence of God when he talks to Korihor, who was teaching his associates that there is no God: "Yea, and all things denote there is a god; yea, even the earth, and all things that are upon the face of it, yea, and its motion, yea, and also all the planets which move in their regular form do witness that there is a Supreme Creator." (Alma 30:44.)

This statement makes me think of a story of a man who was hiking out in the desert and came across a fine watch. He picked it up and noticed that it was running, and that it had the correct time. He was amazed to find something like this so far from civilization. He pondered the meaning of this and reasoned that out here in the desert were many elements, which had, through the effect of wind, water, and sunshine, combined themselves, slowly, over a great period of time, to become the metals and glass, wheels, ratchets, hands and dial, and by perhaps the greatest chance of all, had begun to run, and had adjusted itself to the correct time. The idea that someone had made that watch, that it had a Creator, crossed his mind, but he dismissed it as preposterous. There are those in society today who dismiss the idea that there was a Creator of the universe as preposterous. They prefer to hold a view that somehow all this "just happened" and that there is no governing Intelligence, no laws, no controls. Alma's statement decries this notion, which was advocated by Korihor the Anti-Christ.

The Prophet Joseph Smith addressed this issue, quoting a passage from Psalms 19:1: "If this life were all, we should be led to query, whether or not there was really any substance in existence. . . . But this life is not all; the voice of reason, the language of *inspiration*, and the Spirit of the living God, our Creator, teaches us, as we hold the record of truth in our hands . . . the heavens declare the glory of a God, and the firmament showeth His handiwork; and a moment's reflection is sufficient to teach every man of common intelligence, that all these are not the mere productions of *chance* nor could they be supported by any power less than an Almighty hand." (*Teachings*, p. 56, emphasis included.)

President Howard W. Hunter spoke of this: "'In the beginning, God created the heaven and the earth.' (Gen. 1:1.) There was a divine plan. For every plan there must have been a planner, and for every creation there must have been a creator. Could the perfect universe emerge without a divine plan? Could it have come about by some mechanical chance? Such thoughts are against the stronger reasoning. Such belief could not be supported in view of the tangible evidence which portrays that there is a supreme being, one who had a divine plan, one who was the Creator and the builder of the universe." (CR, *Improvement Era*, December 1968, p. 106.)

Our faith in the Father and the Son is strengthened when we realize this, their omnipotence, their all-wise, eternal power. They created this universe through the power of the priesthood, which is everlasting and unchangeable. Their absolute obedience to eternal law, and their unchanging character make them all-powerful.

The Godhead

God, our Father, His Son, Jesus Christ, and the Holy Ghost comprise what we term the Godhead. They are separate, distinct beings, as shown by several instances in which all three appeared at the same time.

At the baptism of Jesus by John the Baptist, we read:

And Jesus, when he was baptized, went up straightway out of the water: and lo, the heavens were opened unto him, and he saw the Spirit of God descending like a dove, and lighting upon him:
And lo a voice from heaven, saying, This is my beloved Son, in whom I am well pleased. (Matthew 3:16-17.)

And when Stephen the martyr was being stoned,

But he, being full of the Holy Ghost, looked up stedfastly into heaven, and saw the glory of God, and Jesus standing on the right hand of God,
And said, Behold, I see the heavens opened, and the Son of man standing on the right hand of God. (Acts 7:55-56.)

And again in the glorious vision of Joseph Smith and Sidney Rigdon,

And while we meditated upon these things, the Lord touched the eyes of our understandings and they were opened, and the glory of the Lord shone round about.
And we beheld the glory of the Son, on the right hand of the Father, and received of his fulness. (D&C 76:19-20.)

The Father of our Spirits

God, the Father, is the Father of our spirits. It was in His heavenly home that we had our spiritual birth, and progressed until we were ready to take on physical bodies and come to this earth. We were created in the image of God: "So God created man in his own image, in the image of God created he him; male and female created he them." (Genesis 2:27.) We have within us His attributes and characteristics, and as His children we have the potential of becoming as He is.

Our prophet, President Gordon B. Hinckley, made this pointed observation: "Can you imagine a more compelling motivation to worthwhile endeavor than the knowledge that you are a child of God, the Creator of the universe, our all-wise Heavenly Father who expects you to do something with your life and who will give help when help is sought for?" (CR, *Improvement Era*, December 1964, p. 1092.)

Jesus, the Christ

Jesus Christ is the Firstborn of the Father in the spirit, our Elder Brother, who was so obedient that he was perfect and stood as a God before He came to this earth. He assisted in the creation of the earth (see Moses 1:32-33) and offered Himself as our Savior and Redeemer, the Light and the Life of the world. He came to earth begotten of God in the flesh as well as in the spirit, the only one of His spirit children to do so. As both mortal and immortal in this life, He had the power over death, and was able to give His life freely for our sake. This He did through His grace.

God the Father explained to Moses, "And I have a work for thee, Moses, my son; and thou art in the similitude of mine Only Begotten; and mine Only Begotten is and shall be the Savior, for he is full of grace and truth; but there is no God beside me, and all things are present with me, for I know them all." (Moses 1:6.)

The Holy Ghost

Jesus taught of the importance of the Holy Ghost in our quest for salvation: "Except a man be born of water and of the Spirit, he cannot enter into the kingdom of God." (John 3:5.) Indeed, baptism, the cleansing ordinance for the remission of sins, is performed "in the name of the Father, and of the Son, and of the Holy Ghost" (3 Nephi 11:26) after which the Holy Ghost is bestowed by the laying on of hands of one having authority. (See Acts 8:17; 19:6; 3 Nephi 18:37; D&C 20:43.)

To the Nephites, Jesus taught the ordinance of Sacrament, told them that it was to be in remembrance of Him, and then said, ". . . if ye do always remember me ye shall have my Spirit to be with you." (3 Nephi 18:7,11.) We cannot enter the kingdom of Heaven without the Holy Ghost, and we can have it only by authority, by worthiness, and in remembrance of Jesus' sacrifice.

Unity in the Godhead

The Godhead, although three separate and distinct individuals, are one in unity of purpose and mission. Jesus himself declared that a perfect unity abode between Him and His Father: "He that believeth on me, believeth not on me, but on him that sent me. And he that seeth me seeth him that sent me." (John 12:44-45.) And again: "I am the way, the truth, and the life: no man cometh unto the Father, but by me . . . the words that I speak unto you I speak not of myself: but the Father that dwelleth in me, he doeth the works. Believe me that I am in the Father, and the Father in me." (John 14:6,10-11.)

John the Beloved spoke of this unity in testimony of the mission of Jesus Christ: "This is he that came by water and blood, even Jesus Christ; not by water only, but by water and blood. And it is the Spirit that beareth witness, because the Spirit is truth. For there are three that bear record in heaven, the Father, the Word, and the Holy Ghost; and these three are one." (1 John 5:6-7.)

The Lord taught the Nephites: "Verily I say unto you, that the Father, and the Son, and the Holy Ghost are one; and I am in the Father, and the Father in me, and the Father and I are one." (3 Nephi 11:27.)

The Lord affirmed again to the Prophet Joseph: "Which Father, Son, and Holy Ghost are one God, infinite and eternal, without end." (D&C 20:28.)

The word of the Lord in this dispensation taught the bodily characteristics of the three members of the Godhead. "The Father has a body of flesh and bones as tangible as man's; the Son also; but the Holy Ghost has not a body of flesh and bones, but is a personage of Spirit. Were it not so, the Holy Ghost could not dwell in us." (D&C 130:22.)

The Glorious Restoration of Truth

What a glorious and exalted concept was restored when the Father and the Son visited the boy prophet Joseph Smith in the sacred grove! (See PofGP—Joseph Smith History.) By personal experience, he instantly had a firm knowledge of the existence of God, of His personal attributes, of the divinity and living reality of our Savior Jesus Christ, and the power of the Holy Ghost. This sublime moment signalled the refreshing of the flow of revelation from the presence of God to prophets on earth, and the ushering in of the Dispensation of the Fulness of Times, the beginning of the long-awaited Restoration of all things. (See Acts 3:19-21.)

Elder Bruce R. McConkie testifies: "There is a God in heaven who is infinite and eternal. He has all power, all might, and all dominion. He knows all things, and there is nothing which he takes into his heart to do that he cannot accomplish. He is the Creator of all things—this earth and all forms of life and the very universe itself. He is omnipotent, omniscient, and omnipresent." (*The Promised Messiah*, p. 549.)

Understanding our relationship to God as our all-knowing, Eternal Father, Jesus Christ as our Redeemer and the Holy Spirit as the testifier of truth should give us courage to go forward as offspring of Deity with the ability to become pure in heart as they are. This is our quest, our mission—the divine purpose which is the Lord's work and glory.

When Christ taught personally, He said, both in Galilee and among the Nephites, "Blessed are all the pure in heart, for they shall see God." (JST Matthew 5:8; 3 Nephi 12:8.) He taught again in our dispensation, "But blessed are the poor who are pure in heart, whose hearts are broken, and whose spirits are contrite, for they shall see the kingdom of God coming in power and great glory." (D&C 56:18.)

Our commission is to become like them—to pass through this mortal probation, accept of the gifts they have given us, go through the testing and have the dross burned out by the Holy Ghost, and emerge with clean hands and a pure heart, ready to "ascend into the hill of the Lord" and "stand in his holy place" (Psalms 24:3-4). We can do it.

3

Prayer—Communication with Our Father

Our Vital Link

Prayer is the soul's sincere desire,
Uttered or unexpressed,
The motion of a hidden fire
That trembles in the breast.
(Hymns, no. 145.)

When our Father sent us on this journey, He asked that we "call home" often, to communicate our needs and desires, to convey our gratitude, to feel His nearness, to report our progress, and to learn His will. We term this communication "prayer", and it is essential to success on the journey of life and in the quest for purity of heart and eternal life. Therefore one of our tasks is to learn to pray, and to understand the answers that come to our prayers:

"I command thee that thou shalt pray vocally as well as in thy heart; yea, before the world as well as in secret, in public as well as in private." (D&C 19:28.)

President Marion G. Romney said, "No divine commandment has been more frequently repeated than the commandment to pray in the name of the Lord Jesus Christ." (CR, *Ensign*, November 1979, p. 16.)

Prayer is our vital link with our Father in Heaven. We need a channel open between Heavenly Father and ourselves so that He can bless us.

Through sincere, humble prayer we are blessed with comfort, guidance, and peace.

President Spencer W. Kimball expressed his feelings about prayer when he said, "There is a knowledge that our Father in Heaven wants each of us to have, and that is a personal knowledge that He hears and answers our prayers. I have always had very tender feelings about prayer and the power and blessings of prayer. And for this I thank our Heavenly Father and my dear parents and teachers, who taught me by word and example about righteous and heartfelt prayer." ("Pray Always," *Ensign*, October 1981, p. 3.)

Our Father in Heaven is perfect. He has infinite power. He is our Eternal Father. He governs the universe. And yet, He knows each of us personally. Being all powerful, He is able to answer our prayers. His capacity to do good is unlimited. And He desires to bless us. In the Doctrine and Covenants we read, "And, as it is written—Whatsoever ye shall ask in faith, being united in prayer according to my command, ye shall receive." (D&C 29:6.)

The Lord knows each of us by name. He knows our thoughts and the intents of our hearts. "Yea, I tell thee, that thou mayest know that there is none else save God that knowest thy thoughts and the intents of thy heart." (D&C 6:16.)

He also knows the secrets of our hearts: "Shall not God search this out? for he knoweth the secrets of the heart." (Psalms 44:21.) He knows our needs and our desires within ourselves or outwardly.

God always loves us. He is not passive toward his children, He is active. He is always knocking at the door—he waits for us to open to Him. He wants to help us return unto Him and receive all of His blessings. He wants us to exercise faith in Him.

Bishop H. Burke Peterson explained that when we pray, God listens as a loving earthly father would:

> A few years ago . . . I was reflecting on my experiences with my earthly father who has been dead for some time. I remembered that when he was alive, I could always go to him and talk to him about anything, and he would listen to me. He was not a perfect man, but he would listen. I want you to know that I know that whenever one of Heavenly Father's children kneels and talks to him, he listens. I know this as well as I know anything in this world—that Heavenly Father listens to every prayer from his children. I know our prayers

ascend to heaven. No matter what we may have done wrong, he listens to us.

I also believe he answers us. I don't believe he ignores his children when they talk to him. The problem in our communication with him is that not all of us have learned how to listen for his answers, or perhaps we are not prepared to hear him. I believe we receive his answers as we prepare ourselves to receive them. ("Prayer—Try Again," *Ensign*, June 1981, pp. 72-73.)

Our Father in Heaven wants to hear and answer prayers. He loves us as only a Heavenly Father can. He is interested in all of our affairs. He wants to bless us continually if only we will exercise faith in Him and keep His commandments.

How Should We Pray?

O thou by whom we come to God,
The Life, the Truth, the Way!
The path of prayer thyself hast trod;
Lord, teach us how to pray.

In order to gain answers to our prayers, we should learn how to pray properly. The framework of prayer is simple. We start our prayer by addressing our Father in Heaven. We thank Him for all our blessings and ask for the blessings we need. We close our prayer in the name of Jesus Christ, and then we say "amen." The Book of Mormon teaches us to ask in the name of Jesus Christ, who is our advocate: "Whatsoever thing ye shall ask the Father in my name, which is good, in faith believing that ye shall receive, behold, it shall be done unto you." (Moroni 7:26.) "Amen" is a word meaning "so be it." It signifies our faith that it will be done as we have asked. The Lord Himself taught us to use the phrase, "Not my will, but thine be done" in His great intercessory prayer in the garden of Gethsemane. (See Luke 22:42.)

Our prayers do not have a set form. We say the words that are in our hearts. Further, words need not be said at all. President Joseph F. Smith said, "Prayer does not consist of words, altogether. True, faithful, earnest prayer consists more in the feeling that rises from the heart and from the inward desire of our spirits to supplicate the Lord in humility and in faith, that we may receive His blessings. It matters not how simple the words may be, if our desires are genuine and we come before the Lord with a broken heart and a contrite spirit to ask him for that which we need." (*CR*, October 1899, p. 69.)

Prayers do not have to be lengthy to be effective, nor do they have to be beautifully phrased. President Joseph F. Smith also taught:

> We do not have to cry unto him with many words. We do not have to weary him with long prayers. What we do need, and what we should do as Latter-day Saints, for our own good, is to go before him *often*, to witness unto him that we remember him and we are willing to take upon us his name, keep his commandments, work righteousness; and that we desire his Spirit to help us. Then, if we are in trouble, let us go to the Lord and ask him directly and specifically to help us out of the trouble that we are in; and let the prayer come from the heart, let it not be in words that are worn into ruts in the beaten tracks of common use, without thought or feeling in the use of those words. Let us speak the simple words, expressing our need, that will appeal most truly to the Giver of every good and perfect gift. (*Gospel Doctrine*, p. 221, emphasis added.)

The attitude should be sweet and sincere, contrite and humble, with a willingness to learn His will and do it. Do we truly believe that He is all-knowing, that He governs in righteousness, and that He loves us? Then submitting to His will should not be so difficult.

Bishop H. Burke Peterson gave this pattern for praying effectively:

> As you feel the need to confide in the Lord or to improve the quality of your visits with him—to pray, if you please—may I suggest a process to follow: go where you can be alone, go where you can think, go where you can kneel, go where you can speak out loud to him. The bedroom, the bathroom, or the closet will do. Now, picture him in your mind's eye. Think to whom you are speaking, control your thoughts—don't let them wander, address Him as your Father and your friend. Now *tell him things you really feel* to tell Him—not trite phrases that have little meaning, but *have a sincere, heartfelt conversation with him.* Confide in him, ask him for forgiveness, plead with him, enjoy him, thank him, express your love to him, and then listen for his answers. Listening is an essential part of praying. (CR, *Ensign*, January 1974, p. 19, emphasis added.)

Can you find a private place to isolate yourself for your personal petitions so you can pray aloud to your Father in Heaven, your best friend? Can you talk to Him openly about the things you feel deeply about? Can you express to Him your joys, your gratitude, your heart bursting with love? Can you confide to Him your heartfelt need? Can you ask for strength, seek for strength, plead for strength to remove your imperfections and put your life in order? Can you beg, beseech, implore Him for forgiveness? Can you honestly, openly tell Him what is in your heart? It is for *yourself* that you pray. He already knows your heart. He knows your life. You gain by the doing. *Listen* for His answer. Accept His will. He will bless your life.

President Spencer W. Kimball said that there is a price to pay to gain answers to our prayers:

> In our prayers, there must be no glossing over, no hypocrisy, since there can here be no deception. The Lord knows our true condition. Do we tell the Lord how good we are, or how weak? We stand naked before him. Do we offer our supplications in modesty, sincerity, and with a "broken heart and a contrite spirit," or like the Pharisee who prided himself on how well he adhered to the law of Moses? Do we offer a few trite words and worn-out phrases, or do we talk intimately to the Lord for as long as the occasion requires? Do we pray occasionally when we should be praying regularly, often, constantly? Do we pay the price to get answers to our prayers? (*Faith Precedes the Miracle*, p. 207.)

Personal prayers should be a humble and sincere encounter with your Father. We must present ourselves as we really are. This is a time to express your heartfelt gratitude for blessings. It is a time to plead with Him for what is required to enrich your life and make you more able to serve Him effectively. It is a time to plead for the strength to overcome your weaknesses. It is a time to commune with Him and listen to the sweet whispered directions of a Father who loves you and wants you to succeed.

We are then to do everything possible to make those prayers come to pass in our lives. We should not pray "Deliver us from evil" and then walk into temptation. We should not pray for safety and then drive recklessly. We are not to sit, as in the Chinese proverb, with folded arms waiting for roasted duck to fly into our mouths. President Kimball spoke succinctly when he admonished: "A humble prayer on bended knees, followed by the other works, is the invisible switch to tune us with the infinite and bring to us programs of knowledge, inspiration, and faith." (*Teachings of Spencer W. Kimball*, p. 62.)

Gratitude

A feeling of gratitude is a vital part of prayer. We should cultivate the attitude of recognizing blessings and being thankful for them. President David O. McKay said, "The young man who closes the door behind him, who draws the curtains, and there in silence pleads with God for help, should first pour out his soul in gratitude for health, for friends, for loved ones, for the gospel, for the manifestations of God's existence. He should first count his many blessings and name them one by one." (CR, *Improvement Era*, April 1961, p. 390.)

Part of every prayer should be gratefulness. President N. Eldon Tanner said, "As we express our appreciation for our many blessings, we become more conscious of what the Lord has done for us, and thereby we become more appreciative." (CR, *Improvement Era*, December 1967, p. 42.)

President Joseph F. Smith reminded us to acknowledge the hand of the Lord in our lives: "I believe that one of the greatest sins of which the inhabitants of the earth are guilty today is the sin of ingratitude, the want of acknowledgement, on their part, of God and his right to govern and control. . . . Because of this, God is not pleased with the inhabitants of the earth but is angry with them because they will not acknowledge his hand in all things." (*Gospel Doctrine*, pp. 270-271.)

The scriptures admonish us to gratitude: "And in nothing doth man offend God, or against none is his wrath kindled, save those who confess not his hand in all things, and obey not his commandments." (D&C 59:21.) "And he who receiveth all things with thankfulness shall be made glorious; and the things of this earth shall be added unto him, even an hundred fold, yea, more." (D&C 78:19.)

It is important to express gratitude for all the blessings we receive from Him daily. His goodness is immeasurable. In the next life when we come to understand what He truly did for us in this life, we will find that we were unaware of many of the blessings He gave us.

Faith in our Heavenly Father

Prayer is the burden of a sigh,
The falling of a tear,
The upward glancing of an eye
When none but God is near.

It is so important to have faith in our Father in Heaven, that He loves us, that He hears our prayers, and that He will answer them. We must also exercise faith in the Lord Jesus Christ in whose name we ask.

We should have faith that our Father in Heaven desires to bless us, and that He can do so. The Book of Mormon teaches, "The Lord is able to do all things according to his will, for the children of men, if it so be that they exercise faith in him." (1 Nephi 7:12.)

President David O. McKay said that "the first and most fundamental virtue in effective prayer is faith. A belief in God brings peace to the soul. An assurance that God is our Father, into whose presence we can go for comfort and guidance, is a never-failing source of comfort." (*Secrets of a Happy Life*, p. 114.)

The Lord answers our prayers according to our desire and according to our faith. The scriptures tell us, "Verily, verily, I say unto you, even as you desire of me so it shall be done unto you." (D&C 11:8.) "Behold, according to your desires, yea, even according to your faith shall it be done unto you." (v. 17.) It is important that our desires are correct, and that our faith is strong.

We can pray and ask the Lord to increase our faith. It is the upward spiral. When we ask in faith, we receive answers to our prayers. When we receive answers to our prayers, our faith is strengthened. With increased faith we can receive increased blessings. In General Conference Bruce R. McConkie suggested that we pray in terms such as these, "O Lord, increase our faith. . . . O thou God of healing, wilt thou cause him who came with healing in his wings also to heal us spiritually." (CR, April 1984, p. 46.)

As we develop our faith, we will learn to lean heavily on the Lord, and we will gain power to follow the path He has chosen for us. This sweet admonition is given us in the Old Testament: "Trust in the LORD with all thine heart; and lean not unto thine own understanding. In all thy ways acknowledge him, and he shall direct thy paths." (Proverbs 3:5-6.)

Humility before our Maker

Pride can be a great roadblock to our receiving answers to our prayers. In the scriptures the Lord has said, "God resisteth the proud, but giveth grace unto the humble." (James 4:6.)

President David O. McKay explained that we need to pray in "humility—not an outward, hypocritical pretense, but a humility that springs from the heart, from an absence of self-righteousness. Self-respect is a virtue, but self-conceit is an inhibition. The principle of humility in prayer leads one to feel a need of divine guidance. Self-reliance is a virtue, but with it should go a consciousness of the need of superior help—a consciousness that as you walk firmly in the pathway of duty, there is a possibility of your making a miss-step; and with that consciousness is a prayer, a pleading that God will inspire you to avoid that false step." (*Secrets of a Happy Life*, pp. 114-115.)

The importance of humility is illustrated by the experience of Martin Harris, as chronicled in the Doctrine and Covenants. Martin Harris desired to see the golden plates, but before the Lord would allow him to see them, He explained that Martin Harris would have to humble himself. "Behold, I say unto him, he exalts himself and does not humble himself sufficiently before me; but if he will bow down before me, and humble himself in mighty prayer and faith, in the sincerity of his heart, then will I grant unto him a view of the things which he desires to see." (D&C 5:24.)

As we seek the blessings of the Lord, we, too, must humble ourselves. "And it is my will that you shall humble yourselves before me, and obtain this blessing by your diligence and humility and the prayer of faith." (D&C 104:79.)

A sister told her touching experience with answer to prayer in this way:

> "My time alone was a great period of spiritual growth. I had no one to turn to, no place to go, except on my knees. I prayed as I had never prayed before. I fasted faithfully, meaningfully, and often. I read and studied the scriptures from cover to cover for the first time in my life. On my knees, I experienced complete dependence upon God. And he was there. He heard my humble pleadings. He put his arm of love around me. He forgave me of my sins and showed me a better way. I was amazed at the happiness, success, and opportunity that came into my life." ("After Divorce: Clearing The Hurdles," Mary Jane Knights, *Ensign*, August 1985, p. 50.)

Preparation for Prayer

Why does it sometimes appear that God is not listening or answering? Perhaps we have not prepared properly. The Savior said, "Behold, I stand at the door, and knock: if any man hear my voice, and open the

door, I will come in to him, and will sup with him, and he with me."
(Revelation 3:20.)

Of this statement President Spencer W. Kimball said,

The promise is made to everyone. There is no discrimination, no
favored few, but the Lord has not promised to crash the door. He
stands and knocks. If we do not listen, he will not sup with us nor
give answer to our prayers. We must learn how to listen, grasp,
interpret, understand. The Lord stands knocking. He never retreats.
But he will never force himself upon us. If our distance from him
increases, it is we who have moved and not the Lord. And should we
ever fail to get an answer to our prayers, we must look into our lives
for a reason. We have failed to do what we should do, or we have
done something we should not have done. We have dulled our
hearing or impaired our eyesight." (*Faith Precedes the Miracle*, p.
208.)

As President Kimball says, the Lord will never forsake us, but we can
remove ourselves from Him through our actions.

In her insightful book, "The Joy of the Journey," Ardeth Greene
Kapp refers to the preparation needed for two-way communication
through prayer:

This form of work requires some important preparation on our
part if it is to be active. In a talk to Church Education teachers in
1956, President Harold B. Lee, who was then a member of the
Council of the Twelve, talked about a lesson he had learned from
President David O. McKay: "The President made the statement that
. . . when we are relaxed in a private room, we are more susceptible
[to the promptings of the Spirit]; and that so far as he is concerned,
his best thoughts come after he gets up in the morning and is relaxed
and thinking about the duties of the day; that impressions come more
clearly, as if it were a voice." Then President Lee commented,
"Those impressions are right. If we are worried about something and
upset in our feelings, the inspiration does not come. If we so live that
our minds are free from worry and our conscience is clear and our
feelings are right toward one another, the operation of the Spirit of
the Lord upon our spirit is as real as when we pick up the telephone;
but when they come, we must be brave enough to take the suggested
actions." (Talk to seminary and institute of religion teachers, July 6,
1956.)

We learn to talk and we learn to listen, and often while reading the scriptures, we will hear the voice of the Lord in our mind and in our heart by the promptings of the Holy Ghost. (pp. 128-129.)

President Harold B. Lee taught us further: "The thing that all of us should strive for is to so live, keeping the commandments of the Lord, that He can answer our prayers." (*Stand Ye in Holy Places*, p. 144.)

Elder Gene R. Cook explained, "A man does not have to be perfect right now to receive an answer to his prayers, but he has to be humble in his heart and trying his best to fulfill the commandments. Then the Lord will assist him." ("The Grace of the Lord," *New Era*, December 1988, p. 7.)

Sometimes we fail to ask. We feel that since the Lord knows our needs even better than we know them, that we do not need to ask. President Boyd K. Packer explained how vital it is to *ask in prayer*: "You have your agency, and inspiration does not—perhaps cannot—flow unless you ask for it, or someone asks for you. No message in scripture is repeated more often than the invitation, even the command, to pray—to ask. Prayer is so essential a part of revelation that without it the veil may remain closed to you. Learn to pray. Pray often. Pray in your mind, in your heart. Pray on your knees. . . .

"Prayer is *your* personal key to heaven. The lock is on your side of the veil." (CR, *Ensign*, November 1994, p. 59.)

There are other roadblocks to receiving answers. Bishop H. Burke Peterson warned against building a "rock wall" between ourselves and our Father:

As we go through life, we ofttimes build a rock wall between ourselves and heaven. This wall is built by our unrepented sins. For example, in our wall there may be stones of many different sizes and shapes. There could be stones because we have been unkind to someone. Criticism of leaders or teachers may add another stone. A lack of forgiveness may add another. Vulgar thoughts and actions may add some rather large stones in this wall. Dishonesty will add another; selfishness another; and so on.

In spite of the wall we build in front of us, when we cry out to the Lord, he still sends his messages from heaven; but instead of being able to penetrate our hearts, they hit the wall that we have built up and bounce off. His messages don't penetrate, so we say, "He doesn't hear," or "He doesn't answer." Sometimes this wall is very formidable, and the great challenge of life is to destroy it, or, if you please, to cleanse ourselves, purifying this inner vessel so that we can be in tune with the Spirit. ("Prayer—Try Again," *Ensign*, June 1981, p. 73.)

Another thing that can disqualify us from receiving answers to our prayers is a lack of charity, the pure love of Christ, in our lives. Amulek in the Book of Mormon gives a beautiful sermon on prayer, explaining that we should "cry unto the Lord" over every aspect of our lives. He warns, however, that "after ye have done all these things, if ye turn away the needy, and the naked, and visit not the sick and afflicted, and impart of your substance, if ye have, to those who stand in need—I say unto you, if ye do not any of these things, behold, your prayer is vain, and availeth you nothing, and ye are as hypocrites who do deny the faith." (Alma 34:28.)

We must learn to pay the price to get answers to our prayers. God knows each one of us intimately. He knows all our strengths and weaknesses. When we go before Him with a broken heart and a contrite spirit, we are in the attitude of true prayer. When we give up our pride, ask in faith, and pray from our true need, we are in a position to feel the Holy Spirit giving comfort. He is there. He cares. He answers.

Prayer in the Family

> Prayer is the simplest form of speech
> That infant lips can try;
> Prayer, the sublimest strains that reach
> The Majesty on high.

We are under obligation to teach our families how to pray, and the best way to do this is by example. President Heber J. Grant said, "One of the best things in all the world to keep a man true and faithful in the gospel of the Lord Jesus Christ, is to supplicate God secretly in the name of Jesus Christ, for the guidance of His Holy Spirit . . . one of the greatest things that can come into any home to cause the boys and girls in that home to grow up in a love of God . . . is to have family prayer . . . that they may . . . be in harmony, be in tune, to have the radio, so to speak, in communication with the Spirit of the Lord." (*Gospel Standards*, p. 25.)

President Ezra Taft Benson stated: "A father has the responsibility to lead his family by loving God and looking to Him for daily counsel and direction. That means he must have family prayer as well as personal prayer." (*Teachings of Ezra Taft Benson*, p. 430.)

In our own family, we felt it important to have personal and family prayer in the morning and in the evening. While our children were growing up we had kneeling prayer around our table at breakfast and at dinner. In order to give more chances for the children to lead these prayers, after kneeling prayer we would have one of the little children also give a blessing on the food.

Some of the sweetest incidents of our family life have taken place as we have participated in family worship. When our son's wife was struggling with cancer all the extended family taught their children to fast and pray in her behalf. One of the little ones asked if he could eat now, because he was so hungry. His mom said, "Yes, if you have to, but if you wait, it will help Aunt Sherri." The little one understood and continued his fasting. It has been strengthening to all of them to see her improvement.

We found we had to adapt to changing situations. In the days when we had teenagers leaving at various times, Mom would have "family prayer" three or four times, with each one or group who were heading for their daily duties throughout the morning. It was a fortification for all of them.

In addition, we have our sweetheart's prayer when we retire. We hold hands, take turns being voice, and finish with a kiss.

Children learn the power of prayer as they watch parents pray, and as they are allowed to pray in behalf of the family. By praying, they learn the blessings of prayer. The Lord admonishes the Saints: "And they shall also teach their children to pray, and to walk uprightly before the Lord." (D&C 68:28.)

Our six-year-old grandson Andrew began playing soccer, and his world revolved around those games. He looked forward to each one and had his soccer uniform on hours before each game started. Then the weather turned bad and two games were canceled. The third game was scheduled, and he was really worried that this game would also be canceled. He decided that he should pray for good weather. His mother also prayed, because she wanted this little son to have a positive experience with getting answers to prayers.

The day of the game came and the morning was cloudy. Mom and Andrew kept on praying. In the afternoon the skies cleared for awhile, and when game time arrived, the weather was good enough for the game to be played. Andrew was ecstatic! But more importantly, he understood that God heard and answered his prayers.

Elder W. Grant Bangerter told a story concerning protection as answer to prayer. After their usual morning prayer, his wife had tried to drive a tractor on their farm for the first time. She lost control of the vehicle, and could easily have been injured or killed. He said, "As I followed the trail of the tractor, I knew that I wouldn't have been able to drive it over that bank and through that gully without having it tip over on me, but she was spared. No harm had come. Then we thought of what we had asked for that morning, protection against problems, troubles, accidents, and dangers. We made sure we went to the Lord and thanked him right then for the blessing that had come." ("Enjoy It," *Fireside and Devotional Speeches of the Year*, 1982-83, p. 102.)

Pray About Everything in Your Life

> Prayer is the Christian's vital breath,
> The Christian's native air,
> His watchword at the gates of death;
> He enters heav'n with prayer.

When prayer becomes our "vital breath," our "native air," we know that we have truly learned to pray. When we go through the day with a prayer in our hearts, we draw closer to God, and we see his hand in blessing us.

What should we pray about? President Kimball answers,

> We pray for wisdom, for judgment, for understanding. We pray for protection in dangerous places, for strength in moments of temptation. We remember loved ones and friends. We utter momentary prayers in word or thought, aloud or in deepest silence. We always have a prayer in our hearts that we may do well in the activities of our day. Can one do evil when honest prayers are in his heart and on his lips?

We pray over our marriages, our children, our neighbors, our jobs, our decisions, our church assignments, our testimonies, our feelings, our goals. Indeed, we take Amulek's great counsel and we pray for mercy, we pray over our means of livelihood, over our households and against the power of our enemies; we pray "against the devil, who is an enemy to all righteousness," and over the crops of our fields. And when we do not cry unto the Lord, we "let [our] hearts be full, drawn out in prayer unto him continually for [our] welfare, and also for the welfare of those who are around [us]." (See Alma 34:18-27.) ("Pray Always," *Ensign*, October 1981, p. 5.)

President Joseph F. Smith also advised us: "What do you pray for? You pray that God may recognize you, that he may hear your prayers, and that he may bless you with his Spirit, and that he may lead you into all truth and show you the right way; that he will warn you against wrong and guide you into the right path; that you may not fall astray, that you may not veer into the wrong way unto death, but that you may keep in the narrow way . . . . So we pray for what we need." (*Gospel Doctrine*, p. 215.)

The scriptures are full of admonitions about what we should make a matter of prayer. Let's examine what the scriptures counsel us to pray about.

We should pray for forgiveness and for the welfare of our souls. "And my soul hungered; and I kneeled down before my Maker, and I cried unto him in mighty prayer and supplication for mine own soul; and all the day long did I cry unto him; yea, and when the night came I did still raise my voice high that it reached the heavens." (Enos 1:4.)

We should also pray for the welfare of the souls of those around us. "And my prayer to God is concerning my brethren, that they may once again come to the knowledge of God, yea, the redemption of Christ; that they may once again be a delightsome people." (Words of Mormon 1:8.)

"Nevertheless the children of God were commanded that they should gather themselves together oft, and join in fasting and mighty prayer in behalf of the welfare of the souls of those who knew not God." (Alma 6:6.)

Jesus taught us to "Love your enemies, bless them . . . do good to them . . . and pray for them which despitefully use you and persecute you." (Matthew 5:44.)

We all have many opportunities to teach others the gospel. We can pray for the inspiration to teach with the Spirit. "But this is not all; they had given themselves to much prayer, and fasting; therefore they had the spirit of prophecy, and the spirit of revelation, and when they taught, they taught with power and authority of God." (Alma 17:3.)

"And the Spirit shall be given unto you by the prayer of faith; and if ye receive not the Spirit ye shall not teach." (D&C 42:14.)

We can pray that we will be able to overcome temptation. "Yea, and I also exhort you, my brethren, that ye be watchful unto prayer continually, that ye may not be led away by the temptations of the devil, that he may not overpower you, that ye may not become his subjects at the last day; for behold, he rewardeth you no good thing." (Alma 34:39.)

Our prophet Heber J. Grant said that through prayer we can be strengthened to overcome temptation: "I have little or no fear for the boy or the girl, the young man or the young woman, *who honestly and conscientiously supplicate[s] God twice a day for the guidance of His Spirit*. I am sure that when temptation comes they will have the strength to overcome it by the inspiration that shall be given to them. Supplicating the Lord for the guidance of His Spirit places around us a safeguard, and if we earnestly and honestly seek the guidance of the Spirit of the Lord, I can assure you that we will receive it." (*Gospel Standards*, p. 26, emphasis added.)

We need to be very specific in asking for the blessings we need. For example, if we need more self-control, we should pray for it, and then use the self-control the Lord has already blessed us with. If we do this, He will add to our ability to control ourselves.

Fasting as well as prayer may be necessary for special blessings needed from time to time. Elder James E. Talmage said, "Fasting, when practiced in prudence, and genuine prayer are conducive to the development of faith with its accompanying power for good. Individual application of this principle may be made with profit. Have you some besetting weakness, some sinful indulgence that you have vainly tried to overcome? Like the malignant demon that Christ rebuked in the boy, your sin may be of a kind that goeth out only through prayer and fasting." (*Jesus The Christ*, p. 395.)

Fasting and prayer can bring miracles.

When John and Bonnie's small son became critically ill, the doctors diagnosed the illness as spinal meningitis. They told the parents that their boy would either die or be physically and mentally handicapped. As a bearer of the Melchizedek Priesthood, John therefore decided to give his son a blessing. As he prepared to seal the anointing, however, he realized he did not know the Lord's will for his son. And so he simply blessed the boy that he would be comfortable.

After the blessing, John and Bonnie began to fast to know the will of the Lord and to be able to accept it. At the end of their fast, John and Bonnie were in a position to accept the Lord's will. John again blessed his son. This time the Spirit whispered to him to bless the child that he would be healed completely. Their son was healed, and three days later they took him home from the hospital. (*Basic Manual for Priesthood Holders*, Part A, pp. 228-230.)

If we have enemies, we can pray that they are turned into friends. "For he [the prophet Zenos] said: Thou art merciful, O God, for thou hast heard my prayer, even when I was in the wilderness; yea, thou wast merciful when I prayed concerning those who were mine enemies, and thou didst turn them to me." (Alma 33:4.)

Through prayer we increase our spirituality. President Kimball wrote, "Prayer is the passport to spiritual power." (*The Teachings of Spencer W. Kimball*, p. 115.)

If we are true and faithful God will help us solve our problems through revelation. President Kimball wrote, "The blessing of revelation is one that all should seek for. Righteous men and women find that they have the spirit of revelation to direct their families and to aid them in their other responsibilities. But, like Abraham, we must seek to qualify for such revelation by setting our lives in order and by becoming acquainted with the Lord through frequent and regular conversations with him." (*The Teachings of Spencer W. Kimball*, p. 126.)

Elder Boyd K. Packer tells this story of a man who, through prayer, received revelation and found the solution to a financial crisis:

I have a friend who bought a business. A short time later he suffered catastrophic reverses, and there just didn't seem to be any way out for him. Finally it got so bad that he couldn't sleep, so for a period of time he followed the practice of getting up about three o'clock in the morning and going to the office. There, with a paper and a pen, he would ponder and pray and write down every idea that came to him as a possible solution or contribution to the solution of his problem.

It wasn't long before he had several possible directions in which he could go, and it wasn't much longer than that until he had chosen the best of them. But he had earned an extra bonus. His notes showed, after he went over them, that he had discovered many hidden resources he had never noticed before. He came away more independent and successful than he would ever have been if he hadn't suffered those reverses.

There's a lesson in this experience. A year or two later he was called to preside over a mission overseas. His business was so independent and well set up that when he came back he didn't return to it. He now has someone else managing it, and he is able to give virtually all his time to the blessing of others. (*Teach Ye Diligently*, pp. 204-205.)

You, too, can ponder and pray for revelation about your business or employment. Listen to the Spirit, and write down the thoughts that come into your mind. You will find that the Lord knows a great deal about your personal situation.

As a builder, I found this kind of help recently when we were building thirty homes, and were extended heavily. In the midst of the building rush in the area, it was hard to find sub-contractors to work at the times we wanted them, and we often had to wait. In August we were searching for cement contractors. We got some homes done, but in October, most of the flat work was still waiting. It is nearly impossible to pour flat cement in the winter, and terribly expensive if done at all. I knew the bad weather was upon us, and I became desperate. I went to the Lord in sincere humble prayer day after day, still searching for the cement contractors daily. I pled in my prayers that I could be in tune to the Holy Ghost every day, and that God would help me find a solution to the problem.

It came into my mind that I should get the cement forms put into place, and that I would then be able to get the concrete poured and finished as I needed it. I had a carpenter named Jack working on a framing job. The Spirit told me to have Jack start forming for the cement. My foreman really wanted Jack to stay with the framing crew, but the Spirit let me know strongly that I was to immediately have Jack start forming for the cement flatwork. I did as instructed.

I found another man to work with Jack, and adjusted the framing crew as needed. Jack and his partner put the flatwork forms in at a rapid rate. The cement finishers came as the Spirit had indicated they would, and we got the needed work done before the ground froze for the winter.

I have thanked my Father in Heaven many times for this revelation. We had important reasons for not delaying the completion of our houses, and this made a tremendous difference in the outcome of the project. Heavenly Father knows much more about our business requirements than we do. We should ask for the help we need, and then listen and obey the answers that are given.

Pray To Make a Correct Decision

Frequently what we pray for is inspiration in making a decision. The right to receive guidance from the Lord is one of our greatest blessings. The Lord has promised to send his Spirit in answer to our prayers: "Pray always, and I will pour out my Spirit upon you, and great shall be your blessing—yea, even more than if you should obtain treasures of earth and corruptibleness to the extent thereof." (D&C 19:38.)

As this scripture points out, the guidance of the Spirit is beyond price. How can we learn to use prayer and the guidance of the Spirit to successfully make correct decisions?

The pattern was shown to us in the Doctrine and Covenants. Oliver Cowdery was told, "You must study it out in your mind; then you must ask me if it be right, and if it is right I will cause that your bosom shall burn within you; therefore, you shall feel that it is right.

"But if it be not right you shall have no such feelings, but you shall have a stupor of thought." (D&C 9:8-9.)

President Marion G. Romney adds his testimony about making a correct decision with the help of the Lord:

Now, I tell you that you can *make every decision in your life correctly if you can learn to follow the guidance of the Holy Spirit.* This you can do if you will discipline yourself to yield your own feelings to the promptings of the Spirit. Study your problems and prayerfully make a decision. Then take that decision and say to him, in a simple, honest supplication, "Father, I want to make the right decision. I want to do the right thing. This is what I think I should do; let me know if it is the right course." Doing this, you can get the burning in your bosom, if your decision is right. If you do not get the burning, then change your decision and submit a new one. When you learn to walk by the Spirit, you never need to make a mistake. (CR, *Improvement Era*, December 1961, p. 947, emphasis added.)

We have had many experiences with receiving direction through prayer. One that has affected the course of our lives came in the early years of our marriage. After a number of years in the contracting business we decided to build a larger home for our growing family. This home was to be our final home, so we were very interested in securing the right location. We looked over several areas of the city and couldn't really decide where to build. Then we drove through a developing subdivision and noticed a vacant lot which pleased us. As we were looking at it, the Lord made known through the Holy Ghost that this was the place we should build our home, the place where we could serve Him in the Church.

Four months after moving into our new home, Don was called to be in the bishopric. After several years in that calling, he became bishop, serving for over nine years. Then he served as a high councilor for many years, then as counselor in the stake presidency. Now he has the sweet opportunity to serve as stake patriarch. During more than thirty years in this dear home, we reared our family in activity and service. Arda Jean has served in many callings, including Gospel Doctrine teacher and Relief Society president. We feel that in this location has been fulfilled the quiet revelation that assured us this would be a place we could serve the Lord.

"For behold, again I say unto you that if ye will enter in by the way, and receive the Holy Ghost, it will show unto you all things what ye should do." (2 Nephi 32:5.) If we pray earnestly and plead with the Lord for answers to our prayers, He will send the Holy Ghost to guide us.

President Harold B. Lee emphasized the importance of recognizing and of listening to the inspiration of the Lord: "Every man has the privilege to exercise these gifts and these privileges in the conduct of his own affairs; in bringing up his children in the way they should go; in the management of his business, or whatever he does. It is his right to enjoy the spirit of revelation and of inspiration to do the right thing, to be wise and prudent, just and good, in everything that he does. I know that is a true principle . . . all of us should try to strive and give heed to the sudden ideas that come to us, and if we'll give heed to them and cultivate an ear to hear these promptings we too—each of us—can grow in the spirit of revelation. (*Stand Ye in Holy Places*, pp. 141-142.)

Talk to God as you would talk to your earthly father. Be earnest and specific as you pray for solutions to your problems. He will give you impressions by the Spirit to tell you what to do. Following those sudden ideas which come to your mind by inspiration is the way to implement the answers to your prayers. Sometimes this is the hardest part of prayer, but it is one of the most important. If we take heed, we can grow in our ability to receive revelation.

We want to make sure that as we petition the Lord we always say, as the Savior did, "Thy will be done." President Spencer W. Kimball explains why:

> Since our Father in Heaven loves us with more love than we have even for ourselves, it means that we can trust in his goodness, we can trust in him; it means that if we continue praying and living as we should, our Father's hand will guide and bless us.
>
> And so in our prayers we say, "Thy will be done"—and mean it. We would not ask a leader for advice, then disregard it. We must not ask the Lord for blessings and then ignore the answer. Thus, we pray, "Thy will be done, O Lord. Thou knowest best, kind Father. I will accept and follow thy direction gracefully."
>
> We do this because the scriptures remind us that sometimes we may "ask amiss" (James 4:3), or ask for that which is not expedient (see D&C 88:66), or ask for that which may not be "right" (see 3 Nephi 18:20). (*Ensign*, October 1981, p. 5.)

Once we have received an answer from the Lord, we must follow it. Perhaps as time passes after we receive guidance from the Lord our faith may begin to waver and we may begin to doubt the answer we received. Oliver Cowdery was told, when desiring a further witness to an answer he had received, "Verily, verily, I say unto you, if you desire a further witness, cast your mind upon the night that you cried unto me in your heart, that you might know concerning the truth of these things.

"Did I not speak peace to your mind concerning the matter? What greater witness can you have than from God?" (D&C 6:22-23.)

When the Lord gives us guidance, we have a great responsibility to remain faithful to the inspiration we have received. It will help if we will, as Oliver Cowdery did, think back to the moment we received the answer and the sweet feelings borne to us by the Spirit.

By offering faithful, humble, sweet prayers, we can feel the love and peace that comes from God. President Kimball said, "Learning the language of prayer is a joyous, lifetime experience. Sometimes ideas flood our mind as we listen after our prayers. Sometimes feelings press upon us. A spirit of calmness assures us that all will be well. But always, if we have been honest and earnest, we will experience a good feeling—a feeling of warmth for our Father in Heaven and a sense of his love for us. It has sorrowed me that some of us have not learned the meaning of that calm, spiritual warmth, for it is a witness to us that our prayers have been heard." (*Ensign*, October 1981, p. 5.)

Prayer in Overcoming Transgression

> Prayer is the contrite sinner's voice,
> Returning from his ways,
> While angels in their songs rejoice
> And cry, "Behold, he prays!"

How can we, all of us sinners to some extent, cleanse ourselves so that we are worthy to receive answers to our prayers?

All of us have sinned. All of us need God's help in order to be saved. All of us need to humble ourselves before the Lord, go to Him with a broken heart and a contrite spirit, and ask for forgiveness and strength to overcome.

If you have committed a serious sin and wonder if you can be forgiven, President Kimball gives us the answer, "Our loving Father has given us the blessed principle of repentance as the gateway to forgiveness. All sins but those excepted by the Lord—basically, the sin against the Holy Ghost, and murder—will be forgiven to those who totally, consistently, and continuously repent in a genuine and comprehensive transformation of life. There is forgiveness for even the sinner who commits serious transgressions, for the Church will forgive and the Lord will forgive such things when repentance has reached fruition." (*The Miracle of Forgiveness*, p. 14.)

Prayer is a vital part of repentance, and as we strive to bring our contrite hearts back to the Lord, we are admonished to pray: "O then despise not, and wonder not, but hearken unto the words of the Lord, and ask the Father in the name of Jesus for what things soever ye shall stand in need. Doubt not, but be believing, and begin as in times of old, and come unto the Lord with all your heart, and work out your own salvation with fear and trembling before him." (Mormon 9:27.)

As we repent, we should ask the Lord to help us avoid and overcome temptation. President Spencer W. Kimball explained that the Lord is more powerful than the adversary, so that if we depend upon Him, we can conquer temptation: "He who has greater strength than Lucifer, he who is our fortress and our strength, can sustain us in times of great temptation. While the Lord will never forcibly take anyone out of sin or out of the arms of the tempters, he exerts his Spirit to induce the sinner to do it with divine assistance. And the man who yields to the sweet influence and pleadings of the Spirit and does all in his power to stay in a repentant attitude is guaranteed protection, power, freedom and joy." (*The Miracle of Forgiveness*, p. 176.)

When we repent and gain forgiveness of our sins, we can have the Holy Ghost, the Comforter, to be with us and fill us with hope and love. In the Book of Mormon we read, "And the remission of sins bringeth meekness, and lowliness of heart; and because of meekness and lowliness of heart cometh the visitation of the Holy Ghost, which Comforter filleth with hope and perfect love, which love endureth by diligence unto prayer." (Moroni 8:26.)

An important part of the repentance process is forgiveness. "I, the Lord, will forgive whom I will forgive, but of you it is required to forgive all men" (D&C 64:10).

We should forgive all, and that includes ourselves, after we have repented and received forgiveness of the Lord.

Elder Richard G. Scott encourages us to leave our sins behind when we truly repent: "Suffering does not bring forgiveness. It comes through faith in Christ and obedience to His teachings, so that His gift of redemption can apply. . . . Can't you see that to continue to suffer for sins, when there has been proper repentance and forgiveness of the Lord, is not prompted by the Savior but by the master of deceit, whose goal has always been to bind and enslave the children of our Father in Heaven? Satan would encourage you to continue to relive the details of past mistakes, knowing that such thoughts make progress, growth, and service difficult to attain." (CR, *Ensign*, May 1986, pp. 10-11.)

After proper repentance and forgiveness, we should not relive the details of past mistakes. It is a hindrance to our growth. We should forgive ourselves and get on with progress in life.

If we have a hard time forgiving ourselves, we should make it a matter of sincere prayer. Pleading with the Lord to give us strength, then rising above reliving our mistakes, will enable us to overcome this bad habit. He will send peace to our souls. He said, "Learn that he who doeth the works of righteousness shall receive his reward, even peace in this world, and eternal life in the world to come. I, the Lord have spoken it, and the Spirit beareth record." (D&C 59:23-24.)

God Can Help Us Do All Things

The Saints in prayer appear as one
In word and deed and mind,
While with the Father and the Son
Their fellowship they find.

Ammon expressed the spirit of confidence brought by faith and prayer when he said, "Yea, I know that I am nothing; as to my strength I am weak; therefore I will not boast of myself, but I will boast of my God, for in his strength I can do all things." (Alma 26:12.)

There are miraculous instances of the power of prayer in the scriptures.

One of these is the story of Zacharias and his wife Elisabeth. The great desire of their hearts was to have a child, but "they had no child, because that Elisabeth was barren, and they both were now well stricken in years." However, "they were both righteous before God, walking in all the commandments and ordinances of the Lord blameless."

They had been praying for what would now have to be a miracle—the birth of a child to a woman beyond child-bearing years.

One day while Zacharias was serving in the temple, "there appeared unto him an angel of the Lord" who said, "Fear not, Zacharias: for thy prayer is heard; and thy wife Elisabeth shall bear thee a son, and thou shalt call his name John."

What a wonderful blessing! What a miracle. Not only would they have a child, but there were greater blessings in store. The angel continued, "And thou shalt have joy and gladness; and many shall rejoice at his birth.

"For he shall be great in the sight of the Lord, and shall drink neither wine nor strong drink; and he shall be filled with the Holy Ghost, even from his mother's womb.

"And many of the children of Israel shall he turn to the Lord their God.

"And he shall go before him in the spirit and power of Elias, to turn the hearts of the fathers to the children, and the disobedient to the wisdom of the just; to make ready a people prepared for the Lord." (Luke 1:6-17)

Not long after this, Elisabeth conceived, and the child she bore was John the Baptist, who prepared the way for the ministry of Jesus Christ.

Miracles do happen through faith, prayer, and obedience to the commandments of the Lord. Another miracle that occurred because of the prayer of the righteous is recounted in Alma, in the Book of Mormon.

Alma and several other missionaries went to the land of the Zoramites to preach the gospel. When they arrived there, they found such gross wickedness that Alma's soul was grieved and he prayed for the blessings of the Lord as they sought to convert their brethren.

Alma, a righteous man, prayed, "O Lord, wilt thou comfort my soul, and give unto me success, and also my fellow laborers who are with me—yea, Ammon, and Aaron, and Omner, and also Amulek and Zeezrom and also my two sons—yea, even all these wilt thou comfort, O Lord. Yea, wilt thou comfort their souls in Christ.

"Wilt thou grant unto them that they may have strength, that they may bear their afflictions which shall come upon them because of the iniquities of this people.

"O Lord, wilt thou grant unto us that we may have success in bringing them again unto thee in Christ." (Alma 31:32-34.)

After offering this prayer, Alma and his fellow missionaries separated and went about trying to reclaim their brethren. We are told that, "the Lord provided for them that they should hunger not, neither should they thirst; yea, and he also gave them strength, that they should suffer no manner of afflictions, save it were swallowed up in the joy of Christ. Now this was according to the prayer of Alma; and this because he prayed in faith." (Alma 31:38.)

There are also modern-day examples of miracles that occur with a humble prayer of faith.

Don's father had a remarkable missionary experience with the power of prayer. When he had been married for several years and had five children he was called on a mission to the Northwestern States. His first wife, Tillie, stayed home in Hinckley, Utah with the children. Tillie and the children worked long hours on the farm in order to make a living and finance Father's mission.

Soon after he returned home he was called by the stake president to preside over the stake mission. He labored with the missionaries very diligently but found that their attitude was poor. They felt that all the non-members in the area had already heard the gospel message, and that no more would accept it, so there really wasn't any work to be done.

This bothered Father greatly for he had served a good mission in the Northwestern States, being Conference President, and was filled with the missionary spirit. He wanted this same type of work to be done in the Hinckley Stake. He was very upset when missionaries would not go out and do their work.

He talked to his wife about it. One day he told her that he had prayed a great deal and would continue to pray about this matter, but if he didn't receive an answer that night, he would talk the matter over with the stake president.

That night he was awakened by a voice saying, "Joseph, call a testimony meeting with the missionaries tomorrow and bear your testimony to them." Father said, "Whom shall I say is speaking?" The answer came back, "This is Jesus Christ."

Father called the testimony meeting the following day and told the missionaries of the revelation he had received. He said that the testimony meeting was very inspirational. The missionaries felt the power of his testimony, and were caught up in the spirit of the work. Father said he had never seen missionary work move ahead like it did after this spiritual experience.

As we develop faith in God and learn to pray and receive answers to our prayers, miracles will occur in our own lives. I testify to this truth, for I have seen miracles happen in my own life and the lives of the faithful around me.

When I am confronted with a serious problem, I go to the temple. There I pray for a solution to my problem. I always feel the Spirit. In the temple answers come.

I take Alma's counsel to pray over my business. Once when I was building a number of new homes and was heavily obligated for the capital, interest rates started to climb. I worried, "What if they go up too high, as they did once before?" In the temple I prayed sincerely. The assurance came into my mind that I would make a profit on these homes. On my way out of the temple I prayed again. The sentence came into my mind, "You have had your answer." I went home knowing that my business would be secure.

When you have a problem, go to the temple. While there, take some time to meditate and pray about your problem. I know that God will bless you with answers as He has done with me. He has said, "Draw near unto me and I will draw near unto you; seek me diligently and ye shall find me; ask, and ye shall receive; knock, and it shall be opened unto you." (D&C 88:63.) The Lord is always there ready to help us, if we turn to him in humble prayer.

Through prayer we make God a partner in the things we are doing. The Lord is interested in our lives, He wants to help us in everything we do. Elder M. Russell Ballard said, "The heavens are *not* sealed. God does communicate with mortals. . . . What comfort that sweet assurance provides in a world filled with confusion and discouragement! What *peace* and *security* come to the heart that understands that God in heaven knows us and cares about us, individually and collectively, and that He communicates with us, either directly or through His living prophets, according to our needs." (CR, *Ensign*, November 1994, p. 67, emphasis included.)

Heavenly Father is eager to help us with all aspects of our daily endeavors. One man said something like this, "The Lord isn't interested in my small problems. They would bore Him." But I say to you He *is* interested in all your problems, large or small. He wants to help you solve them. If He takes note of every sparrow which falls, every lily of the field (see Matt. 6), how much more will He be interested in the needs of His children, whom He wants to save and exalt?

Sister Dwan J. Young of the Primary General Presidency said, "The important thing to remember is to pray often, talk to Heavenly Father, seek his counsel so that he can guide you. When you draw near to Heavenly Father in prayer, he will draw near to you. You need never feel alone again. I testify to this." (CR, *Ensign*, November 1985, p. 92.)

The journey toward purity of heart will be long and strenuous, but through communion with our Father in Heaven we are not left alone, we have guidance along the way, and we are well-equipped for the task. The end of the search is glorious, and well worth the effort!

As He has promised, "Search diligently, pray always, and be believing, and all things shall work together for your good, if ye walk uprightly." (D&C 90:24.)

4

Through the Atonement of Christ, All Mankind May Be Saved

The Girdle of Truth, the Helmet of Salvation

The most exquisite love story conceivable is that of God creating the world, peopling it with His own children, and providing for their ultimate salvation and exaltation to become beings of triumph, achievement, and glory, like He is. This plan of progression is a declaration of the infinite love of our Eternal Father, and of our Redeemer, Jesus the Christ.

The scriptures abound in passages like "encircled in the arms of His love" (2 Nephi 1:15, D&C 6:20.) and "the love of Christ which passeth knowledge." (Ephesians 3:19.) The Christmas story and the holy anthems of Easter resound with this message of love:

"For God so loved the world, that he gave his only begotten Son, that whosoever believeth in him should not perish, but have everlasting life." (John 3:16.)

"And his name shall be called Wonderful, Counseller, The mighty God, The everlasting Father, The Prince of Peace . . . The zeal of the Lord of hosts will perform this." (Isaiah 9:6-7.)

"Hereby perceive we the love of God, because he laid down his life for us." (1 John 3:16.)

"But God commendeth his love toward us, in that, while we were yet sinners, Christ died for us." (Romans 5:8.)

"And I also beheld that the tree of life was a representation of the love of God. And the angel said unto me again: Look and behold the condescension of God! And I looked, and beheld the Redeemer of the world." (1 Nephi 11:25-27.)

This gospel of love is the girdle of truth and the helmet of salvation Paul used in his analogy of the full armor of God. This truth is the message of the ages, spoken by all the prophets from Adam on. It is the Word personified by Jesus Christ in the flesh. It is the declaration of the prophets of the Restoration, in which all things are brought together again in one.

More than two thousand years ago the Book of Mormon prophets understood the atonement. In Alma we read, "I do know that Christ shall come among the children of men, to take upon him the transgressions of his people, and that he shall atone for the sins of the world. . . . And thus he shall bring salvation to all those who shall believe on his name." (Alma 34:8,15.)

This glorious plan of redemption was explained to all of the children of God in their heavenly home before the foundation of the world was laid. (See D&C 138:56). We shouted for joy (Job 38:7) at the prospect of coming on our earthly missions and receiving the opportunity to progress and become as our Father in Heaven is. We wanted our bodies, we wanted to experience mortality and earth-life. We wanted to prove to our Father that we would follow His plan (Abraham 3:22-28) and return to Him triumphant. We understood that there would be important choices to be made (D&C 29:35,39). We were taught that there would be pain and demanding situations (2 Nephi 2:11). But we knew that we would have His Light and His Spirit to help us, and that there would be those beyond our sight who would assist us.

We also knew that our choices could lead us away from truth and salvation, because there were many of those with whom we had associated who chose not to follow the plan (D&C 29:36-38) but to follow our charming brother, Lucifer, son of the morning. He proposed, as an alternative to the plan of redemption by our Savior, that all would be saved, but at a cost of losing our freedom to choose. Heavenly Father would not abridge our agency (Moses 4:3). He sent Jesus, our Elder Brother, to be the Savior, the Christ, the Messiah, the Redeemer.

Through the power of the holy priesthood, the plan was set into motion. I like to think that we not only shouted for joy, but possibly also sang in the heavenly choir, joining in our first rendition of the Song of Redeeming Love, which was repeated again with the "Glory to God in the Highest" chorus at the time of our Savior's mortal birth. I don't know what we may have sung at the Restoration, but would "The Spirit of God like a Fire is Burning" be a good guess?

The process of creation was set into operation. Heavenly forces were brought into action, and this beautiful earth was made a fit habitation for God's creatures, plant and animal, and at last His children, male and female, created physically in His heavenly image. The process had begun. Our consecrated journey was underway.

Fall and Atonement

In explaining the eternal plan, set forth in plain language in 2 Nephi chapter 2, Lehi sums up the purpose of the Creation, Fall and Redemption: "But behold, all things have been done in the wisdom of him who knoweth all things. Adam fell that men might be; and men are, that they might have joy." (v. 24-25.)

Now, the first effect of the fall was that Adam was cast out of the Garden of Eden, and Eve with him. They were sent from the presence of God, and a two-fold death came into the world—a spiritual death, or banishment from the presence of God, and a mortal death, or death of the body, which would separate body and spirit. "For all mankind, by the fall of Adam being cut off from the presence of the Lord, are considered as dead, both as to things temporal and to things spiritual." (Helaman 14:16.)

Another effect of the fall was that their nature became changed so that they were less sensitive to the workings of the Spirit, and more subject to bodily or carnal desires. (See Alma 42:10.) In this challenging circumstance, Adam and Eve began to bring children into the world, and to teach them the gospel plan as the Lord Jehovah had taught it to them. (See Moses 5:1-5.)

The fall was an important event. It brought about the conditions of mortality, necessary to the plan of progression and testing. It provided means by which Adam and Eve and their children could experience opposition, both in the way they must approach the difficulties of life as obstacles by which to grow, but also in meeting the temptations of Satan, who would still try to persuade them to leave the truth. This, again, would be an opportunity to grow, to overcome, and to progress.

Moses reported the good news given to Adam through the Holy Ghost, when Jehovah told him: "I am the Only Begotten of the Father from the beginning, henceforth and forever, that as thou hast fallen thou mayest be redeemed, and all mankind, even as many as will.

"And in that day Adam blessed God and was filled, and began to prophesy concerning all the families of the earth, saying: Blessed be the name of God, for because of my transgression my eyes are opened, and in this life I shall have joy, and again in the flesh I shall see God.

"And Eve, his wife, heard all these things and was glad, saying: Were it not for our transgression we never should have had seed, and never should have known good and evil, and the joy of our redemption, and the eternal life which God giveth unto all the obedient." (Moses 5:9-11.)

Justice, Mercy, and Resurrection

The laws of justice require that for every offense, there be recompense made. No unclean thing can come into the presence of God. (See 1 Nephi 15:34.) Not only must the transgression of Adam be paid for, but mankind must pay for their own sins, must suffer the penalty for whatever poor choices they make while in this mortal condition.

John the Revelator saw the day of judgment in vision: "And I saw the dead, small and great, stand before God; and the books were opened: and another book was opened, which is the book of life: and the dead were judged out of those things which were written in the books, according to their works." (Revelations 20:12.) We will be judged—with a just judgment—according to that which we have chosen to do while in this life.

Mankind is unable to lift himself above his sinful condition. Fallen man by his own power could never rise from his degraded situation. "And now, there was no means to reclaim men from this fallen state, which man had brought upon himself because of his own disobedience. . . . Now the work of justice could not be destroyed; if so, God would cease to be God. And thus we see that all mankind were fallen, and they were in the grasp of justice; yea, the justice of God, which consigned them forever to be cut off from his presence." (Alma 42:12-14.)

But this is an eternal love story. "Behold, what manner of love the Father hath bestowed upon us, that we should be called the sons of God." (1 John 3:1.)

Jesus Christ, our Elder Brother, Jehovah, loved us from the beginning. Our Eternal Father loves us—"He that spared not his own Son, but delivered him up for us all." (Romans 8:32.)

Alma stated it thus: "And now, the plan of mercy could not be brought about except an atonement should be made; therefore God himself atoneth for the sins of the world, to bring about the plan of mercy, to appease the demands of justice, that God might be a perfect, just God, and a merciful God also." (Alma 42:15.)

Aaron, a young missionary to the Lamanites, taught in these words: "And since man had fallen he could not merit anything of himself; but the sufferings and death of Christ atone for their sins, through faith and repentance, and so forth; and that he breaketh the bands of death, that the grave shall have no victory, and that the sting of death should be swallowed up in the hopes of glory." (Alma 22:14.)

Aaron mentions the other phase of Christ's atonement: to break the bands of the temporal death, or separation of the body and spirit by which mankind were bound, regardless of how righteous or sinful they may have been in their lifetimes. The resurrection is the bringing forth from the grave the bodies which have been separated from the living spirits, and reuniting them again never more to be separated. This is the heralded Easter triumph: "O death, where is thy sting? O grave, where is thy victory?" (I Corinthians 15:55.)

Through Grace We are Saved

The former-day Saints felt the joy of this triumph, as expressed in Romans 5:11: "We also joy in God through our Lord Jesus Christ, by whom we have now received the atonement."

This atonement and resurrection comes through the love and grace of our Savior, Jesus Christ, the culminating offering of love. "Greater love hath no man than this, that a man lay down his life for his friends." (John 15:13.)

Lehi instructed his young son Jacob, "Wherefore, redemption cometh in and through the Holy Messiah; for he is full of grace and truth. Behold he offereth himself a sacrifice for sin, to answer the ends of the law." (2 Nephi 2:6-7.) Moreover, "The way is prepared from the fall of man, and salvation is free." (v. 4.)

This unsurpassed gift was not given because we deserved it, nor because we earned it. The sacrifice was a free gift offered out of the great heart of our Savior, through His grace. It is there, available to every child of our Father in Heaven who has been born into the world. He broke the everlasting chains of death through freely giving up His life when all else was accomplished that He was sent here to do. "For as in Adam all die, even so in Christ shall all be made alive." (I Corinthians 15:22.) Oh, praise to our Savior, God and King, for what He has done in His love for us! It is beyond comprehension to the mortal mind.

We will all be resurrected. This portion of the atonement is unconditional. He made the gift. It is ours. Nephi's testimony stirs us: "As the Lord God liveth, there is none other name given under heaven save it be this Jesus Christ, of which I have spoken, whereby man can be saved." He urges all "to believe in Christ, and to be reconciled to God; for we know that it is by grace that we are saved, after all we can do." (2 Nephi 25:20-23.)

He was perfect. He lived a sinless life. He suffered temptation and overcame it. And yet, through His great love, He accepted the sin, the blame, the guilt, the pain, and the penalty for all the sins of humankind—for all of us. "But he was wounded for our transgressions, he was bruised for our iniquities: the chastisement of our peace was upon him, and with his stripes we are healed." (Isaiah 53:5.)

Can we understand the love He had for us that made it possible for Him to descend below all things, and suffer thus for us? Can we accept that great love, and do what we can for Him, in gratitude for the incomparable thing He did for us through His great mercy, through His benevolence, through His kindness, through His grace?

Remember we are totally dependent on Jesus Christ for the earth we live on, the air we breathe, the food we eat. President David O. McKay illustrated our dependence upon the Lord by quoting this scripture from the Doctrine and Covenants: "All men must repent and believe on the name of Jesus Christ, and worship the Father in his name, and endure in faith on his name to the end, or they cannot be saved in the kingdom of God." (D&C 20:29.)

He then said, "I like to associate that word 'saved' with the power that man gets in this life to rise above his animal instincts and passions, power to overcome or resist social evils that blight men's and women's souls and shut them out not only from the peace of the world, but also from membership in the kingdom of God. Men may yearn for peace, cry for peace, and work for peace, but there will be no peace until they follow the path pointed out by the Living Christ." (CR, *Improvement Era*, May 1948, p. 273.)

We should all be grateful to our Lord, grateful enough to follow His path. Think what we owe Him: He gave us the gospel we live by. He is our Savior and our Redeemer. He atoned for our sins. He made it possible for us to repent, put our lives in' order, and hold to the rod which is the word of God leading us back home. And we are His. He bought us with a price—a price that only He could pay (See I Corinthians 6:20, 7:23.) Only through Jesus Christ can we be saved. How we should love Him!

By Obedience to the Laws and Ordinances of the Gospel

The gift is there, available through His grace and love. But if we wish to receive the full gift, redemption from our personal sins and cleansing by the Atonement, we must qualify ourselves for it by obedience to the laws and ordinances of the Gospel. Lehi went on to explain to Jacob that the atonement for our personal sins is: "unto all those who have a broken heart and a contrite spirit; and unto none else can the ends of the law be answered." (2 Nephi 2:7.)

Mormon described how the resurrection, the free gift of victory over death, comes to all mankind. Following the resurrection we must all stand at the judgment bar of Christ, and receive our reward according to the choices that we made in this life:

"And because of the redemption of man, which came by Jesus Christ, they are brought back into the presence of the Lord; yea, this is wherein all men are redeemed, because the death of Christ bringeth to pass the resurrection, which bringeth to pass a redemption from an endless sleep, from which sleep all men shall be awakened by the power of God when the trump shall sound; and they shall come forth, both small and great, and all shall stand before his bar, being redeemed and loosed from this eternal band of death, which death is a temporal death.

"And then cometh the judgment of the Holy One upon them, and then cometh the time that he that is filthy shall be filthy still; and he that is righteous shall be righteous still; he that is happy shall be happy still; and he that is unhappy shall be unhappy still." (Mormon 9:13-14.)

We must first put our faith in our Savior Jesus Christ. In 2 Nephi 25:29 we read, "The right way is to believe in Christ and deny him not; and Christ is the Holy One of Israel; wherefore ye must bow down before him, and worship him with all your might, mind, and strength, and your whole soul."

Thereafter we must obey the other laws and ordinances of the gospel, which follow in sublime sequence: the favor of repentance, the covenant of baptism, the gift of the Holy Ghost, priesthood covenants, and temple covenants. It is a transcendent journey in truth, with the glorious plan of redemption as our guide and the peace of purity of heart as our goal.

Hope in Christ

Our Savior loves us and wants us to be happy. He knows that the only way we can be truly happy is if we obey His commandments. In Matthew 11:28-30 the Savior said, "Come unto me, all ye that labour and are heavy laden, and I will give you rest.

"Take my yoke upon you, and learn of me; for I am meek and lowly in heart: and ye shall find rest unto your souls.

"For my yoke is easy, and my burden is light."

The yoke is placed upon an ox so his master can direct him, and to enable him to pull. When we take the Savior's yoke upon us, He can guide us. We can learn of Him and keep His commandments, and we can pull our load. He tells us that in this way we truly find rest unto our souls, for with Him helping to carry our load, our burden becomes light. We find peace of mind.

At one point in my life I had much adversity to overcome. I had been sincerely and faithfully praying about my business problems. In the midst of these difficulties I had a remarkable dream. I dreamed that the Savior came to me and took upon himself my heavy burdens. I could see him as plainly as I have ever seen anyone. After this marvelous dream, my difficulties became easy to manage. My burdens truly became light, as He promised.

Our Savior knew that some of the trials of this life, this journey as it were, would be frightening to us. Because He loves us, He comforted us with these words: "Peace I leave with you, my peace I give unto you:

not as the world giveth, give I unto you. Let not your heart be troubled, neither let it be afraid." (John 14:27.)

The Savior gives us peace. When He said, "Let not your heart be troubled," He was telling us to choose not to be troubled. Paraphrasing, "Do not allow your heart to be troubled." Do we have faith that the words of life and light He taught are true? If so, we have no need to be afraid. His peace is not from the world, but His peace is that which comes from heartfelt faith. Faith is the antidote for fear. Faith gives us the hope and expectation that He will attend us, protect us, and lead us along the correct path while in this life. We have hope for a better world than this awaiting us hereafter.

Remembering that our Lord has all power will help us feel at peace, even in this troubled world we must live in. In 1 Nephi 7:12 the prophet Nephi asks his erring brothers, "How is it that ye have forgotten that the Lord is able to do all things according to his will, for the children of men, if it so be that they exercise faith in him? Wherefore, let us be faithful to him."

The Lord is "able to do all things" for us. He gives us all our blessings. He has the power to forgive our sins upon repentance on our part. He has the power to protect us, sustain us, and guide us on the road to eternal life.

In the Book of Mormon we read of the power of a prayer offered in total faith: "Behold, I say unto you that whoso believeth in Christ, doubting nothing, whatsoever he shall ask the Father in the name of Christ it shall be granted him; and this promise is unto all, even unto the ends of the earth." (Mormon 9:21.)

President Brigham Young also stressed the Lord's willingness to grant our desires if we ask in faith: "If the Latter-day Saints will walk up to their privileges and exercise faith in the name of Jesus Christ and live in the enjoyment of the fullness of the Holy Ghost constantly day by day, there is nothing on the face of the earth that they could ask for that would not be given to them. The Lord is waiting to be very gracious unto this people and to pour upon them riches, honor, glory, and power . . . according to the promises He has made through His apostles and prophets." (*Journal of Discourses* 11:114.)

Jesus Christ, our advocate with the Father, is personally involved in our lives. President Howard W. Hunter pointed out that we can gain strength in Christ: "Some of our concerns may come in the form of temptations. Others may be difficult decisions pertaining to education or career or money or marriage. Whatever your burden is, you will find the strength you need in Christ. Jesus Christ is Alpha and Omega, literally the beginning and the end. He is with us from the start to finish, and as such is more than a spectator in our lives." ("Fear Not, Little Flock," given March 14, 1989, *Devotional Speeches of the Year*, Provo, Utah: Brigham Young University Press, 1988-89, p. 115.)

Our daughter Jean bears this testimony of the effect of the Atonement in her life, and of our Savior's love:

> I remember clearly the first time I was aware that I had been touched by the effect of the atonement of Christ, and the Holy Ghost. I was about thirteen and I felt so happy that I skipped all the way home from church. I remember feeling that someone had removed all the sixty watt bulbs from all the light fixtures and had installed 100 watt bulbs instead. There was so much more light in the world! I remember seeing no sense in being mean or grouchy anymore as had been my habit before.
>
> Another time I know I was changed by the Atonement of our Savior was when I went to the temple for my own endowments. When I left the temple I knew that my sins had been forgiven me. Through and through I knew it, and I wept in my weakness and gratitude.
>
> Recently we were given the agony of the death of our 18 month old baby after a brief illness. Many spiritual manifestations have accompanied that event, and any reassurances one can get at a time like that are very much appreciated. I was especially worried about our preschooler, though, five-year-old Robbie, who was closest in age to the baby, and was his daily playmate. He was also present in the midst of the trauma of Jimmy's death and experienced many things his brothers and sister, who were at school, did not have to suffer. Robbie had become very difficult, and my heart ached for him as I tried to figure out how to help.
>
> One morning about six weeks later Robbie slept in late, and when he awoke he came in to me and said, "Mommy, I had a wonderful dream!" He told me that he had been taken to a "crystally" place with beautiful trees where our baby Jimmy and Jesus were. He had played with Jimmy, and Jimmy and Jesus had told him he was a good

boy! Then they had sung him a song. The song they sang was the one from Primary that goes, "I will go, I will do the things the Lord commands."

I began crying as my son told me of his dream. I knew that this dream had been given of the Lord, much as Lehi's dream or King Nebuchadnezzar's dream had been. I was so grateful that in our despair the Lord had seen fit to give us some help for our little son. I am humbled and awestruck that our Lord would take the time to come and personally comfort a little one in distress.

The following week in Primary a sister was showing the children how we feel when the Holy Ghost comes into us. She had cut the silhouette of a body out of cardboard and covered it with beige cloth. To show that when the Holy Ghost is with us we feel filled with light, she shined a flashlight through it. When Robbie saw this he jumped up on his chair, pointed to her illustration and called out, "My dream! That's how it was in my dream!"

Robbie has been better since then, and we have all been reassured of the unfailing love of our Savior, even, or perhaps especially, in our grief.

We have a hope which bears us up. We are able to stand in this troubled world in the midst of uncertainty and doubt, in the midst of turmoil and fear, and stand firm in spite of all the troubles that surround us. This is the promise which was made before the world began, and which continues on even today.

Elder Neal A. Maxwell talked of how this hope brings strength to lift us up and deal with the difficulties of everyday life: "Thus true hope focuses us on the great realities—'things as they really are'—and frees us from unneeded anxiety, but *not* from the necessity of patient endurance. When we are down and discouraged, the hope of Christ can lift us up lest we remain vulnerable overlong." (*Notwithstanding My Weakness*, p. 49, emphasis included.)

This is a hope in Jesus Christ. This hope keeps the eternal picture before our minds, and helps us to realize that the difficulties of this life are just stones in the journey. It can help us see that our own feelings of inadequacy result from lack of faith or from an obscured view of the goal. The glorious ideal is always there. We can depend on it.

Elder Maxwell continues: "Our hope rests upon a dependable expectation. . . . It stiffens, not slackens, the spine. It is anticipation that turns into day-by-day determination. It is an eager and an enthusiastic expectation based upon a dependable and justifiable object of hope, the triumph of the resurrection-generating Lord Jesus Christ. It is this hope, and this hope alone, that permits us to 'endure well' to the end—knowing that the end is but a glorious beginning! It is this same hope that is such a vital and helping virtue when we must 'continue the journey' notwithstanding our weaknesses." (p. 49.)

President Kimball summed it up in these words:

> Christ's atonement gives man hope. We have a hope in Christ here and now. He died for our sins. Because of him and his gospel, our sins are washed away in the waters of baptism; sin and iniquity are burned out of our souls as though by fire; and we become clean, have clear consciences, and gain that peace which passeth understanding. (See Philippians 4:7.)
>
> But today is just a grain of sand in the Sahara of eternity. We have also a hope in Christ for the eternity that lies ahead; otherwise, as Paul said, we would be "of all men most miserable." (I Corinthians 15:19.) (*Teachings of Spencer W. Kimball*, p. 22.)

Our son Glenn bears this fervent testimony of the power of the Atonement in his life:

> I know that Jesus Christ is the Son of God. I know that God lives. I know that He is my Heavenly Father and as my Heavenly Father, He knows me, He loves me, and He is interested in me and my success. I know that Christ is His Only Begotten Son, the King of Kings, the Lord of Lords, my Redeemer, my Elder Brother, and my Friend. He loves me and He died for me.
>
> I know this is true not only because I've read the beautiful story of His life in the scriptures, not only because I've been taught the stories of Jesus since I was a child, not only because of scores of lessons on His life, teachings, and sacrifice, but because His sacrifice has changed me, purified me and made a personal difference in my life.
>
> I know what it is like to feel unclean, unworthy, and to suppose myself unloved. But I also know what it feels like to be cleansed from these feelings and to feel new and whole again. I know that the

story of Jesus is not only the greatest story ever told but that it is
REAL! I know what it feels like to be forgiven and cleansed through
the atonement of Jesus. By personal experience, I have felt the
change in my heart making me pure and whole again. It is through
this personal experience with forgiveness, more than by any other
avenue, that I know it is all true and that Jesus is the Son of God,
that He is the Anointed One—my personal Savior.

I love Christ and I know He lives. I know He was born of a virgin
and died a sinless sacrifice for me. I know that someway, somehow,
when He was suffering the pains of mankind, he saw—through the
corridors of time—me, my life, and my sins, and that he prayed to
the Father, "Father, forgive him, for he knows not what he does."
My heart swells and sings the song of redeeming love for the love I
feel for my Savior.

I thank God, my Heavenly Father, that He was willing to send His
Son to make it possible for me to be purified and return to my
heavenly home.

Faith in the Lord Jesus Christ, The First Principle of the Gospel

Faith, a Shield Against Evil

In our journey toward purity of heart, the principles of the Gospel are the principles of purification. In Paul's analogy, he called Faith the shield. Along with what we already have: our hiking boots (preparation in the gospel of peace), our girdle of Truth, (according to D&C 93:24, an understanding of things as they were, as they are, and as they are to come), and our helmet of Salvation, (a recognition of the mission of Jesus Christ), we now pick up our shield of Faith and move forward with confidence and determination, in the face of whatever may befall us.

According to the Articles of Faith, a concise statement of the doctrines of the Restoration written by the Prophet Joseph Smith, faith is the first principle of the gospel. It is essential to understand and apply this basic principle not only as a basis for our doctrine, but as an active force in our lives.

We are all familiar with the definition of faith in Hebrews 11:1, "Now faith is the substance of things hoped for, the evidence of things not seen." The Prophet Joseph Smith clarified this scripture by translating the word *substance* as *assurance*: "Now faith is the *assurance* of things hoped for, the evidence of things not seen. . . . But without faith it is impossible to please him; for he that cometh to God must believe that he is, and that he is a rewarder of them that diligently seek him." (Hebrews 11:1,6, JST.)

Faith is a reassuring force in our lives. It assures us that the things we hope for, but cannot see, are true. Alma further explains what it is that we hope for when we have faith: "Faith is not to have a perfect knowledge of things; therefore if ye have faith ye hope for things which are not seen, which are true." (Alma 32:21.)

Faith, then, must be an assurance or confidence that the promises we hope for are true, even though the evidence cannot be seen with the eyes. It is not a perfect knowledge, because, as Alma says, "If a man knoweth a thing he hath no cause to believe, for he knoweth it." (Alma 32:18.) Faith has an element of *belief* and *trust* in addition to *hope*.

Faith is the assurance that our Father in Heaven lives and that Jesus is the Christ, the Savior of the world. It is the confidence that if we will repent, we will be forgiven. It is the assurance that we can be healed by the power of the priesthood when we become sick. It is the assurance that we are sons or daughters of God, and that He hears and answers our prayers. It is the assurance that the Savior himself will come and help us carry our heavy loads. It is the assurance that the Holy Ghost will be our constant companion, to lead, guide, and direct our lives, and purify and sanctify us, preparing us to live with our Father in Heaven and His Son Jesus Christ after this life is over, if we are faithful.

The Prophet Joseph Smith taught that "Miracles are the fruits of faith. . . . Faith comes by hearing the word of God. If a man has not faith enough to do one thing, he may have faith enough to do another: if he cannot remove a mountain, he may heal the sick. Where faith is there will be some of the fruits: all gifts and power which were sent from heaven, were poured out on the heads of those who had faith." (*History of the Church of Jesus Christ of Latter-day Saints*, 5:355.)

Referring to this and other statements made by the Prophet Joseph Smith, Elder Bruce R. McConkie said that the Prophet "equates faith with power. He uses the terms interchangeably. Indeed, the possession of power constitutes the test whereby we can measure and determine the quality and the degree of faith we possess. Our faith consists of the degree of power and influence we have with God our Father whereby we work works of righteousness and do many miraculous works." ("Lord, Increase Our Faith," Address at Brigham Young University, October 31, 1967, p. 3.)

So faith, besides being an assurance and a belief in truth, includes *power*. This is stated by other prophets as well. Ammon says that he gained "power according to my faith," (Alma 18:35) and Nephi tells us that the righteous have "power given them to do all things by faith." (2 Nephi 1:10.)

There are innumerable examples of the power of God granted to those who are strong of faith. Helaman's grandson Nephi had such strong faith that he had power to work miracles. We read of his remarkable ministry:

> And Nephi did minister with power and with great authority.
>
> And it came to pass that they were angry with him, even because he had greater power than they, for it were not possible that they could disbelieve his words, for so great was his faith on the Lord Jesus Christ that angels did minister unto him daily.
>
> And in the name of Jesus did he cast out devils and unclean spirits; and even his brother did he raise from the dead, after he had been stoned and suffered death by the people.
>
> And the people saw it, and did witness of it, and were angry with him because of his power; and he did also do many more miracles, in the sight of the people, in the name of Jesus. (3 Nephi 7:17-20.)

This scripture tells us that Nephi's power came because of his great faith. Enoch was another prophet who was able to perform miracles because of his faith. His faith, like Nephi's, gave him power: "And so great was the faith of Enoch that he led the people of God, and their enemies came to battle against them; and he spake the word of the Lord, and the earth trembled, and the mountains fled, even according to his command; and the rivers of water were turned out of their course; and the roar of the lions was heard out of the wilderness; and all nations feared greatly, so powerful was the word of Enoch, and so great was the power of the language which God had given him." (Moses 7:13.)

Moroni reminds us, "Christ hath said: If ye will have faith in me ye shall have power to do whatsoever thing is expedient in me." (Moroni 7:33.) Perhaps it is not "expedient" or necessary that we be able to move mountains through our faith. However it is necessary that we face and overcome the challenges in our daily lives. These challenges may be as important to us as moving a mountain was to Enoch.

President George Q. Cannon said that through faith we can accomplish whatever is required of us: "The strength of the Latter-day Saints is their faith. By that they can accomplish anything they set their hearts to do if it is right. God will be with them and sustain them. He has done it all the time. We have accomplished apparent impossibilities through the power and blessing of God and the faith of the people. If we have faith, we can accomplish all things that are required at our hands. . . . We can do everything that is required of us by the principle of faith, actively exhibited in works." (CR, October 1898, p. 5.)

Elder A. Theodore Tuttle emphasized how necessary this shield of active faith is for us: "We're not going to survive in this world, temporally or spiritually, without increased faith in the Lord—and I don't mean a positive mental attitude—I mean downright solid faith in the Lord Jesus Christ. That is the one thing that gives vitality and power to otherwise rather weak individuals." (*CR, Ensign,* November 1986, p. 73.)

We all have a certain measure of faith. We believe that the sun will rise tomorrow, that there will be winter, spring, summer, and fall. We have an amount of faith in our own abilities. We probably all believe that our Heavenly Father created and set in order those days and seasons. In addition to this, we need faith in the Lord Jesus Christ, acceptance of the reality of His sacrifice and atonement for us, and an application of this acceptance in our daily lives.

Developing Faith

In order to progress in the gospel we must all have faith. How can we develop and increase our faith? Alma taught us simply and beautifully how this can be done (from Alma 32). He compared the word of God to a seed and invited all to "awake and arouse your faculties, even to an experiment upon my words, and exercise a particle of faith, yea, even if ye can no more than desire to believe, let this desire work in you, even until ye believe in a manner that ye can give place for a portion of my words." (Alma 32:27.) First, therefore, we must have a desire to believe.

Alma then tells us that we must allow the word, like a seed, to be planted in our hearts. In other words, we must make a place in our lives for the experiment of faith. We must *try* the gospel in our lives. He says, "If ye give place, that a seed may be planted in your heart, behold, if it be a true seed, or a good seed, if ye do not cast it out by your unbelief, that ye will resist the Spirit of the Lord, behold, it will begin to swell within your breasts; and when you feel these swelling motions, ye will begin to say within yourselves—It must needs be that this is a good seed, or that the word is good, for it beginneth to enlarge my soul; yea, it beginneth to enlighten my understanding, yea, it beginneth to be delicious to me."

After we have begun to give the gospel a place in our lives by living by its precepts, if we are not resisting the Spirit, we will begin to see improvement in our lives. As Alma says, the seed of the gospel will begin to be delicious to us. We will begin to see good results from obeying the commandments.

"Now behold," Alma asks, "would not this increase your faith? I say unto you, Yea; nevertheless it hath not grown up to a perfect knowledge." Because of our obedience in allowing a portion of the gospel into our lives, our faith has increased.

If we now stop the experiment, can we call it a success? Alma warns us that we can't, saying, "Is your knowledge perfect? Behold I say unto you, Nay; neither must ye lay aside your faith, for ye have only exercised your faith to plant the seed that ye might try the experiment to know if the seed was good."

So now we know the seed of the gospel we have planted in our lives is good. We feel enlightened; our souls feel enlarged; we *feel* good! Now, we continue in the experiment. Alma says, "And behold, as the tree beginneth to grow, ye will say: Let us nourish it with great care, that it may get root, that it may grow up, and bring forth fruit unto us. And now behold, if ye nourish it with much care it will get root, and grow up, and bring forth fruit."

What will happen if we neglect the tree we are growing through our faith? Alma says, "But if ye neglect the tree, and take no thought for its nourishment, behold it will not get any root; and when the heat of the sun cometh and scorcheth it, because it hath no root it withers away, and ye pluck it up and cast it out.

"Now, this is not because the seed was not good, neither is it because the fruit thereof would not be desirable; but it is because your ground is barren, and ye will not nourish the tree, therefore ye cannot have the fruit thereof." (See Alma 32:33-39.)

The tree we have planted in our souls is a gift from God. We nourish it and keep it from dying by keeping the commandments of our Heavenly Father. We exercise our faith voluntarily, by choosing to have active confidence in the gospel principles.

First, we continually give the gospel a place in our lives by obeying the commandments. President George Albert Smith said, "Faith is a gift of God; it is the fruitage of righteous living. It does not come to us by our command but is the result of doing the will of our Heavenly Father." (*Latter-day Prophets Speak*, p. 96.)

As we do this, we see that our lives improve. The assurance that this improvement comes from our obedience in turn increases our faith.

Second, we add works of righteousness to nourish our faith and increase its growth; because, as President John Taylor said, "Faith without works being dead, it is evident that living faith and that which is acceptable to God, is that which not only believes in God, but acts upon that belief. It is not only the cause of action, but includes both cause and action. Or in other words it is belief or faith made perfect by works." (*Latter-day Prophets Speak*, p. 97.)

Perhaps you feel that you have tried to exercise faith, but have not received the blessing you desired. Moroni discusses this when he says, "I would show unto the world that faith is things which are hoped for and not seen; wherefore, dispute not because ye see not, for ye receive no witness until after the trial of your faith.

"For it was by faith that Christ showed himself unto our fathers, after he had risen from the dead; and he showed not himself unto them until after they had faith in him; wherefore, it must needs be that some had faith in him, for he showed himself not unto the world." (Ether 12:6-7.)

Sometimes when we think we are not receiving answers to our prayers, it could be that we are undergoing a trial of faith, and that we must continue exercising faith longer, to receive the desired blessing. Elder Richard G. Scott tells of such an experience, as related by President Kimball:

> A relative asked Elder Spencer W. Kimball for a blessing to combat a crippling disease. For some time Elder Kimball prepared himself spiritually; then, fasting, he was prompted to bless her to be healed. Some weeks later she returned, angry and complaining that she was "fed up" with waiting for the Lord to give the promised relief.
>
> He responded: "Now I understand why you have not been blessed. You must be patient, do your part, and express gratitude for the smallest improvement noted."
>
> She repented, followed scrupulously his counsel, and eventually was made well. (CR, *Ensign*, November 1991, p. 85.)

Faith and Works

In the New Testament we read, "Faith without works is dead." (James 2:20.) The dictionary defines "work" as, "physical or mental effort exerted to do or make something; purposeful activity; labor; toil." (*Webster's New World Dictionary of the American Language*, 2nd College Edition, 1970, p. 1638.) So work is a physical or mental effort, and faith without works is dead. We must have a living faith, evidenced by our exerting ourselves mentally and physically in order to exercise our faith.

The importance of combining faith with works is a powerful spiritual principle. There is a wonderful discourse on the link between faith and works in the book of James in the New Testament. There we read,

> What doth it profit, my brethren, though a man say he hath faith, and have not works? can faith save him?
>
> If a brother or sister be naked, and destitute of daily food,
>
> And one of you say unto them, Depart in peace, be ye warmed and filled; notwithstanding ye give them not those things which are needful to the body; what doth it profit?
>
> Even so faith, if it hath not works, is dead, being alone. (James 2:14-17.)

As we read this we can imagine a pompous Pharisee of that day dismissing the poor with a sanctimonious "Be ye warmed and filled," without lifting a hand to actually help those in need. And yet, do we ever find ourselves guilty of the same thoughtlessness? Do we see our own spirit starving for spiritual sustenance and, instead of filling its needs by studying the gospel and praying, do we wave it away with a thoughtless, "Depart in peace"? Can we nourish a flagging faith without works of righteousness?

James' sermon ends with this conclusion: "Ye see then how that by works a man is justified, and not by faith only. . . . For as the body without the spirit is dead, so faith without works is dead also." (James 2:24,26)

There are two aspects to the exercise of our faith. One is the developing and strengthening of our own faith, the other of actively using that faith to make things come to pass. Both forms of "works" are essential. Works coupled with faith will produce spiritual power in our lives.

Elder Bruce R. McConkie said that "faith is a gift of God bestowed as a reward for personal righteousness" (*Mormon Doctrine*, p. 264). The more obedient we are to God's laws, the greater will be our endowment of faith.

Thinking confidently about solutions to a problem is exercising our faith in a positive way. Combining mental exertion with fervent prayer merges faith and works. Elder H. Burke Petersen said, "Prayer strengthens faith. Prayer is the preparation for miracles. Prayer opens the door to eternal happiness." (*A Glimpse of Glory*, p. 23.)

President Gordon B. Hinckley recalled an account of how a young missionary who was overwhelmed by his challenge found his faith strengthened through prayer and fasting:

> I was touched last fall by the heartbreaking statement of a young man in Japan. He said, "I have been here for months. I can't learn the language. I dislike the people. I am depressed by day and weep at night. . . . I wrote my mother and pleaded for an excuse to return home. I have her reply. She says: 'We're praying for you. There is not a day passes that all of us do not kneel together in the morning before we eat and in the evening before we retire and plead with the Lord for his blessing upon you. We have added fasting to our prayer, and when your younger brothers and sisters pray they say, 'Heavenly Father, bless Johnny in Japan and help him to learn the language and do the work he was called to do.'"
>
> This young man then went on to say through his tears, "I will try again. I will add my prayers to theirs and my fasting to their fasting."
>
> Now, four months later, I have a letter from him in which he says, "A miracle has happened. The language has come to me as a gift from the Lord. I have learned to love the people in this beautiful land. God be thanked for the prayers of my family." (CR, *Ensign*, June 1963, p. 532.)

This young elder mentioned a sometimes neglected aspect of exercising our faith through prayer, that of gratitude. Gratitude increases our faith by helping us realize where our blessings really come from. The scriptures admonish us over and over to be thankful for all things. (See Colossians 3:15, Mosiah 26:39, D&C 46:7, D&C 59:7.) We should include gratitude in every prayer we offer, and sometimes take the initiative to make a prayer simply for thankfulness, with no special need to address. Our Father lists ingratitude as one of the few things that offend Him (D&C 59:21).

We can also exercise faith by asking for priesthood blessings when we are ill. Of this President George Q. Cannon said, "Children who are taught by their parents to desire the laying on of hands by the Elders when they are sick receive astonishing benefits therefrom, and their faith becomes exceedingly strong." (*Gospel Truth*, p. 426.) This requires faith, and also strengthens faith.

Another way to strengthen our faith is to study and meditate upon the scriptures. Elder Gene R. Cook writes,

> I would suggest another way to better know the Lord: an intense, continual, and prayerful search to know him through the scriptures. The Lord has revealed in the scriptures much of what we need to know about his characteristics, perfections, and attributes.
>
> The Lord told Martin Harris through the Prophet Joseph Smith, "Learn of me, and listen to my words; walk in the meekness of my Spirit, and you shall have peace in me." (D&C 19:23.) Samuel, the Lamanite, noted that many of the Nephites were "led to believe the holy scriptures, . . . which leadeth them to faith on the Lord." (Helaman 15:7.) Studying the scriptures is a powerful way to learn to know the Lord and develop faith in him. (*Living By The Power of Faith*, p. 38.)

If we prayerfully read the scriptures we will find our faith strengthened day after day. I have found this to be the case as I listen to the Book of Mormon on tape driving from job to job. My eyes get moist as I feel the spirit of those great prophets. It seems I really get to know them well. When one passes away, on to the next prophet I go. The new prophet's personality emanates forth from his writings. What a spiritual feast! I love all of them and look forward to meeting them in the next life.

Another way to nourish our faith is to hear the testimony of others. Elder Gene R. Cook said, "As you hear someone's testimony, your faith has a chance to increase. Your faith in the fact that God lives begins to grow and develop. Think of the words of Paul: 'Faith cometh by hearing, and hearing by the word of God.' (Romans 10:17.) Some ask, 'Do we really need to attend our meetings? Do we need to go where the servants of the Lord are preaching the gospel?' My answer would be, 'If you want your faith to increase, you need to be there.'" (*Living By The Power of Faith*, p. 36.)

We need to listen to general conference, attend stake conference, priesthood meeting, Relief Society, Sunday School, and sacrament meeting. By attending our meetings and prayerfully learning the gospel principles taught, our faith will be strengthened, which will help to keep us on the strait and narrow path that leads to eternal life.

When we mentally exert ourselves by faith, prayer, and meditation, we will see the spiritual power it brings into our lives. Through exercising our faith, rains can come, sickness can be healed, problems can be solved, lives can be mended, love can be regained, challenges can be met.

The Fruits of Faith

As we strengthen our faith we spontaneously increase in good works. In James 2:18 we read, "Yea, a man may say, Thou hast faith, and I have works: shew me thy faith without thy works, and I will shew thee my faith *by my works*." (James 2:18, emphasis added.) When we have faith in the Savior, we naturally reach out to others in love. We care about their needs, and do what we can to help. We treat our families more kindly, we respond positively to the interactions of those around us. We seek for ways to serve in the community.

The Apostle Paul knew how important it was for us to know the faith-empowered works of those who have gone before us, and so he wrote a beautiful sermon on faith, relating numerous examples of the works of faith in the scriptures. We are fortunate to have this sermon recorded in the book of Hebrews:

> By faith Abel offered unto God a more excellent sacrifice than Cain, by which he obtained witness that he was righteous. . . .
>
> By faith Enoch was translated that he should not see death. . . .
>
> By faith Noah, being warned of God of things not seen as yet, moved with fear, prepared an ark to the saving of his house. . . .
>
> Through faith also Sara herself received strength to conceive seed, and was delivered of a child when she was past age, because she judged him faithful who had promised. . . .
>
> By faith Abraham, when he was tried, offered up Isaac. . . .
>
> By faith Moses, when he was come to years, refused to be called the son of Pharaoh's daughter;
>
> Choosing rather to suffer affliction with the people of God, than to enjoy the pleasures of sin for a season;
>
> Esteeming the reproach of Christ greater riches than the treasures in Egypt. . . .
>
> By faith the walls of Jericho fell down, after they were compassed about seven days.
>
> (See Hebrews 11:4-35.)

In the Book of Mormon we find a continuation of this theme of the miracles wrought by faith:

Behold, it was the faith of Alma and Amulek that caused the prison to tumble to the earth.

Behold, it was the faith of Nephi and Lehi that wrought the change upon the Lamanites, that they were baptized with fire and with the Holy Ghost.

Behold, it was the faith of Ammon and his brethren which wrought so great a miracle among the Lamanites.

Yea, and even all they who wrought miracles wrought them by faith, even those who were before Christ and also those who were after.

And it was by faith that the three disciples obtained a promise that they should not taste of death; and they obtained not the promise until after their faith. (Ether 12:13-17.)

President Gordon B. Hinckley continued this recitation of the miracles wrought by faith, naming events that have happened in these latter days:

The history of this Church is a history of the expression of . . . faith. It began with a farm boy in the year 1829 when he read the great promise set forth in the Epistle of James:

"If any of you lack wisdom, let him ask of God, that giveth to all men liberally, and upbraideth not; and it shall be given him.

"But let him ask in faith, nothing wavering, for he that wavereth is like a wave of the sea driven with the wind and tossed." (James 1:5-6.)

It was faith, the simple faith of a fourteen-year-old boy, that took him into the woods that spring morning. It was faith that took him to his knees in pleading for understanding. The marvelous fruit of that faith was a vision glorious and beautiful, of which this great work is but the extended shadow.

. . . It was by faith that a small band of early converts, notwithstanding the very powers of hell brought against them, strengthened and sustained one another, left home and family to spread the word, moved from New York to Ohio and from Ohio to Missouri and from Missouri to Illinois in their search for peace and freedom to worship God according to the dictates of conscience. . .

It was by faith that Brigham Young looked over this valley, then hot and barren, and declared, "This is the place." . . .

With vision, with labor, and with confidence in the power of God working through them, [the pioneers] brought their faith to reality.

Behind us is a glorious history. It is bespangled with heroism, tenacity to principle, and unflagging fidelity. It is the product of faith. Before us is a great future. It begins today. . . .With faith we must go forward. . . .

There is no obstacle too great, no challenge too difficult, that we cannot meet with faith. (CR, *Ensign*, November 1983, pp. 52-53.)

We inherit a great tradition of faith from our brothers and sisters who have lived upon the earth. It is now our turn to lift the torch of faith and move ourselves and the Church forward so that we can partake of the sweet fruits of faith and righteousness. Alma, after explaining the experiment of faith, told us of the promised blessings if we will strengthen our faith until the end:

But if ye will nourish the word, yea, nourish the tree as it beginneth to grow, by your faith with great diligence, and with patience, looking forward to the fruit thereof, it shall take root; and behold it shall be a tree springing up unto everlasting life.

And because of your diligence and your faith and your patience with the word in nourishing it, that it may take root in you, behold, by and by ye shall pluck the fruit thereof, which is most precious, which is sweet above all that is sweet, and which is white above all that is white, yea, and pure above all that is pure; and ye shall feast upon this fruit even until ye are filled, that ye hunger not, neither shall ye thirst.

Then, my brethren, ye shall reap the rewards of your faith, and your diligence, and patience, and long-suffering, waiting for the tree to bring forth fruit unto you. (Alma 32:41-43.)

How sweet are the fruits of faith! How precious to each one of us! If we nourish our faith, we will receive the fruit, which is everlasting life. If faith is still an experiment in your life, begin today. The faith you exercise will gain the reward "which is most precious."

Once we have received our faith and nourished it by our study, prayer, and good works, we will not lose it if we continue doing the things which increased our faith. President Heber J. Grant said, "Faith is a gift of God, and faith comes to each and all of us who serve God and supplicate Him for the guidance of His Spirit. There is no danger of any man or woman losing his or her faith in this Church if he or she is humble and prayerful and obedient to duty. I have never known of such an individual losing his faith. By doing our duty faith increases until it becomes perfect knowledge." (*Latter-day Prophets Speak*, p. 97.)

Faith in God and in His Son Jesus Christ

The first principle of the gospel is to have faith in our Father in Heaven and His Son Jesus Christ. Believe that Christ knows all things. President Ezra Taft Benson said, "Faith in [Jesus Christ] means believing that even though we do not understand all things, He does." (CR, *Ensign*, November 1983, p. 8.) Because He understands all things, we can trust Him to protect us and guide our lives.

Because He has all power, we can have faith that He can help us overcome the obstacles we face in our lives, whatever they may be. President Spencer W. Kimball said, "You will meet Goliaths who threaten you. Whether your Goliath is a town bully or is the temptation to steal or to destroy or the temptation to rob or the desire to curse and swear; if your Goliath is the desire to wantonly destroy or the temptation to lust and to sin, or the urge to avoid activity, whatever is your Goliath, he can be slain. But remember, to be the victor, one must follow the path that David followed: 'David behaved himself wisely in all his ways; and the Lord was with him.' (1 Samuel 18:14)" (CR, *Ensign*, November 1974, p. 82.) Not only does the Lord have power to deliver us, the Lord has power to help us change. Whatever the Goliath that threatens our peace and security, faith in Jesus Christ will enable us to gain the victory.

Jesus Christ has power even over death. Mormon 7:5 tells us that we must "believe in Jesus Christ, that he is the Son of God, and that he was slain by the Jews, and by the power of the Father he hath risen again, whereby he hath gained the victory over the grave; and also in him is the sting of death swallowed up." Through Jesus Christ we will be victorious over death, a free gift to all of us. Beyond that is the reward of the faithful, the promise of eternal life, continuation of family ties, and peace and rest in the presence of our Father and Jesus Christ in the celestial kingdom.

Furthermore, if we have faith in Jesus Christ we will be comforted in knowing that the offered prize of eternal life is worth all the trials, uncertainties, and problems we face.

Faith to Obey the Commandments

In the scriptures, faith is often connected with obedience to the commandments. In 1 Nephi 15:11 Nephi reminds his hard-hearted brothers of the Lord's promise that "if ye will not harden your hearts, and ask me in faith, believing that ye shall receive, *with diligence in keeping my commandments*, surely these things shall be made known unto you." (Emphasis added.)

Later on the Nephites, led by Captain Moroni in defending themselves against the attacking Lamanites, express their faith that "if they were faithful in keeping the commandments of God that he would prosper them in the land." (Alma 48:15.)

In our day, too, it takes faith to obey the commandments. President Kimball said,

> It takes faith—unseeing faith—for young people to proceed immediately with their family responsibilities in the face of financial uncertainties. It takes faith for the young woman to bear her family instead of accepting employment, especially when schooling for the young husband is to be finished. It takes faith to observe the Sabbath when "time and a half" can be had working, when profit can be made, when merchandise can be sold. It takes a great faith to pay tithes when funds are scarce and demands are great. It takes faith to fast and have family prayers and to observe the Word of Wisdom. It takes faith to do home teaching, stake missionary work, and other service, when sacrifice is required. It takes faith to fill full-time missions. But know this—that all these are of the planting, while faithful, devout families, spiritual security, peace, and eternal life are the harvest. (*Faith Precedes the Miracle*, p. 11.)

Faithfulness may require sacrifice on both sides. It may be in things we do, or in things we refrain from doing. We may sacrifice time or goods in the work of the Lord, or we may sacrifice immediate satisfactions in order to fulfill eternal commitments. In either case, it is important to look upon our time here on this earth as limited and very important. It is essential that we choose carefully. Choosing is basically a way of foregoing something in favor of something else—hopefully choosing something eternally better than what we choose to forego.

As fathers and mothers in our homes, we can exercise our faith in God by raising our children in righteousness. Holding a family home evening each week in which we teach our children the gospel is an act of faith. Interviewing children once a month or when they have problems takes faith. Reading the scriptures with our children on a daily basis takes faith. Having family prayer and individual prayer night and morning takes faith. How can we increase our faith so we have enough to raise our families in righteousness? It takes faith to do it, and doing it increases our faith, a process we like to call the "upward spiral to joy."

It takes faith to have individual prayer during each day. Do it, and as the blessings come, thank Him. It takes faith to pay tithing, live the Word of Wisdom, stay morally clean, keep the Sabbath day holy, or obey any other commandment. Strength comes by doing it, and makes it easier to do. He wants us to succeed. He hears every prayer. Ask for the blessings you need. His work and glory is to help us solve our problems. The rewards far outweigh the sacrifice.

President Heber J. Grant tells us that faith helps us listen to the counsel of our Church leaders: "Faith is a gift of God, and when people have faith to live the gospel, and to listen to the counsel of those who preside in the wards and stakes and of the General Authorities of the Church, it has been my experience that they have been abundantly blessed of the Lord, and that many of them have come out of great financial and other difficulties in a most miraculous and wonderful way." (*Latter-day Prophets Speak*, p. 97.)

Note that President Grant equates being obedient to the counsel of those who preside in the wards and stakes, and to the General Authorities of the Church, with obedience to God. The Lord tells us that whether we receive His word "by mine own voice or by the voice of my servants, it is the same." (D&C 1:38.) When our living prophets and leaders counsel us, telling us what the Lord would have us do from day to day, we ought to receive this counsel as though the Lord were speaking directly to us.

Faith in the Promises of the Lord

Abraham received many promises from the Lord, one of which was that he would be the father of many nations. However, he and his wife Sarah grew old and still they had no children. Did Abraham lose his faith in the promises of the Lord? In Romans 4:19-21 we read that Abraham "being not weak in faith, he considered not his own body now dead, when he was about an hundred years old, neither yet the deadness of Sara's womb: He staggered not at the promise of God through unbelief; but was strong in faith, giving glory to God; And being fully persuaded that, what he had promised, he was able also to perform."

Abraham "staggered not" when faced with the seeming impossibility, and the promise was fulfilled. Isaac was born to them, and through him came a posterity as numerous as the sands of the sea—including ourselves.

Matthew Cowley tells of an experience in which a miraculous priesthood blessing was fulfilled:

> I was asked to administer to a baby in New Zealand. I was asked to bless it. The father came up to me with this child, fourteen months old, and he said, "Our child has not been blessed yet, so I want you to give it a name." I said, "All right. What is the name?" He gave me the name of the child, and then he said in a matter-of-fact way, "While you are giving it its name, give it its sight." The child was born blind. He said, "We have had it to the specialists in Wellington. They said it was born blind and they cannot do anything for it. So while you are giving it a name, by the same authority you use to give it a name, give it its vision." Just as simple as that!
>
> Well, I was scared. I never had that faith. The thing came to me just suddenly like lightening out of the blue. But I went on and blessed the baby with a name. It was the longest blessing, I think, I have ever given. I was using all the words I could think of and had ever thought of. I was trying to get enough inspiration—enough nerve, if you want to call it that, to bless that child with its vision. I finally did.
>
> Eight months later I saw the child, and the child saw me. . . . Never let this simple faith get away from your life, never let it get away from you. It is the most precious thing you have in life. (quoted by Henry A. Smith, *Matthew Cowley: Man of Faith*, pp. 138-139.)

This young missionary was able to match his faith to that strong simple faith of the parents. Elder Cowley went on to become a very influential apostle, strengthening the faith of a generation of young people.

Bishop H. Burke Peterson gives this account of a young woman who received a promise in a priesthood blessing:

Some years ago I was a bishop of a ward in the United States. We had a group of young people in our ward who were fine examples of what Latter-day Saints ought to be. They got acquainted with a young teenage girl who was not a member of the Church. This teenage girl was deaf, but she had learned to read lips with her eyes, and if you stood in front of her and spoke to her, she could tell what you were saying by reading your lips. She also had an illness of her heart. She was unable to engage in any athletics with the other girls. The Mormon boys and girls were friendly to her and considerate of her and understanding. She liked the way they treated her. She liked their example. Soon she was invited to listen to the missionaries give the lessons. As they concluded the lessons, she believed what she had been taught and asked her parents if she could be baptized. They also had heard the lessons, but they didn't accept the truth as she did. They did give their permission for her to be baptized, however.

One Saturday afternoon we gathered at the baptismal font as this young deaf girl entered into the water. After the baptism she was to be confirmed a member of the Church. The elders asked me if I would like to stand in the circle. I did. I knew she wouldn't be able to hear the confirmation and blessing from the elder because she couldn't see his lips, so I listened very attentively to the blessing of the elder as he confirmed her a member of the Church. I wanted to tell her what he said after it was over.

The blessing was given by the elder. I could hardly believe my ears when I heard what he said, for he said some things that I would not believe possible. He had full faith that the Lord would grant the blessings he had given.

After the confirmation and blessing I invited the young lady to come to my office. She sat down in front of me as I was prepared now to tell her of the blessing that the elder had just given her. I said, "Nancy, I would like to tell you of the blessing that the elder gave you." She looked at me and said, "Bishop Peterson, I heard the blessing." From that time on Nancy Fuller could hear. She was no longer deaf. From that time on she could play volleyball and play softball and play tennis because her heart had also been healed. (in Conference Report, Korea Area Conference 1975, p. 25, as quoted in Deacon's Course A Manual, 1983, p. 22.)

The vitality of the Church is in the faith of its members, with experiences of the blessings of the Lord happening daily. A lady missionary we knew told of a sweet demonstration of faith rewarded while she was on her mission. One of her companions was from another country, extremely homesick, and having health problems, spending much time being sick in bed. It was a difficult situation, making it hard to do missionary work. On one occasion this troubled sister got angry and struck our friend, knocking her to the floor. She was stunned. Nothing like this had ever happened to her before. Not only was she injured, but her feelings were hurt deeply. She knew that companions should work together in harmony, and she did not know how to handle the situation. At a missionary conference the next day she asked for a priesthood blessing to help her compose her feelings, and know how to proceed. In this blessing, she was given the gift of charity, and was promised strength to be able to help her companion. Struggling within herself, she faced the question of how to deal with her feelings and the need to have peace between companions, so they could accomplish the missions they had been sent to do. The next morning she got on her knees and pled with the Lord for help. She felt she was not strong enough to forgive by herself. She asked for the gift of charity which had been promised. When she walked into the kitchen where her companion was preparing breakfast, she looked at her and suddenly felt a warm glow of peace flow over her from her head to her feet, encompassing her with a feeling of love for her companion. She instantly saw her with new eyes, recognizing her struggle to adjust to a new country and a new language, recognizing her immaturity and insecurity, and feeling a Christlike compassion and true love for her. She put her arms around her and told her in her native language that she loved her, that she was sorry if she had done anything to make her unhappy, and asked her forgiveness and understanding. They both wept tears of love and release, enveloped in the warmth of the sweet, holy moment. It was the beginning of happier times for both of them, and a lesson of strength and faith to last a lifetime—the Lord will fulfill his promises to the faithful.

Our greatest promise from the Lord is that those who remain faithful will inherit eternal life. Moroni 7:41 tells where to anchor our faith: "And what is it that ye shall hope for? Behold I say unto you that ye shall have hope through the atonement of Christ and the power of his resurrection, to be raised unto life eternal, and this because of your faith in him according to the promise." 1 John 2:25 tells us this: "And this is the promise that he hath promised us, even eternal life."

When we read the description in the Doctrine and Covenants of those who have inherited eternal life, we can see that faith is an essential attribute:

They are they who received the testimony of Jesus, and believed on his name and were baptized after the manner of his burial, being buried in the water in his name, and this according to the commandment which he has given—

That by keeping the commandments they might be washed and cleansed from all their sins, and receive the Holy Spirit by the laying on of the hands of him who is ordained and sealed unto this power; *And who overcome by faith."* (D&C 76:51-53, emphasis added.)

We have inherited a beautiful legacy of faith, both from our spiritual ancestors whose lives are told to us in the Bible and the Book of Mormon, and from our more recent spiritual ancestors, who shared in the founding years of the Latter-day Church. Let us exercise our faith in the promises of the Lord, and believe that "he will fulfil all his promises which he shall make unto [us], for he has fulfilled his promises which he has made unto our fathers." (Alma 37:17.) Faith is indeed the power by which our lives are molded, and the tap with which to call down the powers of heaven into our lives. Faith in the Lord Jesus Christ is the impelling power to righteous action.

6

The Blessings of Faith

Power to Overcome the Difficulties of Life

The Lord said to Nephi, "Blessed art thou, Nephi, because of thy faith." (1 Nephi 2:19.) President Spencer W. Kimball explained how faith can bring blessings, saying, "In each of our lives faith can . . . strengthen resolve against temptation, relieve from the bondage of harmful habits, lend the strength to repent and change our lives, and lead to a sure knowledge of the divinity of Jesus Christ. Indomitable faith can help us live the commandments with a willing heart and thereby bring blessings unnumbered, with peace, perfection, and exaltation in the kingdom of God." (*Faith Precedes the Miracle*, p. 12.)

There are many blessings that come through faith—as President Kimball said, "blessings unnumbered." Let's look at some of the blessings we can receive because of our faith.

There is an account in the Book of Mormon of a very faithful people —converted Lamanites. When they joined the Church, they were so fearful that their former sins would return to them, to the destruction of their souls, that they took an oath never again to shed the blood of their brethren, the ferocious Lamanites. When they were attacked, they were so faithful that they refused to break their oath, even though it meant laying down their own lives. The Nephites came to their defense, but it became obvious that the Nephites needed help. The faithful Lamanites would not break their oath, but they had righteous sons, born since their conversion, who had not taken the oath. These young men volunteered to fight for them, and became known as Helaman's stripling warriors. In the battles that followed these young men faced danger and possible death, and yet their faith helped them do what was necessary. The

Nephite leader, Helaman, was so proud of them he called them his "sons." (See Alma, chaps. 53 and 56.) Of these young men Elder Rex D. Pinegar said,

> A prophet-general described [the sons of Helaman] by saying, "They were exceedingly valiant for courage, and also for strength and activity; but behold, this was not all—they were men who were *true at all times in whatsoever thing they were entrusted. . . .*
>
> "Yea, they had been taught by their mothers, that if they did not doubt, God would deliver them. . . .
>
> "And they . . . fought as if with the strength of God; yea, never were men known to have fought with such miraculous strength; and with such mighty power." (Alma 53:20; 56:47,56, emphasis added.)
>
> What gave the sons of Helaman their strength? Their faith in God was their "miraculous strength" and "mighty power." (CR, *Ensign*, November 1982, p. 25.)

Because of their remarkable faith, Helaman's stripling warriors were blessed with protection. Not one of them was killed in battle. Truly, to these young men the blessings of faith were as a "breastplate of righteousness" protecting them from danger.

This same faith can protect us. Elder Pinegar continues, "Do not fear the challenges of life, but approach them patiently, with faith in God. He will reward your faith with power not only to endure, but also to overcome hardships, disappointments, trials, and struggles of daily living. Through diligently striving to live the law of God and with faith in Him, we will not be diverted from our eternal course either by the ways or the praise of the world." (p. 26.)

When we face trials or difficulties in our lives, faith can be the anchor that keeps us from being swept away. Sometimes our problems might cause us to question our belief in God, in His Church, in our own ability to remain steadfast. It is at these critical times in our lives that we need to answer doubt with faith—a state of mind that enables us to have courage—not necessarily for our own desires to be fulfilled, but courage to do what is right with assurance that God is in charge, and things will be best for us in the end.

Job was faced with overwhelmingly difficult challenges. He lost all that he had in life, except for his faith. It was his faith that helped him to persevere and overcome. After losing his children, his health, his home, and the support of his friends, he affirmed, "I know that my redeemer liveth, and that he shall stand at the latter day upon the earth: And though after my skin worms destroy this body, yet in my flesh shall I see God." (Job 19:25-26.)

Like Job, and Helaman's stripling warriors, we can receive strength through our faith. When we face adversity with faith, God can help us endure and ultimately prevail.

Our daughter Mary and her husband Kyle had a test of their faith, in which they learned that steadfast faith required great effort, but also brought great rewards. She says: "After several years of marriage we had not been able to have children, so we decided to adopt. Since we had both served missions in Taiwan, we looked for an agency that placed babies from that country.

"We did all the paperwork and waited, and the day finally came when we were able to go to Taiwan to receive our sweet baby daughter. The first time I looked into my baby's beautiful face I saw that there was a problem with one of her eyes.

"Several weeks were required to complete the adoption, and my husband had to return home, leaving me in Taiwan with our newborn baby.

"I invited a member of the local stake presidency to come over and administer to the baby. She was blessed that her eye would be healed, and that she would grow up normally and bring much joy to her parents. It was a beautiful blessing, and the Spirit attended it.

"In the days that followed I tried to have faith in the blessing, but it was difficult for me, anguished and alone, and I found myself crying over my child again and again.

"One night a friend came to see me, a native missionary I had known while on my mission. When she saw me crying, she was puzzled. Hadn't the baby been blessed that her eye would be healed? Hadn't I received an assurance of this? So why was I still crying?

"It made me think. Where was my faith? We had been promised so much—couldn't I have faith in the Lord's ability to fulfill His promises? I decided that I must exercise my faith and believe in the blessing.

"After I returned to the United States we took our daughter to the hospital to have her eye examined. The doctors determined that she needed surgery within the week to try to correct the defect they found there.

"A few days later my husband and I kissed our sweet baby goodbye and saw her wheeled off in a hospital crib. Even though this was difficult for us as new parents, we had determined that we were going to exercise faith in the promises of the Lord.

"After several hours the doctor appeared in the waiting room, a pleased smile on her face. The surgery had gone in the best possible way. The problem had been corrected, and the outlook was for normal vision. Normal! What a wonderful word."

This dear granddaughter has grown from that helpless baby into a sweet young girl, and her vision has been good, with no lingering problems. The parents, Mary and Kyle, have grown in faith and confidence in the Lord, who has strengthened and blessed them because of their faith.

Through Faith We Can Receive Personal Revelation

Revelation can come into our lives tailored to our personal needs. The Book of Mormon tells us how: "As many as are not stiffnecked and have faith, have communion with the Holy Spirit, which maketh manifest unto the children of men, according to their faith." (Jarom 1:4.)

All of us need the guidance of the Holy Ghost in our lives, and we can receive it by exercising faith. The Doctrine and Covenants tells us that we will receive answers through the Holy Ghost if we ask in faith: "Ask the Father in my name, in faith believing that you shall receive, and you shall have the Holy Ghost, which manifesteth all things which are expedient unto the children of men." (D&C 18:18.) It is "expedient" that we gain guidance for our personal needs, but not for the whole Church—that comes only through the prophets.

President George Q. Cannon assured us:

All may receive personal revelation. It is the privilege of every one to receive revelation. It is the privilege of every mother to receive revelation from God for guidance in the training of her children, to be in communication with the Father through the Holy Spirit. It is the privilege of children to have the same Spirit and to have knowledge from God through that Spirit. . . . It is . . . the privilege of every man, woman and child in the Church to have revelation, to have knowledge, to be instructed of the Lord. (*Gospel Truth*, p. 251).

One of our daughters told of an experience with the principle of personal revelation. She was having trouble with one of her older children teasing his little brother. She tried many ways to solve the problem, but nothing seemed to help, and she was worried about the effect this problem was having on both children.

She knew she needed divine help. With faith she prayed that she would understand what was causing the older child to act this way, in order that she could help him overcome the behavior. In the days that followed her mind was called back to some incidents in the past which helped her see new reasons for this undesirable conduct. She could feel the influence of the Holy Ghost helping her to understand why the teasing was going on, and how she could help the children solve it.

When she implemented the inspiration she had received, she saw marked improvement in both children. As she persisted in following the personal revelation, peace came into the home.

Through the Holy Ghost all of us can gain answers to the problems we face in life. In order to gain this gift, we should go to our Father in Heaven in humble prayer, daily thanking Him for the blessings we receive, and asking for what we need. We then endeavor to make ourselves worthy to receive the revelation we need to guide our lives.

Elder Bruce R. McConkie explained the process for gaining personal revelation:

> Would you like a formula to tell you how to get personal revelation? It might be written in many ways. My formula is simply this:
> 1. Search the scriptures.
> 2. Keep the Commandments.
> 3. Ask in faith.
> Any person who will do this will get his heart so in tune with the Infinite that there will come into his being, from the "still small voice," the eternal realities of religion. And as he progresses and advances and comes nearer to God, there will be a day when he will entertain angels, when he will see visions, and the final end is to view the face of God. ("How to Get Personal Revelation," *New Era*, June 1980, p. 50.)

We can also gain a testimony of any principle of the gospel, and of the gospel as a whole. Speaking of the Holy Ghost, President George Q. Cannon said, "When it descends upon a man, he knows it, and the testimony which it gives cannot be taken away. . . . When the Holy Ghost descends upon a man, God is with him as long as he retains that Spirit, and it is a Spirit that will always bear testimony to him." (*Gospel Truth*,

p. 266). The promise is that if we prayerfully read the Book of Mormon and ask in faith, the Holy Ghost will reveal the truthfulness of it to us (see Moroni 10:4,5). We need this revelation, and we also need personal revelation to help us in making our daily decisions, raising our families, making a living, and magnifying our callings in the Church.

Faith in the Lord Jesus Christ, the first principle of the gospel, is a gift of God, the result of diligent seeking. All of the rewards of the gospel are based upon our faith, and are worth the effort we put forth to secure them. We need guidance from our Heavenly Father to carry us through these last days of trial and uncertainty, and our diligence will be rewarded.

Spiritual and Physical Healing

Faith is a healing influence in our lives, and the healing that comes through faith is real. Our Savior, Jesus Christ, took upon Himself not only our sins, but also our pain and suffering. Needs for healing are both real and diverse, but whatever you are suffering, healing is available. Christ has power to heal, and that healing may be physical, as with the lame or leprous people He cured, or it may be spiritual, as with Mary Magdalene. Faith is the bridge over which that power comes to us. If you have faith that Jesus Christ can take away your pain, you can give it to Him. Let's look at two examples of people who needed healing in different ways.

In the Book of Mormon we read the story of Enos, a man who went into the forest to hunt beasts and ended up on his knees. In fervent prayer he asked the Lord for a remission of his sins and had this experience:

> And there came a voice unto me, saying: Enos, thy sins are forgiven thee, and thou shalt be blessed.
>
> And I, Enos, knew that God could not lie; wherefore, my guilt was swept away.
>
> And I said: Lord, how is it done?
>
> And he said unto me: Because of thy faith in Christ, whom thou hast never before heard nor seen. And many years pass away before he shall manifest himself in the flesh; wherefore, go to, thy faith hath made thee whole. (Enos 1:5-8)

Enos experienced a spiritual healing because of his faith in Christ. President Wilford Woodruff recorded this story of a man who received physical healing because of his faith:

> [The Prophet Joseph] called upon the Lord in prayer, and the power of God rested upon him mightily, and as Jesus healed all the sick around Him in His day, so Joseph, the Prophet of God, healed all around on this occasion. . . .
>
> [We] entered Brother [Elijah] Fordham's house. Brother Fordham had been dying for an hour, and we expected each minute would be his last.
>
> I felt the power of God that was overwhelming His Prophet.
>
> . . . Brother Joseph walked up to Brother Fordham, and took him by the right hand. . . .
>
> He saw that Brother Fordham's eyes were glazed, and that he was speechless and unconscious.
>
> After taking hold of his hand, he looked down into the dying man's face and said: "Brother Fordham, do you not know me?" At first he made no reply; but we could all see the effect of the Spirit of God resting upon him.
>
> He again said: "Elijah, do you not know me?"
>
> With a low whisper, Brother Fordham answered, "Yes!"
>
> The Prophet then said, "Have you not faith to be healed?"
>
> The answer, which was a little plainer than before, was: "I am afraid it is too late. If you had come sooner, I think it might have been."
>
> He had the appearance of a man awaking from sleep. It was the sleep of death.
>
> Joseph then said: "Do you not believe that Jesus is the Christ?"
>
> "I do, Brother Joseph," was the response.
>
> Then the Prophet of God spoke with a loud voice, as in the majesty of the Godhead: "Elijah, I command you, in the name of Jesus of Nazareth, to arise and be made whole!"
>
> The words of the Prophet were not like the words of man, but like the voice of God. It seemed to me that the house shook from its foundation.
>
> Elijah Fordham leaped from his bed like a man raised from the dead. A healthy color came to his face, and life was manifested in every act.

. . . [He] called for his clothes and put them on. He asked for a bowl of bread and milk, and ate it; then put on his hat and followed us into the street to visit others who were sick. (*Leaves from My Journal*, pp. 68-69.)

Faith in our Father in Heaven and His Son Jesus Christ brings power into our lives, power that we need for both spiritual and physical healing. When Christ visited the Nephites He instructed them to "believe in me, that I am Jesus Christ, the Son of God, and...pray unto the Father in my name." (3 Nephi 20:31.) This is one way that we express our faith, and call down His power into our lives.

Exercising Faith

When we use our faith, we gain power from Christ. We often hear the phrase, "exercise our faith." What does this mean? To exercise means to work at something. We don't get into shape by thinking about "pumping iron". Likewise, we don't get into spiritual shape unless we work at believing. When we exercise faith in Christ, we don't simply believe that he will help us solve our problems, but we do our part by keeping the commandments, then expect Him to do His part. When we exercise our faith, we put it into action, and thereby we gain strength.

Elder Rulon G. Craven writes that through faith we can gain the strength to be obedient to those laws which improve our lives:

To perfect ourselves and become like God we must believe that Jesus is the way, the truth, and the life (see John 14:6). He is the way to inner peace, contentment, happiness, joy, growth, development, and the power to overcome personal problems, all of which lead to eternal life in the kingdom of God. During this earth life every person will experience the evils of the adversary, as well as the temptations and influences of sensuality, carnality, devilishness, and worldliness. *The way to thwart these influences and evil enticements is to maintain faith that Christ will help us solve our problems and endure bad conditions if we are diligent in keeping God's commandments.* Christ is the way to overcome sin, degeneracy, sensuality, carnality, and other personal problems with which all of us, to some minor or major degree, are afflicted. The only sure way to self-perfection is through obedience to God's laws, principles, ordinances, and covenants. (*Faith For a Better Life*, pp. 7-8, emphasis added.)

As we exercise our faith in Christ and draw closer to Him, we come to realize what our imperfections are, and gain the desire and power to overcome them. Following is an example of a woman who exercised her faith, and gained in both faith and strength.

> One young convert to the Church realized that she had a personal habit that would not please the Lord. She set about to change this habit by strengthening her resolve with scripture reading and prayer each morning. Within five months she had not only overcome her habit, but she found she had unexpectedly developed a quiet, abiding faith in the Lord's atonement for the sins of the repentant. "I love the Lord so much," she testified. "I feel impelled to even greater works." Her faith in the Lord's help and her work to overcome the habit became the instruments that greatly changed her life. (Relief Society Courses of Study 1979-80, p. 5.)

In order to become members of the Church each of us developed faith in the Lord Jesus Christ, repented of our sins, were baptized, and received the gift of the Holy Ghost by the laying on of hands by one with authority. Now that we are on the strait and narrow path, we too must continue to repent and be true to our covenants. We put faith into action by immediately and humbly repenting of any mistakes and putting our lives in order again. The Holy Ghost will continue to be our companion if we maintain the spirit of repentance.

It is an exercise of faith to repent daily. President George Q. Cannon explained:

> It is not repentance at the time of baptism alone. Some people have an idea that because they have entered the waters of baptism and repented of their sins then that is an end of it. What a mistake! We need to have this spirit of repentance continually; we need to pray to God to show us our conduct every day. Every night before we retire to rest we should review the thoughts, words and acts of the day and then repent of everything we have done that is wrong or that has grieved the Holy Spirit. . . . We may indulge in many things that are not right, indulge in wrong thoughts, be actuated by wrong motives, may have wrong objects in view. . . . Therefore, we need to repent every day and every hour, everyone of us. There is none of us so perfect but that we need to do it, and if we do not we will grieve the Spirit of God and check our progress. (*Gospel Truth*, p. 129.)

President Gordon B. Hinckley talked about how faith helps us in the process of overcoming our weaknesses:

> Regrettably we have not reached perfection. We have a great distance to go. We must cultivate the faith to reform our lives, commencing where we are weak and moving on from there in our work of self-correction, thus gradually and consistently growing in strength to live more nearly as we should.
>
> With faith we can rise above those negative elements in our lives which constantly pull us down. With effort we can develop the capacity to subdue those impulses which lead to degrading and evil actions. (CR, *Ensign*, November 1983, p. 53.)

Faith is a vital element in our quest to improve ourselves. When we believe in Christ's power to help us overcome our weaknesses, we gain power to change. Our determination to succeed becomes stronger and our inclination to disobey becomes weaker.

When President Spencer W. Kimball led the Church he urged the members to be diligent by indicating what a difference active obedience would make in our lives and in the Church:

> Think what would happen if each active family were to bring another family or individual into the Church before next April conference. . . . Imagine, if only one additional mature couple were to be called on a full-time mission from each ward. . . . Contemplate the results if each family were to assist...an inactive family or individual into full activity. . . .
>
> Think of the blessings here and on the other side of the veil if each holder of a temple recommend were to do just one more endowment this next year! And how would our nonmember neighbors and friends feel if we were each to do just one more quiet act of Christian service for them . . . regardless of whether or not they are interested in the Church!
>
> Imagine how much richer our family life would be if our spouses and children were to receive a few more minutes of individual attention each month!
>
> Are we ready . . . to do these seemingly small things out of which great blessings will proceed? (CR, *Ensign*, May 1979, p. 82.)

It takes faith to do what President Kimball asked us to do. It takes faith to follow President Benson's directions to eliminate pride, and to share the Book of Mormon with others. It takes faith to follow President Hunter's counsel to become kinder, more loving, and more Christlike. To implement these teachings in our lives, first we go to our Heavenly Father in humble prayer and ask Him to strengthen our faith—ask Him to make us equal to the task our prophet has given us. We then discuss the task with others involved, or ponder it if it is an individual requirement, and plan the steps we will take to accomplish this work. We should ask for the companionship of the Holy Ghost, who will help us accomplish what the prophet gives us to do. This process of exercising our faith will strengthen us and make us equal to any assignment we get from our priesthood leaders.

Elder Loren C. Dunn relates this experience of a sister who was obedient to the counsel of the Lord's servants and reaped blessings:

> Many years ago during the dark days of World War II, Elvon W. Orme, the president of the Australia Mission was invited to a faithful widow's house for Sunday dinner. Rationing had taken its toll, and many of the good foods had long since disappeared from the shelves of the local stores.
>
> When the president arrived, he was shocked to find a table filled with foods that were in short supply and had not been seen for months.
>
> "I can't eat this," he said, almost embarrassed that he was taking it out of the mouth of a widow.
>
> "I'm afraid you'll have to," she said. "You see, I listened to the Brethren years ago and put in my year's supply, and this is the only kind of food I have."
>
> She showed . . . faith . . . by storing food, and the faith produced a miracle in the time of need. (CR, *Ensign*, May 1981, p. 26.)

This works as an upward spiral to joy. By faith we gain strength to be obedient, and being obedient to the commandments strengthens our faith. It gives us the protection of the breastplate of righteousness. On the other hand, loss of faith is one of the perils of not exercising it—"use it or lose it." In the Doctrine and Covenants we are exhorted to "be diligent in keeping all my commandments, lest judgments come upon you, *and your faith fail you.*" (D&C 136:42, emphasis added.) As we obey the commandments, we are blessed, and as we recognize these blessings in our lives, our faith grows.

Faith That the Lord Will Help Us
Accomplish What He Commands

In the Old Testament we read the story of Abraham who was commanded to leave the land of his fathers and go into a strange land. What was Abraham's response to this commandment from the Lord? "By faith Abraham, when he was called to go out into a place which he should after receive for an inheritance, obeyed; and he went out, not knowing whither he went." (Hebrews 11:8.)

Abraham left his home, not even knowing where he was going, because he had faith that the Lord would make it possible for him to obey the commandment he was given. We also need to develop this kind of faith. Can we trustingly put our hands in His and let Him lead us out of our problems into a better life?

In the scriptures, the Lord frequently promises us that He will provide a way for us to obey Him. 1 Nephi 17:3 says, "If it so be that the children of men keep the commandments of God he doth nourish them, and strengthen them, and provide means whereby they can accomplish the thing which he has commanded them."

Elder A. Theodore Tuttle told of a young boy who had this kind of faith:

> I was told of a conversation by a Primary teacher, who related what transpired in his class. He was teaching the eleven-year-olds. He asked the question, "Suppose the Lord asked you to build a spaceship big enough to take you and your family and provisions off this planet? Could you do it?"
> Steve spoke up and said, "Yes."
> And the teacher said, "Have you ever built a spaceship?"
> "No."
> "Have you ever built a model spaceship?"
> "No."
> "Have you ever seen one?"
> Steve said, "Yes, on TV." But then he declared, "You said the Lord *told* me to build it. If the Lord told me to build it, I could do it." (CR, *Ensign*, November 1986, p. 72.)

This is the same faith Nephi had. His brothers scoffed at him when he began to build a ship, as commanded by the Lord. This was his reply: "And I said unto them: If God had commanded me to do all things I could do them. If he should command me that I should say unto this water, be thou earth, it should be earth; and if I should say it, it would be done.

"And now, if the Lord has such great power, and has wrought so many miracles among the children of men, how is it that he cannot instruct me, that I should build a ship?" (1 Nephi 17:50-51.)

Nephi *did* succeed in building a ship that carried his family to the promised land, and we also can succeed at anything the Lord commands us to do, if we exercise our faith in Him.

One of our daughters is married to a seminary teacher. She has been approached by members of the Church who wonder why she doesn't go to work outside the home and help provide for their six children. She recently gave a talk in sacrament meeting on the topic of following the prophet. Her perception was acute and her testimony strong as she exhorted her listeners to claim the blessings the Lord has promised when we follow Him. She said, "I don't know how the Lord blesses us financially, but He does. We are comfortable and do not lack. I believed the prophet when he told mothers to come home and spend their full efforts rearing righteous children. I took him at his word and claimed the Lord's blessings in return. He has blessed us far beyond my ability to anticipate."

Each of us has needs. What are the trials in individual lives? As varied as the individuals themselves. Do we have financial woes? Are we struggling with habits to overcome? Are we battling disheartening attitudes of despondency? Are we critical and abusive of family members? Are we still fighting evil thoughts? Do we lack motivation to lift ourselves out of base circumstances? Whatever it is, the Lord Jesus Christ, who overcame everything, wants to help. And He will. As Paul said, "I can do all things through Christ which strengtheneth me." (Philippians 4:13.)

President Thomas S. Monson related this touching story of a young man who had faith that the Lord would help him accomplish what he had been commanded to do:

> While serving in Guatemala as a missionary for the Church of Jesus Christ of Latter-day Saints, Randall Ellsworth survived a devastating earthquake that hurled a beam down on his back, paralyzing his legs and severely damaging his kidneys. He was the only American injured in the quake, which claimed the lives of some eighteen thousand persons.

After receiving emergency medical treatment, he was flown to a large hospital near his home in Rockville, Maryland. While Randall was confined there, a newscaster conducted with him an interview that I witnessed through the miracle of television. The reporter asked, "Can you walk?"

The answer: "Not yet, but I will."

"Do you think you will be able to complete your mission?"

Came the reply, "Others think not, but I will. With the President of my church praying for me, and through the prayers of my family, my friends, and my missionary companions, I will walk, and I will return again to Guatemala. The Lord wants me to preach the gospel there for two years, and that's what I intend to do."

There followed a lengthy period of therapy, punctuated by heroic yet silent courage. Little by little, feeling began to return to the almost lifeless limbs. More therapy, more courage, more prayer.

At last, Randall Ellsworth walked aboard the plane that carried him back to the mission to which he had been called—back to the people whom he loved. Behind he left a trail of skeptics and a host of doubters, but also hundreds amazed at the power of God, the miracle of faith, and the example of courage.

On his return to Guatemala, Randall Ellsworth supported himself with the help of two canes. His walk was slow and deliberate. Then one day, as he stood before his mission president, Elder Ellsworth heard these almost unbelievable words spoken: "You have been the recipient of a miracle," said the mission president. "Your faith has been rewarded. If you have the necessary confidence, if you have abiding faith, if you have supreme courage, place those two canes on my desk and walk."

After a long pause, first one cane and then the other was placed on the desk, and a missionary walked. It was halting, it was painful—but he walked, never again to need the canes. (CR, *Ensign*, November 1986, pp. 41-42.)

Let's develop this kind of faith in the Lord by committing ourselves to obey all of His commandments and then working determinedly to accomplish this goal. Let's have faith in the Lord's promise that "I will provide means whereby thou mayest accomplish the things which I have commanded thee." (D&C 5:34.)

These and many other glorious experiences are part of the path through mortality that is lighted by the living Light of our Savior Jesus Christ. Our journey can indeed be joyful if we seek for and claim these blessings by our living faith.

7

Repentance: The Second Principle of Purification

Why is Repentance Necessary?

Our purpose here upon the earth is to prepare to return to God. The scriptures, the light of Christ, the Holy Spirit, and the living prophets show us a direct route back to His presence. However, our own personal course is far from direct. We find ourselves wandering. Thus we are faced with a dilemma. We know from the scriptures that to return to God, we must be pure. In 1 Nephi 15:34 we read, "But behold, I say unto you, the kingdom of God is not filthy, and there cannot any unclean thing enter into the kingdom of God." We come into this world pure and equipped properly for the journey; however as we live our lives, all people except Jesus Christ succumb to sin in one degree or another. "For all have sinned, and come short of the glory of God" (Romans 3:23). What, then, can we do? By sinning we have made ourselves unfit to dwell with God, and we cannot, of ourselves, regain our purity.

Lovingly, the Lord prepared for this extremity. It is possible to make course corrections which return us to that strait and narrow way, that direct course leading to life eternal. Repentance is the answer. Through His sacrifice and atonement, He gave us the power to correct our problems and avail ourselves of His redeeming love. Not only is repentance possible through Him, it is necessary. In Luke 13:3 we read, "Except ye repent, ye shall all likewise perish." Without repentance there is no forgiveness and without forgiveness we cannot have eternal life.

President Spencer W. Kimball explained how we can overcome the effects of sin through repentance: "'Sin is the transgression of the law'

(1 John 3:4.), and for such transgression a punishment is affixed under eternal law. Every normal individual is responsible for the sins he commits, and would be similarly liable to the punishment attached to those broken laws. However, Christ's death on the cross offers us exemption from the eternal punishment for most sins. He took upon himself the punishment for the sins of all the world, with the understanding that those who repent and come unto him will be forgiven of their sins and freed from the punishment." (*The Miracle of Forgiveness*, p. 133.)

President Kimball summarized the process. If we don't repent, we must suffer for our sins. If we do repent and accept Jesus Christ's atonement through the covenant of baptism, He will forgive us. We can become pure.

President Ezra Taft Benson said,

> *Remember that through proper repentance, you can become clean again.* Moroni taught that "despair cometh because of iniquity" (Moroni 10:22). Those who are caught in immorality may be experiencing the devastating effects of despair. But there is an alternative. For those who pay the price required by true repentance, the promise is sure. You can be clean again. The despair can be lifted. The sweet peace of forgiveness will flow into your lives. ("The Law of Chastity," Address at Brigham Young University, 13 October 1987.)

Today the world has a great and obvious need for repentance, and yet we see people turning to rationalization rather than repentance. This road leads only to despair and further sin.

President Benson said that preaching repentance was his most important duty as prophet in this generation: "As I have sought direction from the Lord, I have had reaffirmed in my mind and heart the declaration of the Lord to 'say nothing but repentance unto this generation.' (D&C 6:9; 11:9.)" (*Teachings of Ezra Taft Benson*, p. 69.)

What is true repentance? Our purpose is to explain and explore the process of repentance together with the baptismal covenant of cleanliness, and to invite all to partake of this heavenly gift.

We Must Experience a Change of Heart

The process of repentance involves changing from the natural or carnal state, and turning toward God. This is the mighty struggle of this life. In this endeavor the Spirit entices us to reach upward, replacing the selfish, evil tendencies of the "natural man" with nobility, integrity, and decency.

"For the natural man is an enemy to God, and has been from the fall of Adam, and will be, forever and ever, unless he yields to the enticings of the Holy Spirit, and putteth off the natural man and becometh a saint through the atonement of Christ the Lord, and becometh as a child, submissive, meek, humble, patient, full of love, willing to submit to all things which the Lord seeth fit to inflict upon him, even as a child doth submit to his father." (Mosiah 3:19)

Why is this change of heart necessary? Fallen man responds to the flesh rather than the spirit. He puts his selfish interests first, not relying on the guidance of the Spirit. His self-indulgent, fleshly tendencies lead him to sin, making him unfit to return to God.

"For I the Lord cannot look upon sin with the least degree of allowance;

"Nevertheless, he that repents and does the commandments of the Lord shall be forgiven;

"And he that repents not, from him shall be taken even the light which he has received; for my Spirit shall not always strive with man, saith the Lord of Hosts." (D&C 1:31-33)

If we strive to overcome the natural man, the Spirit will help us repent and change. However, if we continually reject the enticings of the Spirit, it will abandon us and we will lose the light we have received, as warned.

Putting off the natural man, repenting, and coming unto Christ take great discipline and energy. We can do it by becoming "submissive, meek, humble, patient, full of love, willing to submit to all things which the Lord seeth fit to inflict upon us." This really consists of replacing fear with faith, despair with hope, and self-defeating behaviors with peace and love.

More than Just a Change of Actions

President Ezra Taft Benson spoke of this change of heart, explaining that repentance requires more than just a change of actions:

> [An] important principle for us to understand if we would be true members of the Church is that repentance involves not just a change of actions, but a change of heart. . . . When we have undergone this

mighty change, which is brought about only through faith in Jesus Christ and through the operation of the Spirit upon us, it is as though we have become a new person. Thus, the change is likened to a new birth. Thousands of you have experienced this change. You have forsaken lives of sin, . . . and through applying the blood of Christ in your lives, have become clean. You have no more disposition to return to your old ways. You are in reality a new person. This is what is meant by a change of heart. ("A Mighty Change of Heart," *Ensign*, October 1989, pp. 2,4.)

This change of heart is also referred to as being "born of God." Everyone must go through this process of putting off the natural man and being born of God in order to someday return and dwell with God. After his glorious conversion experience, Alma said,

> I have repented of my sins, and have been redeemed of the Lord; behold I am born of the Spirit.
> And the Lord said unto me: Marvel not that all mankind, yea, men and women, all nations, kindreds, tongues and people, must be born again; yea, born of God, changed from their carnal and fallen state, to a state of righteousness, being redeemed of God, becoming his sons and daughters;
> And thus they become new creatures; and unless they do this, they can in nowise inherit the kingdom of God. (Mosiah 27:24-26.)

Repentance is not a single act. Rather "it is composed of many elements, each one indispensable to complete repentance." (Spencer W. Kimball, *The Miracle of Forgiveness*, p. 149.) Neither is it a single event, but a lifetime process in which the repentant person abandons his sins as he recognizes them, always striving for perfection.

Alma stressed the necessity of not only experiencing the change of heart, but continuing on the path of repentance and upward progress. "And now behold, I ask of you, my brethren of the church, have ye spiritually been born of God? Have ye received his image in your countenances? Have ye experienced this mighty change in your hearts?

"And now behold, I say unto you, my brethren, if ye have experienced a change of heart, and if ye have felt to sing the song of redeeming love, I would ask, can ye feel so now?" (Alma 5:14, 26.)

This is a question we should humbly, sincerely, and thoughtfully ask ourselves. The answer is as important as our salvation. It is the difference between being successful in our quest for purity of heart, and being content to remain in mediocrity.

"Little" Sins

Is it true that we need to beware of the "little sins?" In Alma 7:15 we read, "Come and fear not, and lay aside every sin, which doth beset you, which doth bind you down to destruction, yea, come and go forth, and show unto your God that ye are willing to repent of your sins and enter into a covenant with him to keep his commandments."

Have we the courage to lay aside all our sins, including the little ones? Can we do as this scripture suggests and "fear not" to put our hand in the hand of our Lord and Savior, and let Him heal us? Many of us have things, "little things" that we do that we feel are not important enough to think about in regard to our eternal perspective. But the little white lie, the carelessly spoken word, the unkindnesses we practice thoughtlessly, all take away from us spirituality. The vulgar joke, TV shows which grieve the Spirit, grudges and feelings of superiority, tightly held because we feel they don't matter, all erode our sensitivity to the whisperings of the Spirit. They make us callous to the needs of others. They are small threads that bind us to the influence of Satan. They are comfortable, small, habitual tendencies that remove us from our real goal of purity of heart.

"But," one may say, "I obey all the important commandments. I pay my tithing. I obey the Word of Wisdom. I go to church on Sunday." The Lord has told us, "Of him unto whom much is given much is required; and he who sins against the greater light shall receive the greater condemnation." (D&C 82:3.) This scripture means that we are required to live up to the light we have received. Since we are blessed to have the gospel in our lives, we must live in accordance with its precepts . . . *all* of its precepts! We should not rationalize disobeying any commandments, but strive to change our lives completely and be worthy of the great blessings the Lord has blessed us with. Our granddaughter Lexia pointed out to us the passage in Alma 37:6: "By small and simple things are great things brought to pass." She tartly observed that small sins are also the beginning of great destruction!

C.S. Lewis, a Christian writer, has a marvelous way of putting into words the heart of the gospel message. He calls our small sins "souvenirs of Hell." He said many people seem to believe that "some way of embracing both [heaven and hell] can always be found; that mere development or adjustment or refinement will somehow turn evil into good without our being called on for a final and total rejection of anything we should like to retain. This belief I take to be a disastrous error. . . . If we insist on keeping Hell (or even earth) we shall not see Heaven: if we accept Heaven we shall not be able to retain even the smallest and most intimate souvenirs of Hell. I believe, to be sure, that any man who reaches Heaven will find that what he abandoned (even in plucking out his right eye) was precisely nothing." (Preface to *The Great Divorce*, pp. 5-6.)

In the Book of Mormon Nephi describes the people of our day, and says that the devil promotes wickedness among them, thus "he leadeth them by the neck with a flaxen cord, until he bindeth them with his strong cords forever." (2 Nephi 26:22.)

We start down the wrong road by committing little sins, thus allowing Satan to start putting the "flaxen cords" around our necks. The flaxen cords may be smooth. We may think they look good or are fashionable. Worn for long, they even feel good. But at best they make us look and feel like the rest of the world. We may forget that we are a "peculiar people" or a "marked generation" as our prophets have labeled us. We lose some of our commitment, and thus some of our strength. At worst, we continue on and begin to commit larger sins. One or two small cords can be broken easily when we decide to, but as Satan puts more cords around our necks it takes much more effort to remove them, and if we continue in this manner, the cords become ropes and even cables. Satan will have us bound.

How does this happen? Perhaps we decide we must run to the store for milk or bread on the Sabbath. Surely this is no great sin! But unless we make a stand, we tend to repeat the behavior, and shopping on the sabbath becomes a regular pattern. However, as we do this, we violate the spirit of the Sabbath and it becomes just like any other day. We go shopping instead of writing in our journals, visiting the sick, reading the scriptures with our children. Next we may begin to justify this activity, perhaps going out to dinner afterwards.

Eventually the Sabbath seems like any holiday from work—a good day for recreation. We may occasionally go camping or fishing on the Sabbath instead of attending our church meetings. "Isn't this a great way to get close to our children?" we rationalize.

As we allow our Sabbath worship meetings to be replaced frequently, other aspects of Church service seem less important. We forget to say our prayers for days at a time. Tithing becomes more difficult to pay. We resent those we see going to church on Sunday because we feel guilty, so we seek friendship among those who do as we do. Soon we have lost our activity in the Church. Our children have lost the anchor of the gospel that is vital for them in this confusing and decadent world. Slowly and surely Satan has wrapped us with those "flaxen cords" until we are bound.

Now is the Time to Repent

Sometimes when we get into these habits of living that we know are wrong, and yet we have done them for so long we are comfortable in our error, we say to ourselves, "I need to repent. Someday I will change and cleanse my life." However we find it easy to put off our repentance until "tomorrow."

Elder ElRay L. Christiansen said, "We ought not to let personal faults, bad habits, and moral weaknesses persist. They should be overcome and corrected without delay. I have often said: 'You can't repent too soon because you don't know how soon it will be too late.'" (CR, *Ensign*, January 1974, p. 35.)

Alma understood the human tendency for procrastination, and he said, "Yea, I would that ye would come forth and harden not your hearts any longer; for behold, now is the time and the day of your salvation; and therefore, if ye will repent and harden not your hearts, immediately shall the great plan of redemption be brought about unto you.

"For behold, this life is the time for men to prepare to meet God; yea, behold the day of this life is the day for men to perform their labors." (Alma 34:31-32.)

Perhaps we put off our repentance by blaming our sins on others. Elder Marvin J. Ashton said that we must take responsibility for our actions: "We often avoid taking action because we tell ourselves that our problem was caused by circumstances or people beyond our control. Therefore, we think we can abdicate our responsibility, and we find ourselves hoping that other people or a change of conditions will solve our difficulties. Rather, it is our responsibility to repent—to change, and to move forward without delay." (CR, *Ensign*, May 1983, p. 32.)

Procrastination and rationalization only hurt the one who employs them. We must "move forward without delay," because the results of putting off repentance are disastrous. In *The Miracle of Forgiveness* President Kimball reaffirmed the vital importance of repenting without delay:

> In an interview with a young man in Mesa, Arizona, I found him only a little sorry he had committed adultery but not sure that he wanted to cleanse himself. After long deliberations in which I seemed to make little headway against his rebellious spirit I finally said, "Goodbye, Bill, but I warn you, don't break the speed limit, be careful what you eat, take no chances on your life. Be careful in traffic, for *you must not die before this matter is cleared up. Don't you dare to die.*" I quoted this scripture:
>
> > Wherefore, if they should die in their wickedness they must be cast off also, as to the things which are spiritual, which are pertaining to righteousness; wherefore, they must be brought to stand before God, to be judged of their works; and if their works have been filthiness they must needs be filthy; and if they be filthy it must needs be that they cannot dwell in the kingdom of God; if so, the kingdom of God must be filthy also. (pp. 145-6, emphasis included.)

Today is the day to repent and prepare to meet God. Alma pleads with us take advantage of the opportunity to repent in this life:

> I beseech of you that ye do not procrastinate the day of your repentance until the end; for after this day of life, which is given us to prepare for eternity, behold, if we do not improve our time while in this life, then cometh the night of darkness wherein there can be no labor performed.
>
> Ye cannot say, when ye are brought to that awful crisis, that I will repent, that I will return to my God. Nay, ye cannot say this; for that same spirit which doth possess your bodies at the time that ye go out of this life, that same spirit will have power to possess your body in that eternal world. (Alma 34:33-34.)

"The Final State of the Wicked"

Alma continues with a final warning to those who think they can sin now and repent later:

For behold, if ye have procrastinated the day of your repentance even until death, behold, ye have become subjected to the spirit of the devil, and he doth seal you his; therefore, the Spirit of the Lord hath withdrawn from you, and hath no place in you, and the devil hath all power over you; and this is the final state of the wicked. (Alma 34:33-35.)

The results of failing to repent are especially damning to those who have been taught the truth and then reject it:

And now, I say unto you, my brethren, that after ye have known and have been taught all these things, if ye should transgress and go contrary to that which has been spoken, that ye do withdraw yourselves from the Spirit of the Lord, that it may have no place in you to guide you in wisdom's paths that ye may be blessed, prospered, and preserved—

I say unto you, that the man that doeth this, the same cometh out in open rebellion against God; therefore he listeth to obey the evil spirit, and becometh an enemy to all righteousness; therefore, the Lord has no place in him, for he dwelleth not in unholy temples.

Therefore if that man repenteth not, and remaineth and dieth an enemy to God, the demands of divine justice do awaken his immortal soul to a lively sense of his own guilt, which doth cause him to shrink from the presence of the Lord, and doth fill his breast with guilt, and pain, and anguish, which is like an unquenchable fire, whose flame ascendeth up forever and ever.

And now I say unto you, that mercy hath no claim on that man; therefore his final doom is to endure a never-ending torment. (Mosiah 2:36-39.)

The "final state of the wicked" is truly horrifying. The Savior said that those who refuse to repent "must suffer even as I; Which suffering caused myself, even God, the greatest of all, to tremble because of pain, and to bleed at every pore, and to suffer both body and spirit—and would that I might not drink the bitter cup, and shrink." (D&C 19:17-18.)

Compare this awful scenario with the happy state of those who repent and keep the commandments of God: "And moreover, I would desire that ye should consider on the blessed and happy state of those that keep the commandments of God. For behold, they are blessed in all things, both temporal and spiritual; and if they hold out faithful to the end they are received into heaven, that thereby they may dwell with God in a state of never-ending happiness. O remember, remember that these things are true; for the Lord God hath spoken it." (Mosiah 2:41)

The work of the prophets is to warn us, and for this reason they have been unflinching in their descriptions of the punishments awaiting those who procrastinate their repentance, all the while holding out the beautiful promise of the happiness and peace awaiting the repentant.

Faith in Christ is a Prerequisite to Repentance

In the scriptures the words "faith" and "repentance" are frequently used together. Why is faith so important to the process of repentance? It is because of the sacrifice of Jesus Christ that we are able to repent, therefore, our faith in that sacrifice is vital to our sincere and complete repentance.

We must believe in and accept the sacrifice of Jesus Christ in order to gain remission for our sins. In Alma 34:15-17 this principle is beautifully and clearly explained. Notice the repetition of the phrase "faith unto repentance":

> And . . . he shall bring salvation to all those who shall believe on his name; this being the intent of this last sacrifice, to bring about the bowels of mercy, which overpowereth justice, and bringeth about means unto men that they may have *faith unto repentance.*
>
> And thus mercy can satisfy the demands of justice, and encircles them in the arms of safety, while *he that exercises no faith unto repentance* is exposed to the whole law of the demands of justice; therefore only unto him that has *faith unto repentance* is brought about the great and eternal plan of redemption.
>
> Therefore may God grant unto you, my brethren, that ye may begin to exercise your *faith unto repentance*, that ye begin to call upon his holy name, that he would have mercy upon you. (Emphasis added.)

Notice that Jesus Christ Himself makes our faith possible. We can do it!

President Ezra Taft Benson has also explained that faith precedes repentance, saying, "A . . . concept that is important to our understanding is the relationship of repentance to the principle of faith. Repentance is the second fundamental principle of the gospel. The first is that we must have faith in the Lord Jesus Christ. Why is this so? Why must Faith in the Lord precede true repentance? . . .

"Faith in the Lord Jesus Christ is the foundation upon which sincere and meaningful repentance must be built. If we truly seek to put away sin, we must first look to Him who is the Author of our salvation." (*Ensign*, October 1989, p. 2.)

An abiding faith in Jesus Christ is necessary as a foundation for repentance. When we accept His love and help, we will have the courage to change. Elder John A. Widtsoe said that "active faith is repentance." (*A Rational Theology*, p. 95.) Remember we are wearing the armor of God, which includes "taking the shield of faith . . . [by which] ye shall be able to quench all the fiery darts of the wicked." (Ephesians 6:16)

Our Heavenly Father provided the plan of redemption because of His great love for us. "God commendeth his love toward us, in that, while we were yet sinners, Christ died for us." (Romans 5:8. See the beautiful discussion of the atonement in Romans chapter 5.) Because of His great love, the Savior suffered for us so that, if we have faith in Him, and we repent, we can be forgiven and come again into His presence. He loves us. The joy of our Savior is real and divinely exultant when we repent.

"Remember the worth of souls is great in the sight of God;

"For, behold, the Lord your Redeemer suffered death in the flesh; wherefore he suffered the pain of all men, that all men might repent and come unto him.

"And he hath risen again from the dead, that he might bring all men unto him, on conditions of repentance.

"And how great is his joy in the soul that repenteth!" (D&C 18:10-13.)

Christ has His hands outstretched toward us. We are His. He loves us. When we repent and come unto Him, He welcomes us as His own. He will rejoice with us in the forgiveness of our sins.

8

The Process of Repentance

The Key to Progress

Here we are in the midst of our journey to purity of heart. We are well equipped: we have the map, the compass, the armor of God, and a knowledge of the requirements of the journey and the glorious goal.

We have learned that by the Fall of Adam, death came into the world, and that through the Atonement of Jesus Christ, mankind will live again. We have learned that justice requires a penalty for the transgression of the law, and that the mercy of Jesus Christ paid the penalty for all who will repent. We know by sad experience that we have all sinned and come under that penalty.

We have learned that Jesus Christ made it possible for us to repent of our sins in order to be worthy of returning to our Father in Heaven. We know that we are to exercise our faith in Him as a prerequisite to sincere repentance. We know that in order to progress along the route of our quest for purity, we must generate faith and take the action of repentance.

How then do we go about the process of repentance?

Recognizing Our Sins

President Spencer W. Kimball described the beginnings of repentance as a consciousness of guilt. When our faith is strong enough to recognize Jesus Christ, we begin to recognize that we have not done as we ought to have done.

As repentance gets under way, there must be a deep consciousness of guilt, and in that consciousness of guilt may come suffering to the mind, the spirit, and sometimes even to the body. In order to live with themselves, people who transgress must follow one or the other of two alternatives. The one is to sear their conscience or dull their sensitivity with mental tranquilizers so that their transgression may be continued. Those who choose this alternative eventually become calloused and lose their desire to repent. The other alternative is to permit remorse to lead one to total sorrow, then to repentance, and finally on to eventual forgiveness.

Remember this, that forgiveness can never come without repentance. And repentance can never come until one has bared his soul and admitted his actions without excuses or rationalizations. He must admit to himself that he has sinned, without the slightest minimization of the offense or rationalizing of its seriousness, or without soft-pedaling its gravity. He must admit that his sin is as big as it really is and not call a pound an ounce. ("The Gospel of Repentance," *Ensign*, October 1982, p. 4.)

The first step to repentance, then, is to recognize our sins. This means to own them, to admit that what we have done is wrong, and to take responsibility for our actions. To own up to wrong-doing is difficult. Our image of ourselves is attacked. Our perception of what others think of us is assailed. We feel debased.

President Kimball warned plainly: "To avoid the unpleasant recognition of their sins, many rationalize. Some blame God or his laws for their downfall, and by eliminating God and his Church from their lives they seem to think they will get relief. But rationalizing and minimizing sin betrays disregard for or ignorance of the scriptures and the program of God. . . . Someone has said: 'Rationalizing is the bringing of ideals down to the level of one's conduct. Repentance is the bringing of one's conduct up to the level of his ideals.'" (*The Miracle of Forgiveness*, p. 151.)

It takes a humbling of ourselves before God to acknowledge our sins. As long as we tell ourselves that "we have no sin," we are lost. "We deceive ourselves, and the truth is not in us." (1 John 1:8.) Our Creator already knows what we have done—we do not deceive Him! But He stands waiting to receive us as we humbly come to Him: "Be thou humble; and the Lord thy God shall lead thee by the hand, and give thee answer to thy prayers." (D&C 112:10.)

Elder Theodore M. Burton counsels us to face our sins squarely and avoid rationalizing: "We must forget all excuses and recognize fully, exactly, what we have done. We must not say, 'If I hadn't been so angry,' 'If my parents had only been more strict,' 'If my bishop had only been more understanding,' 'If my teachers had only taught me better,' 'If it hadn't been so dark!' There are hundreds of such excuses —none of which matters much in the final analysis.

"To truly repent, we must forget all such rationalizations. We must kneel down before God and openly and honestly admit that what we did was wrong. As we do so, we open our hearts to our Heavenly Father and commit ourselves completely to him." ("The Meaning of Repentance," *Ensign*, August 1988, p. 8.)

We cannot blame others. We must take the full responsibility for our sins, forthrightly acknowledge them and repent of them. This is the only way to happiness in this life. This is the only road that leads to eternal life.

Anguished feelings have their function. The purpose of anxiety is to get us to search for a better way. The purpose of guilt is to bring us to repentance. Alma told his erring son Corianton to let guilt motivate him to the action of repentance: "Let your sins trouble you, with that trouble which shall bring you down unto repentance. . . . Do not endeavor to excuse yourself in the least point." (Alma 42:29-30.)

We must feel even more than guilt, as President Kimball explains: "Of course, even the conviction of guilt is not enough. It could be devastating and destructive were it not accompanied by efforts to rid oneself of guilt. Accompanying the conviction, then, must be an *earnest desire to clean up the guilt* and compensate for the loss sustained through the error . . . one must have an honest desire to right the wrong. (*The Miracle of Forgiveness*, p. 159, emphasis added.)

Following this desire, the sooner we take steps to repent fully, the sooner the guilt will cease.

There are two types of sorrow connected with sin. "For godly sorrow worketh repentance to salvation not to be repented of: but the sorrow of the world worketh death." (2 Corinthians 7:10.)

What is the difference between "godly sorrow" and "the sorrow of the world"? President Ezra Taft Benson explained:

[A] concept I would like to stress is what the scriptures term "godly sorrow" for our sins. It is not uncommon to find men and women in the world who feel remorse for the things they do wrong. Sometimes this is because their actions cause them or loved ones great sorrow and misery. Sometimes their sorrow is caused because they are caught and punished for their actions. Such worldly feelings do not constitute "godly sorrow." . . .

Godly sorrow is a gift of the Spirit. It is a deep realization that our actions have offended our Father and our God. It is the sharp and keen awareness that our behavior caused the Savior, He who knew no sin, even the greatest of all, to endure agony and suffering. Our sins caused Him to bleed at every pore. This very real mental and spiritual anguish is what the scriptures refer to as having "a broken heart and a contrite spirit." (See 3 Nephi 9:20; Moroni 6:2; D&C 20:37, 59:8; Psalms 34:18, 51:17; Isaiah 57:15.) Such a spirit is the absolute prerequisite for true repentance. (*Ensign*, October 1989, p. 4.)

Worldly sorrow is like the man who sorrows because he got caught, but not because he stole. This type of sorrow is short term; he will probably steal again. Godly sorrow, the sorrow that leads to repentance, is a true and humble recognition of wrongdoing, and is part of the process of repentance. Elder F. Burton Howard, speaking to a young man in need of repentance, stated: "In order to be forgiven, a transgressor must experience godly sorrow. He must have anguish of soul and genuine regret. This sorrow must be strong enough and long enough to motivate the additional processes of repentance, or it is not deep enough. Regret must be great enough so as to bring forth a changed person. That person must demonstrate that he is different than before by doing different and better things." (CR, *Ensign*, May 1983, p. 59.)

How much better it is if we will humble ourselves and feel a true, deep sorrow for our sins rather than only being sorry for discovery of our wrong. "Blessed are they who humble themselves without being compelled to be humble; or rather, in other words, blessed is he that believeth in the word of God, and is baptized without stubbornness of heart, yea, without being brought to know the word, or even compelled to know, before they will believe." (Alma 32:16.)

It is not easy to straightforwardly recognize and take responsibility for our sins. Godly sorrow is just that—sorrow. It is painful and difficult—and life-altering. When we humbly acknowledge our unworthiness, God will help us take the next step on the road to complete repentance, and the sweet fruits of forgiveness and peace.

Abandoning Our Sins

The next part of the process of complete repentance is to forsake our sins. President Kimball explained that in order to relinquish a sin, we must abandon anything that leads us to sin:

> The next step in the process of repentance is to abandon the sin. The Lord revealed to the Prophet Joseph Smith, "By this ye may know if a man repenteth of his sins—behold, he will confess them and forsake them." (D&C 58:43.) And to the adulteress, the Master said, "Go, and sin no more." (John 8:11.)
>
> Prayer is important throughout the entire process of repentance, but it is vital now. In the process of abandoning a sin, it is often necessary to abandon *persons, places, things, and situations* that are associated with the transgression. This is fundamental. Substitution of a good environment for a bad can hedge the way between the repenting person and his past sin. (*Ensign*, October 1982, p. 4, emphasis added.)

We must not continue our sins. To insure this, we must change any behavior, activities, or associates which induce us to sin. In plain words, in order to be forgiven of a sin, *we must not repeat it*. The Prophet Joseph Smith wrote regarding repeating the same offense, "Daily transgression and daily repentance is not that which is pleasing in the sight of God." (*Teachings of the Prophet Joseph Smith*, p. 148).

The Lord explains, regarding forgiveness, how essential it is that we give up the sin: "Go your ways and sin no more; but unto that soul who sinneth shall the former sins return, saith the Lord your God." (D&C 82:7.)

This is a sobering warning, that if we repeat the sin, our former sins shall return to us. *Trying* to quit sinning is not enough. True repentance means we are to *abandon* the sin—stop it altogether, turn completely away from it.

God will help us. If we humble ourselves sufficiently, He will give us the strength to stop. Pray unto Him. Plead with Him for that strength.

Though we depend on the Lord for strength, Elder Boyd K. Packer reminds us that we must discipline ourselves. "Repentance is like soap; it can wash sin away. Ground-in dirt may take the strong detergent of discipline to get the stains out, but out they will come." (CR, *Ensign*, May 1989, p. 59.)

Elder Marvin J. Ashton also emphasized the importance of individual effort in overcoming sin: "One may ask, 'What must I do to break the chains that bind me and lead me away from the path our Savior would have us follow?'" These chains cannot be broken by those who live in lust and self-deceit. They can only be broken by people who are willing to change. We must face up to the hard reality of life that damaging chains are broken only by people of courage and commitment who are willing to struggle and weather the pain." (CR, *Ensign*, November 1986, p. 15.)

If we discipline ourselves, "weather the pain," and abandon the sin, President Ezra Taft Benson said that the Lord will help us turn our weaknesses into strengths:

> Moroni . . . was told by the Lord, "If men come unto me I will show unto them their weakness. I give unto men weakness that they may be humble; and my grace is sufficient for all men." It matters not what is our lack or our weakness or our insufficiency. His gifts and powers are sufficient to overcome them all.
>
> Moroni continues with the words of the Lord: "My grace is sufficient for all men that humble themselves before me; for if they humble themselves before me, and have faith in me, *then will I make weak things become strong unto them.*" (Ether 12:27, emphasis added.)
>
> What a promise from the Lord! The very source of our troubles can be changed, molded, and formed into a strength and a source of power. ("A Mighty Change of Heart, *Ensign*, October 1989, pp. 4-5.)

God will help us to change our weaknesses into strengths. However, we should not think that we are stronger or better for having sinned. President Spencer W. Kimball warned:

> [An] error into which some transgressors fall, because of the availability of God's forgiveness, is the illusion that they are somehow stronger for having committed sin and then lived through the period of repentance. This simply is not true. *That man who resists temptation and lives without sin is far better off than the man who has fallen*, no matter how repentant the latter may be. The reformed transgressor, it is true, may be more understanding of one who falls into the same sin, and to that extent perhaps more helpful in the

latter's regeneration. But his sin and repentance have certainly not made him stronger than the consistently righteous person. God will forgive—of that, we are sure. How satisfying it is to be cleansed from filthiness, but how much better it is never to have committed the sin! ("God Will Forgive," *Ensign*, March 1982, p. 7, emphasis added.)

Beginning again requires that we abandon our sins and never repeat them. In this pursuit the Lord will bless us, if we do our part by disciplining ourselves, avoiding any situations or people that may lead us to sin, and seeking strength from the Lord through prayer.

Confession

In Doctrine and Covenants 64:7 we read, "I, the Lord, forgive sins unto those who confess their sins before me and ask forgiveness, who have not sinned unto death." After we have recognized our sins, we are to confess them as part of the repentance process. To whom do we confess? President Kimball includes "ourselves . . . Heavenly Father . . . [and] the bishop":

Confession of the sin is a very important aspect of repentance. We must confess and admit our sins to ourselves and then seriously begin the process of repentance. We must also confess our sins to our Heavenly Father. Especially grave errors such as sexual sins must be confessed to the bishop as well.

One begins the process by going to the Lord in "mighty prayer" as did Enos. Then, if appropriate, one goes to the bishop. The Lord has a constant, orderly plan to bless us in this great law of growth and development, the law of repentance. Every member of the Church is given a bishop or branch president who through his very priesthood ordination or calling is a "judge in Israel." In these matters, the bishop is our best earthly friend. He is one who works with the Spirit of the Lord in blessing our lives and he keeps all matters completely confidential. ("The Gospel of Repentance," *Ensign*, October 1982, p. 4.)

What kinds of sins do we confess to the bishop? Elder Bruce R. McConkie said, "Those sins which involve moral turpitude—meaning serious sins for which the court procedures of the Church could be instituted so that a person's fellowship or membership might be called in

question—such sins must be confessed to the proper church officer."
(*Mormon Doctrine*, p. 293.) President Kimball specified that "adultery,
fornication, other sexual transgressions, and other sins of comparable
seriousness" must all be confessed to "a proper Church authority." (*The
Miracle of Forgiveness*, p. 179.) Homosexuality, abortion, apostasy, and
felonies are of comparable seriousness. If you have questions regarding
confession, talk it over with your bishop.

After we have made a full and honest confession to the bishop, we
follow his counsel. We let him know that we are willing to do whatever
he sees fit to complete our repentance.

Is there anyone else to whom we must confess? President Stephen L.
Richards said that besides the Lord and the bishop, we should confess to
"the aggrieved person or persons, as an essential in making due retri-
bution if that is necessary." (*Conference Report*, April 1954, p. 12, as
quoted in *Mormon Doctrine*, p. 293.)

While confession to God and those we have offended (as well as to
proper priesthood leaders, when required) is necessary for true repentance, Elder Theodore M. Burton warns against unnecessary public confession: "Naturally, the confession that precedes repentance for serious
sins should be made to a bishop or stake president who has the authority
to hear such confession. Confessions to others—particularly confessions
repeated in open meetings, unless the sin has been a public sin requiring
public forgiveness—only demean both the confessor and the hearer."
("The Meaning of Repentance," *Ensign*, August 1988, p. 9.)

Proper confession is a cleansing procedure. When we freely confess
to the Lord that we have violated one of his laws, we demonstrate that
we are ready and willing to cast that sin from our lives. When we
confess a serious sin to the bishop, we recognize the authority of the
Church as the designated representative of God on earth. We demonstrate
that we truly care about our covenants and humbly desire forgiveness and
reinstatement in full communion with the Kingdom of God on the earth.
We show that we are honest in our desire to change, and we make it
possible for the bishop to help us through the steps necessary for
repentance.

Restitution

The next step after confession is restitution. Elder Bruce R.
McConkie has written that restitution is "to return the stolen property,

to make amends for the offense committed, to repair the damage done, to compensate for hardships imposed by one's acts." (*Mormon Doctrine*, pp. 294-95.) Ezekiel describes restitution thus: "If the wicked restore the pledge, give again that he had robbed, walk in the statutes of life, without committing iniquity; he shall surely live, he shall not die. None of his sins that he hath committed shall be mentioned unto him: he hath done that which is lawful and right; he shall surely live." (Ezekiel 33:15-16.)

Sometimes we can't restore everything, but we must do our very best, all that is possible to make full restitution. The thief gives back the stolen merchandise. The liar tells the truth to the people he has lied to. However, one cannot give back stolen virtue. A person who has murdered cannot give back life. This is why these particular sins are so heinous.

Speaking of the difficulty of making restitution for such sins Elder Theodore M. Burton explained,

> If you have stolen money or goods, you can repay them—even sizable amounts, in time. But what if you have robbed yourself of virtue? Is there *anything* you can do, of yourself, to restore your virtue? Even if you gave your very life, you could not restore your virtue. But—perish the thought—does that then mean that it is useless to attempt restitution by performing significant good works or that your sin is unforgivable? No!
>
> Jesus Christ has paid for your sin and has thus satisfied justice. Therefore, he will extend mercy to you—*if* you repent. True repentance on your part, including a change in your lifestyle, enables Christ, in mercy, to forgive your sin. ("The Meaning of Repentance," *Ensign*, August 1988, pp. 8-9.)

As we work to restore that which we have damaged through sin, the Lord will bless our efforts. He is able to bridge the gap between the harm we have done and all we can do to make reparation. In His strength we can be forgiven.

Forgive Others

The problem of forgiving others is as old as humanity. Christ tells us that, while He was on the earth, His disciples struggled with forgiving each other, and paid the price for their unwillingness to forgive:

My disciples, in days of old, sought occasion against one another and forgave not one another in their hearts; and for this evil they were afflicted and sorely chastened.

Wherefore, I say unto you, that ye ought to forgive one another; for he that forgiveth not his brother his trespasses standeth condemned before the Lord; for there remaineth in him the greater sin.

I, the Lord, will forgive whom I will forgive, but of you it is required to forgive all men. (D&C 64:8-10.)

The next step in the process of repentance is to forgive all others who may have offended us. "For, if ye forgive men their trespasses your heavenly Father will also forgive you; But if ye forgive not men their trespasses neither will your Father forgive your trespasses." (3 Nephi 13:14-15.) We must forgive in order to be forgiven. There is no other way.

Christ set the example. He had the spirit of forgiveness toward His executors while they were still in the process of taking His life: "Father, forgive them; for they know not what they do." (Luke 23:34.)

We may think that it was easier for Christ, being perfect, to forgive. But Stephen, the disciple who accepted death rather than renounce his faith, also forgave his executors even while they were stoning him. "[They] cast him out of the city, and stoned him. . . . And he kneeled down, and cried with a loud voice, Lord, lay not this sin to their charge. And when he had said this, he fell asleep." (Acts 7:58-60.)

We should follow the example of our Savior and that of Stephen, and forgive readily, immediately, and completely.

How many times should we forgive others? The answer is found in Matthew 18:21-22: "Then came Peter unto him, and said, Lord, how oft shall my brother sin against me, and I forgive him? till seven times? Jesus saith unto him, I say not unto thee, Until seven times: but, Until seventy times seven."

Peter wanted the Lord to limit the number of times we are to forgive others. Instead the Lord named an impossibly high number, indicating that we do not place limits on our willingness to forgive. We are required to forgive all who offend us as often as the offenses come, even those who are unrepentant, according to President Spencer W. Kimball (see *Miracle of Forgiveness*, p. 283).

This is not easy. Sometimes we are deeply hurt, even by those we love and trust. However, we must overcome our anger or bitterness and forgive in order to *be* forgiven. Elder Hugh W. Pinnock said, speaking of the process of repentance,

> Perhaps the hardest [part] of all, [is to] forgive. Paul said, "To whom ye forgive any thing, I forgive also." (2 Corinthians 2:10.) Certainly part of beginning again is to "love your enemies, do good to them which hate you, Bless them that curse you, and pray for them which despitefully use you." (Luke 6:27-28.) . . .
>
> Think how young Joseph had been wronged by jealous brothers anciently. They sold him into slavery. He had every reason to seek revenge. But when circumstances joined them together in Egypt, Joseph said, "But as for you, ye thought evil against me; but God meant it unto good, . . . to save much people. (Genesis 50:20.)
>
> Yes, so much of heartache and grief eventually become blessings, our earthly instructions, and condition us spiritually. Even if we cannot understand the "whys" of our tribulations, we can still turn to God and rededicate our lives to his safekeeping. (CR, *Ensign*, May 1982, p. 14.)

The fact that we need to forgive others does not mean that we should expose ourselves to abuse by remaining in a situation where we are being abused. If you find yourself or your children in a situation of abuse, consult with your priesthood leaders.

Elder Boyd K. Packer counseled us how forgiving others will bring peace:

> If you resent someone for something he has done—or failed to do—forget it.
>
> Too often the things we carry are petty, even stupid. If you are still upset after all these years because Aunt Clara didn't come to your wedding reception, why don't you grow up and forget it?
>
> If you brood constantly over a loss or a past mistake, look ahead—settle it.
>
> We call that forgiveness. Forgiveness is powerful spiritual medicine. To extend forgiveness, that soothing balm, to those who have offended you is to heal. . . .
>
> Purge and cleanse and soothe your soul and your heart and your mind and that of others.
>
> A cloud will then be lifted, a beam cast from your eye. There will come that peace which surpasseth understanding. (CR, *Ensign*, November 1987, p. 18.)

Following the example of Christ, we can forgive those who have wronged us, even as we hope to be forgiven by those whom we have wronged. It is important that we learn to forgive daily all who offend us. Sometimes we have hurt feelings that are very stubborn; the hurt doesn't want to leave. If we ask in prayer, our Father in Heaven will take the hurt away, though we may need to pray each day until it is gone. Whatever it takes, do it. Giving forgiveness brings peace of mind and happiness back into our lives.

Strive to Obey All of the Commandments

The next step in repentance is to strive keep all of the commandments of God. Of course we know that we are not perfect, but the key is to be *willing* to keep all of the commandments without reservation. "By keeping the commandments they might be washed and cleansed from all their sins." (D&C 76:52.) "Obedience," Elder Boyd K. Packer said, "is a powerful spiritual medicine. It comes close to being a cure-all." (*That All May Be Edified*, p. 67.)

President Kimball wrote that part of our repentance is "total surrender to the program of the Lord":

> In connection with repentance, the scriptures use the phrase, "with all his heart" (see D&C 42:25). Obviously this rules out any reservations. Repentance must involve an all-out, total surrender to the program of the Lord. That transgressor is not fully repentant who neglects his tithing, misses his meetings, breaks the Sabbath, fails in his family prayers, does not sustain the authorities of the Church, breaks the Word of Wisdom, does not love the Lord nor his fellowmen. A reforming adulterer who drinks or curses is not repentant. The repenting burglar who has sex play is not ready for forgiveness. God cannot forgive unless the transgressor shows a true repentance which spreads to all areas of his life. (*The Miracle of Forgiveness*, p. 203.)

Certain commandments are especially important while we are repenting. In Joel 2:12 the Lord commands us to "turn ye even to me with all your heart, and with fasting, and with weeping, and with mourning." Our fasting is a way of purifying ourselves by denying the appetites of the body. As we fast, we should pray for strength "lest ye enter into temptation." (Luke 22:46.)

The purifying power of fasting and prayer is made clear in the Book of Mormon: "Nevertheless they did fast and pray oft, and did wax stronger and stronger in their humility, and firmer and firmer in the faith of Christ, unto the filling their souls with joy and consolation, yea, even to the purifying and the sanctification of their hearts, which sanctification cometh because of their yielding their hearts unto God." (Helaman 3:35.) Through fasting and prayer we gain spiritual strength to overcome our sins.

Jesus commanded us to "search the scriptures." (John 5:39.) This is even more critical while we are in the process of repentance. Elder Richard G. Scott said, "It may be difficult to begin [repenting], but pick up the scriptures and immerse yourself in them. Look for favorite passages. Lean on the Master's teachings, on His servants' testimonies. Refresh your parched soul with the word of God. The scriptures will give you comfort and the strength to overcome." (CR, *Ensign*, May 1990, p. 75.)

We should follow this counsel both during and after the process of repentance, drinking deeply from the well of the scriptures, especially the Book of Mormon.

When we begin to feel the light of repentance and the love of the Lord's forgiveness, it is natural to want to reach out and share that joy and illumination with our fellowmen. It is natural to want to do good works and build up the kingdom of God.

President Kimball reminded us that bearing testimony to others not only raises them up and helps their lives, but insures that our own sins will be forgiven: "Nevertheless, ye are blessed, for the testimony which ye have borne is recorded in heaven for the angels to look upon; and they rejoice over you, and your sins are forgiven you." (D&C 62:3.)

James said that through missionary work and the bringing of souls to Christ, we also sanctify our own souls: "Brethren, if any of you do err from the truth, and one convert him; Let him know, that he which converteth the sinner from the error of his way shall save a soul from death, and shall hide a multitude of sins." (James 5:19-20.) (See *The Miracle of Forgiveness*, p. 205.) It is interesting to note that the Joseph Smith Translation changes "hide" to "prevent" a multitude of sins.

Elder Theodore M. Burton encouraged the repentant to leave the past behind and fill their lives with good causes: "As you undergo the process of repentance, be patient. Be active with positive, righteous thoughts and deeds so that you can become happy and productive again.

"As long as we dwell on sin or evil and refuse to forgive ourselves, we will be subject to return again to our sins. But if we turn from our problems and sins and put them behind us in both thought and action, we can concentrate on good and positive things. As we become fully engaged in good causes, sin will no longer be such a great temptation for us." ("The Meaning of Repentance," *Ensign*, August 1988, p. 9.)

Repentance requires a deep, heart-felt commitment. As we resolutely strive to obey all of the commandments, we make repentance the priority that this life-changing event warrants. Our obedience to the commandments completes our process of repentance and puts us firmly on a new road, with the old painful life behind us. It truly renews us and gives us hope and peace.

Repentance *Is* Possible

Courage to Go On

One of the greatest challenges in our journey toward purity of heart is keeping the eternal viewpoint. When the journey is stony and rough, we can easily lose heart. We may find the pathway clouded by our inadequate faith; we may allow what seems to be important at the moment to steer us aside from our eternal goal. What we need is the courage to keep on. Courage is vital to our progress, because without it we would become disheartened and feel we have to quit. In the jargon of today, we may say we are depressed or that we cannot cope. The Lord knew we would feel like this at some point in our course. He knew we would need to renew our courage in order to move forward. We are promised: "Wait on the Lord: be of good courage, and he shall strengthen thine heart." (Psalms 27:14.) Then He provided the way for us to go forward again and called it repentance. Repentance is so important it is the second principle of purification. It is a principle of regeneration. And we all can do it, if we properly take heart. The Lord *wants* us to succeed: "For verily I say unto you, I will that ye should overcome the world; wherefore I will have compassion upon you." (D&C 64:2.) And further, "Therefore, whosoever repenteth, and hardeneth not his heart, he shall have claim on mercy through mine Only Begotten Son, unto a remission of his sins; and these shall enter into my rest." (Alma 12:34.)

Never Too Late

Satan tries to discourage persons who have committed serious sin. He tries to convince them that they had just as well keep sinning because repentance is now impossible. This is to be recognized as another of Satan's lies. President Harold B. Lee warned us of this great lie: "Satan would have you think . . . that . . . having made one mistake, you might go on and on with no turning back. That is one of the great falsehoods." (CR, *Ensign*, July 1973, p. 122.)

Elder Boyd K. Packer stressed that it is never too late to repent: "Those who make one serious mistake tend to add another by assuming that it is then too late for them. It is never too late! Never! . . . The discouraging idea that a mistake (or even a series of them) makes it everlastingly too late, does not come from the Lord. He has said that *if* we will repent, not only will He forgive us our transgressions, but He will forget them and remember our sins no more." (CR, *Ensign*, May 1989, p. 59.)

Elder Packer said again: "Letters come from those who have made tragic mistakes. They ask, 'Can I *ever* be forgiven?'

"The answer is *yes*!

"The gospel teaches us that relief from torment and guilt can be earned through repentance. Save for those few who defect to perdition after having known a fulness, there is no habit, no addiction, no rebellion, no transgression, no offense exempted from the promise of complete forgiveness." (CR, *Ensign*, November 1995, p. 19.)

And further: "I repeat, save for the exception of the very few who defect to perdition, there is no habit, no addiction, no rebellion, no transgression, no apostasy, no crime exempted from the promise of complete forgiveness. That is the promise of the atonement of Christ." (CR, *Ensign*, November 1995, p. 20.) Then Elder Packer quotes the Prophet Joseph Smith, who said, "There is never a time when the spirit is too old to approach God. *All are within the reach of pardoning mercy, who have not committed the unpardonable sin.*" [*Teachings of the Prophet Joseph Smith*, p. 191; emphasis added.] (CR, *Ensign*, November 1995, p. 21.)

And the mercy of the Lord is always extended. Elder F. Burton Howard reminds us that the Lord cares not what is behind us in our lives: "Some years ago it was fashionable in certain circles to use the phrase, 'You can never go home again.' That is just simply not true. It is possible to return. It is possible for those who have ceased to pray, to pray again. It is possible for those who are lost to find their way through the dark and come home.

"And when they do, they will know, as I know, that the Lord is more concerned with what a man is than with what he was, and with where he is than with where he has been." (CR, *Ensign*, November 1986, p. 78.)

President Spencer W. Kimball holds out the promise of forgiveness as a light in the darkness: "Sometimes a guilt consciousness overpowers a person with such a heaviness that when a repentant one looks back and sees the ugliness, the loathsomeness of the transgression, he is almost overwhelmed and wonders, 'Can the Lord ever forgive me? Can I ever forgive myself?' But when one reaches the depths of despondency and feels the hopelessness of his position, and when he cries out to God for mercy in helplessness but in faith, there comes a still, small, but penetrating voice whispering to his soul, 'Thy sins are forgiven thee.'" ("God Will Forgive," *Ensign*, March 1982, p. 4.)

If We Repent We Will Be Forgiven

"Thy sins are forgiven thee." What a marvelous thought! If we fully and completely repent we *will be* forgiven. "Behold, he who has repented of his sins, the same is forgiven, and I, the Lord, remember them no more." (D&C 58:42.)

Think on that. The Lord remembers our sins no more. What a glorious promise! No video tape, no grand movie of all our transgressions, but the Lord's own voice saying that repented sins are not remembered. The gospel of Hope! Add to that this promise, "If thou wilt do good, yea, and hold out faithful to the end, thou shalt be saved in the kingdom of God, which is the greatest of all the gifts of God; for there is no gift greater than the gift of salvation." (D&C 6:13.) The hope is in Christ who has borne all our iniquities, who suffered for us that we might not suffer if we will repent (D&C 19:16). Then He holds out the promise that if we are faithful in keeping the commandments and serving Him, we shall receive the greatest of all gifts, salvation in the Kingdom of God.

The Lord knows how difficult the road back is, and He encourages us by repeating again and again His promise of forgiveness. Ponder these scriptures:

> Come now, and let us reason together, saith the Lord: though your sins be as scarlet, they shall be as white as snow; though they be red like crimson, they shall be as wool. (Isaiah 1:18-19.)

I, even I, am he that blotteth out thy transgressions for mine own sake, and will not remember thy sins. (Isaiah 43:25.)

For they shall all know me, from the least of them unto the greatest of them, saith the Lord; for I will forgive their iniquity, and I will remember their sin no more. (Jeremiah 31:34.)

And if ye believe on his name ye will repent of all your sins, that thereby ye may have a remission of them through his merits. (Helaman 14:13)

Whosoever transgresseth against me, . . . if he confess his sins before thee and me, and repenteth in the sincerity of his heart, him shall ye forgive, and I will forgive him also. Yea, and as often as my people repent will I forgive them their trespasses against me. (Mosiah 26:29-30.)

How can we know if the Lord has forgiven us? To answer this question, President Harold B. Lee told the story of a young man who sought forgiveness for his sins:

Some years ago, President Romney and I were sitting in my office. The door opened and a fine young man came in with a troubled look on his face, and he said, "Brethren, I am going to the temple for the first time tomorrow. I have made some mistakes in the past, and I have gone to my bishop and my stake president, and I have made a clean disclosure of it all; and after a period of repentance and assurance that I have not returned again to those mistakes, they have now adjudged me ready to go to the temple. But, brethren, that is not enough. I want to know, and how can I know, that the Lord has forgiven me, also."

What would you answer one who would come to you asking that question? As we pondered for a moment, we remembered King Benjamin's address contained in the book of Mosiah. Here was a group of people who now were asking for baptism, and they said they viewed themselves in their carnal state:

". . . And they all cried aloud with one voice, saying: O have mercy, and *apply the atoning blood of Christ that we may receive forgiveness of our sins*, and our hearts may be purified; . . .

". . . After they had spoken these words the Spirit of the Lord came upon them, and they were filled with joy, having received a remission of their sins, and having *peace of conscience*. . . . (Mosiah 4:2-3.)

There was the answer.

If the time comes when you have done all that you can to repent of your sins, whoever you are, wherever you are, and have made amends and restitution to the best of your ability; if it be something that will affect your standing in the Church and you have gone to the proper authorities, *then you will want that confirming answer as to whether or not the Lord has accepted of you.* In your soul-searching, *if you seek for and you find that peace of conscience, by that token you may know that the Lord has accepted of your repentance.*" (CR, *Ensign*, July 1973, p. 122, emphasis added.)

He Means Us

Some find it difficult to feel the forgiveness of the Lord because they cannot forgive themselves for what they have done wrong. The Lord's promise of forgiveness is not just for a select few. It is for everyone. Elder Marion D. Hanks said that when the Lord promises to forgive, he "means us."

> I am one who believes that God loves and will never cease to love all of his children, and that he will not cease to hope for us or reach for us or wait for us. . . . And yet over the earth, across the years, I have met some of God's choicest children who find it very difficult to believe in their hearts that he really means them. They know that he is the source of comfort and pardon and peace and that they must seek him and open the door for him and accept his love, and yet even in their extremity they find it difficult to believe that his promised blessings are for them. Some have offended God and their own consciences and are earnestly repentant but they find the way back blocked by their unwillingness to forgive themselves or to believe that God will forgive them, or sometimes by a strange reluctance in some of us to *really* forgive, to *really* forget, and to *really* rejoice. (CR, *Ensign*, May 1979, pp. 74-75, emphasis included.)

Elder Richard G. Scott, emphasizing the importance of accepting the forgiveness of the Lord and not dwelling on our sins, said, "If you, through poor judgment, were to cover your shoes with mud, would you leave them that way? Of course not. You would cleanse and restore them. Would you then gather the residue of mud and place it in an envelope to show others the mistake that you made? No. Neither should you continue to relive forgiven sin. Every time such thoughts come into your mind, turn your heart in gratitude to the Savior, who gave His life that we, through faith in Him and obedience to His teachings, can overcome transgression and conquer its depressing influence in our lives." (CR, *Ensign*, May 1986, p. 12.)

A dear friend who went through a long and painful repentance process, expressed her feelings: "I believe the necessity of forgiving oneself is an often misunderstood and overlooked part of the repentance process. From my experience, I think we tend to wallow in grief, pain, embarrassment, and even anger associated with our misdeeds, believing ourselves unworthy of forgiveness from anyone. I remained in a tunnel of darkness even after feeling the Lord's forgiveness. I learned in a very personal way that it was necessary to accept His forgiveness by forgiving myself. When I did, the darkness dissipated and the light flooded into my life. I had been told that sadness, darkness, and gloom were not of God. That is right. While I was wallowing, Satan was enjoying. When we allow the light in, Satan has no power. He can't stand the light. Bring the light into your life, and Satan is out of it!"

Don't we all yearn to hear these words from the Lord: "Thy sins are forgiven thee"? His sublime promise is sure to all of God's children who truly repent and follow the Savior. Therefore, "Lift up thy heart and be glad" (Moses 7:44, D&C 25:13) is the Lord's appeal to each of us. We *can* repent, and when we do, we *will* be forgiven.

The Blessings of Repentance

What are the blessings of repentance? Consider the story of Alma. Once a dedicated sinner and opponent of the truth, his life was completely changed through repentance:

> I went about with the sons of Mosiah, seeking to destroy the church of God; but behold, God sent his holy angel to stop us by the way.
>
> And behold, he spake unto us, as it were the voice of thunder, and the whole earth did tremble beneath our feet; and we all fell to the earth, for the fear of the Lord came upon us.
>
> But behold, the voice said unto me: Arise. And I arose and stood up, and beheld the angel.

And he said unto me: If thou wilt of thyself be destroyed, seek no more to destroy the church of God.

And it came to pass that I fell to the earth; and it was for the space of three days and three nights that I could not open my mouth, neither had I the use of my limbs . . .

But I was racked with eternal torment, for my soul was harrowed up to the greatest degree and racked with all my sins . . . even with the pains of a damned soul.

And it came to pass that as I was thus racked with torment . . . behold, I remembered also to have heard my father prophesy unto the people concerning the coming of one Jesus Christ, a Son of God, to atone for the sins of the world.

Now, as my mind caught hold upon this thought, I cried within my heart: O Jesus, thou Son of God, have mercy on me, who am in the gall of bitterness, and am encircled about by the everlasting chains of death.

And now, behold, when I thought this, I could remember my pains no more; yea, I was harrowed up by the memory of my sins no more.

And oh, what joy, and what marvelous light I did behold; yea, my soul was filled with joy as exceeding as was my pain!

Yea, I say unto you, my son, that there could be nothing so exquisite and so bitter as were my pains. Yea, and again I say unto you, my son, that on the other hand, there can be nothing so exquisite and sweet as was my joy. (Alma 36:6-21.)

What a beautiful report of repentance. Alma said, "There can be nothing so exquisite and sweet as was my joy." Joy, then, is one of the fruits of repentance. What other blessings does repentance bring? Consider these scriptures:

"And the remission of sins bringeth meekness, and lowliness of heart; and because of meekness and lowliness of heart cometh the visitation of the Holy Ghost, which Comforter filleth with *hope and perfect love*, which love endureth by diligence unto prayer, until the end shall come, when all the saints shall dwell with God." (Moroni 8:26, emphasis added.)

After we have repented of our sins we secure the remission of our sins. Because of our meekness and lowliness of heart the Holy Ghost will come unto us to comfort, lead and direct us. Furthermore:

"Whosoever repenteth, and hardeneth not his heart, he shall have claim on mercy through mine Only Begotten Son, unto a remission of his sins; and these shall enter into my rest." (Alma 12:34.)

"Pray always, and I will *pour out my Spirit* upon you, and great shall be your blessing—yea, even more than if you should obtain treasures of earth and corruptibleness to the extent thereof. Behold, canst thou read this without rejoicing and lifting up thy heart for gladness? . . . Or canst thou be humble and meek, and conduct thyself wisely before me? Yea, come unto me thy Savior." (D&C 19:38-39,41, emphasis added.)

"Learn of me, and listen to my words; walk in the meekness of my *Spirit*, and you shall have *peace* in me. I am Jesus Christ; I came by the will of the Father, and I do his will." (D&C 19:23-24, emphasis added.)

Joy. Hope and perfect love. The Spirit of the Lord. Peace of conscience. Rest. These are the blessings of repentance. What treasures!

The Savior has given us an invitation to come unto Him. If we repent and come unto him we will be released from a heavy burden. If we follow him and keep his commandments, we will be blessed. The burden of guilt will go away and in its place will come peace and happiness.

In 2 Nephi 31:20 we read, "Wherefore, if ye shall press forward, feasting upon the word of Christ, and endure to the end, behold, thus saith the Father: Ye shall have *eternal life*." (Emphasis added.)

The final and most glorious blessing of repentance is eternal life, "the greatest of all the gifts of God" (D&C 14:7.) All that God has is ours if we will repent and endure to the end. Is it not worth any sacrifice we make along the way?

President Spencer W. Kimball, a dedicated advocate for the power of repentance, said, "Forgiveness of sins is one of the most glorious principles God ever gave to man. Just as repentance is a divine principle, so also is forgiveness. Were it not for this principle, there would be no point in crying repentance. But because of this principle the divine invitation is held out to all of us—come, repent of your sins, and be forgiven!" ("God Will Forgive," *Ensign*, March 1982, p. 7.)

This is a glorious concept! *All* of us have the ability to repent and make ourselves worthy of salvation. We only fail if we make that our choice through our bad conduct. We each have the power to decide our own eternal destiny!

"A Daily Pruning"

After we have repented of all our sins there is still day to day work to be done. President Harold B. Lee said, "To be truly righteous, there is required a daily pruning of the evil growth of our characters by daily repentance from sin." (*Stand Ye in Holy Places*, p. 219.)

Repentance is not to be reserved only for "big" sins. Each of us has a need for daily repentance, because none of us is perfect. When we repent daily, we make ourselves worthy to have the continual companionship of the Holy Ghost.

One of our children asked us, after learning about repentance, "What if I have forgotten something I have done wrong and so I never repent of it? How will I ever repent of things I can't remember?" She was really worried about things she might have forgotten! We answered that she should pray and ask the Lord to reassure her that she had been forgiven—if there was something important, the Holy Ghost would surely have reminded her of whatever might be amiss in her life.

President George Q. Cannon recommended daily review: "When we get up in the morning, let us examine ourselves to see whether the Spirit of God is with us and so at night before we commit ourselves to slumber, review the acts and words of the day and ask God to show unto us wherein we have come short and we may repent; thus, repenting every day and having the forgiveness of our sins every day, there will be no account recorded in heaven against us to be expiated after this life." (*Gospel Truth*, p. 128.)

Daily repentance coupled with seeking the Spirit enable us to make constant refinements in our lives. After we have taken care of the "big ticket items," there are numerous improvements that can be accomplished as they are brought to our attention. President Lee said we should make each day our "masterpiece":

> The righteous man strives for self-improvement knowing that he has daily need of repentance for his misdeeds or his neglect. He is not so much concerned about what he can get but more about how much he can give to others, knowing that along that course only can he find true happiness. He endeavors to make each day his masterpiece so that at night's close he can witness in his soul and to his God that whatever has come to his hand that day, he has done to the best of his ability. His body is not dissipated and weakened by the burdens imposed by the demands of riotous living; his judgment is not rendered faulty by the follies of youth; he is clear of vision, keen of intellect, and strong of body. (*Stand Ye in Holy Places*, p. 333.)

We commend this method. Wonderful blessings will attend the effort. First, with God's help, take care of any "big" sins. Then, ascending the ladder of faithfulness and spirituality, search the heart daily and always strive to change and improve.

President Cannon said that as we do this, we will come to abhor sin and desire to repent instantly whenever we do wrong: "We should have the spirit of repentance constantly in our hearts. Our hearts should be touched and softened by it, so that we will be mellowed under its influence and that we shall have such a horror of sin and such a desire for righteousness that when we become conscious that we have thought or said or done anything contrary to the mind and will of God, we will instantly bow down and acknowledge our sins before the Lord and repent of them with all our hearts and obtain forgiveness for them." (*Gospel Truth*, p. 127.)

The spirit of repentance is a spirit of sweetness. It is an asmosphere of progression, enhancement, and encouragement. In this disposition each day can be one of challenge and fulfillment, accompanied by an awareness of the Lord's sweet love.

President Kimball spoke of the peace that comes from this repentant attitude: "The essence of the miracle of forgiveness is that it brings peace to the previously anxious, restless, frustrated, perhaps tormented soul. In a world of turmoil and contention this is indeed a priceless gift. . . . It is not easy to be at peace in today's troubled world. Necessarily peace is a personal acquisition . . . it can be attained only through maintaining constantly a repentant attitude, seeking forgiveness of sins both large and small, and thus coming ever closer to God." (*Miracle of Forgiveness*, pp. 363, 366.)

Let us remember that our Father in Heaven is our *Father*. He loves us tenderly, and wants us to succeed.

President Cannon's beautiful words confirm the love our Father in Heaven has for us, and promises that He will forgive us and bless us: "I can say for the encouragement of all who are struggling that God is very, very merciful. He is willing to forgive all who come unto Him in humility. All who will ask Him for light, He will give light. All who ask Him for strength, He will give strength. All who ask Him for peace, He will give peace. All who ask Him for joy and happiness of soul, to them He will give these blessings. None will go away unsatisfied." (*Gospel Truth*, p. 132.)

We have felt the power of repentance in our own lives. We have tasted of the sweet peace that comes with forgiveness. We testify that the Lord is waiting for you and for each of us to come unto Him, repent, and receive the forgiveness and peace He wants to give us. We urge you to accept His invitation. By following the steps outlined, take your personal journey toward joy.

The Lord's Grace

Your Companion for the Journey

When we were set upon this journey of mortality, our Savior Jesus Christ, himself already having achieved perfection and Godhood, promised his love and grace to be with us through the entire trek. He continually reaffirms this promise: "My arms are outstretched still." "I will be with you." "Come unto me." "My peace I give unto you." "Behold, I stand at the door and knock."

We are not alone. We are never alone. If we have removed ourselves from Him, our Savior, He is still just a prayer away. "My grace is sufficient for all men that humble themselves before me." (Ether 12:27.)

"Lord, How is it Done?"

This word "grace" resounds through the scriptures of every dispensation, assuring us that our Father in Heaven, and the Lord Jesus Christ, love us, stand by us, and want us to succeed. We may plead for understanding of His grace, as Enos did, when he felt the Lord's forgiveness flood his anguished soul, "Lord, how is it done?" (Enos 1:7.)

Enos was amazed at the power which came to him. The Lord told him it was because of his faith, and when he poured out his soul in behalf of his fellowmen, the Lord assured him that He would "visit [them] according to their diligence" in keeping His commandments (v. 10). The atonement which makes forgiveness possible is provided through the grace of Jesus Christ, and is universally available to all.

"Grace" is a term perhaps not totally understood. It reappears throughout the scriptures with a number of various applications. To help us understand how it impacts our lives, and "how it is done," we will explore some of the various meanings this lovely word has in the scriptures.

Grace is often used as a synonym for "favor" as in "Noah found grace in the eyes of the Lord." (Moses 8:27.)

It may mean a "free gift," as when Enoch was speaking to the Lord: "Thou hast made me, and given unto me a right to thy throne, and not of myself, but through thine own grace." (Moses 7:59.)

It is often applied to the equally "free gift" given by Jesus Christ when He wrought out the atonement for us: "For by grace are ye saved through faith; and that not of yourselves: it is the gift of God." (Ephesians 2:8.)

Grace sometimes refers to attributes of character, as when the boy Jesus is described as growing "from grace to grace" (D&C 93:11,12.) This may refer to strength, or to knowledge, as it is often combined with truth: "Wherefore, redemption cometh in and through the Holy Messiah; for he is full of grace and truth." (2 Nephi 2:6.)

It is also used as the attribute of gratitude, a word closely allied to grace: "Wherefore we receiving a kingdom which cannot be moved, let us have grace, whereby we may serve God acceptably with reverence and godly fear." (Hebrews 12:28.) This relates to the term sometimes used in the world as gratitude for the food provided, "saying grace."

It refers to the attribute of love, as in Alma 5:48: "Jesus Christ shall come, yea, the Son, the Only Begotten of the Father, full of grace, and mercy, and truth. And behold, it is he that cometh to take away the sins of the world."

Again, it refers to the attribute of strength, as in D&C 106:8: "And I will give him grace and assurance wherewith he may stand."

This is closely allied with the idea of divine assistance in D&C 109:44: "Help thy servants to say, with thy grace assisting them: Thy will be done, O Lord, and not ours."

"Power" is referred to as grace in D&C 88:78: "Teach ye diligently and my grace shall attend you," and again in D&C 76:94-95: "They who dwell in his presence are the church of the Firstborn; and they see as they are seen, and know as they are known, having received of his fulness and of his grace; and he makes them equal in power, and in might, and in dominion."

"An Enabling Power"

Perhaps the most important meaning of grace to us is "an enabling power." The Bible Dictionary defines "grace", explaining that "the main idea of the word is divine means of help or strength, given through the bounteous mercy and love of Jesus Christ. . . . This grace is an enabling power that allows men and women to lay hold on eternal life and exaltation after they have expended their own best efforts." (p. 697.)

Examples of this "enabling power" are: in Mosiah 18:26, "And the priests were not to depend upon the people for their support; but for their labor they were to receive the grace of God, that they might wax strong in the Spirit." Again in Jacob 4:7, "Nevertheless, the Lord God showeth us our weakness that we may know that it is by his grace, and his great condescensions unto the children of men, that we have power to do these things." And in D&C 17:8, "And if you do these last commandments of mine, which I have given you, the gates of hell shall not prevail against you; for my grace is sufficient for you, and you shall be lifted up at the last day."

We must have that divine power. We are commanded to work out our own salvation, but even as we work at this, we know that the laws of justice demand that a penalty be paid for sin. Our sins preclude us from gaining exaltation and returning to our Father in Heaven, because no unclean thing can enter the Kingdom of God. We can strive to overcome our sins and change our lives; however, there is still that eternal debt to be paid. There is, therefore, a gap between what *we can do* to achieve exaltation, and what *must be done*. This is why grace is necessary. After we have expended our own best efforts, the grace or "enabling power" of Jesus Christ fills that gap, pays the price for our sins, cleanses us, and allows us to gain eternal life. "For we know that it is by grace that we are saved, after all we can do." (2 Nephi 25:23).

Another aspect of grace is the power we gain through Christ to overcome whatever trials beset us in this life. It is a "divine means of help or strength." In this sense it is also an enabling power, because we combine our efforts with the power of the Savior to complete something we would be unable to do alone.

Elder Gene R. Cook spoke of this type of grace, saying, "A scriptural word used to define this ability to overcome the trials of the world through the love of God is *grace*. The word *grace* is not an easy term to define. Perhaps the best definition I know is 'enabling power,' the power the Lord has given us to accomplish all things (see Bible Dictionary)." ("The Grace of the Lord," *New Era*, December 1988, pp. 4,6.)

Now, knowing how much we need the grace of Christ, how can we take advantage of this enabling power in our own lives? We first exercise our faith in Christ, and His ability. Consider these scriptures:

> Yea, and how is it that ye have forgotten that the Lord is able to do all things according to his will, for the children of men, if it so be that they exercise faith in him? Wherefore, let us be faithful to him. (1 Nephi 7:12.)

> If ye will have faith in me ye shall have power to do whatsoever thing is expedient in me. (Moroni 7:33.)

> And inasmuch as ye are humble and faithful and call upon my name, behold, I will give you the victory. (D&C 104:82.)

"There Is No Human Problem Beyond His Capacity to Solve"

As we learn to rely on our Savior through our growing faith, we can then enlist the help of the Lord in overcoming the temptations, trials, and trouble we may encounter in life. President Ezra Taft Benson said, "Faith in Jesus Christ consists of complete reliance on Him. As God, He has infinite power, intelligence, and love. *There is no human problem beyond His capacity to solve.* Because He descended below all things (see D&C 122:8), He knows how to help us rise above our daily difficulties. . . . *There is no evil which He cannot arrest.*" (CR, *Ensign*, November 1983, p. 8, emphasis added.)

We should realize the important truth that we are totally dependent upon Jesus Christ. Why do we flaunt our own puny powers? We depend on Him for the very air we breathe, the food we eat, the clothes we wear and the homes we live in. All that we "own" on earth is His; we are stewards of His property. He created the earth. He governs the universe.

Recognizing His might and our dependence on Him can be the first step to progress. We may have much ability—where did we get it? We may have much learning—where did we get our minds? Why did we receive the opportunity to learn? When we claim these as our own, we act like Lucifer who wanted God to give him His glory. But when we humbly put Jesus Christ into the center of our lives and have faith in Him, He adds His power to ours, multiplies our talents, and makes us mighty in ways we could never before imagine.

Elder James M. Paramore tells this story of a man with a seemingly insurmountable problem:

> [A man] had what was thought to be an incurable alcohol problem. Every day after work for twenty years, he bought alcohol and consumed it until he could hardly find his way home. He received friendship and encouragement to pray to heaven for help. One day after his work, while he was driving into the countryside with his bottle, a voice came into his heart to stop his car, walk out into the field, and pray to Father in Heaven for help. His simple prayer was heard by his Father in Heaven, and as he stood up and walked back to his car, all desire to drink liquor left his life. The powers of heaven had descended upon him, and he knew that God lived and loved him. (CR, *Ensign*, May 1986, p. 69.)

Alone, this man was incapable of overcoming his dependence on alcohol. However, when he combined his efforts with a sincere, fervent plea for help from God, he was successful.

Don tells of experiencing this enabling power in his life. His words: On my mission in Finland representing the Church of Jesus Christ of Latter-day Saints I found the language extremely difficult. I did everything in my power to learn the language. Although I would get up at 5:00 o'clock every morning and study Finnish, when people spoke it sounded to me like one long word. Two Finns were trying to teach me, but I had not learned enough to converse. I felt helpless and ineffective.

After several weeks went by in this way, I went to the Lord in solemn prayer. I told Him that I knew He had brought me to Finland to teach the gospel, and He knew I had a testimony of Jesus Christ. I pled with him to give me the Finnish language so I could do my work.

Later we were at a youth outing. My two friends came over to greet me. It was as if someone had pulled plugs out of my ears. I could understand them, and further, when I spoke they could understand me.

While on my mission I also saw the grace of Christ enable people to overcome personal difficulties in their attempt to embrace the gospel. We had an investigator, Sister Nyland. We taught her the discussions, but she was too embarrassed to pray. Time went on, and she could not get a testimony of the gospel of Jesus Christ. At the end of one of our cottage meetings, we all knelt down to pray as usual. I told her we could not do her praying for her any longer, and called on her to pray at this time.

A long time passed in silence while we waited on our knees, and then I heard a tiny sweet voice talking to her Father in Heaven, thanking Him for the missionaries and asking for a testimony of the gospel.

One of her problems was giving up coffee. One night she had a dream in which she was in heaven. She said the streets were so clean and perfect. She was really enjoying herself, looking around at the beauty of the scene. Suddenly she looked down and saw her old black coffee pot in her hand. She said she looked all over heaven to find a place dirty enough to put that coffee pot. She woke up in a sweat. She told us, "I went into the kitchen, got the black coffee pot, went into the back yard, dug a hole in the grass, and buried it. I said, 'There! You are not going to go to heaven with me!'" She was soon baptized.

Bishop H. Burke Petersen told of his own experience where he needed the help of the Lord in overcoming some unforgiving feelings:

> I suppose we have all had someone do something to us that we didn't like, and that made us angry. We can't forget it, and we don't want to be around that person. This is called being unforgiving. Now, the Lord has had some very strong words to say to those who will not forgive one another. Many years ago I had an experience with being unforgiving. I felt I had been taken advantage of, and I did not like the person. I did not want to be around him; I would pass on the other side of the street if he came down it; I wouldn't talk to him. Long after the issue should have been closed, it was still cankering my soul. One day my wife, who is very astute and knows when I'm not doing everything I should, said, "You don't like so and so, do you?"
>
> "No, I don't," I said. "But how could you tell?"
>
> "Well, it shows—in your countenance it shows. Why don't you do something about it?" she said.
>
> "Like what?"
>
> "Why don't you pray about it?"
>
> I said, "Well, I did pray once, and I still don't like him."
>
> "No," she said, "why don't you *really* pray about it?"
>
> Then I began to think, and I knew what she meant. So I decided that I was going to pray for a better feeling about this person until I had one. That night I got on my knees, and I prayed and opened up my heart to the Lord. But when I got up off my knees, I still didn't like that person. The next morning I knelt and prayed and asked to have a feeling of goodness toward him; but when I finished my

prayers, I still didn't like him. The next night I still didn't like him; a week later I didn't like him; and a month later I didn't like him—and I had been praying every night and every morning. But I kept it up, and I finally started pleading—not just praying, but pleading. After much prayer, the time came when without question or reservation I knew I could stand before the Lord, if I were asked to, and that he would know that at least in this instance my heart was pure. A change had come over me after a period of time. That stone of unforgiveness needs to be removed from all of us, if it happens to be there, and I suggest that persistent prayer might be a way to remove it. ("Prayer—Try Again," *Ensign*, June 1981, p. 73.)

When Bishop Petersen really humbled himself and pled with the Lord, he got an answer. The change that came over him cleansed his heart from the canker of unforgiveness, and he received a new attitude toward the man.

People can overcome other human failings through dependence on the Lord. A man we will call Joshua decided he wanted to overcome the bad habit of swearing. Knowing this habit to be long-standing and hard to remove, he decided to ask Heavenly Father in prayer for help every time it happened. Joshua would ask for forgiveness and strength to overcome this bad habit every time he swore. At first he found he had to ask several times a day. But as he continued with determination, he found that the need to pray for forgiveness and strength dwindled down to something like once a day, once a week, then once a month. One of the last times Joshua had to pray regarding swearing was on a cold winter day. In a hurry to get to the top of some stairs, he stumbled and fell. His hand hit the ice-cold steel and began to bleed. The angry swear word tumbled out, and he instantly remembered. The pain in his bleeding hand was not nearly so bad as the terrible remorse in his heart. He prayed quickly, "Father, forgive me and strengthen me, that I may overcome, I ask in the name of Jesus Christ. Amen." He felt so foolish to have again succumbed to his weakness that he redoubled his effort, praying daily, and soon was free from this bad habit.

Almost any weakness or sin can be overcome in this manner. Say, for example, you have the problem of watching "R", "NC-17", or "X" rated movies, of reading or looking at books with pornography in them, or of watching indecent TV. Make an agreement with the Lord to pray for strength to overcome every time you are tempted. You may find you will give in a few times, but you will soon gain the strength you lack. As you withstand and begin to put your mind to more worthwhile pursuits, pornography in any form will sicken you. You will come to abhor this vile practice. Romans 12:9 exhorts us to "Abhor that which is evil; cleave to that which is good." What a great gift it would be to have our natures changed so that we would abhor sin in any form!

Some feel that they will overcome their weaknesses by themselves and then come unto Christ and He will save them. This discredits the atonement of Jesus Christ, who overcame the world. Without His help we cannot succeed. When we do all in our power, then rely on Him, we cannot fail.

Only Christ Can Change Our Nature

As we seek to overcome, through the grace of Christ, whatever problems are blocking our progression in the gospel, we come to recognize that it is our very nature, not just our actions, that needs change. We are bound by our mortal birth to mortal abilities. We are indeed children of our Heavenly Father, but placed into this mortal condition for the testing probation. We are in this state because of the fall of Adam, and will remain thus until acted upon by the redeeming power of Jesus Christ, through his grace. Abinadi explains:

"Even that old serpent . . . did beguile our first parents, which was the cause of their fall; which was the cause of all mankind becoming carnal, sensual, devilish, knowing evil from good, subjecting themselves to the devil.

"Thus all mankind were lost; and behold, they would have been endlessly lost were it not that God redeemed his people from their lost and fallen state." (Mosiah 16:3-4.)

We are dependent upon Christ for that salvation which lifts us above this mortal condition. Brother George W. Pace of Brigham Young University wrote, "We cannot enjoy the greater powers available in the restored gospel unless we sense in a profound way our total dependence on the Son of God and realize that only in and through him can our nature be changed and our character become like his. To know that Jesus is literally the Son of God is to acknowledge that because of that divine sonship he was able to come to the earth, break the bands of sin and death, and offer through his divine gospel the power to become like him and in so doing add to the honor and glory of the Father." (*Our Search to Know the Lord*, p. 74.)

In the Book of Mormon there is a group of people who experienced this very change in their nature through the grace and power of Christ. As King Benjamin spoke to his people, admonishing them of their sins, a great change came upon the people and they fell to the earth because "they had viewed themselves in their own carnal state, even less than the dust of the earth. And they all cried aloud with one voice, saying: O have mercy, and apply the atoning blood of Christ that we may receive forgiveness of our sins, and our hearts may be purified; for we believe in Jesus Christ, the Son of God, who created heaven and earth, and all things; who shall come down among the children of men." (Mosiah 4:2.)

These people became aware of their weaknesses, which caused them to be humble. In their humility they realized their need for the grace of Christ, and they called upon God to help them repent. When they received a remission of their sins, *their very natures were changed.* Alma described it thus, speaking of the experience to their descendants: "And behold, he [Alma the Elder] preached the word unto your fathers, and a mighty change was also wrought in their hearts, and they humbled themselves and put their trust in the true and living God. And behold, they were faithful until the end; therefore they were saved." (Alma 5:13.)

Over and over again in the scriptures we are assured of what we can do through the power of the Lord:

I can do all things through Christ which strengtheneth me. (Philippians 4:13.)

The LORD will give strength unto his people. (Psalms 29:11.)

He giveth power to the faint; and to them that have no might he increaseth strength. (Isaiah 40:29.)

And if it so be that the children of men keep the commandments of God he doth nourish them, and strengthen them, and provide means whereby they can accomplish the thing which he has commanded them . . . (1 Nephi 17:3).

For behold, I do not require at their hands to fight the battles of Zion; for, as I said in a former commandment, even so will I fulfil—I will fight your battles. (D&C 105:14.)

Exercising our faith in these promises will help us begin to make the necessary changes in ourselves. But we must always keep in mind that we cannot overcome deep-seated habits alone. Brother Stephen R. Covey explained that, after exercising faith in Christ, we can enter into a contract with Him through our covenants and personal prayer:

> We can't fully overcome . . . habits and impacted tendencies by ourselves. Our own resolves, our own will, our own effort—all this is necessary but is not sufficient. We need the transforming power of the Savior, born of faith in him and his atoning sacrifice and of entering into a contract with him. In such a contract, made in ordinance work and in private prayer, we covenant, or promise, or witness to take upon ourselves his name and to keep his commandments. He, in turn, promises us to give us his spirit, which, if we are true to our promises, will renew and strengthen and transform us. In this way we combine our power with the power of the Almighty. (*Spiritual Roots of Human Relations*, p. 93.)

President Ezra Taft Benson said that through Christ we can overcome worldly influences and human failings: "Only Jesus Christ is uniquely qualified to provide that hope, that confidence, and that strength to overcome the world and rise above our human failings." (CR, *Ensign*, November 1983, p. 6.)

Plead With Him Daily

Jesus invited us to welcome Him into our lives when He said, "Behold, I stand at the door, and knock: if any man hear my voice, and open the door, I will come in to him, and will sup with him, and he with me." (Revelation 3:20.)

We need to take our Savior up on this invitation and open the door and let Him into our lives. President Marion G. Romney said, "Prayer is the key which unlocks the door and lets Christ into our lives." (CR, *Ensign*, May 1978, p. 50.) And President Benson said, "When you choose to follow Christ, you choose to be changed." (CR, *Ensign*, November 1985, p. 5.)

As we follow Christ and change our lives, we should start with whatever the Holy Spirit indicates to us is our present concern. Maybe we have trouble forgiving a person who has offended us. When we make this a matter of fervent prayer, when we cry unto the Lord to take the bitterness out of our heart, when we beg the Lord to free us of these bad feelings and keep praying over a period of time, the bitterness will leave and we will only feel love for the person. I know it will work because I have taken this step and found the peace and love that only Jesus Christ can give.

After one weakness is conquered, we can go on to the next, and treat it in the same manner. In this way, with the help of the Lord, we can overcome all our imperfections. We need to plead with Him daily for the strength to overcome the ones we are working on at the time. There is a price to be paid for the answers we receive from our prayers. That price is to humble ourselves, have faith in Him, to be humble and contrite. He promised "my grace is sufficient for all men that humble themselves before me; for if they humble themselves before me, and have faith in me, then will I make weak things become strong unto them." (Ether 12:27.) This should give us encouragement to totally trust the Lord, to lean upon Him, have faith in Him, and pray for His help in everything we do. With such trust and faith we can overcome whatever obstacles are before us in our efforts to purify our lives.

11

Baptism

Accepting the Commission

The common goal of every person born into the world is to obtain exaltation. This was established as our goal in the premortal existence when we shouted for joy because the plan of salvation was presented to us. Because of the veil drawn over our minds for the purpose of our probation here, many do not recognize this goal. However, the whispering of the still small voice, the Light of Christ, gives us the feeling of truth when we hear it. Missionaries go into the mission field to preach the gospel of Jesus Christ. Some people recognize the whispering of truth, accept the message, have faith in Jesus Christ, repent of their sins, and wish to start on the road for that newly-remembered goal.

The path leading to eternal life is a long one, and baptism is the gate. "For the gate by which ye should enter is repentance and baptism by water; and then cometh a remission of your sins by fire and by the Holy Ghost." (2 Nephi 31:17.) In our analogy of the path through life as a journey to purity of heart, baptism is seen as our acceptance of the commission by God to pass through mortality and come back to Him having overcome. In this sense, and in actuality, it is a covenant with Him that we take upon ourselves this mission, and the name of Jesus Christ, to bear before the world.

In the Book of Mormon the story is told of a group of people who received the gospel, felt the urging of its message, and desired to make a covenant with their Savior. As they were gathered together, their leader Alma said to them:

Behold, here are the waters of Mormon (for thus were they called) and now, as ye are desirous to come into the fold of God, and to be called his people, and are willing to bear one another's burdens, that they may be light;

Yea, and are willing to mourn with those that mourn; yea, and comfort those that stand in need of comfort, and to stand as witnesses of God at all times and in all things, and in all places that ye may be in, even until death, that ye may be redeemed of God, and be numbered with those of the first resurrection, that ye may have eternal life—

Now I say unto you, if this be the desire of your hearts, what have you against being baptized in the name of the Lord, as a witness before him that ye have entered into a covenant with him, that ye will serve him and keep his commandments, that he may pour out his Spirit more abundantly upon you?

And now when the people had heard these words, they clapped their hands for joy, and exclaimed: This is the desire of our hearts. (Mosiah 18:8-11.)

As Alma thus prepared his people for baptism, he named several prerequisites. The first is a desire to be called the people of God. Next is a love for our brothers and sisters, and a willingness to "bear one another's burdens." After this, Alma says that they were to be willing to "stand as witnesses of God at all times." His people, having expressed their willingness to do these things, were then baptized in the waters of Mormon. Alma says of these waters, "how beautiful are they to the eyes of them who there came to the knowledge of their Redeemer" (Mosiah 18:30).

Immersion is Symbolic

What is the significance of this mode of acceptance of the gospel principles? Baptism by immersion is a symbol of the Savior's burial and resurrection: "Therefore we are buried with him by baptism into death: that like as Christ was raised up from the dead by the glory of the Father, even so we also should walk in newness of life." (Romans 6:4.) Baptism symbolizes that we bury the old person and rise from the water a new converted person, one who is willing to live up to the covenants to bear His name worthily before the world, to live righteously, to purify one's heart, and to bless the lives of others.

Baptism is also a symbol of birth, as explained by Jesus: "Except a man be born again, he cannot see the kingdom of God. . . . Except a man be born of water and of the Spirit, he cannot enter into the kingdom of God." (John 3:3,5.) The Lord taught this plainly to Adam: "Teach these things freely unto your children, saying: That by reason of transgression cometh the fall, which fall bringeth death, and inasmuch as ye were born into the world by water, and blood, and the spirit, which I have made, and so became of dust a living soul, even so ye must be born again into the kingdom of heaven, of water, and of the Spirit, and be cleansed by blood, even the blood of mine Only Begotten; that ye might be sanctified from all sin, and enjoy the words of eternal life in this world, and eternal life in the world to come, even immortal glory; For by the water ye keep the commandment; by the Spirit ye are justified, and by the blood ye are sanctified." (Moses 6:58-60.)

Baptism is a Covenant

A covenant is a contract between two parties in which each party agrees to do something for the other. What we promise in the covenant of baptism is obedience to the Lord and His commandments, and to bear His name before the world. In return the Lord promises us several things. He promises to cleanse us of our sins (see D&C 33:11). Through baptism we gain membership in His church (see Moroni 6:4). We are also promised the gift of the Holy Ghost if we are baptized (see 2 Nephi 31:12-13). We receive the Holy Ghost by the laying on of hands of one who has authority. If we have faith in Jesus Christ and have repented of all our sins, we will receive the Holy Ghost to be our constant companion. Finally, the greatest blessing that comes through baptism is that if we are faithful to our covenants, we will receive eternal life (see Alma 7:15-16).

President Marion G. Romney said, "By accepting membership in the Church, through baptism and the laying on of hands for the gift of the Holy Ghost, a person enters into a covenant with the Lord to obey and live by all the requirements of the gospel. The Lord's promise, conditioned upon such obedience, is the gift of eternal life." (CR, *Ensign*, November 1978, p. 87.)

The Doctrine and Covenants further describes those who will receive eternal life: "They are they who received the testimony of Jesus, and believed on his name and were baptized after the manner of his burial, being buried in the water in his name, and this according to the commandment which he has given—That by keeping the commandments they might be washed and cleansed from all their sins, and receive the Holy Spirit by the laying on of the hands of him who is ordained and sealed unto this power." (D&C 76:51-52.)

After Baptism

President Joseph Fielding Smith said that the gospel teaches us what we are to do after we are baptized: "One of the great purposes of the true church is to teach men what they must do after baptism to gain the full blessing of the gospel. . . . We must endure to the end; we must keep the commandments after baptism; we must work out our salvation with fear and trembling before the Lord; we must so live as to acquire the attributes of godliness and become the kind of people who can enjoy the glory and wonders of the celestial kingdom." ("The Plan of Salvation," *Ensign*, November 1971, p. 5.)

President Spencer W. Kimball said that our baptismal covenant includes a promise "to work righteousness as well as to avoid evil." (*The Miracle of Forgiveness*, p. 94.) Let's look at a group of people who were baptized into the church. What did they do to "work righteousness as well as to avoid evil"?

And the church did meet together oft, to fast and to pray, and to speak one with another concerning the welfare of their souls.

And they did meet together oft to partake of bread and wine, in remembrance of the Lord Jesus.

And they were strict to observe that there should be no iniquity among them; and whoso was found to commit iniquity, and three witnesses of the church did condemn them before the elders, and if they repented not, and confessed not, their names were blotted out, and they were not numbered among the people of Christ.

But as oft as they repented and sought forgiveness, with real intent, they were forgiven.

And their meetings were conducted by the church after the manner of the workings of the Spirit, and by the power of the Holy Ghost; for as the power of the Holy Ghost led them whether to preach, or to exhort, or to pray, or to supplicate, or to sing, even so it was done. (Moroni 6:5-9.)

After baptism and confirmation we are to continue to pray to our Father in Heaven—to seek guidance and strength, and thank Him for our many blessings. We should fast and pray as needed. It is important to attend all of our meetings and go the extra mile in magnifying our callings in the Church. We have the opportunity to do our home teaching and visiting teaching every month. We can bless the lives of our neighbors as we see need. We should listen to the inspiration of the still, small voice which leads us to do important errands in the Lord's service. We should "do many things of [our] own free will, and bring to pass much righteousness." (D&C 58:27.)

We may make mistakes after baptism; we are to repent of them and get back on the right road. We need to live a worthy life so we can have the companionship of the Holy Ghost. This attitude of humility as we live our lives, this constant correcting of course, leads us toward perfection.

The Sacrament, Renewal of Our Covenant

God has provided a way by which we can renew our baptismal covenants. We do this when we partake of the sacrament. Elder Bruce R. McConkie stated: "In his church we partake often of the sacrament, to renew our baptismal covenant, to assert anew that we will 'always remember him and keep his commandments,' and to plead that we 'may have his Spirit' to be with us. (D&C 20:77.) When this is done in righteousness, by those who are just and true, the Spirit of the Lord comes to dwell in their hearts; and as we have seen, Christ himself thereby dwells in them and they in him. Thus we find our Lord teaching: 'He that eateth my flesh, and drinketh my blood, dwelleth in me, and I in him.' (John 6:56.)" (*The Promised Messiah*, pp. 127-128.)

President Joseph Fielding Smith emphasized the need for worthy actions to accompany our partaking of the sacrament:

Again, I have wondered how members of the Church can go to the sacrament service and partake of these emblems, and make these solemn covenants, and then immediately after the close of the meeting go out to some place of amusement, to attend a picture show, a baseball game, or some resort, or to gather at some home to play cards.

When any of these things is done, the guilty person violates this sacred covenant so recently made or renewed. Do they who do this pay so little attention to their obligations that they really do not sense their significance? . . .

When we indulge in habits of this kind we are *covenant breakers*. (*Doctrines of Salvation*, vol. 2, p. 345, emphasis included.)

Faithfulness to Our Covenants Brings Joy in This Life and Exaltation in the Next

Not only will our willingness to receive the covenant of baptism and remain faithful until the end bring us eternal life in the life to come, it will also bring us joy and happiness in this life. Elder S. Dilworth Young said, "You will find happiness such as you cannot understand if you keep the commandments and covenants of the Lord. . . . Men or women who keep the covenants . . . find joy, peace, comfort, and forgiveness of sin as the Lord has promised." (*Covenants and Commandments*, Brigham Young University Speeches of the Year [Provo, 3 Aug 1971], p. 8.)

All the commandments we are given and asked to obey are for our earthly and eternal benefit. President Joseph Fielding Smith, Jr. promised this when he said, "We should fully and sincerely comprehend the fact that *no requirement, request, or commandment made of man by the Father or the Son is given except for the purpose of advancing man on the path of eternal perfection.* Never at any time has the Lord given to man a commandment which was not intended to exalt him and bring him nearer to eternal companionship with the Father and the Son." (*Doctrines of Salvation*, vol. I, p. 155.)

When we understand the importance of our baptismal covenants, we will find the strength we need to live up to those covenants, and as we do so we will receive the promised blessings of forgiveness for our sins, the gift of the Holy Ghost, joy in this life, and eventually, exaltation in the mansions of our Father in Heaven.

12

The Sacrament

Sacrifice and Sacrament

During the period of the Old Testament, under the law of Moses, the firstborn lamb was offered as a sacrifice to the Lord. The lamb was symbolic of the sacrifice the Savior would make in the future. Jacob the brother of Nephi exulted: "Behold, my soul delighteth in proving unto my people the truth of the coming of Christ; for, for this end hath the law of Moses been given; and all things which have been given of God from the beginning of the world, unto man, are the typifying of him." (2 Nephi 11:4.) The coming of Christ was in fulfillment of these expectations. To those in Galilee, Jesus declared: "Think not that I am come to destroy the law, or the prophets: I am not come to destroy, but to fulfil." (Matthew 5:17.) And to the Nephites, after His resurrection, He said: "Behold, by me redemption cometh, and in me is the law of Moses fulfilled." (3 Nephi 9:17.)

He warned the unbelieving Jews: "Verily, verily, I say unto you, Except ye eat the flesh of the Son of man, and drink his blood, ye have no life in you. Whoso eateth my flesh, and drinketh my blood, hath eternal life; and I will raise him up at the last day." (John 6:53-54.)

When He had finished His work, having taught the gospel freely, having called and commissioned the leadership of His church and endowed them with power, and being ready in all things to make His eternal sacrifice, just before Gethsemane and Calvary Christ instituted the sacrament among His Apostles. In Matthew 26:26-28 we read, "And as they were eating, Jesus took bread, and blessed it, and brake it, and gave it to the disciples, and said, Take, eat; this is my body.

"And he took the cup, and gave thanks, and gave it to them, saying, Drink ye all of it;

"For this is my blood of the new testament, which is shed for many for the remission of sins."

This was a replacement for the sacrifice of animals in the lives of His followers. The Law of Moses was fulfilled with His last sacrifice, and they were then to look back on His Sacrifice in love and obedience. Acts 2:42 tells us that under the ministry of Peter, newly baptized members of the infant Church of Jesus Christ "continued stedfastly in the apostles' doctrine and fellowship, and in breaking of bread, and in prayers." It was a great comfort to them to meet thus and rejoice in the mercy and grace of their Lord.

At the Feet of Jesus

When Jesus appeared on the American continent, he also introduced the ordinance of the sacrament to the Nephites. How would it have been to be present and seated at the feet of Jesus Christ when this occurred:

> And it came to pass that Jesus commanded his disciples that they should bring forth some bread and wine unto him.
>
> And while they were gone for bread and wine, he commanded the multitude that they should sit themselves down upon the earth.
>
> And when the disciples had come with bread and wine, he took of the bread and brake and blessed it; and he gave unto the disciples and commanded that they should eat.
>
> And when they had eaten and were filled, he commanded that they should give unto the multitude.
>
> And when the multitude had eaten and were filled, he said unto the disciples: Behold there shall one be ordained among you, and to him will I give power that he shall break bread and bless it and give it unto the people of my church, unto all those who shall believe and be baptized in my name.
>
> And this shall ye always observe to do, even as I have done, even as I have broken bread and blessed it and given it unto you.
>
> And this shall ye do in remembrance of my body, which I have shown unto you. And it shall be a testimony unto the Father that ye do always remember me. And if ye do always remember me ye shall have my Spirit to be with you.
>
> And it came to pass that when he said these words, he commanded his disciples that they should take of the wine of the cup and drink of it, and that they should also give unto the multitude that they might drink of it.

And it came to pass that they did so, and did drink of it and were filled; and they gave unto the multitude, and they did drink, and they were filled.

And when the disciples had done this, Jesus said unto them: Blessed are ye for this thing which ye have done, for this is fulfilling my commandments, and this doth witness unto the Father that ye are willing to do that which I have commanded you.

And this shall ye always do to those who repent and are baptized in my name; and ye shall do it in remembrance of my blood, which I have shed for you, that ye may witness unto the Father that ye do always remember me. And if ye do always remember me ye shall have my Spirit to be with you. (3 Nephi 18:1-11.)

What a beautiful experience! Can you imagine partaking of the sacrament at the very feet of the Savior? I'm sure that each time they partook of the sacrament thereafter they thought about this holy and exalting experience.

Today, as in the Savior's day, the sacrament symbolizes the sacrifice He made in our behalf. Jesus Christ atoned for our sins. He made it possible for us to accept Him, repent of our sins, be baptized by water and the Spirit by those who have authority, and receive a remission of our sins through His atonement.

Worthiness, Devotion, and Reverence

The sacrament is a holy ordinance and requires worthiness, devotion, and reverence when we partake of it. Elder Melvin J. Ballard said, "Each time we partake of these emblems, we manifest before the Father that we do remember his Son; and by the act of partaking of the bread and the water, we make a solemn covenant that we do take upon us the name of our Redeemer, and that we do, further, make a pledge and an agreement by that act that we will keep his commandments." (*Sermons and Missionary Services of Melvin J. Ballard*, p. 147.) When we partake of the sacrament we renew the covenant we made at baptism. We, like the Nephites, agree to keep the Lord's commandments.

In regard to the covenants made when we partake of the sacrament President David O. McKay said, "Who can measure the responsibility of such a covenant? How far reaching! How comprehensive! It excludes from man's life profanity, vulgarity, idleness, jealousy, drunkenness, dishonesty, hatred, selfishness, and every form of vice. It obligates him to industry, to kindness, to the performance of every duty in church and state. He binds himself to respect his fellowmen, to honor the Priesthood, to pay his tithes and offerings and to consecrate his life to the service of humanity." (*Millenial Star*, December 1923, 85:778, as quoted in Deacon's manual, course B, 1984, p. 74.)

An early apostle, Elder George A. Smith, spoke of how we should receive the emblems of our Savior's sacrifice.

> We enjoy the privilege of partaking of the sacrament in commemoration of the death and suffering of our Lord and Saviour, to witness to each other that we are willing to keep his commandments, and to observe the requirements of the fulness of the Gospel until he shall come. Under these circumstances we assemble and call together our wandering thoughts and minds. We review our conduct, our feelings to our Heavenly Father, our actions and doings in relation to His laws, and also our faith towards our brethren, and make a kind of settlement with ourselves, a balance of accounts in our minds, repenting of our sins and follies, and we lay the foundation in our own minds to renew our diligence and exertions in future, that wherein we have failed to walk up to the line of our duty we may improve, and that we may partake of those emblems under an express influence, and with a perfect understanding of a covenant that we will remember Him in all things until He come[s]. (*Journal of Discourses*, vol. 5, p. 11.)

Such a review will help us be sure that we are truly worthy to partake of the sacrament. The Lord warned, "Ye shall not suffer any one knowingly to partake of my flesh and blood unworthily, when ye shall minister it;

"For whoso eateth and drinketh my flesh and blood unworthily eateth and drinketh damnation to his soul." (3 Nephi 18:28-29.)

Elder John H. Groberg explained how we can know if we are worthy to partake of the sacrament:

> What does it mean to partake of the sacrament worthily? Or how do we know if we are unworthy?
>
> If we desire to improve (which is to repent) and are not under priesthood restriction, then, in my opinion, we are worthy. . . . If, however, we refuse to repent and improve, if we do not remember him and keep his commandment, then we have stopped our growth, and that is damnation to our souls.

The sacrament is an intensely personal experience, and we are the ones who know [if we] are worthy or otherwise. (CR, *Ensign*, May 1989, p. 38.)

Elder Groberg gives us excellent guidance to help us decide whether we are worthy of partaking of the sacrament. It is up to each person to look deep into his own heart and ask himself if he truly desires to repent, and is working to do so, in order to be worthy of partaking of the sacrament.

In the Book of Mormon we are commanded, "See that ye partake not of the sacrament of Christ unworthily; but see that ye do all things in worthiness, and do it in the name of Jesus Christ, the Son of the living God; and if ye do this, and endure to the end, ye will in nowise be cast out." (Mormon 9:29.) When we partake of the sacrament worthily, we keep ourselves on the road that leads to eternal life.

The Cleansing Power of the Sacrament

Partaking of the sacrament is an important part of repentance. We may wish that we could go into the waters of baptism again and be washed clean of our sins; however, this is not necessary. Elder Melvin J. Ballard explains that, when partaken of worthily and as part of the repentance process, the sacrament performs the same cleansing action as baptism:

> We do things for which we are sorry and desire to be forgiven, or we have erred against someone and given injury. If there is a feeling in our hearts that we are sorry for what we have done, if there is a feeling in our souls that we would like to be forgiven, then the method to obtain forgiveness is not through rebaptism; it is not to make confession to man, but it is to repent of our sins, to go to those against whom we have sinned or transgressed and obtain their forgiveness and then [go] to the sacrament table where, if we have sincerely repented and put ourselves in proper condition, we shall be forgiven, and spiritual healing will come to our souls. It will really enter our being." (*Sermons and Missionary Services of Melvin J. Ballard*, p. 149.)

Elder Groberg also spoke of the cleansing power of the sacrament when he said,

Do you remember the feeling you had when you were baptized—that sweet, clean feeling of a pure soul, having been forgiven, washed clean through the merits of the Savior? If we partake of the sacrament worthily, we can feel that way regularly, for we renew that covenant, which includes his forgiveness.

Those who would deny themselves the blessing of the sacrament by not attending sacrament meeting or by not thinking of the Savior during the services surely must not understand the great opportunity to be forgiven, to have his Spirit to guide and comfort them! What more could anyone ask? (CR, *Ensign*, May 1989, p. 38.)

In the Book of Mormon we are invited to "Come unto Christ, and be perfected in him." (Moroni 10:32.) One way we do this is through the sacrament. Elder Royden G. Derrick explained how repentance and the partaking of the sacrament help us to progress: "It is important that we partake of the sacrament regularly. When we do so, in sincere repentance, our baptismal covenants are renewed, the Lord forgives us, and we start anew. It is truly a marvelous and a merciful process, one which enables us to grow and progress." (CR, *Ensign*, May 1989, p. 77.)

When we partake of the sacrament sincerely, repentantly, we renew our baptismal covenants, and we receive the forgiveness of the Lord. "We start anew."

Consider this story, related by Elder Groberg, of someone who repented and came to a deep appreciation of the blessing of worthily partaking of the sacrament:

Some years ago, a young couple we will call the Joneses visited with their bishop about a problem the wife had. The details are not important, but through the direction of the Spirit, the bishop's decision was that, among other things, Sister Jones would not partake of the sacrament for a period of time while she worked out some attitudes and problems.

With lots of love and support, she continued to attend meetings with her family, and few but her husband and the bishop were aware of the situation or even noticed that week after week she did not partake of the sacrament. At first she didn't feel much difference; but as time went on, she became more and more desirous to be worthy to partake of the sacrament. She thought she had repented before, but as the real soul-searching deepened and as her desire to worthily partake of the sacrament increased, true fundamental changes began to take place in her life and in her actions and in her thinking.

More time passed. Finally, during one sacrament meeting, the Spirit bore witness to the bishop and to Brother and Sister Jones that the time had come for her to again partake of the sacrament. "Next Sunday," the bishop said.

Next Sunday came, and Sister Jones sat again with her family, nervous, yet excited and full of anticipation. "Am I really worthy? How I want to be!" she thought. The sacrament hymn was more meaningful than ever. She sang with such feeling that it was difficult to hold back the tears. And the sacrament prayers—how profound! She listened so intently that every word sank deep into her soul—to take his name, always remember him, keep his commandments, always have his Spirit. (See D&C 20:77-79.) "Oh, how I desire this," she thought.

. . . Tears streamed down her face. There was a barely audible sob of joy, "Oh!" as she reached for the emblem of the Lord's love for her. The congregation did not hear the sob, but they did notice the tears in the bishop's eyes.

Life and hope and forgiveness and spiritual strength had been given and received. No one could be more worthy. Sister Jones truly *wanted* to have his Spirit. She *wanted* to take his name upon her. With all her heart, she *wanted* to remember him and keep his commandments. She *wanted* to repent, to improve, and to follow the guidance of his Spirit. (CR, *Ensign*, May 1989, p. 39.)

We each need to make partaking of the sacrament a sacred, personal experience. When we truly have the desire to appreciate the experience of taking the sacrament, we too can feel as deeply as this woman did our desire to take upon ourselves the name of Christ, remember Him and keep His commandments. We also can have the guidance of the Spirit.

The Lord has promised that if we are worthy as we partake of the sacrament, the Holy Ghost will be with us. What more can we ask for? What greater blessing is there than to have the third member of the Godhead with us? The Spirit will teach us, strengthen us, protect us, and cleanse us.

What does this mean in our daily lives? We are His disciples, we bear His name, and have covenanted to always remember Him. This will stand us in good stead when a temptation comes before us. If we remember Him, we will be less likely to explode with temper when someone cuts in front of us on the freeway. We will be less likely to cheat on our income taxes. We will be more likely to give assistance where needed, more likely to offer a kind word and a smile. It will make us more ready to reach out to our companions on the journey and make their way a little easier.

Our daughter Rachel had an experience that impressed upon her what a privilege it is to be able to partake of the sacrament. For a period of about twelve weeks she wasn't able to attend sacrament meeting, first because of illness among her four children, and then because of problems in her pregnancy, which required her to stay in bed for an extended period of time.

As one week after another went by she began to miss the opportunity of attending her meetings, and especially of partaking of the sacrament. She describes a feeling of yearning down deep in her soul, a hunger for the emblems of the Lord's supper. Then one Sunday morning she woke up feeling better than usual, and so her husband helped her get all their children ready and they went to sacrament meeting. She had to return home immediately after the meeting to rest, but she was really grateful that she had been able to partake of the sacrament. She says, "I hadn't realized what an important part of my life it was until it was gone."

When we partake of the sacrament, let us revere it as a blessed, exalting experience. Look upon it as a step in your eternal progression. Elder Dallin H. Oaks taught us this, saying:

> Our willingness to take upon us the name of Jesus Christ affirms our commitment to do all that we can to be counted among those whom he will choose to stand at his right hand and be called by his name at the last day. In this sacred sense, our witness that we are willing to take upon us the name of Jesus Christ constitutes our declaration of candidacy for exaltation in the celestial kingdom. Exaltation is eternal life, "the greatest of all the gifts of God." (D&C 14:7.)
>
> That is what we should ponder as we partake of the sacred emblems of the sacrament. As we do so, we glory in the mission of the risen Lord, who lived and taught and suffered and died and rose again that all mankind might have immortality *and eternal life.* (CR, *Ensign,* May 1985, p. 83, emphasis included.)

The Lord has provided us with a weekly opportunity to reaffirm our willingness to bear His name, and to receive anew His sacrifice for us. It is important that we be worthy and make partaking of the sacrament a sacred, uplifting, cleansing experience.

The Holy Ghost

The Sword of the Spirit

Paul's description of the whole armor of God advises us to take "the sword of the Spirit, which is the word of God." (Ephesians 6:17.) In another analogy, he advises us to "put on the armour of light." (Romans 13:12.) This is one of the most important parts of our protective gear for our journey through life.

Light, truth, Spirit, the word of God, are all attributes of the Holy Ghost, the Comforter, whose work it is to purge us of dross, to burn out our impurities, to baptize us with fire, as it were, and make us clean and ready to stand before our Creator. This purification is the essence of our quest.

Elder Bruce R. McConkie said, "The Holy Ghost is . . . a *Purifier* in that, because of Christ and the atonement, this Spirit member of the Godhead has power given him to cleanse, sanctify, and purify the human soul. (3 Ne. 27:19-21.)" (*Mormon Doctrine*, p. 612.)

Who Is the Holy Ghost and What Does He Do?

Our Father in Heaven; His Son, Jesus Christ, our Redeemer; and the Holy Ghost, make up what we term the Godhead. They preside over us and direct the Grand Plan of eternity in which we are all involved. We understand our relationship to our Father, and our dependence upon our Elder Brother and Savior, but sometimes it is hard to grasp the concept of the Holy Ghost, who He is and what He does.

The Prophet Joseph taught that He is a personage of Spirit, unlike the other two who have physical, glorified, resurrected bodies: "The Father has a body of flesh and bones as tangible as man's; the Son also; but the Holy Ghost has not a body of flesh and bones, but is a personage of Spirit. Were it not so, the Holy Ghost could not dwell in us." (D&C 130:22.)

Jesus taught the disciples the closeness between Himself and His Father who sent Him: "If ye had known me, ye should have known my Father also: and from henceforth ye know him, and have seen him . . . he that hath seen me hath seen the Father." (John 14:7,9.) In His intercessory prayer, preparing to return to His Father, He emphasized that oneness: "And now I am no more in the world, but these [the Apostles] are in the world, and I come to thee. Holy Father, keep through thine own name those whom thou hast given me, that they may be one, as we are." (John 17:11.)

This same unity characterizes the Holy Ghost. Jesus consoled the Apostles facing His departure by promising that He would send the Comforter, the Holy Ghost, to abide with them. "But the Comforter, which is the Holy Ghost, whom the Father will send in my name, he shall teach you all things, and bring all things to your remembrance, whatsoever I have said unto you" (John 14:26); "He shall testify of me" (John 15:26); and "He will guide you into all truth: for he shall not speak of himself; but whatsoever he shall hear, that shall he speak: and he will shew you things to come. He shall glorify me: for he shall receive of mine, and shall shew it unto you. All things that the Father hath are mine: therefore said I, that he shall take of mine, and shall shew it unto you." (John 16:13-16.)

Comfort, guidance, truth, testimony of Jesus, revelation of things to come. Such as these are the mission of the Holy Ghost, a member of the Godhead, a personage of spirit, one in unity with Jesus Christ and the Father.

Before one joins the Church of Jesus Christ of Latter-day Saints, the Holy Ghost can come from time to time. He can testify that the message the missionaries are teaching is true. However, the Holy Ghost will not stay permanently. (See D&C 130:23.)

It isn't until after one gains a testimony of the gospel, repents of one's sins, is baptized and receives the gift of the Holy Ghost by the laying on of hands through the power of the Melchizedek Priesthood that one can receive the gift of the Holy Ghost, or receive the Holy Ghost to be a constant companion.

Elder Bruce R. McConkie explained this by quoting the Prophet Joseph Smith, who said, "There is a difference between the Holy Ghost and the gift of the Holy Ghost," (*Teachings*, p. 199.) Elder McConkie further explained, "As the third member of the Godhead, the Holy Ghost is a Personage of Spirit; the gift of the Holy Ghost, however, is the right, based on faithfulness, to the constant companionship of that member of the Godhead. It is the right to receive revelation, guidance, light, and truth from the Spirit." (*Mormon Doctrine*, p. 313.)

If we are faithful members of the Church, we have the right to have the constant companionship of the Holy Ghost.

Elder Parley P. Pratt described the effect of the Holy Ghost on a man or woman's character:

The gift of the Holy Ghost . . . quickens all the intellectual faculties, increases, enlarges, expands and purifies all the natural passions and affections, and adapts them, by the gift of wisdom, to their lawful use. It inspires, develops, cultivates and matures all the fine-toned sympathies, joys, tastes, kindred feelings and affections of our nature. It inspires virtue, kindness, goodness, tenderness, gentleness and charity. It develops beauty of person, form and features. It tends to health, vigor, animation and social feeling. It develops and invigorates all the faculties of the physical and intellectual man. It strengthens, invigorates and gives tone to the nerves. In short, it is, as it were, marrow to the bone, joy to the heart, light to the eyes, music to the ears, and life to the whole being. (*Key to the Science of Theology*, pp. 101-102.)

One of the functions of the Holy Ghost is as a refiner's fire. This refers to a process of using high heat to purify metal. In the procedure dross and impurities are burned away, and the metal becomes stronger and worth more. In this crucible, according to the analogy, we can become sanctified by the Holy Spirit by having our dross, our evil tendencies, burned out. This process may be painful, but it leaves us stronger, clean, and more capable for the experience we have been through.

The Importance of Heeding the Holy Ghost

Elder Melvin J. Ballard said, "I know of nothing today that the Latter-day Saints need more than the guidance of the Holy Spirit in the solution of the problems of life." (*Conference Report*, April 1931, pp. 37-38.) Why is the companionship of the Holy Ghost, the *gift* of the Holy Ghost, so important in our lives? Elder Ballard elaborated: "How important it is for us today, as perhaps never before, to stir up the gift of God that is in us, that has been given us through the putting on of the hands of those authorized servants of God, that we, by the guidance of that holy inspiration may be able in these troublesome times . . . to enjoy the gift of discernment." (p. 36.)

Into every life problems come, and in each case there is a solution that will move us along the path of life in a positive direction. Sometimes it is difficult for us to see the right answer when faced with a perplexing problem. At these crucial turnings in the road of life we are in special need of the guidance of the Holy Spirit. With the help of the Spirit we can make the decisions that will bless our lives and the lives of those around us.

President Wilford Woodruff had an experience in which Brigham Young returned from the spirit world with a message about the importance of the Holy Spirit in our lives. During this visitation President Young said, "I want you to teach the people—and I want you to follow this counsel yourself—that they must labor and so live as to obtain the Holy Spirit, for without this you cannot build up the kingdom; without the spirit of God you are in danger of walking in the dark, and in danger of failing to accomplish your calling as apostles and as elders in the church and kingdom of God." (*Journal of Discourses*, 21:318.)

Life is made up of a series of decisions, the effect of which is to determine our course in this life and in the eternities. Perhaps we do not see the connection between our everyday decisions and our eternal condition, but line upon line we build a life that is either leading us downward to spiritual destruction, or is preparing us for exaltation. When Jesus Christ comes in His glory, the righteous believers will be caught up to meet Him. These happy ones are those "that are wise and have received the truth, and have taken the Holy Spirit for their guide, and have not been deceived" (D&C 45:57). Those who have not chosen to follow the Holy Spirit will be "hewn down and cast into the fire" on that fateful day.

We need the Holy Spirit for our guide—and the gift of the Holy Ghost has been given to us as members of the Church. What must we do now to make sure we *receive* this gift? President Marion G. Romney said, "Everyone of us who are members of the Church has had hands laid upon our heads, and we have been given, as far as ordinance can give it, the gift of the Holy Ghost. But, as I remember, when I was confirmed, the Holy Ghost was not directed to come to me; I was directed to 'Receive the Holy Ghost.' If I receive the Holy Ghost and follow his guidance, I will be among those who are protected and carried through these troubled times. And so will you, and so will every other soul who lives under his direction." (CR, *Ensign*, December 1961, p. 947.)

According to these quotations, our Apostles felt times were troubled in 1931 and in 1961. Are they less troubled today? We still need the guidance of the Holy Ghost, and will continue to need it more and more as we prepare for the coming of our Savior.

How To Gain the Constant Companionship of the Holy Ghost

What a great blessing is promised if we will follow the guidance of the Holy Ghost! Can you envision what President Romney called being "protected and carried through these troubled times" would do to your life? Surely this is a blessing worth striving for. What can we do to be able to have the constant companionship of the Holy Ghost?

President Lorenzo Snow said, "From the time we receive the Gospel, go down into the waters of baptism and have hands laid upon us afterwards for the gift of the Holy Ghost, we have a friend, *if we do not drive it from us by doing wrong.* That friend is the Holy Spirit, the Holy Ghost, which partakes of the things of God and shows them unto us." (CR, April 1899, p. 52, emphasis added.) When we do wrong we drive the Holy Ghost away. We must choose to keep our minds and actions clean in order to be worthy of and to understand His influence. President Snow said further: "It will reveal to [us] even in the simplest of matters, what [we] should do, by making suggestions to [us]." How dearly do we need this Spirit of revelation!

What does it mean to be worthy of His presence? We have been given detailed guidance on this subject from our latter-day leaders and prophets.

Live Worthy of the Spirit

Most importantly, we must keep the commandments of the Lord. President Harold B. Lee compared our spiritual selves with a radio, explaining that we, like the radio, can only receive messages from the Spirit when we are obedient to the commandments:

> In my home I have a beautiful instrument called a radio. When everything is in good working order we can dial to a certain station and pick up a speaker or the voice of a singer . . . across the continent. . . . But, after we had used it for a long time, the little delicate instruments . . . on the inside called radio tubes began to wear out. . . . The radio may sit there looking quite like it did before, but because of what has happened on the inside, we can hear nothing.
>
> Now, . . . you and I have within our souls something like . . . those radio tubes. We might have what we call a "go-to-sacrament-meeting" tube, "keep-the-Word-of-Wisdom" tube, "pay-your-tithing" tube, . . . "have-your-family-prayers" tube, "Read-the-Scriptures" tube, and, . . . the "keep-yourselves-morally-clean" tube. If one of these becomes worn out by disuse or inactivity . . . it has the same effect upon our spiritual selves that a worn-out tube has on a radio."
> ("Tune in the Lord," *Ensign*, February 1974, p. 17.)

If we feel that our prayers are not being answered, then perhaps we need to look at our obedience to the commandments and see if there is not a worn out tube, a commandment we are not obeying, that is keeping us from receiving the messages of the Spirit. Today, instead of radio tubes, we have transistors, personal computers, cellular telephones, and "FAX" machines but the principle is the same. If all aspects of the receiver are not in working order, the communication is not received. The Lord is sending, and He will not fail. It is we who must be prepared and open to accept.

President Boyd K. Packer spoke of keeping the body pure in order to receive guidance:

"Your body is the instrument of your mind. In your emotions, the spirit and the body come closest to being one. What you learn spiritually depends, to a degree, on how you treat your body. That is why the Word of Wisdom (D&C 89) is so important.

"The habit-forming substances prohibited by that revelation—tea, coffee, liquor, tobacco—interfere with the delicate feelings of spiritual communication, just as other addictive drugs will do.

"Do not ignore the Word of Wisdom, for that may cost you the 'great treasures of knowledge, even hidden treasures' (D&C 89:19) promised to those who keep it. And good health is an added blessing." (CR, *Ensign*, November 1994, p 61.)

We are commanded, "Be ye clean, that bear the vessels of the Lord." (Isaiah 52:11.) We must not violate this commandment by willfully putting into our bodies, or our minds, things that are evil, because if we do, the Holy Ghost cannot enter into us.

If we do our duty, which is to obey the commandments, the Holy Ghost will be able to stay with us. If we live worthy lives, the Holy Ghost will be our friend.

President Joseph F. Smith named some important ways our lives would improve if we "possessed the Spirit of the Lord Jesus Christ. There would be no contention, dishonor, nor dishonesty among neighbors nor in the communities of the people. None would take advantage of the unwary, the weak or unsuspecting; no one would seek to wrong another." (*Gospel Doctrine*, p. 214.)

We ought to pray each day that the Holy Ghost may be our constant companion for that day, and then live in such a way that this Spirit will stay with us. We should choose to do whatever it takes to live by the Spirit.

President Brigham Young was a bold spokesman for doing what is right. He said, "I never have cared but for one thing, and that is, simply to know that I am now *right* before my *Father in Heaven*. If I am this *moment*, this *day*, doing the things *God requires* of my *hands*, and precisely where my *Father in Heaven wants me to be*, I care no more about tomorrow than though it never would come." (*Journal of Discourses*, 1:132, emphasis included.)

Develop Spirituality

Beyond simply not breaking the commandments, it is important that we develop ourselves spiritually in order to understand the promptings of the Spirit. President Spencer W. Kimball taught that personal spirituality is necessary if we are to receive the gift of the Holy Ghost: "Each person on whom authoritative hands have been placed will receive the Holy Ghost. . . . If one does not receive the great gift of the Holy Ghost, then it is his fault, that he hasn't been spiritual enough or close enough to Heavenly Father." (*The Teachings of Spencer W. Kimball*, p. 23.)

Elder ElRay L. Christiansen outlined several steps that will enhance our spirituality when he said, "Study of the scriptures, prayer, faithful living of the commandments of the Lord, the discharge of church obligations and duties, being a considerate neighbor, and using the heaven-sent program of family home evenings can provide a basis for having the Holy Ghost as a constant companion and protector, which will result in peace and happiness." ("Power Over Satan," CR, *Ensign*, November 1974, p. 24.)

Do we love the scriptures? Do we make scripture study an indispensable part of our daily routine? President Spencer W. Kimball recommended scripture study as a remedy for waning spirituality:

> I find that when I get casual in my relationship with divinity and when it seems that no divine ear is listening and no divine voice is speaking, that I am far, far away. If I immerse myself in the scriptures the distance narrows and the spirituality returns. I find myself loving more intensely those whom I must love with all my heart and mind and strength, and loving them more, I find it easier to abide their counsel. ("What I Hope You Will Teach My Grandchildren and All Others of the Youth of Zion," address to Seminary and Institute Personnel, Brigham Young University, July 11, 1966, p. 6.)

Another way to maintain spirituality and keep the Holy Ghost with us is to partake of the sacrament regularly and worthily. Confirming the importance of the sacrament in maintaining spirituality, President Marion G. Romney said, "The purpose of the sacrament is to promote the maintenance of spirituality. Both the revealed prayers over the bread and over the water contain the phrase, 'that they [who partake] may . . . have his Spirit to be with them' (see D&C 20:77,79)." (CR, *Ensign*, November 1979, p. 16.)

The first principles of the gospel are tightly interrelated. Faith prepares us for repentance, which is made possible by our faith. Repentance prepares us for baptism, wherein our sins are then remitted. Cleansed by baptism, we are then ready to receive the Holy Ghost, which guides us on the path of truth, and testifies of Jesus Christ. The sacrament is a renewal of the baptismal covenant, and makes us ready to have the Holy Spirit to be with us. The Holy Spirit reaffirms the importance of the emblems of the Savior's sacrifice, and helps strengthen our faith in Him. So it seems that the sacrament and the Holy Spirit have much to do with each other. In your efforts to invite the Holy Ghost to be with us always, remember the importance of the sacrament. We should approach it with a contrite heart and a worshipful, grateful spirit, making the effort to always remember Him. Then we may always have His Spirit to be with us.

When we partake of the Sacrament, do we choose to prepare ourselves so it will be a serious, sacred part of our Sabbath worship? Elder Graham W. Doxey suggested some ways we can make the sacrament a solemn experience: "*Partake* of the sacrament. Don't merely *take* the sacrament. Think of the covenants you are remaking. Truly witness unto the Father that you will take upon yourself the name of his Son, even Jesus Christ. Recommit yourself to always remember him, to keep the commandments which he has given you. Your obedience will entitle you to have his Spirit to be with you." (CR, *Ensign*, November 1991, p. 26.)

As we develop our spirituality, we will be able to depend upon the companionship of the Holy Ghost, and as we depend upon His companionship, we will find that we are able to make the right decisions through the gentle promptings of the Spirit. We will find that we are comforted by the Spirit in our times of need. We will find the strength to overcome our weaknesses. We will find a friend in our loneliness, relief from our pain, solace for our grief, hope for the future, cheer in the daily routine, elation in special occurrences, and undiluted joy in the journey of life.

How to Hear the Still Small Voice

If you have been feeling that you are obeying the commandments and still are not receiving the guidance from the Holy Spirit that you seek, perhaps what you are lacking is a "peaceful setting" in which to receive inspiration. Elder Boyd K. Packer said,

> Inspiration comes more easily in peaceful settings. Such words as *quiet, still, peaceable, Comforter* abound in the scriptures: "Be *still*, and know that I am God." (Psalms 46:10; italics added.) . . .
>
> Elijah felt a great wind, an earthquake, a fire. The Lord was not in any of them; then came "a still small voice." (1 Kings 19:12.)
>
> Helaman said of that voice of revelation, "It was not a voice of thunder, neither was it a voice of a great tumultuous noise, but behold, it was a still voice of perfect mildness, as if it had been a whisper, and it did pierce even to the very soul." (Heleman 5:30.)
>
> It was Nephi who reminded his brothers that an angel "hath spoken unto you in a still small voice, but ye were past *feeling*, that ye could not *feel* his words." (1 Nephi 17:45; italics added.) . . .

Irreverence suits the purposes of the adversary by obstructing the delicate channels of revelation in both mind and spirit. (CR, *Ensign*, November 1991, pp. 21-22.)

As we seek for a peaceful setting in which to open the "delicate channels of revelation" we can use the scriptures to help us. President Ezra Taft Benson encouraged us to set aside the cares of the world and meditate on the scriptures, citing remarkable instances of revelation that have come when this is done:

Take time to meditate. Meditation on a passage of scripture—James 1:5—led a young boy into a grove of trees to commune with his Heavenly Father. That is what opened the heavens in this dispensation.

Meditation on a passage of scripture from the book of John in the New Testament brought forth the great revelation on the three degrees of glory.

Meditation on another passage of scripture from the Epistle of Peter opened the heavens to President Joseph F. Smith, and he saw the spirit world. That revelation, known as the Vision of the Redemption of the Dead, is now a part of the Doctrine and Covenants.

Ponder the significance of the responsibility the Lord has given to us. The Lord has counseled, "Let the solemnities of eternity rest upon your minds." (D&C 43:34.) You cannot do that when your minds are preoccupied with the cares of the world. ("Seek the Spirit of the Lord," *Ensign*, April 1988, p. 2.)

Is the Lord speaking to us? Can He be heard? Can we receive the answers we need to the problems of our own lives through the Holy Ghost? Elder Graham W. Doxey answered these questions, saying,

My testimony is that the Lord *is* speaking to you! But with the deafening decibels of today's environment, all too often we fail to hear him. . . .

Time to listen. The *ability* to listen. The *desire* to listen. On religious matters, too many of us are saying, "What did you say? Speak up; I can't hear you." And when he doesn't *shout* back, or cause the bush to burn, or write us a message in stone with his finger, we are inclined to think he doesn't listen, doesn't care about us. Some even conclude there is no God. . . .

The questions are not, "Does God live? Does God love me? Does God speak to me?" The critical question is, "Are you listening to him?" Have you removed your shoes? It is the same for *you* as it was for Elijah, as it is with the modern-day prophets: *"The still, small voice is still small."* . . .

This still, small voice is speaking personally to you. Please be *still* and *listen*! (CR, *Ensign*, November 1991, pp. 25-26, emphasis included.)

Another thing to be alert to is that the Holy Ghost can easily be offended. If we fight and quarrel with those around us the Holy Ghost will leave us. In the Book of Mormon we read, "For verily, verily I say unto you, he that hath the spirit of contention is not of me, but is of the devil, who is the father of contention, and he stirreth up the hearts of men to contend with anger, one with another. Behold, this is not my doctrine, to stir up the hearts of men with anger, one against another; but this is my doctrine, that such things should be done away." (3 Nephi 11:29-30.)

The Prophet Joseph Smith had an experience that taught him that contention would deprive him of the blessings of the Spirit. David Whitmer was present and told of it. One day the Prophet was upset about something Emma had done. He went upstairs to translate, but could not. He went back downstairs and out into an orchard and prayed for an hour. After he got up off his knees he came back into the house and asked Emma's forgiveness. He then returned to his translation and was able to do his work. David said, "He could do nothing save he was humble and faithful." (From a statement by David Whitmer given September 15, 1882, *Comprehensive History of the Church*, vol. 1, p. 131.)

It is the same with us. If we fight and quarrel with our spouse, our children, or anyone else, the Holy Ghost will leave us. A home where the Holy Spirit is felt is happy and peaceable. Love is cultivated. Charity is chosen. We should strive to be at peace with all people so that we can have the guidance and blessing of the Holy Ghost to grace our lives. He will make our homes a haven of compatibility for those who reside there.

Another condition that can build a wall between us and the promptings of the Spirit is lack of reverence in our lives. Do we set aside times for prayer and meditation, or are our lives so busy that we have no time to sit still and listen to the Spirit? Do we provide ourselves with peaceful times wherein we can meditate upon our lives and the gospel and allow the gentle influence of the Holy Ghost to tell us what we need to know?

President David O. McKay related this story a number of times, showing how being "too busy" can deprive us of marvelous spiritual experience:

> One day in Salt Lake City a son kissed his mother good morning, took his dinner bucket, and went to City Creek Canyon where he worked. He was a switchman on the train that was carrying logs out of the canyon. Before noon his body was brought back lifeless. The mother was inconsolable. She could not be reconciled to that tragedy —her boy just in his early twenties so suddenly taken away. The funeral was held, and words of consolation were spoken, but she was not consoled. She couldn't understand it.
>
> One forenoon, so she says, after her husband had gone to his office to attend to his duties as a member of the Presiding Bishopric, she lay in a relaxed state on the bed, still yearning and praying for some consolation. She said that her son appeared and said, "Mother, you needn't worry. That was merely an accident. I gave the signal to the engineer to move on, and as the train started, I jumped for the handle of the freight car, and my foot got caught in a sagebrush, and I fell under the wheel. I went to Father soon after that, but he was so busy in the office I couldn't influence him—I couldn't make any impression upon him, and I tried again. Today I come to you to give you that comfort and tell you that I am happy."
>
> . . . I cite it today as an instance of the reality of the existence of intelligence and environment to which you and I are "dead," so to speak, as was this boy's father." (*Gospel Ideals*, pp. 525-6.)

Are we sometimes so busy that spiritual forces cannot reach us? Perhaps even too busy doing good to stop and let the Holy Spirit refresh us? Awakening to things spiritual will help us realize that today is part of a great eternal picture, of which we can now see only a part.

We don't need to be perfect to seek for the Spirit. The Lord will help us from whatever point we find ourselves. In the Doctrine and Covenants we are told that the gifts of the spirit "are given for the benefit of those who love me and keep all my commandments, *and him that seeketh so to do*." (D&C 46:9, emphasis added.) If we have faith in God and a repentant and receptive spirit, striving to keep the commandments, the Lord will work with us as we seek to improve ourselves.

Receiving the gift of the Holy Spirit is vital to our spiritual well-being. It is our right to claim it. As we do so, as we perfect our lives, the sweet influence of the Spirit will guide us, comfort us, and lead us and those we love toward eternal life.

President Ezra Taft Benson told us how important this is: "Spirituality —being in tune with the Spirit of the Lord—is the greatest need we all have. We should strive for the constant companionship of the Holy Ghost all the days of our lives. When we have the Spirit, we will love to serve, we will love the Lord, and we will love those with whom we serve, and those whom we serve." ("Seek the Spirit of the Lord," *Ensign*, April 1988, p. 5.)

We need the influence of the Holy Ghost in all aspects of our lives. President George Q. Cannon said,

> The only way to maintain our position in the Kingdom of God is . . . to live so that the Spirit of the Lord may be a constant and abiding guest with us, whether in the privacy of our chamber, in the domestic circle or in the midst of the crowded thoroughfares, the busy scenes and anxious cares of life. He who will pursue this course will never lack for knowledge; he will never be in doubt or in darkness, nor will his mind ever be clouded by the gloomy pall of unbelief; on the contrary his hopes will be bright; his faith will be strong; his joy will be full; he will be able each succeeding day to comprehend the unfolding purposes of Jehovah and to rejoice in the glorious liberty and happiness which all the faithful children of God enjoy. (*Gospel Truth*, p. 267.)

Let's seek to receive and retain the companionship of the Holy Ghost. Let's pray and plead daily with the Lord, exercising all possible faith that the Lord will grant this blessing of constant guidance. Let's increase our spirituality so that, with the help of the Holy Spirit we can avoid doubt and darkness. Thus we can have peace of mind and comfort on this earth, and we can look forward with hope and joy to the glories which are promised in the eternities to come.

14

How Can We Recognize the Influence of the Holy Ghost?

A Guide for Every Step of the Way

On our quest toward purity of heart we have available to us a guide for every step of the way. The ninth Article of Faith says, "We believe all that God has revealed, all that He does now reveal, and we believe that He will yet reveal many great and important things pertaining to the kingdom of Heaven." This principle of ongoing revelation is most essential to the true church of Jesus Christ, led by living prophets.

Elder Richard L. Evans stated: "This brings us to the question of communication between God and man, between a loving, all-knowing Father and his searching, seeking children. This communication includes prayer, inspiration, impressions from the divine source upon the mind of man, the findings of truth through earnest seeking and research, and also what is called revelation, to which the ninth Article of our Faith refers." (CR, *Improvement Era*, October 1963, p. 41.)

Revelation is not only for leading the Church, but also for leading the individuals within the Church who seek to listen to the promptings of the Holy Spirit. The Book of Mormon tells us, "For behold, again I say unto you that if ye will enter in by the way, and receive the Holy Ghost, it will show unto you all things what ye should do." (2 Nephi 32:5.) We have the promise that the Holy Ghost will tell us what to do in "all things." It is a reliable guide, and vital to our success.

Many of us are not aware of heavenly guidance when it comes to us. We may have been inspired by this guide as we have faced the decisions of life, but perhaps we need help to recognize it for what it is. How can we know if we are being inspired by the Holy Spirit?

President Harold B. Lee tells us that there are many ways that revelation from the Holy Ghost comes to us: "If we will live worthy, then the Lord will guide us—by a personal appearance, or by His actual voice, or by His voice coming into our mind, or by impressions upon our heart and our soul. And oh, how grateful we ought to be if the Lord sends us a dream in which are revealed to us the beauties of the eternity or a warning and direction for our special comfort. Yes, if we so live, the Lord will guide us for our salvation and for our benefit." (*Stand Ye in Holy Places*, p. 144.)

Feelings

President Lee spoke of receiving "impressions upon our heart and our soul." This is the most common way the Holy Ghost influences us—through our thoughts and feelings. President Ezra Taft Benson confirmed that we are most often inspired through our feelings: "We hear the words of the Lord most often by a feeling. If we are humble and sensitive, the Lord will prompt us through our feelings. That is why spiritual promptings move us on occasion to great joy, sometimes to tears. Many times my emotions have been made tender and my feelings very sensitive when touched by the Spirit." ("Seek the Spirit of the Lord," *Ensign*, April 1988, p. 5.)

President Boyd K. Packer also presented this idea, saying, "The Holy Ghost speaks with a voice that you *feel* more than you *hear*. It is described as a "still, small voice." (D&C 85:6) And while we speak of 'listening' to the whisperings of the Spirit, most often one describes a spiritual prompting by saying, 'I had a *feeling* . . .'

". . . Revelation comes as words we *feel* more than *hear* . . .

"This voice of the Spirit speaks gently, prompting you what to do or what to say, or it may caution or warn you." (CR, *Ensign*, November 1994, p. 60.)

President Benson and Elder Packer tell us that we usually receive inspiration by a feeling, and yet some of us expect and seek for something different, some grand manifestation of the will of the Lord. Of this President Spencer W. Kimball said,

> In our day, as in times past, many people expect that if there be revelation it will come with awe-inspiring, earth-shaking display. For

many it is hard to accept as revelation those numerous ones in Moses'
time, in Joseph's time, and in our own year—those revelations which
come to prophets as deep unassailable impressions settling down on
the prophet's mind and heart as dew from heaven or as the dawn dis-
sipates the darkness of night.

Expecting the spectacular, one may not be fully alerted to the
constant flow of revealed communication. (CR, *Ensign*, May 1977,
p. 78.)

And so, as we seek to understand the voice of the Spirit, we should
remember that the voice we are listening for is "still" and "small." It
comes to our hearts when we need it and when we are prepared, usually
in a quiet, unspectacular way that should nevertheless be a powerful
force in shaping our lives.

President Benson talked about the kinds of feelings the Holy Ghost
causes in us:

> The Holy Ghost causes our feelings to be more tender. We feel
> more charitable and compassionate with each other. We are more
> calm in our relationships. We have a greater capacity to love each
> other. People want to be around us because our very countenances
> radiate the influence of the Spirit. We are more godly in our char-
> acter. As a result, we become increasingly more sensitive to the
> promptings of the Holy Ghost and thus able to comprehend spiritual
> things more readily. (*Ensign*, April 1988, p. 5.)

It is sweet to experience this tenderness of feeling brought through the
Spirit. At times when I knew I had difficult interviews coming up, I have
prayed sincerely that the Holy Ghost could be with me as I conducted
these interviews. As I have started such discussions I notice that my
feelings have been very responsive, and my emotions close to the
surface. Heavenly Father has answered my prayers and sent the Holy
Ghost to guide thoughts and words. The persons being interviewed have
also felt this soothing Spirit. We have been able to accomplish much
under these ideal circumstances. How grateful I am when I feel the Holy
Spirit in this way.

Sister Myrna Behunin told of an experience in her family when her
feelings were calmed and made tender by the Spirit:

> It was about a week after we had taken ten-year-old Wayne into
> our home through the Church Indian Placement Program. . . .

I received a phone call from his school teacher. The teacher informed me that he was having trouble with Wayne at school. Wayne was disrespectful to him and to other teachers. This was a blow to me. I had never had a problem like that with my own children, and it greatly upset me . . . my temper flared, as it so often does . . .

To make matters worse, Wayne was late coming home from school because of a fight with a neighbor boy. They fought all the way from the bus stop. . . .

Shaking with anger, I slipped into my own bedroom and knelt and prayed. I prayed for wisdom in handling the problem, and I also asked that through the Spirit I would know what to say. As I stood up after praying, I felt a warm, calm feeling consume me. It started at my head and gently flowed to my feet . . . a million thoughts raced through my mind. . . .

I sat on the edge of the bed next to him, and put my arm around his shoulders. The first words I spoke surprised even me, for I said, "Wayne, forgive me for being so cross with you." Then I told him of the phone call from his teacher and gave him an opportunity to explain himself. We had a wonderful talk; he confided in me, and as we spoke, we did so in whispers. This was much different from the tone I had expected to use before asking my Heavenly Father for help . . . it did more for the relationship between Wayne and me than any other thing.

Thank goodness we have prayer and the gift of the Holy Spirit to guide us if we ask for it." (Myrna Behunin, "We Talked in Whispers," *Ensign*, January 1976, pp. 51-52.)

When we have an experience wherein our feelings are tempered by the Spirit, the influence is unmistakable. When our whole being is filled with assurance and peace, we can know that what we are feeling is the power of the Holy Ghost.

Knowledge

There are two components of personal revelation. When we receive an answer from the Lord through His Spirit, we are given knowledge and we are given a feeling. In the Doctrine and Covenants we read, "Yea, behold, I will tell you in your *mind* and in your *heart*, by the Holy Ghost, which shall come upon you and which shall dwell in your heart." (D&C 8:2, emphasis added.) The two components of personal revelation are "mind" and "heart" or in other words, thoughts and feelings. Personal revelation often comes in the form of an idea that comes to our minds which we feel good about in our hearts.

President Benson referred to these two elements when he said, "Do you take time to listen to the promptings of the Spirit? Answers to prayer come most often by a still voice and are discerned by our deepest, innermost *feelings*." (CR, *Ensign*, November 1977, p. 32, emphasis included.)

Our daughter Mary had an experience which caused her to recognize these two elements clearly in answer to her prayer:

"As I grew up I had always considered going on a mission, especially since my mother was a returned missionary. As I approached my 21st birthday, I had it in the back of my mind that when I turned 21 I would begin to think about a mission.

"One night about five months before my birthday I was saying my evening prayers when the words came into my mind, 'Ask about your mission.' I was startled because I wasn't really ready to consider this question, however I was obedient and said, 'Father, should I go on a mission?'

"Immediately there came into my heart a feeling of joy and excitement that was unmistakable. If I ever experienced a "burning in the bosom," it was definitely that night! Not only that, but for the next few days every time I thought about going on a mission my heart was filled with anticipation and peace and assurance. I soon went to my bishop and began the paperwork that led to my mission call.

"I have been so grateful for this inspiration that came to my mind and my heart. My decision to go on a mission has changed my life. Not only did I grow in the service of the Lord, but I was blessed to meet a fine fellow missionary who, after we returned home and were better acquainted, became my eternal companion. We have since then adopted children from our mission country and had them sealed to our eternal family."

The Holy Ghost can come to us at these pivotal moments in our lives to guide us to do what will lead to our future happiness. The gift of the Holy Ghost may also be with us in our everyday affairs, helping us feel comfortable as we make ordinary decisions that lead us to do good, to fulfill our proper responsibilities, and to assist others in righteousness.

Arda Jean tells this account:

"Once when I was talking things over with my mother I explained in a rather puzzled way that, being a busy mother, sometimes I have gone for some length of time without checking on my active children. Then suddenly, something makes me look up from what I was involved in and glance about quickly for a particular child, being impelled to locate that child immediately. When I find her, there is a real problem or danger that I am able to resolve at that exact time.

"My mother helped me to understand this is the Holy Spirit guiding me—arousing my attention at the very time it is needed. As we reared our family, I learned to recognize and act on uneasy feelings with dispatch, being grateful for the holy source from which they came.

"One experience stands out in my memory. Our youngest daughter had some health problems which caused concern as she was growing up. One was being prone to allergic reactions, and we have learned to watch for and deal with them. One afternoon, Memorial Day holiday, the extended family had gathered, and we were having a delightful visit and supper. Several of the young people had gone to ride the ATVs in the private wooded area behind our home. They were taking turns, having a lot of fun on the first good-weather weekend of the summer.

"As we were talking, someone noticed Ruth coming up from the field, looking very swollen in the face and puffy around the eyes. I recognized these symptoms immediately. Apparently the bikes were stirring up the pollen in the field, and she was having an allergic reaction. I took her into the house to treat her. We did all the usual things, but the Spirit was urging me that this reaction was much more than the usual one, and I began to hurry. I called to her father. He and her brothers gave her a priesthood blessing, promising her that she would recover. I took her to an evening pediatric clinic for help.

"It was a long evening for Ruth and me. The doctors immediately gave her the antidote by injection, then they came in and out, seeing other patients in need, while we waited out the treatment. It was a severe reaction. Over and over again as the swelling in her air passages increased, she would quit breathing. I watched for those moments, patting her face to rouse her and telling her to 'Breathe!'

"It was hard to watch her struggle so, and realize how close she was to the other side of the veil. And yet, as I went through what now looks like an ordeal, I was full of faith and confidence because of the priest-hood blessing which had been pronounced. It seemed to me that the Spirit led me to be calm. I felt sure that she would be all right.

"Many years later, Ruth related what a comfort it was to her to rouse time and again, open her eyes, and see me there, holding her face and commanding her to take a breath.

"After the urgency passed, she was admitted to the hospital where she was given oxygen and other treatment during the last week of school. This distressed our lively pre-teen, who didn't want to be confined during the fun days of the closing of school for the summer recess. But we were so grateful for knowledge from the Spirit—knowledge of what to do, and assurance that she would come through all right."

As illustrated in these two stories, the knowledge we gain through the Spirit will always be accompanied by a feeling of peace and assurance.

Guideposts

We must be careful as we seek to understand the inspiration that comes to us so that we are not deceived. The First Presidency gave this guiding instruction on the subject of individual revelation: "In secular as well as spiritual affairs, Saints may receive Divine guidance and revelation affecting themselves, but this does not convey authority to direct others, and is not to be accepted when contrary to Church covenants, doctrine, or discipline, or to known facts, demonstrated truths, or good common sense." (*Messages of the First Presidency*, vol. 4, p. 286.)

Here, then, are the guideposts. Apply these questions: Is what we are considering contrary to Church covenants, doctrine, or discipline? Is it contradictory to known facts, demonstrated truths, or common sense? The Holy Spirit will not lead us contrary to what we already know, or to what the prophets and the gospel plainly teach. Are we attempting to lead or direct others not of our family or Church stewardship? Are we using any kind of force or coersion? Is this outside the Lord's revealed pattern? The scriptures warn us not to be deceived:

> And again, I will give unto you a pattern in all things, that ye may not be deceived; for Satan is abroad in the land, and he goeth forth deceiving the nations—
>
> Wherefore he that prayeth, whose spirit is contrite, the same is accepted of me if he obey mine ordinances. (D&C 52:14-15.)
>
> Wherefore, beware lest ye are deceived; and that ye may not be deceived seek ye earnestly the best gifts, always remembering for what they are given;
>
> For verily I say unto you, they are given for the benefit of those who love me and keep all my commandments, and him that seeketh

so to do; that all may be benefited that seek or that ask of me, that ask and not for a sign that they may consume it upon their lusts. (D&C 46:8-9.)

And this shall be a law unto you, that ye receive not the teachings of any that shall come before you as revelations or commandments;

And this I give unto you that you may not be deceived, that you may know they are not of me.

For verily I say unto you, that he that is ordained of me shall come in at the gate and be ordained as I have told you before, to teach those revelations which you have received and shall receive through him whom I have appointed. (D&C 43:5-7.)

The Lord then consoles us:

And whoso treasureth up my word, shall not be deceived. (Pearl of Great Price: Joseph Smith—Matthew 1:37.)

For they that are wise and have received the truth, and have taken the Holy Spirit for their guide, and have not been deceived—verily I say unto you, they shall not be hewn down and cast into the fire, but shall abide the day. (D&C 45:57.)

Elder S. Dilworth Young said, referring to someone who feels that he has received guidance from the Holy Ghost, "He may . . . know that if this revelation is in harmony with revealed principles, that it is right. No one will ever receive revelation that is contrary to the word given to the living prophet." (CR, *Ensign*, May 1976, p. 23.)

Elder Boyd K. Packer added, "In the Church we are not exempt from common sense. You can know, to begin with, that you will not be prompted from any righteous source to steal, to lie, to cheat, to join anyone in any kind of moral transgression." (*That All May Be Edified*, p. 12.)

If you feel you have received an answer to prayer, you can apply these tests to see if it is from a true source. How wonderful that we have these guideposts as we find our way in life!

How to Ask Correctly

In order to gain answers to our prayers through the Holy Ghost, it is important to ask correctly. President Marion G. Romney described how he set about getting answers to his prayers in these words:

The most satisfying solutions to problems and the best answers to questions that I have been able to make in my own life, I have arrived at as follows:

1. From my youth I have searched the scriptures.
2. I have tried to honestly face the challenge or question presented with a sincere desire to solve it as Jesus would solve it.
3. I have, through diligent study and prayer, sought to weigh alternatives in light of what I knew about gospel principles.
4. I have made a decision in my own mind.
5. I have then taken the matter to the Lord, told him the problem, told him that I wanted to do what was right in his view, and asked him to give me peace of mind if I have made the right decision. ("What Would Jesus Do," *New Era*, September 1972, p. 6.)

This method suggested by President Romney is outlined in the scriptures. "But, behold, I say unto you, that you must study it out in your mind; then you must ask me if it be right, and if it is right I will cause that your bosom shall burn within you; therefore, you shall feel that it is right." (D&C 9:8.) When we use this method to gain answers to specific questions, the Lord can guide and inspire us to make the right decisions.

Consider this story about a young woman who needed guidance and used this method to gain it:

A young woman attending college testified that she had felt the direction of the Holy Ghost in her life and that, through following these whisperings, had been greatly blessed. She said that from childhood she was taught by her parents that when she had an important decision to make, she should heed the advice found in scripture: [D&C 9:8 quoted.]

"On one occasion [she related], I had what I believed to be a fine job opportunity for summer work in a distant community. I was trying to finance my own college education and this work would have been very rewarding financially, even after paying for my living expenses. I made a thorough investigation of all factors concerned and found some things questionable. I would be living with two other girls about whom I knew nothing, yet the money sounded so attractive. . . .

"I spent much time prayerfully searching for the right answer and yielding my own feelings to the promptings of the Holy Ghost. I finally said frankly to my Heavenly Father, 'I want this job very much, but I do want to do the thing that will be best for me. Deep down I don't believe that I should accept this job. Please let me know if I'm making the right choice in not accepting it.' I received such a warmth of feeling, such a glow of assurance that I knew I had made the correct decision. My decision was further confirmed at the end of the summer when I learned that the two girls who were to have been my roommates were not desirable companions." (Relief Society Courses of Study, 1985, pp. 6-7.)

It may not always be easy to follow the promptings of the Holy Ghost, but it is important to do so. Our lives will be better for it. Elder F. Enzio Busche tells us,

It takes courage and commitment to follow the promptings of the Spirit because they may frighten us as they lead us to walk along new paths, sometimes paths that no one has walked before, paths of the second mile, of acting totally differently from how worldly people act. For instance, we may be prompted to smile when someone offends us, to give love where others give hate, to say thank you where others would not find anything to be thankful for, to accept jobs that others would be too proud to do, to apologize where others would defend themselves, and to do all the seemingly crazy things that the Spirit prompts a righteous, honest, listening heart to do." ("The Only Real Treasure," *New Era*, December 1979, p. 5.)

The Holy Ghost and Man's Agency

In following the promptings of the Holy Ghost, do we lose our freedom, or our agency? It seems that some find themselves fearful of submitting to the will of God, lest they lose their own freedom to choose. Let's look in the scriptures and the statements of the prophets for an answer to this question.

In the Doctrine and Covenants we read, "Verily I say, men should be anxiously engaged in a good cause, and do many things of their own free will, and bring to pass much righteousness; For the power is in them, wherein they are agents unto themselves. And inasmuch as men do good they shall in nowise lose their reward." (D&C 58:27-28.)

The Lord says that, instead of waiting to be directed in all things, we should "do many things of [our] own free will." The whole plan of progression is based on our agency and our development as we learn to choose right over wrong. The Lord is delighted when we are anxiously engaged in doing good things of our own free will.

The only time agency becomes a problem to us is when we use it to choose wrong, and our choices drag us down. Why do we want the freedom to do that? And yet we have it! For our Father will never abridge our right to choose. What is important is that we bring to pass righteousness by our exercise of will.

How vital it is that we *choose* to follow the promptings of the Spirit as we move forward in life. Choosing right increases our ability, that is, we are able to do more. Our freedom to choose increases as we have more options due to our increased capability. Even the mind is expanded by the light of the Holy Spirit, making it more able to make choices, and more able to act on those choices. Rather than losing freedom when we submit to the Spirit, we gain more ability to choose.

President Lorenzo Snow said,

> I believe in the independence of men and women. I believe that men and women have the image of God given them—are formed after the image of God, and possess Deity in their nature and character, and that their spiritual organization possesses the qualities and properties of God, and that there is the principle of God in every individual. It is designed that man should act as God, and not be constrained and controlled in everything, but have an independency, an agency, and the power to spread abroad and act according to the principle of Godliness that is in him, act according to the power and intelligence and enlightenment of God, that he possesses, and not that he should be watched continually, and be controlled, and act as a slave in these matters." (*Journal of Discourses*, 20:367.)

We, then, being created in the image of God and, indeed, being His offspring, possess Deity in our nature as the prophet said. We are free to choose for ourselves, and part of achieving that divine potential is to learn to choose good over evil.

President Brigham Young also addressed the issue of agency and obedience when he wrote, "In rendering that strict obedience, are we made slaves? No, it is the only way on the face of the earth for you and me to become free, and we shall become the slaves of our own passions, and of the wicked one, and servants to the devil, if we take any other course." (*Journal of Discourses*, 18:246.)

We lose our agency not by obedience, but by following the path of evil. We see it prevalent in our society. A person who uses tobacco becomes a slave to that habit. People who use drugs and alcohol find the same situation, becoming slaves to their habit, and to the requirements of supporting it. When the first choice was offered, they were free to choose to accept or reject, but the choice of evil led them to the slavery of addiction.

We can also become addicted to pornographic movies, books and TV. The Holy Ghost will not remain with people who are so addicted—the Spirit leaves as soon as one becomes involved with such material. It leaves when we wilfully violate any of the commandments of God. He will not be a part of our sins. We should stay away from any evidence of this type of evil.

My father-in-law, Irvin L. Warnock, told me something that struck me as profound. We observed a man who was obviously an alcoholic, and somewhat a derelict. Dad Warnock said that he, himself, had more freedom than this man had, because he could choose whether to drink or not, while the drunk could not choose, because he was addicted to his alcohol. He also noted that he had more freedom because he could choose to go to the temple, while the drunk had not that choice. Some may think the commandments restrict our freedom; however, as Dad Warnock said, just the opposite is true. The commandments are enablers. They enable us to keep our agency. We become free by keeping the commandments and living God's plan of life. We also gain the companionship of the Holy Ghost in this manner.

Elder Bruce McConkie had some pointed words in regard to agency: "All things are governed by law. Through obedience and righteousness men are able to receive revelation from the Holy Spirit; through disobedience and wickedness (which course constitutes conformity to the laws which govern in this field) men are able to receive impressions, guidance, and even revelation from the Evil Spirit. Judas was in this latter category; he had descended to that depth of spiritual depravity where he consorted with and was subject to the will of evil spirits. There is no curtailment of agency in either of these courses; both are pursued by deliberate choice." (*Doctrinal New Testament Commentary*, vol. 1, p. 702.)

It is our blessing to be able to choose, and it is our responsibility to choose correctly. The Light of Christ, the Holy Ghost, and our own common sense will help us to choose the right. We are well endowed, and it is up to us to use our agency in an upward course. Our faith in the Lord Jesus Christ and His love for us should convince us of our ability to recognize the influence of the Holy Ghost and desire the Lord's righteous purposes in our lives.

15

Blessings That Come Through the Holy Ghost

Answers

The gift of the Holy Ghost is one of the greatest blessings of our lives, because it brings with it other wonderful and necessary blessings. What blessings do we need? What problems are vexing our lives? If we choose the way of peace, we make ourselves ready for the comforts of the Holy Ghost to be with us and abide.

President James E. Faust spoke beautifully to our daily needs as he named some of these blessings available through the Holy Ghost. We have inserted, between President Faust's answers, some of the troublesome questions and problems faced by so many of us today.

Is there help for the sorrow in our lives?

The comforting Spirit of the Holy Ghost can abide with us twenty-four hours a day: when we work, when we play, when we rest. Its strengthening influence can be with us year in and year out. That sustaining influence can be with us in joy and sorrow, when we rejoice as well as when we grieve.

What can we do about the stresses we face?

I believe the Spirit of the Holy Ghost is the greatest guarantor of inward peace in our unstable world. It can be more mind-expanding and can make us have a better sense of well-being than any chemical or other earthly substance. It will calm our nerves; it will breathe peace to our souls. This Comforter can be with us as we seek to improve. It can function as a source of revelation to warn us of impending danger and also help keep us from making mistakes. It can enhance our natural senses so that we can see more clearly, hear more keenly, and remember what we should remember. It is a way of maximizing our happiness.

What about my troubled past?

The Spirit—the Holy Ghost—will help us work out our insecurities. For instance, it can help us learn to forgive. There comes a time when people must move on, seeking greater things rather than being consumed by the memory of some hurt or injustice. Dwelling constantly on past injuries is, by its nature, limiting to the Spirit. It does not promote peace.

What about my doubts?

The Holy Ghost will also help us solve crises of faith. The Spirit of the Holy Ghost can be a confirming witness, testifying of heavenly things. Through that Spirit, a strong knowledge distills in one's mind, and one feels all doubt or questions disappear.

Where can I turn for peace?

The Apostle Paul said, "For the kingdom of God is not meat and drink; but righteousness, and peace, and joy in the Holy Ghost." (Romans 14:17.) He added elsewhere that true Saints are the "temple of the Holy Ghost." (1 Corinthians 6:19.) (See CR, *Ensign*, May 1989, pp. 32-33.)

Comfort, strength, peace, guidance, remembrance, happiness, security, forgiveness, faith. The very things we seek! What marvelous blessings these are! Let's look at some of these more closely.

Guidance

One of the greatest blessings given us through the Holy Ghost is guidance. Sometimes this guidance takes the form of an answer to a specific question we ask the Lord through prayer.

A young man returned home after faithfully serving a mission. His greatest desires were to choose a profession and find a wife with whom he could build an eternal marriage. He faithfully worked to maintain the spirituality he had developed on his mission, while he continued his studies at a university. He also began to date attractive young women. Several times he wondered if he had found the right young woman to marry, and yet each time there seemed to be something missing, and as he prayed, he knew that he must keep looking. One time the answer came as a definite "no," while another time the guidance was simply to "wait." As each relationship ended the pained young man wondered when his search would be successful.

Then one day he met a young woman, also a faithful returned missionary. He was attracted to her lovely face and her spiritual strength. He noticed how being with her made him feel motivated to achieve. She seemed to him to be everything he had ever dreamed of in a companion and a friend. He hoped he had found his wife. This time as he prayed, he felt a positive affirmation that *this* young woman was the one for whom he had waited. His heart filled with joy and love as the Holy Spirit confirmed to his soul that he had made the right decision. How vital it is to have this most important decision receive the affirmation of the Holy Ghost—what a solid foundation upon which to build a life of spiritual success and happiness.

Reiterating the "grand privilege of every Latter-day Saint" to receive guidance in his or her life, President Lorenzo Snow urged us to keep within us:

> . . . the Spirit of God, which is the spirit of revelation to every man and woman. . . . We should try to learn the nature of this spirit, that we may understand its suggestions, and then we will always be able to do right. This is the grand privilege of every Latter-day Saint. We know that it is our right to have the manifestations of the spirit every day of our lives. . . . The spirit is in every man and every woman so that they need not walk in the darkness at all . . . they have it within them; there is a friend that knows just exactly what to say to them. . . . That friend is the Holy Spirit, the Holy Ghost, which partakes of the things of God and shows them unto us. This is a grand means that the Lord has provided for us, that we may know the light, and not be groveling continually in the dark. (*Conference Report*, April 1899, p. 52.)

We need not "grovel" constantly in the dark, but we can flood our lives with the brilliant illumination of the Spirit of God. We can be assured that the decisions we make under this influence are correct and will lead us upward along the right path.

Another type of guidance that comes through the Holy Ghost is an urging that prompts us to do something *right now*. This type of inspiration sometimes leads us to a certain action that is different from what we have planned. Elder F. Burton Howard tells of some of these promptings that have come to him through the Spirit:

> As I have better understood my relationship with the Holy Ghost, I have come to know:
>
> What it is to unexpectedly change airplanes in a distant city, only to find after arriving home that an originally scheduled flight has been indefinitely delayed.
>
> What it is to begin a missionary interview with the question, never asked before or since, "Elder, who have you been fighting with?"— and to hear the astonished reply, "President, how did you know?"
>
> What it is to pay a surprise visit to a distant city only to hear someone say, "I have been praying for days that you would come."
>
> Occasionally I have had time to pray and ponder before acting on the promptings of the Comforter. More often, I have found myself as Nephi, "led by the Spirit, not knowing beforehand the things which I should do." (1 Nephi 4:6.) ("The Gift of Knowing," *Ensign*, September 1983, p. 33.)

Another experience with this type of revelation was related by President Marion G. Romney. He concluded a funeral sermon and was ready to sit down, when:

> There came into my mind the words, "Turn around and bear your testimony." And this I did. I thought no more about the event for several months until my sister, then living in a neighboring stake, paid us a visit and told us this incident:
>
> She said: "There lives in our ward a woman who for many years has taken no interest in the Church. Our efforts to activate her have been fruitless. Recently she has completely changed. She pays her tithing, attends sacrament meetings regularly, and participates in all Church activities. When asked what caused the reformation, she said: 'I went to Salt Lake City to the funeral of my mother. During the services a man by the name of Romney spoke. After he had given an ordinary talk, I thought he was going to sit down; but instead he turned around to the pulpit and bore a testimony which greatly impressed me. It awakened in me a desire to live as my mother had always taught me.'" (CR, *Ensign*, May 1978, p. 50.)

Sometimes these promptings can come when there is danger and immediate action is necessary. There must be no hesitation when this type of revelation comes. Elder Bruce R. McConkie gives this incident from his childhood:

> One of my earliest childhood recollections is of riding a horse through an apple orchard. The horse was tame and well broken, and I felt at home in the saddle.
>
> But one day something frightened my mount, and he bolted through the orchard. I was swept from the saddle by the overhanging limbs, and one leg slipped down through the stirrup. I desperately hung to an almost broken leather strap that a cowboy uses to tie a lariat to his saddle. My weight should have broken the strap, but somehow it held for the moment. Another lunge or two of the stampeding horse would have broken the strap or wrenched it from my hands and left me to be dragged to injury or death with my foot entangled in the stirrup.
>
> Suddenly the horse stopped, and I became aware that someone was holding the bridle tightly and attempting to calm the quivering animal. Almost immediately I was snatched up into the arms of my father.
>
> What had happened? What had brought my father to my rescue in the split second before I slipped beneath the hoofs of my panic-driven horse?
>
> My father had been sitting in the house reading the newspaper when the Spirit whispered to him, "Run out into the orchard!"
>
> Without a moment's hesitation, not waiting to learn why or for what reason, my father ran. Finding himself in the orchard without knowing why he was there, he saw the galloping horse and thought, *I must stop this horse.*
>
> He did so and found me. And that is how I was saved from serious injury or possible death. (*The Friend*, September 1972, p. 10, emphasis included.)

What if Elder McConkie's father had been unworthy of receiving guidance through the Holy Ghost? What if he had never learned to listen to the whisperings of the Spirit? What if he had delayed in responding?

Warning by the Spirit has also happened in our family. Our son Evan was a missionary in Minnesota, the land of ten thousand lakes. The winters there are extremely cold, and most of the lakes freeze over.

People in Minnesota enjoy ice fishing, and they build little houses on the frozen lakes from which to fish.

One day when Evan and his companion were walking home from church they decided to cross one of these lakes and do some "ice house" tracting on the way. Evan was walking about four feet behind his companion. Suddenly in his mind's eye he could see the ice cracking and his companion falling through it into the lake. At first he dismissed the image, but it came again, this time with more intensity. He knew that he was being warned.

He called to his companion, who didn't respond. His companion said later that he could hear Evan, but thought he was across the lake and not really close to him. Impelled to action, Evan ran forward, taking hold of his companion's shoulder. At that moment they both heard the ice begin to crack under them.

Evan told his companion to run one way, and he ran the other. They both were soon off the ice, greatly relieved to have escaped the danger. When they arrived at their apartment, the phone was ringing. It was their mission president inquiring if they were all right, because he had a feeling they were in trouble, and he was calling to see what had happened.

Evan is still grateful today that the Lord intervened to save his companion and himself from tragedy. He is thankful that he was worthy to receive this warning inspiration when it was so vital.

The Holy Ghost can be our best friend. We have the right to have his influence with us twenty-four hours a day. Besides warning us when we are in danger, he will show us correct ways to solve our problems even in the simplest matters. We will be able to do right in all cases. By always doing right we can keep our consciences clear before God and man. As we keep the commandments the Holy Ghost will guide us.

Strength to Resist Temptation

President Hugh B. Brown gave a brief statement that sums up our strength to resist: "Purity is power." (CR, *Ensign*, June 1964, p. 483.) We need that power, therefore we need to be pure, so we can receive it.

Our world is full of temptation, and the Holy Ghost can strengthen us so that we will be able to resist the temptation that presents itself to us. The Lord has promised to stand by us in the hour of temptation. When we are tempted to do evil, the Spirit of the Lord gives us a strong feeling of disapproval that helps us avoid that which is wrong. The Lord speaks of this chastening influence, and how it prepares us for deliverance: "Verily, thus saith the Lord unto you whom I love, and whom I love I also chasten that their sins may be forgiven, for with the chastisement I prepare a way for their deliverance in all things out of temptation." (D&C 95:1.) It has probably never been easy to live the gospel, but in our dispensation it is especially difficult because of the wickedness of the world.

President James E. Faust pointed out how our standards are being assaulted today, saying, "We need a sure compass because many of the standards, values, vows and obligations which have helped us preserve our spirituality, our honor, our integrity, our worth, and our decency have little by little been assaulted and discarded. I speak, among other values, of the standards of chastity, parental respect, fidelity in marriage, and obedience to God's laws—such as Sabbath observance—which have been weakened, if not destroyed. Society has been misled." (CR, *Ensign*, May 1989 p. 32.)

Sometimes it seems that we are surrounded by temptation, and yet we have a guide that can help us stay on a true course even when many around us are falling prey to the lures of the exciting action in this sophisticated world. What is that "sure compass"? President Faust says, "The Book of Mormon, the Bible, and other scriptures, along with the guidance of modern prophets, provide true standards of conduct. In addition, the gift of the Holy Ghost is available as a sure guide, as the voice of conscience, and as a moral compass. This guiding compass is personal to each of us. It is unerring. It is unfailing. However, we must listen to it in order to steer clear of the shoals which will cause our lives to sink into unhappiness and self-doubt." (CR, *Ensign*, May 1989, p. 32.)

Being very exact with ourselves about learning and keeping God's laws will help us avoid areas of danger. Laws—rules—are the means by which we achieve our progress. There are reasons for each of them. If we rationalize them away, we lose their benefit. We trade our happiness for a momentary counterfeit. Satan deludes us.

What a source of strength it is to know that we have the power of the Holy Ghost to help us recognize fallacy and resist temptation. When we learn to draw down that power and make it interactive in our lives, the very powers of heaven can function in our behalf.

President Faust told us, "The gift of the Holy Ghost will prompt us to resist temptation by reminding us of the gospel law in the very moment of temptation." (CR, *Ensign*, May 1989, p. 32.)

The Apostle Peter averred, "The Lord knoweth how to deliver the godly out of temptations." (2 Peter 2:9). The prophet Alma counseled his brethren, active members of the Church: "I wish from the inmost part of my heart . . . that ye would humble yourselves before the Lord, and call on his holy name, and watch and pray continually, that ye may not be tempted above that which ye can bear, and thus be led by the Holy Spirit, becoming humble, meek, submissive, patient, full of love and all long-suffering; Having faith on the Lord; having a hope that ye shall receive eternal life; having the love of God always in your hearts, that ye may be lifted up at the last day and enter into his rest." (Alma 13:27-29).

Many active, hard-driving, success-oriented young men and women of today don't like the sound of those words *humble, meek, submissive, patient, and long-suffering*. But these very attributes activate the power of heaven, the power of the priesthood, the power of the Holy Ghost, the actual creative powers of the universe into operation in our earthly lives. It is already happening in many of these same successful lives where people are loving the Lord and looking heavenward for His help. The Lord is eager for us to succeed. When we apply the scriptures to our lives with this new outlook, we must be alert to what will transpire!

Knowledge and Truth

Truth is one of our greatest weapons against the deceit of Satan, and one of the most effectual enablers available. Jesus Christ promised that if we know the truth, "The truth shall make you free." (John 8:32.)

Read the many scriptures which promise strength from the truth and knowledge available through the Holy Ghost. Let this precious understanding enlighten and invigorate your mind, your heart, and your daily activities. In the Doctrine and Covenants we read,

> God shall give unto you knowledge by his Holy Spirit, yea, by the unspeakable gift of the Holy Ghost. (D&C 121:26.)

> Truth is knowledge of things as they are, and as they were, and as they are to come. (D&C 93:24.)

Behold, thou knowest that thou hast inquired of me and I did enlighten thy mind; and now I tell thee these things that thou mayest know that thou hast been enlightened by the Spirit of truth. (D&C 6:15.)

If thou shalt ask, thou shalt receive revelation upon revelation, knowledge upon knowledge, that thou mayest know the mysteries and peaceable things--that which bringeth joy, that which bringeth life eternal. (D&C 42:61.)

Think of these promises! Apply them to your business, your career, your family; to relationships with your spouse, your parents, or your colleagues. The Lord knows you, and He knows the answers to all the things you are struggling with. Part of your purpose in life is to learn, and some of that is to learn how, when, and whom to ask!

One of our daughters states emphatically that because she and her husband pay a full tithing and do their best to live the gospel, they are able to make their rather small income reach to all the needs of their growing family. She shops sales, including "gently used" items at yard sales and thrift shops. She has a style of buying food items in bulk and storing them away for daily and future use. She sews as creatively as she shops, and cooks with equal ingenuity. She finds enterprising ways to supplement their income. She says, unabashed, "I pray over my shopping. I ask the Lord to help me find the things I need at a price I can pay. And He does it." Her husband increases his take-home pay by gaining more education and by teaching extra classes. They find inexpensive ways of having the family enjoy time together, and often use natural resources as entertainment. They both affirm that they are prompted by the Holy Spirit, that their minds are quickened and their bodies strengthened because of their obedience to the law of tithing and the Word of Wisdom. Their family is anchored to faith in Christ, and they are happy.

President Brigham Young spoke of the knowledge and truth that can be revealed by the Spirit when he said, "The Holy Ghost takes of the Father, and of the Son, and shows it to the disciples. It shows them things past, present, and to come. It opens the vision of the mind, unlocks the treasures of wisdom, and they begin to understand the things of God. . . . It leads them to drink at the fountain of eternal wisdom, justice, and truth; they grow in grace, and in the knowledge of the truth as it is in Jesus Christ, until they see as they are seen, and know as they are known." (*Journal of Discourses,* 1:241.)

Elder John A. Widtsoe added: "Above all, therefore, I have been and am grateful for the restored gospel of Jesus Christ. It explains, to the heart's satisfaction, the mystery of man's life on earth. It gives courage to meet the day's toil. It transmutes sorrows and disappointments into understanding and contentment. It opens a vision of the stream of time from eternity to eternity. With such knowledge, and a surrender to truth, happiness comes pleading for acceptance." (*In a Sunlit Land*, p. 243.)

Testimony

Important as day-to-day knowledge is, the most important knowledge we can gain in this life is a testimony of the gospel. Our son Martin was involved in an ongoing sequence of events in the life of a young man in one of his Scout troops. For our story, we will call him Jim. Being a Scouter at heart, Martin took notice of Jim one of the first days in his new ward—a friendly, likeable boy. When he became president of the elders quorum, Martin was able to make assignments for Jim to go home teaching, and at this time became better acquainted with the family, a single mother struggling to raise teenage sons. Later as Scoutmaster, although Jim was beyond the regular age for the troop, Martin took a particular interest in this boy, and noted that Jim needed only three more merit badges and a project to get his Eagle award. At age sixteen Jim was not really interested in completing it. Jim was slipping from activity, coming to church only occasionally. He became unhappy, going out with friends who were drinking, losing interest in attending school.

His mother was concerned, the bishop was concerned, other adult friends were concerned. All were praying for Jim. Each was listening to the Holy Spirit, and did what he or she felt impressed to do, but the boy continued acting confused, depressed, and overwhelmed. Sometimes he would not get out of bed; he missed a lot of school. Jim was asked to be Senior Patrol Leader in Scouts, and when he came he did a good job. He did take interest in the younger Scouts and he liked going camping.

Martin would sometimes hire Jim to do odd jobs on his construction site. This gave him the challenge of doing a job and completing it, and the reward of having some of his own money to spend. A pattern of improvement began to emerge. The prayers of the faithful leaders were being answered as each was prompted to give help in the way he or she could. Jim was made Assistant Scoutmaster, and gave good help to the younger Scouts.

One night as Martin, the Scoutmaster, lay in bed after his evening prayer, the thought suddenly struck him that Jim had only three months to complete his Eagle requirements before he would pass the age deadline. He felt compelled to take the matter into his own hands and urge it through. Jim responded to his enthusiasm and moved forward. The badges were completed quickly, and the Eagle project loomed ahead. Jim enlisted the help of the bishop and other ward members, who were eager to see him succeed. Under his initiative, the Scouts inspected, repaired, sold or donated as needed, smoke alarms in nearly 400 homes. Here was real, tangible success, accomplished by many people being prompted by the Spirit and acting upon those feelings. His Eagle Court of Honor was a highlight for the whole ward.

About this time he graduated from high school. By now, he was becoming more interested in Church, but wanted to have a testimony for himself, not merely to accept it on the assertion of others. The bishop wanted to advance him in the priesthood, but Jim was holding back. He discussed with his Scoutmaster his questions about the reality of God. Martin shared with him his own experiences; taught him the real substance of prayer; taught him to perceive the blessings of the Lord in his life; and helped him to recognize the influence of the Spirit. But the young man still wanted an affirmation that he could recognize. One night, his heart reaching out for an answer, he read Moses 1:39: "This is my work and my glory, to bring to pass the immortality and eternal life of man." The words pierced his heart with the assertion: God is real! A feeling of peace flooded his soul, and he found he could not sleep. The next Fast meeting the congregation rustled as he stood to speak. After stating his testimony, he added, "I told the bishop that when I was ready to be advanced in the priesthood I would let him know. I am telling him now, I am ready."

More days of growth followed. He asked his older brother to ordain him a priest, and a year later, he asked his Scoutmaster to ordain him an elder. Only a few months later, this changed young man received his mission call. At his farewell, he tearfully thanked all those who had worked so hard with him over several years, grateful that they "never gave up on him." All felt their prayers had been answered.

Through the Spirit any of us can know that the gospel is true, that God lives, that Jesus Christ is our Savior. This is the sweetest experience of a lifetime. It may come quickly, but more often is the result of a process of learning and living. But all true testimonies are given through the Holy Spirit. Listen to the testimonies borne by some of our prophets:

President Joseph F. Smith:

> The office and duty of the Holy Ghost is to bring to our remembrance things that are past, to make clear to our understanding things that are present, and to show us things that are to come. It is his duty also to testify of the Father and of the Son, and reveal them unto us. I say to this congregation that the Holy Spirit of God has spoken to me—not through the ear, not through the eye, but to my spirit, to my living and eternal part,—and has revealed unto me that Jesus is the Christ, the Son of the living God. I testify to you that I know that my Redeemer lives. (October 18, 1896. In *Collected Discourses*, vol. 5, p. 230.)

President Joseph Fielding Smith, Jr.:

> I bear testimony of the divine mission of Jesus Christ.
> I know he was born of Mary in Bethlehem of Judea; that God was his Father; and that he came into the world to die upon the cross for the sins of the world.
> I know that he and his Father appeared to Joseph Smith to usher in the dispensation of the fulness of times, and that he will soon come again to live and reign with men on earth a thousand years.
> I pray that all of us who believe in his name will be worthy, whether in life or in death, to abide the day of his coming; and that we shall dwell with him forever in the kingdom of his Father. (Pamphlet, Christmas, 1971.)

President Marion G. Romney:

> I know that my Redeemer lives. I shall not know it better when I stand before the bar of God to be judged. I bear that witness to you, not from what people have told me; I bear it out of a knowledge revealed to me by the Holy Spirit. . . . I know that the Prophet Joseph Smith was a prophet of God. I know he saw God, the Eternal Father, and his Son, Jesus Christ, as he says he did. I was not there, but I have read his account many, many, many times. From his

account I get in my mind a mental picture, but I did not get my knowledge that he had the vision from that source. I received it from the whisperings of the Holy Spirit. (*Look to God and Live*, pp. 252-253.)

We should all strive to gain a strong testimony of the gospel the same way President Romney gained his—through the whisperings of the Spirit. If we seek to gain knowledge of the things of God, He will send truth and knowledge by the Holy Ghost. Fortified with that knowledge we will be able to progress toward eternal life, and better able to solve the dilemmas of today.

A Change in Our Nature

Sometimes we struggle with a problem and it seems we never have the power to resolve it. It will help to realize that as part of the eternal plan, we are in a carnal condition brought on by the Fall. Also as part of the eternal plan, we can overcome our carnal nature only with the help of Jesus Christ through the Holy Spirit. Paul talked about this quandary in Romans 8:13-14: "For if ye live after the flesh, ye shall die: but if ye through the Spirit do mortify the deeds of the body, ye shall live. For as many as are led by the Spirit of God, they are the sons of God."

Simply trying to live the law is not enough. The very best we can do is not sufficient—we cannot pay the price. We must accept Jesus Christ in faith so we can receive the Holy Spirit, which can burn out our impurities. President John Taylor explained our need the Holy Spirit, saying, "What will enable you, brethren and sisters, to govern yourselves? The Spirit of God; and you cannot do it without the Spirit of the living God dwelling in you,—you must have the light of revelation, or else you cannot do it." (*Journal of Discourses*, 10:57.)

Total trust in Jesus Christ and acceptance of His Atonement are needed to obtain the mighty change in nature received by the people of King Benjamin. Alma said, "Behold, he (Christ) changed their hearts; yea, he awakened them out of a deep sleep, and they awoke unto God. Behold, they were in the midst of darkness; nevertheless, their souls were illuminated by the light of the everlasting word." (Alma 5:7.) When their natures had been changed through the Spirit, they had the Christlike attributes of concern for the welfare of each other, love in its pure form, unselfishness, and willingness to bear the burdens of others. All good and noble attributes are included in the condition of the faithful who receive this blessing, including redemption from the Fall.

All Things Brought to Our Remembrance

Jesus taught His Apostles another of the responsibilities of the Holy Ghost when He said "the Comforter . . . the Holy Ghost . . . shall teach you all things, and bring all things to your remembrance, whatsoever I have said unto you." (John 14:26.) The mission of the Holy Ghost is also to remind us, as well as the Apostles, of the Lord's teachings. In time of need, the gospel principles we have learned will be brought back into our minds.

Elder Henry B. Eyring spoke of this:

The Holy Ghost brings back memories of what God has taught us. And one of the ways God teaches us is with his blessings; and so, if we choose to exercise faith, the Holy Ghost will bring God's kindnesses to our remembrance. . . .

You could have an experience with the gift of the Holy Ghost today. You could begin a private prayer with thanks. You could start to count your blessings, and then pause for a moment. If you exercise faith, and with the gift of the Holy Ghost, you will find that memories of other blessings will flood into your mind. If you begin to express gratitude for each of them, your prayer may take a little longer than usual. Remembrance will come. And so will gratitude. (CR, *Ensign*, November 1989, pp. 12-13.)

In addition to blessings, sometimes the Holy Ghost will bring to our remembrance a scripture that will help us through a time of need. He may bring to mind a happy memory that will ease us through a troubled time. Perhaps it may be a lesson learned and then forgotten. The Holy Ghost helps us remember what we need to remember.

Our daughter had an experience in which the Holy Ghost brought a scripture to her remembrance when she needed it:

"My husband had just graduated from the university, and we were deciding which law school to attend. He applied to three, but we really favored one of them. When school got out we had to decide what to do. We received acceptances from two of the schools, even a scholarship offer by one, but the one we really wanted to attend had not responded. We had to move out of our apartment or commit to another year. What should we do?

"We took the problem to the Lord in prayer, and felt that we should move to the city where our preferred law school was located. We felt the Spirit of the Lord confirming this decision, so we acted on the prompting and moved.

"As the summer wore on, we still had not received acceptance from that law school. I tried to maintain faith in the inspiration we had received, but I found myself worrying again and again. One day I was really fretting over what we had done, and so I went into a room away from everyone else and prayed. I asked the Lord to confirm our decision so that I could be at peace.

"The answer I received surprised me. A scripture from the Doctrine and Covenants came clearly to my mind: 'Verily, verily, I say unto you, if you desire a further witness, cast your mind upon the night that you cried unto me in your heart, that you might know concerning the truth of these things.

"'Did I not speak peace to your mind concerning the matter? What greater witness can you have than from God?' (D&C 6:22-23.)

"What surprised me was not this scripture, it was the tone of the answer. I could feel that the Lord was displeased with me for doubting the answer He had so clearly given us. I knew that He expected more from me, and I determined to be more trusting and to exercise my faith.

"The summer continued to pass with no reply, but I wanted to show the Lord that I had learned the lesson and that I had faith. At last, two weeks before classes started that fall, we received our acceptance to the law school. Our prayers had been answered, and an important lesson had been learned."

Love, Peace, Joy

President Ezra Taft Benson said, "Having the Holy Ghost brings forth certain fruits.

"The Apostle Paul said 'the fruit of the Spirit is love, joy, peace, longsuffering, gentleness, goodness, faith, Meekness, [and] temperance.' (Galatians 5:22-23.)

"The most important thing in our lives is the Spirit. I have always felt that. We must remain open and sensitive to the promptings of the Holy Ghost in all aspects of our lives." ("Seek the Spirit of the Lord," *Ensign*, April 1988, p. 3.)

We should seek the gifts of the Spirit. If we have love, joy, peace, longsuffering, gentleness, goodness, faith and meekness in our hearts at all times, think how much better we will relate to our spouses, our children, and others. It is worth the effort.

President George Q. Cannon said, "When a man or woman, or a boy or girl receives the Holy Ghost, it brings peace, joy, love and happiness;

and the person who is in possession of this Spirit has a feeling of kindness and charity towards all mankind. His mind is enlightened and the things of God are made plain unto him. Society is benefited and the world is purified by its bestowal." (*Gospel Truth*, p. 502.)

The ideal marriage would be one where each partner strove for the constant companionship of the Holy Ghost. In such a marriage love would abound. Husband and wife would be gentle with each other; joy and peace would be in their hearts. They would not offend each other because the Holy Ghost does not offend. They would give freely of themselves. Selfishness would be unheard of—sacrifice to fill each other's needs would be the order of the day. Difficult problems would be solved by fasting and praying together. Revelation would come so that correct solutions would be found to all of the problems. That marriage would be a little bit of heaven here on earth.

Happiness comes from listening to the Spirit of the Lord and living by its precepts. Our purpose on earth is to find joy (2 Nephi 2:25) and our Heavenly Father provided the means for us to find it. We don't have to wait for another world to receive this blessing. By walking the path of righteousness we find peace, love, happiness, and joy, and we have hope of it in perfection in the eternal world to come.

Sealing by the Holy Spirit of Promise

All the essential saving ordinances pertaining to our membership in God's kingdom on the earth must be ratified by the Holy Spirit of Promise, another name for the Holy Ghost, in order to be sealed and valid in Heaven after this earth life. Our hearts, our real intent, our worthiness to receive the eternal blessings are all known by this Holy Spirit and affirmed or sealed by that power, eternally on earth and in heaven.

The power of sealing was given to the Prophet Joseph Smith in the Restoration, and continues down in an unbroken chain from him to our present prophet. This includes the power of earthly ordinances like baptism, confirmation, and ordinations to the priesthood, and also the power of other sacred ordinances like baptism for the dead, temple work, sealing of families for eternity, and other ordinances of the holy temple. They are performed on the earth, and sealed for eternity in the heavens by the power of the priesthood, then sealed by the Holy Spirit of Promise. This title for the Holy Ghost is used in the powerful sections of the Doctrine and Covenants referring to the solemnities of the eternal worlds to follow, particularly in sections 76, 124, and 132:

> For all who will have a blessing at my hands shall abide the law which was appointed for that blessing, and the conditions thereof, as were instituted from before the foundation of the world . . .
>
> And . . . the conditions of this law are these: All covenants, contracts, bonds, obligations, oaths, vows, performanmces, connections, associations, or expectations, that are not made and entered into and sealed by the Holy Spirit of promise, . . . are of no efficacy, virtue, or force in and after the resurrection from the dead; for all contracts that are not made unto this end have an end when men are dead. (D&C 132:5,7.)

The sealing power is one of the dearest blessings the gospel has to offer, the assurance that our associations with our loved ones need not end when we are dead. Having only moved to another address, so to speak, we may continue on, knowing as we are known, loving each other as we do now, and being sealed in eternal family relationships. It is the hope and glory of the gospel!

Brother George W. Pace summed it up when he said,

> Surely as we reflect that it is the . . . power of the Spirit . . . that enables us to gain control over our bodies; that it is the Spirit that conveys a remission of sins and cleanses and purifies sin-laden souls; it is the Spirit that distills the very nature of the Redeemer into our beings as we live by faith; that it is the Spirit that endows faithful believers in Christ with charity, the pure love of Christ; that it is the Spirit that seals all ordinances according to the faithfulness of the members so that heavenly assurances of eternal life can be obtained while we are yet in mortality—as we reflect on all of these and many more, surely we will exclaim, "What a privilege, what a blessing to have the gift and power of the Holy Ghost." (*Our Search to Know the Lord*, p. 121.)

Realizing the power and blessings that come through the Spirit should motivate us to bring our lives into harmony with the gospel. Then we will be worthy to have the companionship of the Holy Ghost and its blessings.

16

Being Born Again

The Destination

In our quest for purity of heart, the destination is the newness of life referred to as being "born again." It is the reward for all of the efforts we have put forth, all the trials we have overcome, all the work we have done in behalf of ourselves and our associates.

President John Taylor teaches us a great truth:

> The time will come on this earth when every knee shall bow to Him, and every tongue shall confess that Jesus is the Christ, to the glory of God the Father. That time will come. It is not here now; but as I have said He has introduced this Gospel as the entering wedge, as the little leaven by which He can operate, that He may have a people under the influence of the Holy Ghost, a people that can hold communion with Him, like so many thousand strings penetrating the eternal worlds and drawing down blessings from the Almighty, drawing fire, and life, and intelligence from Him; for we ourselves are sparks struck from the blaze of His eternal fire, emanating from God our Father, and we wish to operate with Him and for Him and under His guidance, for the accomplishment of His purposes here upon the earth. This is what we are here for. (*Journal of Discourses*, vol. 24, p. 128.)

Spiritual rebirth is taught as a process, not an event. We will search the scriptures and the prophets for a better understanding of this divine condition.

A New Birth

When I was working in a community service project, I was associated with a woman who had a lot of ability, but was very difficult to work with. She had a quick temper, and showed it in our planning meetings, although she would take assignments and follow through very well. About midway through the project her whole demeanor changed. I was astonished at the change in her attitude, her cooperativeness, even her looks. She had a softness in her face that had never been evident before, smiled readily, and had a radiant appearance. Our meetings became much more focused and productive without the constant discord. I learned that she had joined the Church, and later went through the temple. The light was truly in her life.

This marvelous change occurs when we are born again. Jesus said that to enter into the kingdom of God one must be born again. (See John 3:5.) What does it mean to be born again? President Joseph Fielding Smith, Jr. tells us: "Every child that comes into this world is carried in water, is born of water, and of blood, and of the spirit. So when we are born into the kingdom of God, we must be born in the same way. By baptism, we are born of the water. Through the shedding of the blood of Christ, we are cleansed and sanctified; and we are justified, through the Spirit of God, for baptism is not complete without the baptism of the Holy Ghost. You see the *parallel* between birth into the world and birth into the kingdom of God." (*Doctrines of Salvation*, vol. II, p. 324, emphasis included.)

Elder Bruce R. McConkie explains further that this comes about through the Holy Ghost: "The first birth takes place when spirits pass from their pre-existent first estate into mortality; the *second birth or birth "into the kingdom of heaven" takes place when mortal men are born again and become alive to the things of the Spirit and of righteousness.* . . . The second birth begins when men are baptized in water by a legal administrator; it is completed when they actually receive the companionship of the Holy Ghost, becoming new creatures by the cleansing power of that member of the Godhead." (*Mormon Doctrine*, p. 101, emphasis added.)

We see, then, that our second birth begins at baptism and is completed when we receive and are cleansed by the companionship of the Holy Ghost. Being born again means that we abandon what Paul calls "our old man", or self, ". . . that the body of sin might be destroyed, that henceforth we should not serve sin. For he that is dead to sin is freed from sin." (Inspired Version, Romans 6:6-7.)

When we abandon our old, sinful self, we become a man or woman of God. This rebirth literally causes us to become "new creatures," as we read in Mosiah 27:25-26: "Marvel not that all mankind, yea, men and women, all nations, kindreds, tongues and people, must be born again; yea, born of God, changed from their carnal and fallen state, to a state of righteousness, being redeemed of God, becoming his sons and daughters;

"And thus they become new creatures; and unless they do this, they can in nowise inherit the kingdom of God."

This rebirth comes about through the power of the Holy Ghost. Elder Bruce R. McConkie, speaking of the role of the Holy Ghost in the "new birth," described the "covenant of exaltation" and explained: "Of those who keep their part of the covenant [the Lord] says: '[They] are sanctified by the Spirit unto the renewing of their bodies.' That is, they are born again; they become alive in Christ; they are new creatures of the Holy Ghost; they become the sons of God and thus joint-heirs with Christ." (*A New Witness for the Articles of Faith*, p. 313.)

To apply this directly to our own lives, each of us should ask ourselves these questions: "Have [I] spiritually been born of God? Have [I] received his image in [my countenance]? Have [I] experienced this mighty change in [my heart]?" (Alma 5:14.)

All of us must be born again. To have the ordinances performed is not sufficient if we have not fully made the commitment in our hearts. When we wholeheartedly accept Christ's atonement and seek perfection in our lives, we can then have the iniquity removed from our hearts "as if by fire," thus becoming new creatures "by the power of the Holy Ghost."

President Harold B. Lee explained that being born again involves a change in the inner man: "Conversion must mean more than just being a "card carrying" member of the Church with a tithing receipt, a membership card, a temple recommend, etc. It means to overcome the tendencies to criticize and to strive continually to improve inward weaknesses and not merely the outward appearances." (*Conference Report*, April 1971, p. 92.)

Life is a constant process of refining our mortality and our weaknesses. When we have been baptized and received a remission of our sins, the Holy Ghost will make us aware of the areas in our inner lives that still need refining. We can talk over with our Heavenly Father what needs working on. A broken heart and a contrite spirit invite the Holy Ghost to enter in and cleanse our lives. His guidance on a daily basis will help to solve our problems, and will lift us above the petty cares of this world. We are energized, animated, and invigorated by the holy power.

President Lee said that an important part of conversion is having a testimony that the leaders of the Church are inspired and chosen by God: "Now I want to impress this upon you. Someone has said it this way, and I believe it to be absolutely true: 'That person is not truly converted until he sees the power of God resting upon the leaders of this church, and until it goes down into his heart by fire.' Until the members of this church have that conviction that they are being led in the right way, and they have a conviction that these men of God are men who are inspired and have been properly appointed by the hand of God, they are not truly converted." (*Conference Report*, April 1972, p. 118.)

In our personal search for this divine conviction, let us do our part by avoiding any criticism of the leadership in the Lord's Church, and by giving our full support to them, in word and deed. When we feel the power of the Holy Ghost in our lives we will know that they also work under this power. We will recognize the divine mission of His Church and its leaders, and be able to give our minds and strength full-heartedly to His cause.

Let's make Christ the center of our lives, and allow Him to change us. Let's depend on Him completely. Let's keep His commandments, build His kingdom, and rejoice in His way of life.

A Newness of Life

Reading some actual instances of people who have been born again will help us learn a great deal about what it means to be born again.

President Joseph F. Smith tells of this experience after his baptism: "The feeling that came upon me was that of pure peace, of love and of light. I felt in my soul that if I had sinned—and surely I was not without sin—that it had been forgiven me; that I was indeed cleansed from sin; my heart was touched, and I felt that I would not injure the smallest insect beneath my feet. I felt as if I wanted to do good everywhere to everybody and to everything. I felt a newness of life, a newness of desire to do that which was right." (*Gospel Doctrine*, p. 96.)

Another prophet, President Lorenzo Snow tells this remarkable event:

> Some two or three weeks after I was baptized, one day while engaged in my studies, I began to reflect upon the fact that I had not obtained a *knowledge* of the truth of the work . . . and I began to feel very uneasy. I laid aside my books, left the house, and wandered around through the fields under the oppressive influence of a gloomy, disconsolate spirit, while an indescribable cloud of darkness seemed to envelop me. I had been accustomed, at the close of the day, to retire for secret prayer, to a grove a short distance from my lodgings, but at this time I felt no inclination to do so. The spirit of prayer had departed and the heavens seemed like brass over my head. At length, realizing that the usual time had come for secret prayer, I concluded I would not forego my evening service, and, as a matter of formality, knelt as I was in the habit of doing, and in my accustomed retired place, but not feeling as I was [accustomed] to feel.
>
> I had no sooner opened my lips in an effort to pray, than I heard a sound, just above my head, like the rustling of silken robes, and immediately the Spirit of God descended upon me, completely enveloping my whole person, filling me from the crown of my head to the soles of my feet, and Oh, the joy and happiness I felt! No language can describe the almost instantaneous transition from a dense cloud of mental and spiritual darkness into a refulgence of light and knowledge . . . that God lives, that Jesus Christ is the Son of God, and of the restoration of the holy Priesthood, and the fulness of the Gospel. It was a complete baptism—a tangible immersion in the heavenly principle or element, the Holy Ghost; and even more real and physical in its effects upon every part of my system than the immersion by water; dispelling forever, so long as reason and memory last, all possibility of doubt or fear . . .
>
> I cannot tell how long I remained in the full flow of the blissful enjoyment and divine enlightenment, but it was several minutes before the celestial element which filled and surrounded me began gradually to withdraw. On arising from my kneeling posture, with my heart swelling with gratitude to God . . . I *knew* that He had conferred on me what only an omnipotent being can confer—that which is of greater value than all the wealth and honors worlds can bestow. That night, as I retired to rest, the same wonderful manifestations were repeated, and continued to be for several successive nights. The sweet remembrance of those glorious experiences, from that time to the present, bring them fresh before me, imparting an inspiring influence which pervades my whole being, and I trust will to the close of my earthly existence. (Eliza R. Snow, comp.,

Biography and Family Record of Lorenzo Snow, pp. 7-9, from quotation in *The Holy Ghost*, McConkie and Millett, pp. 98-99.)

This is a moving and dramatic account of being born again. This man went on to become a prophet. Does everyone who is born again have such an experience? What can *we* expect?

Elder Bruce R. McConkie explained that, although in some miraculous instances conversion is instantaneous, it usually involves a process: "Being born again is a gradual thing, except in a few isolated instances that are so miraculous that they get written up in the scriptures. As far as the generality of the members of the Church are concerned, we are born again by degrees, and we are born again to added light and added knowledge and added desires for righteousness as we keep the commandments." ("Jesus Christ and Him Crucified," *1976 Devotional Speeches of the Year*, p. 399, as quoted in *The Holy Ghost*, p. 102.)

Whether the manifestation of being born of the Spirit happens at the time of baptism or later in one's life, it is a blessing all of us should strive for.

Let's see what effect being born again had on the life of yet another man, and through him, his family:

David's father was president of the stake. David had never been to the stake president's office; but last evening at dinner he had raised some questions about spiritual rebirth, and his father had invited him to come to the stake president's office to discuss the matter. As he settled into a chair, David noticed a picture on his father's desk. It was a picture of the stake presidency; there was his father, smiling and dignified. David was early for the appointment; and as he waited, the thought occurred to him that if ever anyone knew anything about spiritual rebirth, it must be his father.

David's father had worked in the mines most of his adult life. Nothing had ever really mattered to him beyond food and sleep. Seldom had he been much of a father until the day the missionaries knocked at their door. After weeks of questions, some patience on the part of the missionaries, and many prayers by David's mother (who herself had immediately accepted the gospel taught by the missionaries), David's father had joined the Church. The rest of the family joined within weeks after their father led the way.

David hadn't noticed it at first, but gradually his father had changed. There had been nothing spectacular—no visions, no outward manifestations—but just gradual change. First they had begun to attend church. Later David's father had announced at the dinner table that they would never eat another meal in their home without having a blessing on the food. That had been twelve years ago. Then they had commenced holding a regular family home evening. David still remembered the family journey to the Los Angeles Temple, where they had been sealed together as a family for time and eternity. Later, when David and his brothers had spoken harshly about one of the leaders of their ward, he remembered his father's justified anger and instant rebuke, for although David's father had controlled his temper, he made it very clear to his sons that they must never say such things about any of the Church officers again. While his father's change had occurred quietly and gradually, it was nevertheless a powerful change. David had often wondered to himself what possibly could have taken a hard-headed man like his father and literally turned him around. And now that he was on the proper course, it seemed that his dedication and zeal in the cause of the Master increased every day.

David's father had been called to serve in the ward MIA [Young Men] and later in the stake. Then just two years later he had been called as a counselor in the stake presidency. David noticed that his father was gone from home a great deal, but the time he did manage to spend at home with his wife and four sons was quality time. As a contrast to twelve years ago, their home was now truly a house of love, prayer, and order. David had listened to his father's testimony in conferences and as he had shared it with his sons and with others who had been in their home. During one home evening, he told his sons: "I am not the father you used to have; I have been changed. And I want you to know that for whatever else I may say or do, I know that Jesus lives and is my Redeemer, because I have tasted of his goodness and I know of his love for me." David knew his father well enough to know that he testified of the reality of Jesus and of the truth of the gospel from the depths of his soul. And now his father was president of the stake.

As David sat there waiting, he suddenly realized that he lived in the very shadow of a man who had been born again! Hastily he scribbled a note to his father and then left. The note read: "Dad, I won't need to talk to you after all. I have the answers to my question. See you at dinner. David." (*The Life and Teachings of Jesus and His Apostles*, pp. 40-41.)

Being born again brings wonderful blessings. It actually brings a new course to our lives, as it did for David's father.

Each member of the Church can see his or her life change as they seek to be born again. One day a sister picked up a novel she had read several years earlier. She was surprised by the immoral behavior in the book. Why hadn't she been repulsed by the book years before when she had read it?

As she thought about it, she realized that she had become more selective in all her entertainment choices. She thought about a movie she and her husband had walked out of recently and she remembered feeling that she *had* to leave because of the way she felt while sitting there.

Why had it become less a matter of deciding to leave than simply being unable to sit there any longer? The answer came to her as she read in Alma 13:12 about some people who had purified themselves through faith and repentance until they "could not look upon sin save it were with abhorrence." She knew that although she was not perfect, she could see that she was beginning to abhor evil from her heart.

She knelt down and thanked God for the gift of the Holy Ghost that had helped her make these changes in her life—in fact, had made them impossible not to make.

What an improvement there will be in our lives if we will put off the natural man and become saints. We will find that we begin to abhor sin, and that it grows easier and easier to live the commandments. As we do this, our lives will become purer and the blessings of the Lord will rain down upon us. We will find comfort, solace, and joy even in the most difficult circumstances.

Elder John A. Widtsoe described what he witnessed in his work as an apostle:

> The greatest miracle of the gospel is the transformation for good of those who embrace it and live it. That was sensed in meeting with the people, officially and in their homes. Despite origin, education, and position they are changed to the easy vision of all, when eternal truth settles in their hearts. It is marvelous to me how men and women called into office, rise to a new dignity with added power when the spirit of their callings comes upon them. And there are other miracles, thousands of them, healing of the sick, guidance in human affairs, and others, that proclaim the reality of the gift of the priesthood of God—the power and authority of God. Indeed, in this work the testimony grows that we are indeed living in a day when the power of the spirit flows in rich abundance among those who are faithful to the truth. (*In a Sunlit Land*, p. 167.)

"These Are They Who Have Overcome the World"

When we are born again and have the constant companionship of the Holy Ghost, we will steadily follow the path the Lord has for us in this life. We will be able to make proper decisions that will lead us into further service and further joy. Those who lead lives of this kind will find that when they lay down the burdens of mortality, they are received into a glorious state described by President David O. McKay (*Cherished Experiences*, pp. 59-60). We pray this may be your reward.

I . . . fell asleep, and beheld in vision something infinitely sublime. In the distance I beheld a beautiful white city. Though it was far away, yet I seemed to realize that trees with luscious fruit, shrubbery with gorgeously tinted leaves, and flowers in perfect bloom abounded everywhere. The clear sky above seemed to reflect these beautiful shades of color. I then saw a great concourse of people approaching the city. Each one wore a white flowing robe and a white headdress. Instantly my attention seemed centered upon their leader, and though I could see only the profile of his features and his body, I recognized him at once as my Savior! The tint and radiance of his countenance were glorious to behold. There was a peace about him which seemed sublime—it was divine!

The city, I understood, was his. It was the City Eternal; and the people following him were to abide there in peace and eternal happiness.

But who were they?

As if the Savior read my thoughts, he answered by pointing to a semicircle that then appeared above them, and on which was written in gold the words:

These are they Who Have Overcome the World—
Who Have Truly Been Born Again!

Section II

How to Do It

17

You Can Overcome Pride

The Root of the Sin of Pride

One of the most insidious evils of our time, perhaps of all time, is the sin of pride. It enters into our thinking, and from there, into our choices and actions. It colors our reactions to others, our attitudes, and consequently our relationships with those around us. President Ezra Taft Benson addressed this problem forcefully in General Conference, both in April, 1986 and again in April, 1989. He urged us to examine ourselves and to do our best to root out this evil.

Our prophets have always warned against the sin of pride. Alma cautions us, "Behold, are ye stripped of pride? I say unto you, if ye are not ye are not prepared to meet God. Behold ye must prepare quickly; for the kingdom of heaven is soon at hand, and such an one hath not eternal life." (Alma 5:28.)

To help us understand this problem in our personal lives, President Benson pointed out the root of the sin of pride: "Most of us think of pride as a self-centeredness, conceit, boastfulness, arrogance, or haughtiness. All of these are elements of the sin, but the heart, or core, is still missing.

"The central feature of pride is enmity—enmity toward God and enmity toward our fellowmen. *Enmity* means 'hatred toward, hostility to, or a state of opposition.' It is the power by which Satan wishes to reign over us." (CR, *Ensign*, May 1989, p. 4.)

Pride, then, is a sin because of this root of enmity—including hatred, hostility or opposition. Never before have we seen enmity in greater evidence than now—country against country; groups, factions, causes setting themselves against others; nationalities in civil war against their former neighbors. In smaller headlines we see gang rivalries, families in disarray, abuse, revenge, cheating in competition, many kinds of hostility. How can we resist this great sin?

In the New Testament Christ was asked, "Master, what is the great commandment in the law?" Jesus answered, "Thou shalt love the Lord thy God with all thy heart, and with all thy soul, and with all thy mind.

"This is the first and great commandment.

"And the second is like unto it, Thou shalt love thy neighbor as thyself.

"On these two commandments hang all the law and the prophets." (Matthew 22:37-40.)

Love, being the opposite of enmity, is the antidote for pride, and is the basis for all success, not only in the gospel, but in all interactions with people. Pride causes us to break both these great commandments through enmity or hatred for God and our fellowmen. When a person has love in his heart, he esteems others as himself. He seeks for that which is good for them as well as good for himself. He strives to help and uphold others, because he has this good feeling about them in his heart. It is an attitude of caring, of responsibility, and of benevolence.

We need to take stock of our individual lives and see how we measure up. It is easy for pride to creep in unless we make the choice to love sincerely.

Results of the Sin of Pride

President Benson pointed out that pride as he described it is always a sin: "In the scriptures there is no such thing as righteous pride. It is always considered as a sin. We are not speaking of a wholesome view of self-worth, which is best established by a close relationship with God. But we are speaking of pride as the universal sin, as someone has described it. . . .

"Essentially, pride is a 'my will' rather than 'thy will' approach to life. The opposite of pride is humbleness, meekness, submissiveness (see Alma 13:28), or teachableness." (CR, *Ensign*, May 1986, p. 6.)

President Benson's description shows that the sin of pride leads to more sin by causing us to value our own will above God's will. Elder Neal A. Maxwell concurs, "Just as meekness is in all our virtues, so pride is in all our sins. . . .

"According to *The Interpreter's Dictionary of the Bible*, 'at least six Hebrew roots contain the idea of pride, and almost all of them mean "to lift up," "to be high."' These are translated into English as *arrogance, loftiness, presumption, boasting.*' (p. 896.)" (*Meek and Lowly*, p. 50.)

Elder Maxwell uses some pithy phrases in his descriptions of pride, as well as its blessed opposite, meekness: "Arrogance and disobedience are cellmates. . . . Scriptural warnings often couple pride and selfishness. . . . The gospel seeks to make us a community of saints, a city on a hill, but pride and selfishness produce just the opposite result. . . . Meekness creates the ultimate openness, the openness to spiritual things. . . . It is a heroic thing for individuals to reverse themselves, their attitudes, and their patterns of behavior in order to pursue discipleship." (pp. 50-66.)

President Benson tells how pride has led to sin in the past:

> The scriptures abound with evidences of the severe consequences of the sin of pride to individuals, groups, cities and nations. "Pride goeth before destruction." (Prov. 16:18.) It destroyed the Nephite nation and the city of Sodom. (See Moro. 8:27; Ezek. 16:49-50.)
>
> It was through pride that Jesus Christ was crucified. The Pharisees were wroth because Jesus claimed to be the Son of God, which was a threat to their position, and so they plotted His death. (See John 11:53.)
>
> Saul became an enemy to David through pride. He was jealous because the crowds of Israelite women were singing that "Saul hath slain his thousands, and David his ten thousands." (1 Sam. 18:6-8.) (CR, *Ensign*, May 1989, p. 5.)

Pride grows in our hearts when we feel that we are better than others because we dress better, have more of the goods of the world, or are educated better than some. We may be able to accumulate riches. We may have talents of which we are prideful. We may grasp for power. Even the poor do not escape the sin of pride if they resent others who have more, or if they claim to be better because they do not have more! Rich or poor may take advantage of their neighbor, withhold their goods from the needy, and look down with scorn on others of God's children. There are those who mock persons with handicaps; there are those who scorn persons with "less beauty" or "less personality" or lesser skills. Pride is the mark of the people in the great and spacious building spoken of in Lehi's dream.

President Benson spoke of these people when he said,

> The great and spacious building which Lehi saw was the pride of the world where the multitude of the earth was gathered. (See 1

Nephi 11:35-36.) Those who walked the straight and narrow path and held onto the word of God and partook of the love of God were mocked and scorned by those in the building. (See 1 Ne. 8:20, 27, 33; 11:25.)

"The humble followers of Christ" are few. (2 Ne. 28:14.)

Pride does not look up to God and care about what is right. It looks sideways to man and argues who is right. Pride is manifest in the spirit of contention. (CR, *Ensign*, May 1986, p. 6.)

Another way pride can cause us to sin is that, like those in the great and spacious building, we become more concerned about what others think than about what God thinks of us. President Benson spoke of this:

> The proud stand more in fear of men's judgment than of God's judgment. (See D&C 3:6-7; 30:1-2; 60:2.) "What will men think of me?" weighs heavier than "what will God think of me?" . . .
>
> Fear of men's judgment manifests itself in competition for men's approval. The proud love "the praise of men more than the praise of God." (John 12:42-43.) Our motives for the things we do are where the sin is manifest. Jesus said He did "always those things" that pleased God. (John 8:29.) Would we not do well to have the pleasing of God as our motive rather than to try to elevate ourselves above our brother and outdo another? (CR, *Ensign*, May 1989, p. 5.)

We should realize that men's opinions of us are transitory; it is only our standing before God that has eternal importance. It actually matters little what men think of us; Heavenly Father looks on the heart and knows us for what we really are, prideful or humble. We can be assured that God is just; His opinion of us will be based on what we are inside, not what pride or opinion makes of us. He will take us as we are when we reach out to Him, and He will lovingly help us go forward and improve our lives.

We have noted how pride leads to extremely serious consequences in the lives of individuals. Combined into a collective way of living, it can be socially disastrous. President Benson explained that pride caused the fall of a whole nation—the people of the Book of Mormon:

> The Doctrine and Covenants tells us that the Book of Mormon is the "record of a fallen people." (D&C 20:9.) Why did they fall? This is one of the major messages of the Book of Mormon. Mormon gives

the answer in the closing chapters of the book in these words: "Behold, the pride of this nation, or the people of the Nephites, hath proven their destruction." (Moroni 8:27.) And then, lest we miss that momentous Book of Mormon message from that fallen people, the Lord warns us in the Doctrine and Covenants, "Beware of pride, lest ye become as the Nephites of old." (D&C 38:39.) (CR, *Ensign*, May 1989, p. 4.)

President Benson stressed this great message of the Book of Mormon because it has direct application to us today. Our time is very similar. Nephi, Alma, all the prophets and the faithful were anticipating the coming of the Savior. Before His coming, those who were not steadfast in the faith were destroyed, leaving only the more righteous to welcome Him. In like manner, we are now anticipating His second coming, and the warning is clear, both from the ancient prophets and from our modern prophets.

We read, "For the hour is nigh and the day soon at hand when the earth is ripe; and all the proud and they that do wickedly shall be as stubble; and I will burn them up, saith the Lord of Hosts, that wickedness shall not be upon the earth." (D&C 29:9. Other scriptures relating to the second coming include D&C 64:22-24; 3 Nephi 25:1-2.) The Lord finishes His warning with these words: "Wherefore, if ye believe me, ye will labor while it is called today." (D&C 64:25.)

The Lord is calling us to cleanse ourselves of pride and wickedness, and with full hearts apply ourselves to preparing for the great events that will usher in the thousand years of peace and righteousness. We have the privilege and responsibility to make sure we are valiant and ready for Jesus Christ's second coming!

Pride Causes People to Mistreat Others

As President Benson said, pride causes some to want to be above others. They feel competition and enmity, not love, toward fellow beings. In the Book of Mormon Jacob denounced the pride that had entered the hearts of the people, causing them to persecute their brethren:

> The hand of providence hath smiled upon you most pleasingly, that you have obtained many riches; and because some of you have obtained more abundantly than that of your brethren ye are lifted up in the pride of your hearts, and wear stiff necks and high heads

because of the costliness of your apparel, and persecute your brethren because ye suppose that ye are better than they.

And now, my brethren, do ye suppose that God justifieth you in this thing? Behold, I say unto you, Nay. But he condemneth you, and if ye persist in these things his judgments must speedily come unto you. . . .

And now, my brethren, I have spoken unto you concerning pride; and those of you which have afflicted your neighbor, and persecuted him because ye were proud in your hearts, of the things which God hath given you, what say ye of it?

Do ye not suppose that such things are abominable unto him who created all flesh? And the one being is as precious in his sight as the other. (Jacob 2:13-14, 20-21.)

Isn't it ludicrous to look down on one's fellow beings because of being "proud . . . of the things God has given you?" One is being proud of what came from God, not oneself—but neglecting to give Him the credit.

How can we keep wealth from causing us to persecute and look down on those around us? We should first remember the tender love that God has for all of His children, and then remember the two great commandments, to love God with all our hearts and to love our fellow beings. He loves all His children, and so should we. What is the purpose for the substance with which the Lord has blessed us? Jacob counsels:

Think of your brethren like unto yourselves, and be familiar with all and free with your substance, that they may be rich like unto you.

But before ye seek for riches, seek ye for the kingdom of God.

And after ye have obtained a hope in Christ ye shall obtain riches, if ye seek them; and ye will seek them for the intent to do good—to clothe the naked, and to feed the hungry, and to liberate the captive, and administer relief to the sick and the afflicted. (Jacob 2:17-19.)

The pride that causes people to persecute others has plagued mankind through the ages. Mormon prophesied this about the day when the Book of Mormon would come forth (our day!):

I know that ye do walk in the pride of your hearts; and there are none save a few only who do not lift themselves up in the pride of their hearts, unto the wearing of very fine apparel, unto envying, and strifes, and malice, and persecutions, and all manner of iniquities because of the pride of your hearts.

For behold, ye do love money, and your substance, and your fine apparel, and the adorning of your churches, more than ye love the poor and the needy, the sick and the afflicted. . . .

Why do ye adorn yourselves with that which hath no life, and yet suffer the hungry, and the needy, and the naked, and the sick and the afflicted to pass by you, and notice them not? (Mormon 8:36-37,39.)

Does this description strike at the heart when we read it on the printed page? Overcoming pride is the test and trial of today. Can we pass it? We must not walk in the pride of our hearts. We must not love money and fine apparel more than we love the poor and the needy, the sick and the afflicted. Rather than seek the praise of the world, we are to seek to do the will of God, to keep His commandments and build His kingdom, living together in love.

Pride impels us to adorn ourselves with "that which hath no life," while ignoring our neighbors. The Savior's love urges us to be our neighbor's keeper, to help those who are oppressed, in any way we can. Our prayers are to be followed with service to our fellow men and our God. Alma pleads with us thus: "After ye have done all these things, if ye turn away the needy, and the naked, and visit not the sick and the afflicted, and impart of your substance . . . to those who stand in need . . . behold, your prayer is vain and availeth you nothing." (Alma 34:28).

President Benson cautioned, "Was it not through pride that the devil became the devil? Christ wanted to serve. The devil wanted to rule. Christ wanted to bring men to where He was. The devil wanted to be above men." (CR, *Ensign*, May 1986, p. 6.)

Is there any room for pride in our relationships? Rather than look down on other children of God, shouldn't we esteem them as ourselves? Shouldn't we, like our Master, strive to lift them up—at least to where we are?

Alma 38:14 counsels us, "Do not say: O God, I thank thee that we are better than our brethren; but rather say: O Lord, forgive my unworthiness, and remember my brethren in mercy—yea, acknowledge your unworthiness before God at all times."

Pride in the Church

Pride is still a problem in the Church today. The Lord has warned in the latter-days, "Beware of pride, lest ye become as the Nephites of old." (D&C 38:39.)

President Spencer W. Kimball admonished ordinary members of the Church: "Sometimes we find members who have an overdose of false pride. They want their way or they will quit. Have you ever seen anybody leave the ward and never 'darken the door' of the ward building again because of a little altercation perhaps with the bishop or someone there?" (CR, *Ensign*, May 1975, p. 78.)

Let us make sure we do not allow our pride to stand between us and receiving blessings in the Kingdom of God. Look on pride as another temptation that is to be overcome as we strive to enjoy the gospel light. Can we sustain one another and not try to place ourselves above others?

The Prophet Joseph Smith counsels, "Beware of pride, and [do] not seek to excel one above another, but act for each other's good, and pray for one another, and honor our brother or make honorable mention of his name, and not backbite and devour our brother. Why will not man learn wisdom by precept at this late age of the world, when we have such a cloud of witnesses and examples before us, and not be obliged to learn by sad experience everything we know." (*Teachings of the Prophet Joseph Smith*, p. 155.)

Another situation that creates difficulty for some members of the Church is becoming prideful in serving in positions of authority in the Church. It is a privilege to serve. The object of our service is to help bring people to Christ, and to alleviate suffering. Wherever we are called, we ought to serve humbly and sincerely, knowing that we get our strength and inspiration from God. We should also be gracious when we are released, and someone else fills the position we held. What is important is the work of saving souls, not the honor of the position. Some serve well as administrators, but at the center of the work are those who serve as ministers—dedicated home teachers and visiting teachers are at the heart of compassionate service. Knowing this, we should strive to go the extra mile in all of our service, not seeking the honor and praise of man, but rather pleasing God and bringing about Zion by service to His individual children.

In the Church we should have a feeling of charity, esteem each other as equals and pray for one another continually. If we honor our brothers and sisters, as the Prophet said, we will not be tempted to criticize each other or those in authority, but instead will sustain and support each other in our positions of responsibility.

Pride in the Home

Pride can also be a very destructive force in the home. Each of us has a tendency to think that we, ourselves, are a little wiser, a little saner, a little better in any stated way than those around us. Consequently, our relationships with those nearest us are at risk. Even in Latter-day Saint homes we can find backbiting, faultfinding, envying, selfishness, jealousy, and unforgiveness. These actions cause contention, irritation, and disharmony, even abuse, in that precious home that should be a fortress and a refuge for our dearest and best, our family members.

Contrast this with a home of love where each member is concerned with the welfare of each other, where sharp words are repressed, where encouragement is freely given, where gratitude is expressed, where understanding is expected and forgiveness is received. This is the ideal Latter-day Saint home, and it requires continual effort.

Pride is a big factor in most broken marriages. Pride manifests itself in marriage partners bent on divorce in many if not all of the following ways:

1. Refusal to forgive, harboring past offenses.
2. Fault-finding.
3. Withholding words of praise and gratitude that would encourage a partner.
4. Living beyond their means.
5. Fighting and quarreling with each other.
6. Thinking of self before others.
7. Being defensive.
8. Indulging in self-pity.
9. Backbiting, murmuring, "badmouthing" the other.
10. Blaming, instead of taking responsibility for what is going wrong.

In order to improve such a marriage each partner needs to stop, take a good look at himself or herself, admit what he or she is doing that is destructive to harmony and peace in the marriage, then repent and put his or her life in order. Neither can force the spouse to reform, but either can surely improve himself or herself.

When one tries to make things better in the relationship, in a spirit of love, cooperation, kindness and caring, the way is cleared for the spouse to respond in like manner. However, remember that many factors are present—changes may come quickly, or they may take some time. In any case, love and patience will produce better results than harshness.

Elder Rulon G. Craven of the Second Quorum of the Seventy tells this story:

> I recall the story of the man who went to his lawyer because he wanted to divorce his wife. He told the lawyer that before the divorce he wanted to do whatever would make her most miserable. The lawyer said, "I know just how to make that happen, if you are willing to do it." The man agreed, so the lawyer gave these instructions: "Wait for a period of time before you tell her you want a divorce. Between now and that date, work very hard at being kind, sensitive, pleasant, and helping your wife in ways that you have never thought of before. Instead of reading the paper and watching television while she prepares dinner, help her. Hang up your clothes and put your things where they belong. Do the repair work she wants done without having to be asked repeatedly."
>
> The man began to speak: "Just a minute . . ."
>
> The lawyer said, "Let me finish. And then, on that planned day, when you have done so many good things for her, tell her you want a divorce. She will be most miserable at the thought of your leaving her."
>
> The man thought that sounded like a good plan, so he followed the counsel of his lawyer. When the time came that he was to indicate to his wife that he wanted a divorce, a call came from the lawyer about preparing papers for the divorce.
>
> "What divorce?" he said to the lawyer. "I do not want to divorce my wife. She is the kindest, pleasantest, most sensitive person, and I have no intention of divorcing her." The man learned from this experience the great force love has for creating good, and that love begets love. (*The Pursuit of Perfection*, pp. 83-84.)

Overcoming Pride Through Humility

How can we combat the destructive force of pride in all of our relationships, including our relationship with God? We should understand that the opposite of pride is humility, a virtue exemplified by Christ Himself. Elder Bruce R. McConkie lists it as a requirement in many situations: "Humility must accompany repentance to qualify a person for baptism (D&C 20:37); It is required of all engaged in gospel service (D&C 12:8); is an essential attribute for all who embark in the service of God (D&C 4:6); precedes the acquiring of wisdom from the Spirit D&C (136:32-33); is needed to qualify the righteous to see God (D&C 67:10); and without it no one can gain entrance to the kingdom of God hereafter. (2 Nephi 9:42.)" (*Mormon Doctrine*, p. 370.)

What is this essential attribute? Webster's Third International Dictionary defines the word "humble": "Modest or meek in spirit, manner, or appearance: not proud or haughty." . . . 'A spot where a man feels his own insignificance and may well learn to be humble,' —Samuel Butler. . . . Humble suggests absence of vanity or pride . . . patient, subdued, retiring mildness, . . . lack of boastfulness, or conceited or jealous demand for recognition." (p. 1101.)

This excellent rendition goes along with the gospel definition. President Kimball said, "Humility is teachableness—an ability to realize that all virtues and abilities are not concentrated in one's self." (*Teachings of Spencer W. Kimball*, p. 233.)

Elder Neal A. Maxwell explained how the quality of being teachable makes us more able to receive truth: "Teachableness puts man in a relationship to truth in which he does not flinch from the implications of the truth, but is open to receive it. Thus being realistic, the humble man can cope with this world and with the world to come with greater competency than those who are not teachable. (*That My Family Should Partake*, p. 81.)

Jesus, speaking to people who "trusted in themselves that they were righteous, and despised others," spoke a parable that teaches us to be humble, not even being proud of our good works:

> The Pharisee stood and prayed thus with himself, God, I thank thee, that I am not as other men are, extortioners, unjust, adulterers, or even as this publican. I fast twice in the week, I give tithes of all that I possess. And the publican, standing afar off, would not lift up so much as his eyes unto heaven, but smote upon his breast, saying, God be merciful to me a sinner. I tell you, this man went down to his house justified rather than the other: for every one that exalteth himself shall be abased, and he that humbleth himself shall be exalted. (Luke 18:9-14.)

The Pharisee really did all these good works he boasted of, but he did them for the praise of men, and that was his reward. He failed to gain God's reward because of his lack of humility—the Lord looks upon the heart and judges the real intent, not the outward show. It was the humble publican who was "justified."

Another attribute of humility is obedience. A humble, teachable, meek and seeking person is obedient to the truths he learns. John A. Widtsoe spoke succinctly, "Joseph Smith was an obedient man. Humility always breeds obedience." (*Joseph Smith, Seeker after Truth, Prophet of God*, p. 333.)

Humility is Learned from Chastisement

When we are humble we are willing to receive counsel and even chastisement. Sometimes the Lord has reasons to chasten us—we need to remember that He chastens those whom He loves (Hebrews 12:6; Revelation 3:19). We can learn, therefore, humbly to receive the Lord's rebuke and chastening, even welcome it. President Ezra Taft Benson said, "We can choose to humble ourselves by receiving counsel and chastisement." (CR, *Ensign*, May 1989, p. 7.) The purpose of such chastening is to encourage us to learn, to repent, and to continue on our upward path to purification and eternal life. We can try to use new insights thus gained to better our lives, and to be more compassionate to those around us. By this manner we can refine our lives and become more Christ-like.

This state of humble submission to God's will is counterpart to happiness—it is the process of choosing happiness. It is not a matter of pretending that things are good when we are suffering. It is, rather, a matter of recognizing the purpose of suffering, and remembering that the Lord has promised to make us equal to our burdens. It is a matter of claiming His promises, and making ourselves worthy of them. "All is well, all is well," the hymn which sustained the pioneers through deserts and death reminds us that the "big picture"—the eternal viewpoint—is focused on the unfolding story of God's love, His plan for us, and our rejoicing in it. We can recognize when the Lord blesses and protects us. We can accept the gladness with which the Spirit fills our hearts. We still have to carry loads—that is part of the accomplishment—but our loads will feel light.

Christ is Our Example

Jesus Christ is our example of a life dedicated to doing the will of God. President Benson said, "Christ removed self as the force in His perfect life. It was not *my* will, but *thine* be done." (CR, *Ensign*, May 1986, p. 6.)

The Savior said, "I am meek and lowly in heart." (Matthew 11:29.) If the Savior, the God of this earth, is humble and teachable in His heart, shouldn't we be also?

President Kimball suggested that "Humble and meek properly suggest virtues, not weaknesses." He elaborated: "Humility is not weakness but strength. . . . One can be bold and meek at the same time. One can be courageous and humble. If the Lord was meek and lowly and humble, then to become humble one must do what he did in boldly denouncing evil, bravely advancing righteous works, courageously meeting every problem, becoming the master of himself and the situations about him and being near oblivious to personal credit." (*Teachings of Spencer W. Kimball*, p. 232.)

And he warned, "When one becomes conscious of his great humility, he has already lost it." (p. 233.)

Moroni saw the Savior and talked with Him. He said, "I have seen Jesus, and . . . he hath talked with me face to face, and . . . he told me in plain humility, even as a man telleth another in mine own language, concerning these things." (Ether 12:39.) Can you imagine how it would be to talk with the Savior face to face? If the God of this earth spoke to Moroni in plain humility, shouldn't you and I speak with each other in plain humility whenever we converse? Take note that Jesus talked with Moroni in his own language. That seems significant in the observation of His humility.

Humility Accepts Dependence upon our Savior

Are we not totally dependent upon God, our Savior, for the air we breathe, the food we eat, the clothes we wear, and the good land we live on? What cause have we to be proud?

We are also dependent upon Christ for the Atonement in our behalf. Without the Savior we would all be lost; through His grace we are candidates for eternal life.

We are reminded of this dependence on the Lord in Mosiah 2:23-26:

> And now, in the first place, he hath created you, and granted unto you your lives, for which ye are indebted unto him.

And secondly, he doth require that ye should do as he hath commanded you; for which if ye do, he doth immediately bless you; and therefore he hath paid you. And ye are still indebted unto him, and are, and will be, forever and ever; therefore, of what have ye to boast?

And now I ask, can ye say aught of yourselves? I answer you, Nay. Ye cannot say that ye are even as much as the dust of the earth; yet ye were created of the dust of the earth; but behold, it belongeth to him who created you.

Helaman says we are even less than the dust: "O how great is the nothingness of the children of men; yea, even they are less than the dust of the earth. For behold, the dust of the earth moveth hither and thither to the dividing asunder, at the command of our great and everlasting God." (Helaman 12:7-8.) The dust is obedient to the Lord. We who claim to be so much could take a lesson from it.

When we receive strength from the Lord to overcome a problem or a weakness, we have a tendency to say to ourselves, "Now I am stronger than I was" and go forward in self-assurance rather than acknowledging the hand of the Lord in strengthening us. This is pride in action. It manifests itself in another way when we receive administration at the hands of the elders for an illness, and then fail to acknowledge the Lord's power in the healing.

If we are going to overcome pride, a series of steps will help us become submissive to the Lord. First we should open our hearts to Him and love him with full faith. We can in humility recognize our total dependence on Him with gratitude, not feeling debased, but as an heir to all that He offers. Then we are in a position to respect and love our fellow beings who are also his children. Choosing thus, we are on a proper base to accept Him and to welcome his commandments as enablers, tools with which to build a happy life.

Blessings Attend Humility

The Lord always promises rewards for obedience. For humility He promises extensive blessings.

Be thou humble; and the Lord thy God shall lead thee by the hand, and give thee answer to thy prayers. (D&C 112:10.)

And inasmuch as they were humble they might be made strong, and blessed from on high, and receive knowledge from time to time. (D&C 1:28.)

Always retain in remembrance, the greatness of God, and your own nothingness, and his goodness and long-suffering towards you, unworthy creatures, and humble yourselves even in the depths of humility, calling on the name of the Lord daily, and standing steadfastly in the faith of that which is to come . . . if ye do this ye shall always rejoice, and be filled with the love of God, and always retain a remission of your sins, and you shall grow in the knowledge of the glory of him that created you. (Mosiah 4:11-12.)

Humble yourselves in the sight of the Lord, and he shall lift you up. (James 4:10.)

How to Do It

Jesus taught us that we should choose humility: "He that is greatest among you shall be your servant. And whosoever shall exalt himself shall be abased; and he that shall humble himself shall be exalted." (Matthew 23:11-12.)

President Benson taught us how to humble ourselves. We select his "antidotes" for the poison of pride:

We can choose to humble ourselves by conquering enmity toward our brothers and sisters, *esteeming them as ourselves*, and lifting them as high or higher than we are. . . . We can choose to humble ourselves by receiving counsel and chastisement. . . . We can choose to humble ourselves by forgiving those who have offended us. . . . We can choose to humble ourselves by rendering selfless service. We can choose to humble ourselves by going on missions and preaching the word that can humble others. . . . We can choose to humble ourselves by getting to the temple more frequently. We can choose to humble ourselves by confessing and forsaking our sins and being born of God. . . . We can choose to humble ourselves by loving God, submitting our will to His, and putting Him first in our lives. (CR, *Ensign*, May 1989, pp. 6-7, emphasis added.)

Note President Benson's counsel to *choose* to humble ourselves by esteeming our brothers and sisters as ourselves. Yes, even our spouse.

Even the leaders of the ward and the Church. Yes, even the poor, the sick and the afflicted. All are children of God and therefore our brethren and sisters. As Saints, we are expected to love one another, as Jesus Christ loves us. This really works.

When we esteem others as ourselves we start to feel good about them. Instead of putting them down we want to build them up. A new attitude of love settles down upon us. We choose to make forgiveness a way of life by forgiving immediately those who may offend us. We render selfless service to our fellowmen, recognizing that God loves them dearly, and choosing to love them in the same way. We live charitably, volunteer for service assignments, work in the community, make our neighborhoods more friendly. Our attitude is, "I want to do whatever God wants me to do." Remember who it was that insisted on having his own will in the pre-mortal council?

Elder Bruce R. McConkie explains that the purpose of our mortal life "is to test men and see whether they will seek for worldly things— wealth, learning, honors, power—or whether they will flee from pride, humble themselves before God, and walk before him with an eye single to his glory. Without this basic Christian virtue of humility there is neither spiritual progression here nor eternal life hereafter. With it men are able to gain every godly attribute in this life and to qualify for full salvation in the mansions on high." (*Doctrinal New Testament Commentary*, vol. 1, p. 500.)

From time to time we should check ourselves to see if we are becoming proud. To do so, one can ask the following questions:

1. Do I pray, "Thy will, not mine, be done"?
2. Am I jealous of other people's accomplishments?
3. Do I fear men more than God? Do I love and seek for the praise of men over the praise of God?
4. Do I love money and the things money can buy—fine homes, fine clothing, fast cars, vacations, even fine education—more than I love my fellowmen, especially the sick and afflicted, the poor and the hungry?
5. Am I lifted up in the pride of my heart because I have greater learning or more material goods than my neighbor?
6. Do I resent those who have more than I have in the way of learning, material goods, or social position?
7. Am I helping the poor, the sick, the needy, and the afflicted? Be specific!

8. Am I meek and lowly of heart? (The Savior is!)
9. Do I express gratitude and praise to family members?
10. Do I refuse to forgive anyone on earth? Am I holding a grudge against anyone?
11. Am I truly supportive of Church leaders, refraining from criticism? Am I envious of anyone in a "higher" position?
12. Do I esteem others (even the "least of these") as myself?
13. Do I express my gratitude to my Eternal Father daily?
14. Do I say, "'What would God have me do with my life?' rather than 'What do I want out of life?'"

Remember what President Benson said: "My beloved brethren and sisters, as we cleanse the inner vessel, there will have to be changes made in our own personal lives, in our families, and in the Church. The proud do not change to improve, but defend their position by rationalizing. Repentance means change, and it takes a humble person to change. But we can do it." (CR, *Ensign*, May 1986, p. 7.)

President Benson stated his faith in us. We can change. We can repent, humble ourselves before the Lord, and cleanse the inner vessel.

Jesus Christ told Moroni the reward for overcoming his imperfection: "Because thou hast seen thy weakness thou shalt be made strong, even unto the sitting down in the place which I have prepared in the mansions of my Father." (Ether 12:37.)

The Lord will also strengthen us if we will be humble and have faith in Him. He will enable us to overcome our pride, follow Him, live His commandments and gain eternal life.

18

You Can Forgive
and Receive Forgiveness

We Are Required to Forgive

From time to time in our lives all of us are offended by the words or actions of another. In the scriptures we read, "Woe unto the world because of offences! for it must needs be that offences come; but woe to that man by whom the offence cometh!" (Matthew 18:7.) Offenses come, and people are hurt. It is no problem for us as mortals to understand the law of justice: punishment is justly deserved by an offender. But what of the innocent one, the offended one? What course of action should one choose when offenses come? We know we are to avoid giving offense, but is something more expected of one seeking to live a law of Christ-like love? If we are on a quest for purity of life, for peace and harmony in our lives, we do have a standard to which we should adhere.

What is our obligation when offended by another? Elder Marion D. Hanks said,

What is our response when we are offended, misunderstood, unfairly or unkindly treated, or sinned against, made an offender for a word, falsely accused, passed over, hurt by those we love, our offerings rejected? Do we resent, become bitter, hold a grudge? Or do we resolve the problem if we can, forgive, and rid ourselves of the burden?

The nature of our response to such situations may well determine the nature and quality of our lives, here and eternally. . . .

It is required of us to forgive. Our salvation depends upon it. (CR, *Ensign*, January 1974, p. 20.)

All too often in these situations we focus on the duty of the offender to apologize and make things right. However, it is also the obligation of the *offended* one to forgive. Elder Hanks was referring to the Lord's words in the Doctrine and Covenants:

> My disciples, in days of old, sought occasion against one another and forgave not one another in their hearts; and for this evil they were afflicted and sorely chastened.
>
> Wherefore, I say unto you, that ye ought to forgive one another; for he that forgiveth not his brother his trespasses standeth condemned before the Lord; for there remaineth in him the greater sin.
>
> I, the Lord, will forgive whom I will forgive, but of you it is required to forgive all men. (D&C 64:8-10.)

Those who refuse to forgive when offenses happen become the greater sinners!

We Are to Forgive Regardless of the Attitude of the Offender

President Spencer W. Kimball referred to the same scripture (D&C 64:8-10) in the following account:

> I was struggling with a community problem in a small ward in the East where two prominent men, leaders of the people, were deadlocked in a long and unrelenting feud. . . . Nearly all the people of the ward were involved. Rumors spread and differences were aired and gossip became tongues of fire until the little community was divided by a deep gulf. . . . I was sent to clear up the matter. I arrived at the frustrated community about 6 p.m., Sunday night, and immediately went into session with the principal combatants.
>
> How we struggled! How I pleaded and warned and begged and urged! Nothing seemed to be moving them. Each antagonist was so sure that he was right and justified that it was impossible to budge him.
>
> The hours were passing—it was now long after midnight . . . the atmosphere was still one of ill temper and ugliness. Stubborn resistance would not give way. Then it happened. I aimlessly opened my Doctrine and Covenants again and there before me it was . . . the very answer.

[Section 64] It was an appeal and an imploring and a threat and seemed to be coming direct from the Lord. I read from the seventh verse on, but the quarreling participants yielded not an inch until I came to the ninth verse. Then I saw them flinch, startled, wondering. Could that be right? The Lord was saying to us—to all of us—

"Wherefore, I say unto you, that ye ought to forgive one another."

This was an obligation. They had heard it before. They had said it in repeating the Lord's Prayer. But now: ". . . for he that forgiveth not his brother his trespasses standeth condemned before the Lord . . ."

In their hearts, they may have been saying: "Well, I might forgive if he repents and asks forgiveness, but he must make the first move." Then the full impact of the last line seemed to strike them: "For there remaineth in him the greater sin."

"What? Does that mean I must forgive even if my antagonist remains cold and indifferent and mean?" There is no mistaking it.

. . . Sometimes men get satisfactions from seeing the other party on his knees and grovelling in the dust, but that is not the gospel way.

Shocked, the two men sat up, listened, pondered a minute, then began to yield. This scripture added to all the others read brought them to their knees. Two a.m. and two bitter adversaries were shaking hands, smiling and forgiving and asking forgiveness. Two men were in a meaningful embrace. This hour was holy. Old grievances were forgiven and forgotten, and enemies became friends again. No reference was ever made again to the differences . . . peace was restored. (*The Miracle of Forgiveness*, pp. 281-82.)

We have all been in situations where we feel justified in our resentment against another, even to the point of involving others in our dispute, or doing something to get even. But from this account we learn that revenge is a response of the carnal, not the spiritual man, and that forgiving others is an obligation, if we wish to receive the blessings and avoid the condemnation of the Lord. We also learn that forgiving others is required no matter what their attitude is. As with these two men, that holy moment of joy and peace will come to us after we have truly forgiven one who has offended us.

The requirement is that we forgive all who offend us regardless of whether they make amends or not. President Kimball added,

"Yes, to be in the right we must forgive, and we must do so *without regard to whether or not our antagonist repents*, or how sincere is his transformation, or whether or not he asks our forgiveness." (*Miracle of Forgiveness*, p. 283.)

Peter asked Jesus the question, "Lord, how oft shall my brother sin against me, and I forgive him? till seven times?

Jesus answered, "I say not unto thee, Until seven times: but, Until seventy times seven." (Matthew 18:21-22)

President Kimball quoted a former prophet in admonishing us to forgive others regardless of their attitude:

> . . . The admonition of President Joseph F. Smith in 1902 is as applicable now as then:
>
> "We hope and pray that you will . . . forgive one another and never from this time forth . . . bear malice toward another fellow creature.
>
> ". . . It is extremely hurtful for any man holding the gift of the Holy Ghost to harbor a spirit of envy, or malice, or retaliations, or intolerance toward or against his fellow man. We ought to say in our hearts, "Let God judge between me and thee, but as for me, I will forgive." I want to say to you that Latter-day Saints who harbor a feeling of unforgiveness in their souls are more censurable than the one who has sinned against them. Go home and dismiss envy and hatred from your hearts: dismiss the feeling of unforgiveness; and cultivate in your souls that spirit of Christ which cried out upon the cross, "Father, forgive them; for they know not what they do." This is the spirit that Latter-day Saints ought to possess all the day long."
>
> . . . We must follow the example and the teaching of the Master, who said: ". . . Ye ought to say in your hearts—let God judge between me and thee, and reward thee according to thy deeds." (D&C 64:11.) But men often are unwilling to leave it to the Lord, fearing perhaps that the Lord might be too merciful, less severe than is proper in the case. (*The Miracle of Forgiveness*, pp. 282-83.)

Isn't it interesting that we who are so in need of mercy ourselves are so unwilling to extend mercy to our fellow beings? As King Benjamin said, "Are we not all beggars? Do we not all depend upon the same Being, even God, for all the substance which we have? . . . Ye have been calling on his name, and begging for a remission of your sins. And has he suffered that ye have begged in vain? Nay; he has poured out his Spirit upon you, and has caused that your hearts should be filled with joy." (Mosiah 4:19-20.)

We plead with the Lord to extend His mercy toward us and forgive us of our sins, and at the same time we want Him to exact justice on those who have offended us! For this reason the Savior told the parable of the king which took account of his servants. The king forgave a great debt to one of his servants who begged, "Lord, have patience with me." This servant then went out, found a fellow servant who owed him a debt and, forgetting his own plea for patience, cast the other man into prison.

When the king heard of this, he called the unmerciful servant to him and said, "O thou wicked servant, I forgave thee all that debt, because thou desiredst me: Shouldest not thou also have had compassion on thy fellowservant, even as I had pity on thee?" So saying, the king "delivered him to the tormenters, till he should pay all that was due unto him." (Matthew 18:23-34.)

The Savior said it will be the same with us if we refuse to forgive each other. "So likewise shall my heavenly Father do also unto you, if ye from your hearts forgive not every one his brother their trespasses." (v. 35.)

Elder Marion D. Hanks explained that "not only our eternal salvation depends upon our willingness and capacity to forgive wrongs committed against us. Our joy and satisfaction in this life, and our true freedom, depend upon our doing so. . . .

". . . Even if it appears that another may be deserving of our resentment or hatred, none of us can afford to pay the price of resenting or hating, because of what it does to us. . . .

"God help us rid ourselves of resentment and pettiness and foolish pride; to love, and to forgive, in order that we may be friends with ourselves, with others, and with the Lord." ("Even as Christ Forgave," *New Era*, June 1974, pp. 5-6.)

The *New Era* had some advice for its young readers on how to forgive:

> How do you free yourself from this parasitic emotion? First of all, you ask a kind and loving Father for his help. Tell him of your pain and of your struggle to forgive. Pray specifically for charity, for the power to forgive, and for the ability to understand the friend who hurt you. Heavenly Father knows and loves both you and your friend, and he will help you heal the hurt.
>
> Of course, he will expect you to do all you can for yourself. That means first of all really *wanting* to let go of your grudge—even if it is a shield against further hurt. Then, as feelings of anger come to you, refuse to indulge them. Do not fantasize about telling your

friend off. Do not replay the incident that hurt you over and over again in your mind. Do not think of ways to get even. Refuse to do anything that nourishes your anger, and it will begin to grow weak from starvation. (Q&A, *New Era*, January 1989, p. 18.)

This is one of the hardest adjustments we can face in our lives, but Heavenly Father will help us if we ask in sweet, humble prayer. Our goal should be to learn to forgive offenses instantly, so that when the offense is complete, our forgiveness is also complete. This way we don't have to suffer the bitterness, hatred, and revengeful feelings that come to those who fail to forgive. These feelings not only make us miserable, but decrease our spirituality and prevent our growth. Let us extend mercy to others, even as we hope for the mercy of the Lord to be extended to us in our unworthiness.

We Must Forgive Others Completely

When we forgive others, we are to do so completely. It is not enough to simply *say* we forgive. We must forgive from our hearts and cleanse ourselves of any bitterness and hard feelings. President Spencer W. Kimball spoke of the need to completely forgive when he said:

Many people, when brought to a reconciliation with others, say that they forgive, but they continue to hold malice, continue to suspect the other party, continue to disbelieve the other's sincerity. This is sin, for when a reconciliation has been effected and when repentance is claimed, each should forgive and forget, build immediately the fences which have been breached, and restore the former compatibility. . . . Forgiveness means forgetfulness. One woman had 'gone through' a reconciliation in a branch and had made the physical motions and verbal statements indicating it, and expressed the mouthy words forgiving. Then with flashing eyes, she remarked, "I will forgive her, but I have a memory like an elephant. I'll never forget." Her pretended adjustment was valueless and void. She still harbored the bitterness. . . . Worse still, she stood "condemned before the Lord," and there remained in her an even greater sin than in the one who, she claimed, had injured her.
Little did this antagonistic woman realize that she had not forgiven at all. . . . [True forgiveness] must be a purging of feelings and thoughts and bitternesses. Mere words avail nothing. (*The Miracle of Forgiveness*, pp. 262-63.)

Here President Kimball tells us true forgiveness is from the heart, and is much more than just our outward actions. Further, if we do not make the full forgiveness in our hearts, we ourselves are sinning. If we truly forgive, we purge our feelings, our thoughts, and our emotions of harbored bitterness. No one says that is easy, but it is truly necessary. It is one of the stated requirements of receiving forgiveness for our own transgressions.

Elder Theodore M. Burton said, "It is wicked to reject a child of God simply because he made an error." He clarified, "We need not be tolerant of the sin, but we must become tolerant and forgiving of the sinner." (CR, *Ensign*, May 1983, p. 71.)

"Agree With Thine Adversary Quickly"

When we are offended we should forgive quickly. Jesus taught that if we are angry with our brother and come to leave an offering at the altar, we should first go and be reconciled before we are worthy to make offering to the Lord. He admonished us to "Agree with thine adversary quickly." (See Matthew 5:21-26.) He warns that failure to do so will require that we pay "the uttermost farthing."

Elder Robert L. Simpson said, "Not one of us is incapable of calling to mind, this very instant, a person who has offended in some way; and if my understanding of the scriptures is correct, we had better make it a matter of urgent business to forgive that person, whether he asks it or not. Woe unto that man who stands stubbornly in the way of another's plea for repentance by failure to forgive, 'for he that forgiveth not his brother his trespasses standeth condemned before the Lord; for there remaineth in him the greater sin.' (D&C 64:9) . . . Slow forgiveness is almost no forgiveness." (CR, *Improvement Era*, December 1966, p. 1149.)

Bishop H. Burke Petersen said,

What will you do when hurt by another? The safe way, the sure way, the right way is to look inward and immediately start the cleansing process. The wise and the happy person removes first the impurities from within. The longer the poison of resentment and unforgiveness stays in a body, the greater and longer lasting is its destructive effect. As long as we blame others for our condition or circumstance and build a wall of self-justification around ourselves, our strength will diminish and our power and ability to rise above our situation will fade away. The poison of revenge, or of unforgiving thoughts or attitudes, unless removed, will destroy the soul in which it is harbored . . . instead, approach men in the spirit of the Master, even those who "despitefully use you." (Matthew 5:44.) Let us pray —rather, let us plead for the spirit of forgiveness. Let us look for the good in each other—not the flaws. (CR, *Ensign*, November 1983, pp. 59-60.)

We should make a commitment to forgive all offenses as they are happening, or at least to forgive daily. Through sincere prayer the Lord will help us keep this commitment.

However, if we choose not to forgive, if we allow ourselves to dwell on the offense, bad feelings will grow. The hurt will turn to resentment and then to bitterness. By being unforgiving we give Satan an opportunity to come into our lives—he will intensify the process by putting more evil thoughts in our minds. If we still don't forgive we will probably start seeking revenge. From here it will take a lot of work and a lot of prayer to get rid of the bad feelings—we may have to beg our Father in Heaven to take away the cruel emotions and restore the love. But we cannot allow the poison of unforgiveness to destroy our souls. We must take action with ourselves before we commit a terrible wrong. We must persist in our effort, and in our sincere prayers, and Heavenly Father will take away the hurt and restore our feelings of love, forgiveness, and peace again.

President David O. McKay said, "I cannot think that a Latter-day Saint will hold enmity in his heart if he will sincerely, in secret, pray God to remove from his heart all feelings of envy and malice toward any of his fellow men." (CR, *Improvement Era*, June 1961, p. 390.)

Peace and Joy Come Through Forgiveness

When we forgive those who have offended us, we make it possible for the Spirit to enter our hearts and bring us peace and joy. As Elder Hanks said, true forgiveness brings joy, satisfaction, and true freedom.

President Kimball relates the story of a man who discovered blessings that come when we truly forgive those who have wronged us. This man, Glenn Kempton, lost his father to a murderer's bullet when just a small boy. He hated his father's assassin for many years. In his own words:

. . . One day while reading the New Testament, I came to Matthew, fifth chapter, verses 43 to 45, wherein Jesus said:

"Ye have heard that it hath been said, Thou shalt love thy neighbour, and hate thine enemy. But I say unto you, Love your enemies, bless them that curse you, do good to them that hate you, and pray for them which despitefully use you, and persecute you; that ye may be the children of your Father which is in heaven. . . ."

Here it was, the words of the Savior saying we should forgive. This applied to me. I read those verses again and again and it still meant forgiveness. Not very long after this, I found in the 64th section of the Doctrine and Covenants, verses 9 and 10, more of the Savior's words:

"Wherefore, I say unto you, that ye ought to forgive one another; for he that forgiveth not his brother his trespasses standeth condemned before the Lord; for there remaineth in him the greater sin. I, the Lord, will forgive whom I will forgive, but of you it is required to forgive all men."

He knew in his heart he must forgive the man, but procrastination held him, and years went by before he took action. He struggled with feelings of guilt at not having the courage to go forward and forgive the man. He continues,

A few years ago, just shortly before Christmas, a season when the love of Christ abounds and the spirit of giving and forgiving gets inside of us, my wife and I were in Phoenix on a short trip. Having concluded our business in the middle of the second afternoon, we started home. As we rode along, I expressed the desire to detour and return home via Florence, for that is where the state prison is located. My wife readily assented.

It was after visiting hours when we arrived but I went on inside and asked for the warden. I was directed to his office.

After I had introduced myself and expressed a desire to meet and talk to Tom Powers, a puzzled expression came over the warden's face, but after only a slight hesitation, he said, "I'm sure that can be arranged." Whereupon he dispatched a guard down into the compound who soon returned with Tom. We were introduced, and led into the parole room where we had a long talk. We went back to that cold, gray February morning thirty years before, re-enacting that whole terrible tragedy. We talked for perhaps an hour and a half.

Finally, I said, "Tom, you made a mistake for which you owe a debt to society for which I feel you must continue to pay, just the same as I must continue to pay the price for having been reared without a father."

Then I stood and extended my hand. He stood and took it. I continued, "With all my heart, I forgive you for this awful thing that has come into our lives."

He bowed his head and I left him there. I don't know how he felt then, and I don't know how he feels now, but my witness to you is that it is a glorious thing when bitterness and hatred go out of your heart and forgiveness comes in.

I thanked the warden for his kindness, and as I walked out the door and down that long flight of steps I knew that forgiveness was better than revenge, for I had experienced it.

As we drove home in the gathering twilight, a sweet and peaceful calm came over me. Out of pure gratitude I placed my arm around my wife, who understood, for I know that we had now found a broader, richer and more abundant life.

President Kimball concludes: "Not only had Glenn Kempton found the joy of forgiving, but the example he set as a faithful Latter-day Saint has had far-reaching influence on many others who know his story and have heard his testimony.

"'Blessed are the merciful: for they shall obtain mercy.'" (*The Miracle of Forgiveness*, pp. 289-293.)

This is a great example of forgiveness for all of us. After this man had rid himself of unforgiving feelings, the darkness went out of his heart and peace came in. In the gospel light, he found true freedom in a "more abundant life."

If Glenn Kempton could forgive the man who killed his father, surely we can forgive those who offend us.

Our Willingness to Forgive Others Affects Our Own Lives

Just as we can, by forgiving others, find peace and joy, so, when we refuse to forgive those who have offended us, we poison our own souls and destroy our own peace. By being unforgiving we wither our spirits. We develop some of the following problems: a proud heart, bad feelings, resentment, ill will, bitterness, hatred, anger, malice, grudges, revengeful hearts, rationalization that unforgiveness is all right. We deprive ourselves of abundance in our lives. It goes both ways. Consider these stories told by President Kimball:

> There was a young mother who lost her husband. The family had been in poor circumstances, and the insurance policy was only $2,000. The company promptly delivered the check for that amount as soon as proof of death was furnished. The young widow concluded she should save this for emergencies, and accordingly deposited it in the bank. Others knew of her savings, and one kinsman convinced her that she should lend the $2,000 to him at a high rate of interest.
>
> Years passed, and she had received neither principle nor interest and she noticed that the borrower avoided her and made evasive promises when she asked him about the money. Now she needed the money and it could not be had.
>
> "How I hate him," she told me, and her voice breathed venom and bitterness and her dark eyes flashed. To think that an able-bodied man would defraud a young widow with a family to support! "How I loathe him!" she repeated over and over. Then I told her the Kempton story. She listened intently. I saw she was impressed. At the conclusion there were tears in her eyes, and she whispered: "Thank you. Thank you, sincerely. Surely I, too, must forgive my enemy. I will now cleanse my heart of its bitterness. I do not expect ever to receive the money, but I leave my offender in the hands of the Lord."
>
> Weeks later she saw me again and confessed that those intervening weeks had been the happiest in her life. A new peace had over-shadowed her and she was able to pray for the offender and forgive him, even though she never received back a single dollar.
>
> I saw a woman once whose little girl had been violated. "I will never forgive the culprit so long as I live," she repeated every time it came into her mind. Vicious and ugly was the act. Anyone should be shocked and disturbed at such a crime, but to be unwilling to forgive is not Christ-like. The foul deed was done and could *not* be undone. The culprit had been disciplined. In her bitterness the woman shriveled and shrank. (*The Miracle of Forgiveness*, pp. 293-94.)

In the first story the woman forgave her offender. She found peace when she was able to pray for the offender and forgive him. In the second story, the woman didn't forgive her offender. She cultivated her own anguish. Her bitterness poisoned her own life. What a terrible price we must pay if we fail to forgive!

Bishop H. Burke Petersen said, "I want to speak of a weakness that has thwarted the spiritual growth of men through the ages. . . . It poisons the spirit of a person to the point that one is hobbled by its debilitating power. It has the power to drag people to the depths of hell; yet, when released from its hold, they may soar to celestial heights. It has kept many from rising to their full potential. It has been a roadblock to the talented and to the favored. It is one of the most effective tools of Satan. We are speaking of an unforgiving and unforgetting spirit." (CR, *Ensign*, November 1983, p. 59.)

The best way to combat Satan's influence in this area of our lives is to be a forgiving person. I believe we need God's help to succeed. Our prayers in this regard are among the most important pleadings we may have with our Father in Heaven. To become a forgiving and forgetting person is vital to our successful relationships with others, and essential to a feeling of well-being and acceptance of ourselves. If we keep praying sincerely, this will happen.

The law of love comes into play here most particularly. Jesus taught: "Love your enemies, bless them that curse you, do good to them that hate you, and pray for them which despitefully use you, and persecute you." (Matthew 5:44.) Having the courage to pray for our offender—bless them, serve them—will lead to loving them, which is what Jesus commanded us. What joy that will cause!

President Gordon B. Hinckley adds: "So many of us are prone to say we forgive, when in fact we are unwilling to forget. If the Lord is willing to forget the sins of the repentant, then why are so many of us inclined to bring up the past again and again? Here is a great lesson we all need to learn. There is no true forgiveness without forgetting." ("The Order and Will of God," *Ensign*, January 1989, p. 5.)

It is a great challenge to cleanse one's heart of all envy, hatred, bitterness, grudges, and revengeful feelings, but to have restored happiness, contentment, and peace of mind is the reward of those who forgive and forget.

Forgiveness in the Eternal Plan

Eternal life is conditioned upon being a forgiving person, "For, if ye forgive men their trespasses your heavenly Father will also forgive you; But if ye forgive not men their trespasses neither will your Father forgive your trespasses." (3 Nephi 13:14-15) If our Father in Heaven does not forgive us our trespasses, we cannot receive eternal life.

Elder Marion D. Hanks asks, "Does it not seem a supreme impudence to ask and expect God to forgive when we do not forgive?—openly? and 'in our hearts'?" (CR, *Ensign*, January 1974, p. 20.)

However, if we do forgive others we are promised, "Inasmuch as you have forgiven one another your trespasses, even so I, the Lord, forgive you." (D&C 82:1.)

Elder Robert L. Simpson spoke of the connection between repentance and forgiveness, saying:

Not only need we forgive to be forgiven, but we must also repent to earn this great blessing. . . . (D&C 58:42.)

This, brothers and sisters, is the hope of mankind, to have our mistakes wiped clean. There is no other way; there are no shortcuts in the kingdom of God. We repent, we forgive, we progress, and may we remind ourselves once more, it all starts with our own willingness to forgive one another. Yes, after all is said and done, the Golden Rule still stands supreme, "Do unto others as you would have others do unto you." (See Matthew 7:12.) First forgive and then stand eligible in the sight of God to be forgiven. The simplicity of the process testifies of its divinity." (CR, *Improvement Era*, December 1966, p. 1148.)

The divine process is centered on the idea of forgiveness. We sin, we err, we require forgiveness to be reconciled to the divine will. And we must forgive in order to be forgiven—it is an essential part of our repentance. Our baptism shows our willingness to accept the Lord's Atonement. The sacrament represents both that willingness and the Lord's promise of forgiveness. We should take these things seriously and make being forgiving an integral part of our desire to become Christlike.

Elder Jeffrey R. Holland wrote: "The Latter-day Saint who faithfully goes to sacrament meeting but is no more merciful or patient or forgiving as a result, . . . [goes] through the motions of the ordinances without loyalty to or understanding of the reasons for which these ordinances were established—obedience, gentleness, and loving kindness in the search for forgiveness of their sins." ("I Stand All Amazed," *Ensign*, August 1986, p. 70.)

And Elder Dallin Oaks said, "Among the things we should remember about the Savior is that there are things we should forget about our fellowmen—the wrongs they have done us. . . . If we always remember our Savior, we will forgive and forget grievances against those who have wronged us." (CR, *Ensign*, May 1988, pp. 30-31.)

In order to be Christlike, we must always forgive, regardless of the offense or of the attitude of the offender. If we do not forgive others, should we partake of the sacrament? President Kimball says, "Unless a person forgives his brother his trespasses *with all his heart* he is unfit to partake of the sacrament." (*The Miracle of Forgiveness*, p. 264.) Being unforgiving is a willful holding on to hard feelings. We should make it a practice to earnestly rid ourselves of these feelings, and thus make ourselves worthy and ready to take the emblems of the Lord's sacrifice.

Elder Holland's perceptive words explain this in the eternal viewpoint: "Surely the reason Christ said "Father, forgive them" was because even in the weakened and terribly trying hour he faced, he knew that this was the message he had come through all eternity to deliver . . . that not *in spite of* injustice and brutality and unkindness and disobedience but precisely *because* of them had he come to extend forgiveness to the family of man." (*Ensign*, August 1986, p. 72.)

"It must needs be that offenses come . . ." (Matthew 18:7) and so, our Savior's mission extended the hope of forgiveness to all.

Elder Holland continued: "Perhaps the highest and holiest and purest act of cleansing . . . would be to say in the face of unkindness and injustice that you do yet more truly 'love your enemies and bless them that curse you, do good to them that hate you, and pray for them that despitefully use you, and persecute you.' That is the demanding pathway of perfection." (Matthew 5:44.) (p. 72.)

President Harold B. Lee shared a precious experience not long after he was called into the Quorum of the Twelve:

> I bear you my humble testimony, as one of the humblest among you: I know there are powers that can draw close to one who fills his heart with the kind of love of which . . . has [been] spoken. . . . I came to a night, some years ago, when on my bed, I realized that before I could be worthy of the high place to which I had been called, I must love and forgive every soul that walked the earth, and in that time I came to know and I received a peace and a direction and a comfort, and an inspiration, that told me things to come and gave me impressions that I knew were from a divine source. I know that these things are true and that God lives, that Jesus is the Christ, and that each of us might live the abundant life by drawing thus close to him. (CR, *Improvement Era*, November 1946, p. 760.)

Forgiving Ourselves

The principle of forgiveness includes forgiving ourselves. After we have repented of a sin we need to accept God's forgiveness. We need to forgive ourselves and get on with our lives. "Behold, he who has repented of his sins, the same is forgiven, and I, the Lord, remember them no more." (D&C 58:42.) "But as oft as they repented and sought forgiveness, with real intent, they were forgiven." (Moroni 6:8.) The Lord is quick to forgive us once we have repented of our sins.

If the Lord remembers our sins no more, neither should we. Once we have repented of our sins we should forgive ourselves completely. If we continue to dwell on them they will fester in our souls and hold us back.

Elder Sterling W. Sill tells this account of someone who didn't forgive herself, and the consequences in her life:

> Sometime ago I talked with a woman 53 years of age who had committed a moral transgression at age 18. She understood that her sin was very serious, but because she had repented a thousand times we can depend on the Lord's promise that he had forgiven her. But she had never forgiven herself. Because she felt unclean and inferior, she withdrew from her friends, refused to marry, and became a kind of social and spiritual recluse. For 35 years she downgraded herself with bitter regrets and accusations. Her life looking back upon her sin has turned her into something far below the wonderful person that God intended her to be. Her sin at age 18 was very serious. But for 35 years she has been adding to her sin by wasting the most valuable thing in the world, which is a splendid human life. (*What Doth It Profit*, p. 183.)

Through Jesus Christ's atonement and our repentance we become clean—if the Lord has pronounced us clean, should we pronounce ourselves unclean? When we repent, our debt of sin is then paid in full and we are once more innocent before God. We are then free indeed—clean and free to move ahead with our lives in the full service of the Lord.

Forgiveness in the Family

Forgiveness is a particularly important attribute in the close personal relationships in the family. Because of the private and intimate nature of family life, we can give offense easily, and we are vulnerable to being offended by those who are most important to us. Great care should be taken to preserve these most precious attachments and show love in all our associations with family members.

President Gordon B. Hinckley told this story of what can happen in a marriage when people fail to forgive one another:

> Not long ago I listened at length to a couple who sat across the desk from me. There was bitterness between them. I know that at one time their love was deep and true. But each had developed a habit of speaking of the faults of the other. Unwilling to forgive the kind of mistakes we all make, and unwilling to forget them and live above them with forbearance, they had carped at one another until the love they once knew had been smothered. It had turned to ashes with the decree of a so-called no fault divorce. Now there is only loneliness and recrimination. I am satisfied that had there been even a small measure of repentance and forgiveness, they would still be together, enjoying the companionship that had so richly blessed their earlier years. (CR, *Ensign*, November 1980, p. 62.)

Marriage, the closest of all relationships, may require forgiveness on a daily basis. It is crippling to our partner when we continually dwell on their shortcomings, bringing up offenses, real or imagined, from the past. If a person is having trouble forgiving, a good place to start is with one's wife or husband. There may be things that rankle from times past, making today's interactions more bristly than they need be. Clearing up any such problems would be so beneficial to the relationship with each other and with the children as well.

We suggest this approach. Be humble. Use prayer, and fasting if necessary, telling Heavenly Father how important this matter is. Ponder and pray until your heart is right. Then go to your spouse and say that you are sorry for offenses which you have given, and that you intend to avoid giving offense in the future. Suggest that together you seek complete forgiveness from each other of all hard feelings between you. Have a clean heart, freely offering forgiveness for any offenses that may have troubled you. Promise sincerely that you intend to be more accepting in the future, because your marriage is most precious to your life. If your spouse is ready for this, it can be a beautiful beginning. Maybe you will need to fast and pray together in order to effect complete forgiveness, but be understanding, be patient, and do whatever it takes to purge your souls of any resentment, unkindness, or revengeful feelings.

Then forgive and forget daily. When you have your sweetheart's prayer before retiring to bed each night, make sure you have resolved any difficulty that the day may have brought. We humbly suggest that this will increase the happiness in any home.

This checklist will help to identify a truly forgiving attitude toward a marriage partner:

Avoid:

1. Ill will, resentment, bitterness, hatred, or revengeful feelings.
2. Condemnatory words.
3. Coldness or indifference.
4. Suspicion.
5. Harboring past grievances.

Apply:

1. Acceptance.
2. Warmth, consideration, and caring.
3. Trust and respect.
4. Words of praise, commendation, and admiration.
5. Feelings of peace, conciliation, and love.

Forgiving increases our love for each other. When the whole family lives the law of forgiveness, a sweet spirit will fill the home. Resentment, annoyance, critical feelings, grudges, and malice, are the opposite of forgiveness. Satan laughs at the misery we get into by our unforgiving attitudes. Patience, love, tenderness, approval, thoughtfulness, and kindness are of God. He is pleased when family members are thoughtful and pleasant to each other.

Young people growing up may have a hard time forgiving a family member or a friend for an offense that happened. It is easy for them to rationalize that they are justified because of the hurt they felt, or the consequences of the offense. Harboring unforgiving feelings will affect their whole life in a negative way. It is important to help young family members understand the law of forgiveness, to promote family happiness and solidarity, and to help them resolve problems early in life.

Offenses happen. That cannot be changed. What makes the difference is the way we react at the time of the offense, and afterward. Will we compound the original injustice by injuring the offender? Arda Jean's mother had a truism: "Two wrongs never made a right." Wrong is wrong, even if done in retaliation for wrong.

The full law of forgiveness includes penalties for being unforgiving, and blessings that attend forgiveness and mercy. We should pray that

Heavenly Father will soften our hearts and make us forgiving—pray that He will remove the hurt. Then we must do our part by consciously exchanging feelings of resentment for feelings of acceptance. Doing acts of service for the offending person will generate love. We must continue to pray until our heart is changed.

Elder Robert L. Simpson said, "As we forgive, we increase our capacity for light and understanding. . . . As we forgive, our capacity for love expands toward heaven." (CR, *Improvement Era*, December 1966, p. 1149.)

Think of living in a home where everyone forgives all offenses as they happen, where family members are more understanding, more kind and generous with time and talents—think of working together in unity and kindness, making sacrifices for each other, caring sincerely about the welfare of each other.

What an opportunity for growth and development. Forgiveness is an important tool to help solve problems and grow closer together. Under these conditions the Spirit of the Lord abounds in the home. The Savior's love becomes an actual presence. The Holy Ghost can rest upon the family. Hearts will be filled with gladness. Love will be encircling and joy will be full.

Sometimes offenses happen when children are growing up, and in later years, children have a hard time forgiving the parent for these offenses. These are especially painful, because of the emotion involved. The offended child feels deprivation of love, plus betrayal of trust. The agony grows with time, and bitterness towards the parent colors their perspective. This is a particularly difficult situation to resolve. The offenses may be very real, or they may be enlarged by the emotions and memory of pain and passing time. The real solution is in a change of outlook and the process of forgiving. The harm one causes by anger and alienation is an offense on the part of the other. Much better to overlook, pardon, and forgive.

Elder Richard G. Scott spoke about therapy wherein a person is encouraged to remember details of events in their childhood: "Detailed leading questions that probe your past may unwittingly trigger thoughts that are more imagination or fantasy than reality. They could lead to condemnation of another for acts that were not committed. While likely few in number, I know of cases where such therapy has caused great injustice to the innocent from unwittingly stimulated accusations that were later proven false. Memory, particularly adult memory of childhood experiences, is fallible. Remember, false accusation is also a sin." (CR, *Ensign*, May 1992, p. 33.)

A son or daughter who is harboring offenses would do well to forgive the parents today. It is important to restore a loving relationship with them. This forgiveness may be difficult to achieve. It may take a lot of prayer and effort but the peace that comes with a forgiving heart is worth any effort.

Sometimes a person is in a situation where family members are abusive. Do not suppose that forgiveness means a person must be submissive to abuse or adverse circumstances. Seek help, and still be forgiving.

Elder H. Burke Peterson said, "No one can be classed as a true follower of the Savior who is not in the process of removing from his heart and mind every feeling of ill will, bitterness, hatred, envy, or jealousy toward another." (CR, *Ensign*, November 1983, p. 60.)

A Story of Forgiveness

We are familiar with heart-tugging stories from the scriptures where our heroes were abused or killed by wicked offenders in the most heinous fashion. And yet they were able to keep pure charity in their hearts and forgive and pray for the perpetrators. Most of us will never be offended as deeply as our Savior, Paul, and Stephen were. However, into every life comes those moments when we face a personal Gethsemane, when forgiving another will seem very difficult. Elder Boyd K. Packer tells such an account:

> Many years ago I was taught a lesson by a man I admired very much. He was as saintly a man as I have ever known. He was steady and serene, with a deep spiritual strength that many drew upon . . .
>
> On one occasion when we were alone and the spirit was right, he gave me a lesson for my life from an experience in his. Although I thought I had known him, he told me things I would not have supposed. . . .
>
> He married a lovely young woman, and presently everything in his life was just right. He was well employed, with a bright future. They were deeply in love, and she was expecting their first child.
>
> The night the baby was to be born there were complications. The only doctor was somewhere in the countryside tending to the sick.

They were not able to find him. After many hours of labor the condition of the mother-to-be became desperate.

Finally the doctor arrived. He sensed an emergency, acted quickly, and soon had things in order. The baby was born and the crisis, it appeared, was over.

Some days later the young mother died from the very infection that the doctor had been treating at the other home that night.

My friend's world was shattered. Everything was not right now; everything was all wrong. He had lost his wife, his sweetheart. He had no way to take care of a tiny baby and at once tend to his work.

As the weeks wore on his grief festered. "That doctor should not be allowed to practice," he would say. "He brought that infection to my wife; if he had been careful she would be alive today." He thought of little else, and in his bitterness he became threatening.

Then one night a knock came at his door. A little youngster said, simply, "Daddy wants you to come over. He wants to talk to you."

"Daddy" was the stake president. A grieving, heartbroken young man went to see his spiritual leader. This spiritual shepherd had been watching his flock and had something to say to him.

The counsel from this wise servant was simply: "John, leave it alone. Nothing you do about it will bring her back. Anything you do will make it worse. John, leave it alone."

My friend told me then that this had been his trial, his Gethsemane.

How could he leave it alone? Right was right! A terrible wrong had been committed, and somebody must pay for it.

He struggled in agony to get hold of himself. It did not happen at once. Finally he determined that whatever else the issues were, he should be obedient. . . .

He determined to follow the counsel of that wise spiritual leader. He would leave it alone.

Then he told me, "I was an old man before I finally understood. It was not until I was an old man that I could finally see a poor country doctor—overworked, underpaid, run ragged from patient to patient, with little proper medicine, no hospital, few instruments. He struggled to save lives, and succeeded for the most part.

"He had come in a moment of crisis when two lives hung in the balance and had acted without delay.

"I was an old man," he repeated, "before I finally understood. I would have ruined my life," he said, "and the lives of others."

Many times he had thanked the Lord on his knees for a wise spiritual leader who counseled simply, "John, leave it alone."

And that is my counsel to you. If you have festering sores, a grudge, some bitterness, disappointment, or jealousy, get hold of yourself. You may not be able to control things out there with others, but you can control things here, inside of you.

I say, therefore: John, leave it alone. Mary, leave it alone. (CR, *Ensign*, November 1977, p. 60.)

You Can Do It

How will we treat our own "Gethsemane?" Will we be able to take the inspired advice and *leave it alone*? Our own lives hang in the balance. We can choose peace, virtue, and service, or we can choose revenge, suffering, and hindrance in our lives and those around us. The choice is ours—we have the ability to carve a path of harmony, accord, and inspiration. With our own determination and the help of the Lord, we can learn to forgive others.

Elder Robert L. Simpson said, "Biblical history tells us that no mortal man has ever been subjected to the humility, the pain, the suffering that were experienced by the Savior of the world during his final hours of mortality.

". . . There he hung, his body broken and bleeding, still taunted by his enemies; and it was in the midst of all this that Jesus pled perhaps quietly, with deep reverence, 'Father, forgive them; for they know not what they do. . . .' (Luke 23:34.)" (CR, *Improvement Era*, December 1966, p. 1148.)

Surely the Savior is our best example of forgiveness. He asked "What manner of men ought ye to be?" He then answered, "Even as I am." (3 Nephi 27:27.)

To summarize and restate the things we have learned in this chapter:

1. God has commanded us to forgive. "I, the Lord will forgive whom I will forgive, but *of you it is required to forgive all men.*" (D&C 64:9-10, emphasis added.)

2. We must forgive regardless of the attitude of the offender. "To be in the right we must forgive, and we must do so *without regard to whether or not our antagonist repents*, or how sincere is his transfor-

mation, or whether or not he asks our forgiveness" (Spencer W. Kimball, *The Miracle of Forgiveness*, pp. 282-83).

3. Our willingness to forgive others affects our own lives. "It has kept many from rising to their full potential. It has been a roadblock to the talented and to the favored. It is one of the most effective tools of Satan. We are speaking of an unforgiving and unforgetting spirit." (Bishop H. Burke Peterson, CR, *Ensign*, November 1983, p. 59.)

4. If we do not forgive others we should not partake of the sacrament. President Kimball says, "Unless a person forgives his brother his trespasses *with all his heart* he is unfit to partake of the sacrament." (*The Miracle of Forgiveness*, p. 264.)

5. We should forgive others quickly. "The longer the poison of resentment and unforgiveness stays in a body, the greater and longer lasting is its destructive effect. As long as we blame others for our condition or circumstance and build a wall of self-justification around ourselves, our strength will diminish and our power and ability to rise above our situation will fade away. The poison of revenge, or of unforgiving thoughts or attitudes, unless removed, will destroy the soul in which it is harbored." (Bishop H. Burke Peterson, CR, *Ensign*, November 1983, p. 59.)

6. Forgiving others is necessary for our salvation. "For if ye forgive men their trespasses, your heavenly Father will also forgive you: But if ye forgive not men their trespasses, neither will your Father forgive your trespasses." (Matthew 6:14-15.)

7. Forgiving others brings peace and joy. "Not only our eternal salvation depends upon our willingness and capacity to forgive wrongs committed against us. Our joy and satisfaction in this life, and our true freedom, depend upon our doing so." (Marion D. Hanks, *New Era*, June 1974, pp. 5-6.)

You can do it. Be humble in your pleading, and the Lord will help you be free at last from the pain of unforgiveness. You can feel the peace of mind, the satisfaction of reconciliation, and the triumph of victory over self that comes into the heart of a forgiving, forgetting person.

19

You Can Overcome Anger

In his excellent article on controlling anger, Burton C. Kelly, of the Counseling Center faculty and professor of educational psychology at Brigham Young University, said "Imagine, for a moment, a world where few, if any, marriages end in divorce, few children shout at their parents, no parents abuse their children. Imagine a world of safe neighborhoods, peaceful governments, and healthy citizens—largely without hypertension, headaches, or backaches.

"Sound like a never-never land, unpeopled by mortals? Yet I have just described some of the probable effects of a world absent only one simple emotion—anger." ("The Case Against Anger," *Ensign*, February 1980, p. 9.)

Anger is such a destructive force for evil, it is no wonder that anger is a sin. "Anger, a sin?" you may say. "I've never thought of it as a sin, just a weakness." Let's look at some scriptures that tell us that anger is a sin.

The Sin of Anger

Solomon in the Bible calls anger *transgression*: "An angry man stirreth up strife, and a furious man aboundeth in transgression." (Proverbs 29:22.) In the New Testament Jesus forbids us from getting angry with a brother. He repeated it to the Nephites:

> Therefore come unto me and be ye saved; for verily I say unto you, that except ye shall keep my commandments, which I have commanded you at this time, ye shall in no case enter into the kingdom of heaven.

Ye have heard that it hath been said by them of old time, and it is also written before you, that thou shalt not kill, and whosoever shall kill shall be in danger of the judgment of God;

But I say unto you, that *whosoever is angry with his brother* shall be in danger of his judgment. And whosoever shall say to his brother, Raca, shall be in danger of the council; and whosoever shall say, Thou fool, shall be in danger of hell fire. (3 Nephi 12:20-22, emphasis added.)

President Spencer W. Kimball also addressed the subject of anger as sin, saying: "Killing is an act of aggression. But *anger is a thought-sin.* It may be the forerunner of murder. But if one's *thoughts* do not get vicious nor violent, he is unlikely to take life." (*The Miracle of Forgiveness*, p. 112, emphasis added.)

If we keep our minds free of anger, we avoid this "thought-sin." Elder Dallin H. Oaks also emphasized that thoughts can be a sin: "The New Testament also condemns anger and unrighteous feelings—another example of sins committed solely on the basis of thoughts. (See Matthew 5:22.)" ("The Desires of Our Hearts," *Ensign*, June 1986, p. 65.)

There are many more scriptures that condemn anger: "Let all bitterness, and wrath, and anger, and clamour, and evil speaking, be put away from you, with all malice." (Ephesians 4:31.) "Be . . . slow to wrath: For the wrath of man worketh not the righteousness of God." (James 1:19-20.)

We are to put away from us all anger. "Cease from anger, and forsake wrath: fret not thyself in any wise to do evil." (Psalms 37:8.)

The latter-day prophets also warn us against anger. President Brigham Young said, "Never suffer anger to arise in your bosoms; for, if you do, you may be overcome by evil." (*Journal of Discourses*, 6:290.) He also counseled, "Cease your anger, and sullenness of temper." (*Discourses of Brigham Young*, p. 268.) Wilford Woodruff said, "The moment a man or woman becomes angry they show a great weakness." (*Journal of Discourses*, 4:98.) President David O. McKay said, "Anger that leads a man . . . to condemn his brother is a crime." (*Pathways to Happiness*, p. 321.)

The Book of Mormon warns us that when children fight and quarrel, they commit sin: "And ye will not suffer your children that they go hungry, or naked; neither will ye suffer that they transgress the laws of God, and fight and quarrel one with another, and serve the devil, who is the master of sin, or who is the evil spirit which hath been spoken of by our fathers, he being an enemy to all righteousness.

"But ye will teach them to walk in the ways of truth and soberness; ye will teach them to love one another, and to serve one another." (Mosiah 4:14-15.)

Adults also transgress the laws of God when they "fight and quarrel one with another." We ought to control ourselves, and not get angry, fight and quarrel with our spouses, our children, or anyone else, for this is sin. President Kimball discusses this: "While the major sins . . . call for confession to the proper Church authorities, clearly such confession is neither necessary nor desirable for all sins. Those of lesser gravity but which have offended others—marital differences, *minor fits of anger*, disagreements and such—should instead be confessed to the person or persons hurt and the matter should be cleared between the persons involved." (*Miracle of Forgiveness*, p. 185, emphasis added.)

The Savior condemned anger when He told the Nephites: "There shall be no disputations among you, as there have hitherto been; . . . he that hath the spirit of contention is not of me, but is of the devil, who is the father of contention, and he stirreth up the hearts of men to contend with anger, one with another. Behold, this is not my doctrine, to stir up the hearts of men with anger, one against another; but this is my doctrine, that such things should be done away." (3 Nephi 11:28-30.)

You Can Control Your Anger

Some days tension comes into our lives. Self-control dissolves into angry outbursts. Is it really possible to overcome anger in our lives? Elder ElRay L. Christiansen said that each of us has the power to control our anger: "Why is it inexcusable to explode with anger and become vindictive? Simply because the power has been given us to control and to overcome such tendencies. If not curbed, such tendencies soon lose for us the respect and love of others." (CR, *Ensign*, June 1971, p. 38.)

President George Q. Cannon said:

"It is very difficult to be angry and sin not. The anger which is not unto sin is that which God and his servants feel against the wicked and their evil ways; but the anger of children one with another is not from God, but from that source from which all evils flow and sorrows rise. It is the temptation of the evil one to lead us astray.

"We have all to learn to govern our tempers and passions. It matters not if we be big or little, old or young, we must not let them control us.

If they do, they will destroy us. A man with passions he cannot govern is like a run-away locomotive engine; no one knows where it will go or the injury it will do, but it is sure to come to destruction at last." (*Gospel Truth*, p. 441.)

Since we have the power to control our reactions, it is important to not let our children see us in uncontrolled anger. Think what such an example is implanting in their tender minds. Not only is it a bad example, which passes the sins of the fathers and mothers on to their sons and daughters, but we see all around us the direct damage it can do. The police are continually being called out to stop family fights. Uncontrolled anger results in wives being beaten, children being abused. Some family fights end up in death for a family member.

Surely there is plenty of evidence to condemn anger. And yet some will defend this emotion. Some say they inherited their bad temper so they are unable to control it. Consider this different opinion:

> Almost daily we come in contact with someone who is impatient, touchy, or easily irritated. There are those who excuse this fault as a family trait or personal weakness. It should not be dismissed in this manner. The components of ill temper are made up of jealousy, envy, anger, conceit, harshness, cruelty, and unkindness. Each of these imperfections is a vice within itself capable of producing misery, laying waste to homes, suspending cherished friendships, embittering people, and generating disunity. To engender hatred is to plant the seeds of revenge, the spirit of which is retaliation and reprisal. Such an attitude can never be expected to produce anything but resentment. ("Study Guide for Ward Teachers", *Improvement Era*, September 1958, p. 669.)

Passing on such weaknesses from generation to generation is also a sin. It is possible to be the one to break the chain. It is possible to live in peace with those we love the most.

We must learn to control anger we may feel against our family members. President David O. McKay said, "No member of this Church —husband, father—has the right to utter an oath in his home or ever to express a cross word to his wife or to his children. . . . Never must there be expressed in a Latter-day Saint home an oath, a condemnatory term, an expression of anger or jealousy or hatred. Control it! Do not express it! You do what you can to produce peace and harmony, no matter what you may suffer." (CR, *Improvement Era*, June 1963, pp.

534-536.) There we have it. Anger is always out of place. The prophet spoke directly to our daily needs. Peace and harmony in the home are essential to achieving the goals of a true Latter-day Saint family. Anger destroys family communication and family relationships. It destroys marriages. It destroys the very conditions that produce peace in our lives. We need to make the choices that will exclude anger from our homes and our lives. We must control anger and live without it, no matter how hard it is to overcome, no matter what pride and sins we have to give up to do it.

Take Responsibility for Your Anger

Elder Rulon G. Craven of the Second Quorum of the Seventy tells us that taking responsibility for our state of mind is a beginning step toward controlling it:

> When we take personal responsibility for our condition (and for the consequences), we begin to control our lives.
> When things are not right and you don't feel right, check your thinking. If you find yourself mentally expecting others to change, to apologize, to make you happy, change your thinking. When you assume responsibility for your disposition, you can think differently and act differently. You can choose to be happy, and then act happy. (*The Pursuit of Perfection*, pp. 94-95.)

We must accept personal responsibility for all of our feelings and emotions. We are in charge of ourselves. We have the power to choose what we will or will not do. We actually do choose, whether we admit it to ourselves or not.

We can better take responsibility and control our anger if we look at what causes anger. Remember that these causes are within a person, and not in surrounding circumstances or people.

All our emotions are preceded by thoughts. "We select our thoughts, make our decisions, and are responsible for our reaction to emotion. If in our thinking we give place to the ugly and sordid, it is sure to find expression. If on the other hand our thoughts are elevated to the joyful and sublime, then those qualities will be reflected in our behavior: 'Whatsoever ye sow, that also shall ye reap.' (Galatians 6:7.)" (Study Guide for Ward Teachers, *Improvement Era*, September 1958, p. 669.)

What kind of thoughts precede anger? Anger is a secondary emotion. We first feel the effect of an emotion triggered by some circumstance around us. We may feel frustration, disappointment, fear, or insult. Our reaction to that is anger. All this happens within ourselves. It is our choice. Consciously or unconsciously, we elect to become angry, or allow ourselves to become angry.

An effective way to control anger is to recognize and deal with the first emotion. Acknowledging it may diffuse the anger. If the problem requires resolution, do so, attacking the problem, but not the person involved.

"I am upset because I wanted to arrive at the movie on time" (frustration). Acknowledge the frustration to yourself. Plan your approach to the problem, and discuss it with those to whom it applies, in a kind and caring manner.

"My anger is because I think this circumstance will reflect on my ability to hold my own at work. I am afraid I might lose my job" (fear). Taking responsibility for the first, causative emotion can help you to think sub-consciously, "I know why I am upset. Being angry will get me nowhere. I choose to be in control in this situation."

"That sounded like an insult! I could get really angry and retaliate. But I really want to have a good relationship with this person, so I will make a choice. I prefer to: A) ignore the remark as though I hadn't heard; B) reflect it back on a positive tone and see if I could have been mistaken; or C) discuss the matter privately with this person when we can have a chance to come to an understanding."

It may take practice to learn to read the first emotion. A sensible approach is to take some reflective time, perhaps in the evening when you can be by yourself, and ponder the incident. Ask yourself, "Why did I react the way I did? What happened as a result of my action? Is this what I want to happen? What are my eternal goals, and how is this behavior fitting with those goals? How can I do better the next time I am faced with a (frustrating) (fearful) (insulting) situation?" When we can make our decisions according to our eternal goals we will have made an important beginning.

Elder ElRay L. Christiansen named pride as one of the causes of anger: "Why does one rise to anger? The dominant cause is, undoubtedly, pride." ("Be Slow To Anger," *The Improvement Era*, September 1958, p. 667.)

All of us recognize the effects of pride. Pride causes us to think that we are right and all others are wrong. Pride causes us to look down on others and resent them. Pride causes us to treat others and their feelings and needs with contempt. Recognizing pride as a cause for our anger may uncover a great realm of emotions in ourselves we had not discovered.

It is easy to get angry at a neighbor if we allow ourselves to dwell on his failings, judging and condemning him. However, judging unrighteously is also a sin, and carries with it a grievous risk (see also Matthew 7:1) but forgiving gains forgiveness. In Luke 7:37 we read,

> Judge not, and ye shall not be judged: condemn not, and ye shall not be condemned: forgive, and ye shall be forgiven:
> Give, and it shall be given unto you; good measure, pressed down, and shaken together, and running over, shall men give into your bosom. For with the same measure that ye mete withal it shall be measured to you again.

The same type judgment we use against others will be used against us, but if we give, the Lord's bounty will be showered down upon us in good measure. If we spend the effort to get rid of our own faults, we may be humbled to the point that we will no longer have the desire to judge our neighbor. This will remove the tendency to become angry at him.

When we allow our thoughts to dwell on ourselves and our own desires, then we get angry when the actions of others do not match what we want or expect them to do. We need to know it is not their action that causes our anger, but rather our attitude about their action, our response. We have only ourselves to blame for getting angry.

Brother Burton C. Kelly further explains this when he says, "We must be able to recognize not only our anger but the reasons for our anger. We must realize that we make ourselves angry, that our anger comes not because of what others say or do but because we are condemning them, making selfish demands of them, or trying to control them." ("The Case Against Anger," *Ensign*, February 1980, p. 12.)

We also find that allowing anger to rise is a habit. Often we react in a certain way just because we have done it so much we do it automatically. Taking responsibility for our actions brings the problem to our attention so that we can choose to overcome habitual anger.

We are responsible for our own thoughts. If we allow ourselves to dwell on negative thoughts such as jealousy, envy, and conceit, we tend to allow our tempers to run wild and we reap a terrible harvest. These emotions run contrary to our previously established eternal goals, which include the quest for purity of heart. One by one they can be replaced with more noble motives. Pride is a sin. Selfishness is a sin. Uncontrolled anger is a sin.

Forgive Immediately

Forgiveness is a vital part of controlling our anger. Forgiveness relieves us of many of the unkind thoughts and feelings which precede anger. Elder Rulon G. Craven explained this principle:

> The Savior outlined the perfect method for relieving ourselves of negative thoughts and feelings, and overcoming inner traumas, which can cause illness, frustration, and possibly mental depression. It is by using the principle of forgiveness. Though it is often hard for us to forgive because of ego and pride, in the forgiving there is a *clearing of the mind* and a feeling of goodness that enters our hearts. The Savior said: "For, if ye forgive men their trespasses your Heavenly Father will also forgive you; But if ye forgive not men their trespasses neither will your Father forgive your trespasses" (3 Nephi 13:14-15). (*The Pursuit of Perfection*, pp. 95-96, emphasis added.)

Being a forgiving person gives us a great deal of control over our feelings. Much of the anger we feel is our response to offenses from other people. Since offenses will always be available, we could remain constantly angry if we chose. Anger can be controlled much easier if we could learn to forgive people on the spot. Forgiveness will not only help us control our anger, it will help us maintain good relationships with others, thus avoiding potential situations of anger. Forgiveness, like all of God's commandments, it is a tool. By choosing and using this tool we can build ourselves a better life.

Love Others

Anger is the opposite of the divine injunction to look outward with love to others, to care about their needs and their welfare. Anger is selfish; peace comes from service and love.

Elder Bernard P. Brockbank explained this, saying:

> Brothers and sisters, if you desire to eliminate hate and contention
> entirely from your lives, you must strengthen your mastery to love.
> All of us feel that we have love in our hearts but sometimes it does
> not control our acts.
> If we keep the first and great commandment on love, we will
> strengthen our ability to overcome contention and evil. We all know
> the first great commandment. It is spoken of on many occasions.
> Jesus said:
>> Thou shalt love the Lord thy God with all thy heart,
>> and with all thy soul, and with all thy mind. (Matthew 22:37.)
> ("Love Versus Contention," Address at Brigham Young University,
> January 14, 1969, p. 7.)

Love, then, is a key to removing anger from our lives. But we can
train ourselves to forbear when provoked. Brother Burton C. Kelly tells
this story:

> You may remember the story of the two missionaries in Germany
> who were standing on the porch talking to the woman of the house
> when her husband came up. When he found out they were Latter-day
> Saint missionaries, he became very angry. After inviting the elders
> off the porch, he slugged one elder and knocked him down. The elder
> calmly got up, brushed off his pants, picked up his hat, put it on, said
> "Thank you," and walked away with his companion. The man was
> so impressed by the elder's response that, after recovering from his
> amazement and astonishment, he ran after the elders, invited them to
> return, and had them teach him the gospel. (Yes, he joined the
> Church.) (*Ensign*, February 1980, p. 9.)

This elder was in charge of his thoughts. He loved the people he was
sent to serve. If we love and serve others, we will be less likely to
become angry with them. We will try to understand and serve them,
instead of controlling and resenting them. Love makes us want the best
for them as well as for ourselves.

A woman met a newcomer in her neighborhood. They became friends
immediately, conversing freely and enjoying the time they spent together.
The woman was grateful for her new friend, and came to love her and
her family. One day it struck the woman that this friend had several

habits which really annoyed her when she saw them in other people. Why, then, didn't they bother her when she saw them in this friend? As she thought about it, she realized that because she loved her friend, she was forgiving of these things that usually irritated her. She realized that if she loved everyone the way she loved her friend, she would not become angry or annoyed with them. What a great lesson this is!

We can learn to live without anger in our lives. We can be in charge of our thoughts so we can always give the appropriate response and avoid getting angry. By applying true repentance we can overcome our tendency to this sin. By being forgiving we can develop better relationships. By fostering the love of God in our hearts we can avoid contention. When we keep the commandments in these ways, the Holy Ghost will promote an attitude of peace and conciliation within us. We have the power to forgive or hold a grudge, to get angry or be happy. It is all up to us. If we feel we need additional strength, we can pray for it.

The Lord has told us how to work in a righteous manner with our fellow beings:

> No power or influence can or ought to be maintained by virtue of the priesthood, only by persuasion, by long-suffering, by gentleness and meekness, and by love unfeigned;
>
> By kindness, and pure knowledge, which shall greatly enlarge the soul without hypocrisy, and without guile—
>
> Reproving betimes with sharpness, when moved upon by the Holy Ghost; and then showing forth afterwards an increase of love toward him whom thou hast reproved, lest he esteem thee to be his enemy;
>
> That he may know that thy faithfulness is stronger than the cords of death. (D&C 121:41-44.)

Pray for Strength

Elder Theodore M. Burton tells us that when we get angry, the Spirit leaves us: "Unless we live very close to God and listen carefully to the whisperings of the Holy Spirit, we will find dissension creeping into our own lives. . . . Whenever you get red in the face, whenever you raise your voice, whenever you get 'hot under the collar' or angry, rebellious, or negative in spirit, then know that the Spirit of God is leaving you and the spirit of Satan is beginning to take over." (CR, *Ensign*, November 1974, p. 56.)

When we feel some of these symptoms coming on us, a plan for success is to pray to our Father in Heaven for strength to overcome our anger. Jesus said, "Ask, and it shall be given you; seek, and ye shall find; knock, and it shall be opened unto you: For every one that asketh receiveth; and he that seeketh findeth; and to him that knocketh it shall be opened." (Matthew 7:7-8.)

If we humbly ask for strength, it will be sent to us in times of need.

President Brigham Young suggests prayer as a means of controlling anger:

> Many men will say they have a violent temper, and try to excuse themselves for actions of which they are ashamed. I will say, there is not a man in this house who has a more indomitable and unyielding temper than myself. But there is not a man in the world who cannot overcome his passion, if he will struggle earnestly to do so. If you find passion coming on you, go off to some place where you cannot be heard; let none of your family see you or hear you, while it is upon you, but struggle till it leaves you; *and pray for strength to overcome.* As I have said many times to the Elders, pray in your families, and if, when the time for prayer comes, you have not the spirit of prayer upon you, and your knees are unwilling to bow, say to them, "Knees, get down there"; make them bend, and remain there until you obtain the Spirit of the Lord. If the spirit yields to the body, it becomes corrupt; but if the body yields to the spirit it becomes pure and holy. (Widtsoe, *Discourses of Brigham Young*, p. 267, emphasis added.)

President Young refers to the spirit and body combination we have in mortal life. The spirit comes from our Father in Heaven and the body from the elements of the earth. We may have to force the body to obey the will of the spirit, as he suggests. This is an interesting view on controlling anger, and it certainly will succeed.

President Brigham Young also said, "Our Spirits were pure and holy when they entered our tabernacles; and if they have been defiled, it has been by the influence of Satan, through the weakness of the flesh. . . . [when] the spirit overcomes the flesh, it yields obedience to the whisperings of the eternal Spirit of truth, which elevates it above the power of all unholy desires and passions." (*Journal of Discourses*, 8:138-39.)

Subjecting the body to the will of the spirit enables us to gain control of our baser inclinations.

President Gordon B. Hinckley reminds us of the terrible harm caused by unrestrained anger, and tells us how to combat it through prayer:

> Who can calculate the wounds inflicted, their depth and pain, by harsh and mean words spoken in anger? How pitiful a sight is a man who is strong in many ways but who loses all control of himself when some little thing, usually of no significant consequence, disturbs his equanimity. In every marriage there are, of course, occasional differences. But I find no justification for tempers that explode on the slightest provocation.
>
> Said the writer of Proverbs: Wrath is cruel, and anger is outrageous." (Proverbs 27:4.)
>
> A violent temper is such a terrible, corrosive thing. And the tragedy is that it accomplishes no good; it only feeds evil with resentment and rebellion and pain. To any man or boy within the sound of my voice who has trouble controlling his tongue, may I suggest that you plead with the Lord for the strength to overcome your weakness, that you apologize to those you have offended, and that you marshal within yourselves the power to discipline your tongue. (CR, *Ensign*, November 1991, pp. 50-51.)

There is real strength in prayer. God loves us. He wants us to succeed. If we pray for strength to overcome, if this is the desire of our heart, if we persist, he will help us overcome this imperfection. Uncontrolled anger is a sin, and therefore must undergo repentance and be overcome as any other sin. Repentance requires acknowledgment of sin, confession to the Lord through prayer, and forsaking the sin.

If we make an agreement with ourselves to pray for forgiveness and for strength to overcome every time we get angry, we will overcome. Just making the agreement will give us confidence. Using this method calls the problem of anger to our attention. It marshalls our determination. When we recognize the feeling of anger, every time we find the voice rising or feel hot under the collar, we immediately pray until we feel the anger leave. Then we thank God for the strength He sent. Combining our own self-discipline and our exercise of choice with the help of the Lord, we will be able to extinguish the problem of uncontrolled anger from our lives.

We will gradually improve until we will go a month or more without getting angry. How refreshing. It really works. We will find that we were using anger as a substitute for using our creative mind to solve our problems. When the mind is at work, the temptation to get angry is lessened.

"The Key to Happiness Is To Get the Spirit"

Jesus Christ spoke in this dispensation, and gave us a key to living in this difficult world. "Learn of me, and listen to my words; walk in the meekness of my Spirit, and you shall have peace in me." (D&C 19:23).

These precepts make a righteous, scriptural formula for dealing with those around us in a way that promotes peace, satisfaction, and gladness. President Marion G. Romney said, "The key to happiness is to get the Spirit and keep it. The right to [the Spirit] we were given when we were confirmed members of this Church. Walk by it back into the presence of God." (CR, *Improvement Era*, December 1961, p. 949.) These statements summarize the principle of controlling anger. Further, they are the only means of achieving the happiness we desire in this earth life. We gain peace in Christ when we keep the Spirit of the Holy Ghost with us, and let it guide our actions.

President Harold B. Lee told of a young couple who were angry with each other:

> The girl, heartbroken because of the unhappiness in her home, had visited an attorney and taken the preliminary steps toward a divorce. She had sought to invite her husband to have an interview with one of the local Church leaders but he had steadfastly refused, and so she came asking if I would meet with them. I invited her and her husband to be at a stake conference where I was to be in attendance, so that we could arrange a time to sit down together. They came up at the close of the conference, where there had been a marvelous spirit. There, with their arms around each other and with my arms about both of them, I heard them say, with tears streaming down their cheeks, "Brother Lee, after the wonderful spirit that we have felt here in this conference today, it is unlikely that we will have need to talk further with you." (*Stand Ye in Holy Places*, pp. 112-113.)

President George Q. Cannon explained how the Holy Spirit improves our temperament: "The Spirit of God produces peace and quiet and good-temper. Men and women who have the Spirit are amiable, are kind and loving one toward another. They control their tempers, because the Spirit of God will not dwell where the spirit of anger and hatred and violence exist.

"We should, of all people upon the face of the earth, be the best tempered, the kindest, the most forbearing, the most loving, the least disposed to quarrel." (*Gospel Truth*, p. 441.)

Wouldn't life be sweeter if you lived this way? Wouldn't you like to live with people who possess these qualities? Wouldn't you like your children to possess these qualities? It is all possible.

> Peace is the gift of God. Do you want peace? Go to God. Do you want peace in your families? Go to God. Do you want peace to brood over your families? If you do, live your religion, and the very peace of God will dwell and abide with you, for that is where peace comes from. (President John Taylor, *Journal of Discourses*, Vol. 10, p. 56.)

With anger under control, with contention gone, we are ready to enjoy the love of God in our hearts. We are ready for the Holy Ghost to be in our lives. We are ready to enjoy the guidance, peace, and happiness promised to the faithful who love the Lord.

20

You Can Gain Strength From the Scriptures Daily

The Word of God is the Sword of the Spirit

Our lives are truly busy. We have many things to accomplish each day—work, meals, appointments, music lessons, sports, homework, meetings, housekeeping—things of importance. Things that crowd in upon our time and attention, things that fight for center stage in our lives. Sometimes the mundane things that keep us so busy cause us to neglect things of eternal importance. The scriptures often fall in the category of neglected things.

Paul makes the analogy that the word of God is the sword of the Spirit. A sword may be a sure defense against enemies of the soul. And it may double as a tool for cutting through the thick underbrush of choking trivia which clogs our path toward our eternal goal. All the choices with which we fill our time may be important—the tasks may be vital. But if we are hacking at the jungle with a short blade or a dull edge, we are wasting a precious portion of our mortal probation. Daily portions of the word of God will shine the steel and hone the blade, making all our functions more efficient. Can we afford not to do it? It's like paying tithing: the rest of the money goes so much further after our act of faith.

Elder Carlos E. Asay spoke of the things that we busy ourselves with: "I fear that many of us rush about from day to day taking for granted the holy scriptures. We scramble to honor appointments with physicians, lawyers, and businessmen. Yet we think nothing of postponing interviews with Deity—postponing scripture study. Little wonder we develop anemic souls and lose our direction in living. How much better it would be if we planned and held sacred fifteen or twenty minutes a day for reading the scriptures. Such interviews with Deity would help us recognize his voice and enable us to receive guidance in all of our affairs." (CR, *Ensign*, November 1978, pp. 53-54.)

Think how much better our daily lives would be if we structured them around the study of the scripture! The soul sufficiently strengthened by scripture study and prayer will be much better able to cope with the demands of a challenging life.

President Harold B. Lee pointed out the danger of neglecting our study of the scriptures: *"I say that we need to teach our people to find their answers in the scriptures.* . . . But the unfortunate thing is that so many of us are not reading the scriptures. We do not know what is in them, and therefore we speculate about the things that we ought to have found in the scriptures themselves. I think that therein is one of our biggest dangers of today." (*Ensign*, December 1972, p. 3, emphasis added.)

The scriptures tell us what we are to do to have eternal life. We need to know what is in them. Someone once said that we cannot draw water from an empty well. We need to have the words of life in our minds and hearts so that we can use them as needed.

Further, we need the direction of the Lord in our lives constantly if we are to make the right choices. As we seek to accomplish spiritual goals of progression and service, the scriptures make a vehicle for the Lord to reveal His will to us. Many have had words of scripture brought to their minds as an answer to a heartfelt prayer. A woman Don taught as a missionary in Finland wrote of her experience:

"I was 19 when the missionaries began teaching me the gospel of Jesus Christ. The Church was new to my country. In my town of Jyvaskyla, in the heartland of Finland, there was not one member, except the missionaries.

"I had felt the Spirit in meetings with the missionaries, but never anything more sweet and nice than when Elders Udell E. Poulsen and Don M. Christensen challenged me to be baptized. I still wasn't sure if what these two young men told me was true or not, but they obviously believed it was true . . .

'Pray about it,' counselled the missionaries.

"Early the next morning I knelt and poured out my heart to Heavenly Father, 'Was it true? How would my family react if I joined? Would my friends make fun of me?' I had never studied the scriptures, but the answer came as clearly as if I had read it—"'Seek ye first the Kingdom of God, and his righteousness; and all these things shall be added unto you.' (Matt 6:33.)

"I walked to a store that morning to get milk for breakfast. It was an extremely cold January day. Remembering the answer to my prayer, I thought, 'It's true, it's true. And nothing else matters anymore because I'm going to get baptized.' A warm feeling that defied the coldness of the morning settled over me.

"Since then, life has had its highs and lows, but all the things I worried about were taken care of more magnificently than I could have ever imagined. I have been able to study at BYU, marry a good man, rear five marvelous children, and be a wife to a man who has served as a bishop and mission president. My testimony, started that cold January morning, has never wavered." (Lea Mahoney, "Touched by the Scriptures," *Church News*, May 4, 1986.)

Strengthen the Family

Family scripture study is a way to draw our families together in love, and teach them the important lessons they need in order to return back to their Heavenly Father. No one can take the place of a parent in teaching children to read and love the scriptures. Elder H. Burke Peterson related some of his experiences with families in the Church who study scriptures together:

> As I have traveled to the stakes of the Church, I have found many dedicated parents who gather their families about them daily to study the revelations of the Lord as recorded in the holy scriptures. I remember one family of 12 children who studied together daily in two groups, one for the older children and another for the younger children in their family. Think of the time and effort this has taken over the years. Think how the blessings to this family have multiplied, as many of their children have now reached adulthood and are raising young families of their own.
>
> I was in another home where ten children, all young, were given a daily treat of the scriptures. I know of a mother, alone, with four children. She has them get ready early for bed and reads to them from the scriptures before they go to sleep each night. What a blessing for thoughtful parents to shower on their most important responsi-

bility, their little ones. There shouldn't be—there mustn't be—one family in this Church that doesn't take the time to read from the scriptures every day. Every family can do it in their own way. I have a testimony of this. (CR, *Ensign*, May 1975, pp. 53-54.)

President Marion G. Romney was a great advocate of the blessings of studying the Book of Mormon. He told this heartwarming story about an experience he had studying the scriptures with his son:

I remember reading [the Book of Mormon] with one of my lads when he was very young. On one occasion I lay in the lower bunk and he in the upper bunk. We were each reading aloud alternate paragraphs of those last three marvelous chapters of Second Nephi. I heard his voice breaking and thought he had a cold, but we went on to the end of the three chapters. As we finished, he said to me, "Daddy, do you ever cry when you read the Book of Mormon?"

"Yes, son," I answered. "Sometimes the Spirit of the Lord so witnesses to my soul that the Book of Mormon is true that I do cry."

"Well," he said, "that is what happened to me tonight." I know not all of them will respond like that, but I know that some of them will, and I tell you this book was given to us of God to read and to live by, and it will hold us as close to the Spirit of the Lord as anything I know. Won't you please read it?" (CR, *Improvement Era*, May 1949, p. 330.)

Sometimes I have the same experience when I read the Book of Mormon. The spirit of the book is strong, and when my spirit is in tune, I, too, am touched with its truth. It is important that we make opportunity for the Holy Spirit to instill that testimony into the hearts of our family members. You might try taking turns reading from the Book of Mormon during part of your family home evening.

Arda Jean tells this experience:

"One day a sister bore her testimony in Relief Society to the great benefit received by bringing the spirit of the Book of Mormon into her home through daily study. I was so touched by the strength of her witness that I decided we should make it a practice in our home as well. Now I, too, can testify that it does, indeed, bring an increase of consideration for each other, and that its spirit gentles the rambunctious little hearts that are in the process of growing up in our homes.

"Since that time I read the Book of Mormon once each year, and try also to complete the reading of whichever of the standard works is the current study course. In this way I have come to know all of the scriptures much better, and find continual joy in the many ways this blesses me. I was thrilled as a Relief Society president to listen to President Kimball exhort the sisters to become scriptorians."

Our daughter Jolene and her husband Bill Dew and their five children read and discuss the Book of Mormon every morning for about a half an hour. They feel they are receiving in their home the blessings that accompany reading of the Book of Mormon promised by President Marion G. Romney, namely that "the spirit of reverence will increase; mutual respect and consideration for each other will grow. The spirit of contention will depart. Parents will counsel their children in greater love and wisdom. Children will be more responsive and submissive to the counsel of their parents. Righteousness will increase. Faith, hope and charity—the pure love of Christ—will abound in our homes and lives, bringing in their wake peace, joy, and happiness" (CR, *Ensign*, May 1980, p. 67).

Imagine having all these blessings in your home! Is there any home that would not benefit by an increase in "mutual respect and consideration for each other"? And wouldn't we all appreciate it if in our homes the "spirit of contention" would depart. Think about how much good could be accomplished in a home filled with "peace, joy, and happiness"! All these blessings are available if we will read the scriptures, and especially the Book of Mormon, with our families and by ourselves.

Elder Bruce R. McConkie urged the sisters, "We would like each of you to read [the scriptures], either by yourself, or with your husband, or with your families, and not simply read the words but ponder and pray about their content so that there will come into your lives the desires for righteousness that grow out of the study of the pure, perfect word of God. We would like the Church to start drinking at the fountain— undiluted—the pure, perfect message that the Lord has given by the mouths of his prophets, the message found in the Standard Works of the Church." ("Drink from the Fountain," *Ensign*, April 1975, p. 70.)

When we read, study, ponder, and pray about the scriptures, there comes into our lives the desire for righteousness. It is the fastest way to improve our character. It is the surest way of filling our lives with good.

Every Latter-day Saint, every family, should find time to read the scriptures every day. You can read them early in the morning before school and work, during lunch breaks, before or after dinner, or as a bedtime story. You can read them together as husband and wife. Read them while traveling. When Don was in the army he carried his small servicemen's editions in his pocket, and read the scriptures during breaks throughout the day.

One of the nicest things in our lives was when we decided to put a cassette tape player in the car and listen to the scriptures on tape. Now we listen to them as we travel around town. We have listened to all of the standard works plus many talks given by General Authorities. We recommend this highly. Perhaps you only travel a few minutes a day, but it adds up. We also have small tape recorders available at home to use while loading the dishwasher, folding the laundry, raking leaves, or the like. Some people use a headset and listen while they jog or walk.

You can expand your study of the gospel by purchasing good religious tapes from the bookstore on almost any subject you are interested in. You can gradually become an authority on many subjects. If you have a weakness you are trying to overcome such as thinking bad thoughts, not paying a full tithing, or being too judgmental of other children of our Father in Heaven, try listening to tapes on the subject. As you immerse yourself in the Gospel you will become stronger.

A good way to start studying the scriptures is to follow President Benson's admonition to read the Book of Mormon. A few minutes every day, faithfully, will change your life.

"Feasting On the Words of Christ"

Scripture study is part of the path leading to eternal life. By being baptized, we have entered in at the gate, but what else is necessary for us? Nephi explains:

> And now, my beloved brethren, after ye have gotten into this strait and narrow path, I would ask if all is done? Behold, I say unto you, Nay; . . .
> Wherefore, ye must press forward with a steadfastness in Christ, having a perfect brightness of hope, and a love of God and of all men. Wherefore, if ye shall press forward, *feasting upon the word of Christ*, and endure to the end, behold, thus saith the Father: Ye shall have eternal life. (2 Nephi 31:17-20.)

How do we feast upon the word of Christ? Scripture study is food for our souls. Without sufficient nourishment, our bodies suffer. Our spirits also suffer if they are denied regular spiritual sustenance. We need to be sure that we are as active in feeding our spirits by feasting upon the scriptures daily as we are in feeding our physical body. Do we ever just "forget" to eat for days on end? And yet, we are often guilty of neglecting the nourishment of our spirits for long spaces of time. Are you feeling discouraged, and lacking in spiritual insights? Are your problems overwhelming you? Perhaps what you are feeling is the hunger pains of your spirit.

We can nourish our souls by attending our church meetings, but to prepare ourselves to inherit eternal life, we need to actively seek to understand what is required of us in the way of obedience and righteousness. President Spencer W. Kimball said, "Only the faithful will receive the promised reward, which is eternal life. For one cannot receive eternal life without becoming a 'doer of the word' (see James 1:22) and being valiant in obedience to the Lord's commandments. And one cannot become a 'doer of the word' without first becoming a 'hearer.' And to become a 'hearer' is not simply to stand idly by and wait for chance bits of information; it is to seek out and study and pray and comprehend." ("How Rare a Possession—the Scriptures!" *Ensign*, Sept. 1976, p. 2.)

To truly comprehend and internalize the truths in the scriptures, we are exhorted to "ponder." President Marion G. Romney said, "As I have read the scriptures, I have been challenged by the word *ponder*, so frequently used in the Book of Mormon. The dictionary says that *ponder* means 'to weigh mentally, think deeply about, deliberate, meditate.' *Pondering* is, in my feeling, a form of prayer. . . . Desiring, searching, and pondering over 'the words of eternal life,' all three of them together, as important as they are, would be inadequate without prayer." (CR, *Ensign*, July 1973, pp. 90-91, emphasis included.)

How can we begin to ponder the scriptures?

A Sample Scripture Study Session

President Howard W. Hunter advised us as to the "how" of scripture study. He said, "We should not be haphazard in our reading but rather develop a systematic plan for study. There are some who read to a schedule of a number of pages or a set number of chapters each day or week. This may be perfectly justifiable and may be enjoyable if one is reading for pleasure, but it does not constitute meaningful study. *It is better to have a set amount of time to give to scriptural study each day than to have a set amount of chapters to read.* Sometimes we find that the study of a single verse will occupy the whole time." (CR, *Ensign*, November 1979, p. 64, emphasis added.)

One way to organize your scripture study is to choose a topic you would like to know more about, and then use the resources in the LDS editions of the scriptures to help you learn all you can from the scriptures on this subject. You could choose a topic you feel you need help with, or perhaps an area of gospel doctrine that you would like to understand better.

Let's see how a sample scripture study session might go:

First you kneel in prayer and ask that your Father in Heaven will guide you and give you insight as you research your topic in scripture study today.

You have had a lot of negative feelings towards others lately, and you realize that what you are doing is judging them. You know that there is a scripture somewhere about judging. You decide to begin there.

To find that scripture, you look in the back of your scriptures for the topical guide. Under "judge," and you see that the scripture you are thinking of is in Matthew 7:1-5. You turn to that scripture and read,

> Judge not, that ye be not judged.
>
> For with what judgment ye judge, ye shall be judged: and with what measure ye mete, it shall be measured to you again.
>
> And why beholdest thou the mote that is in thy brother's eye, but considerest not the beam that is in thine own eye?
>
> Or how wilt thou say to thy brother, Let me pull out the mote out of thine eye; and, behold, a beam is in thine own eye?
>
> Thou hypocrite, first cast out the beam out of thine own eye; and then shalt thou see clearly to cast out the mote out of thy brother's eye.

You ponder this scripture:

"'Judge not, that ye be not judged.' I'll put that scripture in my own words. Maybe that means that I shouldn't judge others, because if I do, I will also be judged. It could mean that if I am feeling negatively about others, they may be doing the same about me. I don't like that idea!"

You look at the notes at the bottom of the page and see that the Joseph Smith Translation renders this passage this way: "Judge not unrighteously, that ye be not judged: but judge righteous judgment."

"Hmm. Is what I am doing righteous judgment? I am looking at others and disliking them because of things they do. Jesus said we should love even our enemies. Disliking others can't be righteous judgment."

The next verse seems to back up what you learned from the first—the same measure you use on others will be used on you.

What else does this scripture say? "And why beholdest thou the mote that is in thy brother's eye, but considerest not the beam that is in thine own eye?"

"Oh dear, it is becoming so clear to me. I am judging others, disliking them for what I see; and because I am involved in judging others, I am not looking at myself, and seeing things *I* need to improve on. I guess I'm really saying to others, 'Let me pull out the mote out of thine eye' while my vision is obstructed by my own weakness.

"I really need to cast the beam out of my own eye, before I can see clearly enough to cast out the mote out of my brother's eye. I guess that is what I am trying to do by studying these scriptures today."

You would like to read more about this subject, so you look down in the footnotes. Under 1a you see Alma 41:14-15. You turn to that scripture and read,

> Therefore, my son, see that you are merciful unto your brethren; deal justly, judge righteously, and do good continually; and if ye do all these things then shall ye receive your reward; yea, ye shall have mercy restored unto you again; ye shall have justice restored unto you again; ye shall have a righteous judgment restored unto you again; and ye shall have good rewarded unto you again.
>
> For that which ye do send out shall return unto you again, and be restored; therefore, the word restoration more fully condemneth the sinner, and justifieth him not at all.

"This scripture gives me hope. It encourages me to treat those around me well, with mercy and justice. Then mercy, justice, righteous judgment, and good will come back to me. I know I have been judging my neighbors, the Young family, pretty harshly. I keep thinking of ways they need to improve their lives—last Sunday I kept thinking how much I wished they had heard the lesson! I didn't even think how much the lesson applied to me. That isn't using mercy in my relationships with others. How can I judge righteously if I don't even know their family well? Maybe I could get to know them better. Maybe that's why this scripture tells me to "do good continually."

"Hmmm . . . I wonder if there are any people feeling about me as I do about the Youngs? This scripture promises that good will come back to me if I send good into the lives of others. I can see that I would be happier if I do."

Another reference you find in the footnotes is D&C 1:10. You turn to this scripture and read,

> Unto the day when the Lord shall come to recompense unto every man according to his work, and measure to every man according to the measure which he has measured to his fellow man. (D&C 1:10)

"Is it possible that God will measure me the same way I measure others? I know at that last judgment I will certainly need mercy from the Lord! I think I had better start looking upon my neighbors with the mercy that *I* need to receive."

There is one more footnote reference you want to look up. It is D&C 11:12:

> And now, verily, verily, I say unto thee, put your trust in that Spirit which leadeth to do good—yea, to do justly, to walk humbly, to judge righteously; and this is my Spirit.

"Put my trust in the Spirit. I guess that means that I need to let the Spirit of the Lord guide my actions—lead me to do good and judge righteously. I think I have judged others harshly in an attempt to to make myself feel better in comparison. The Spirit whispers to me that I don't climb higher by walking on others. President Benson told us that pride is a terrible sin. I guess that judging unrighteously is really pride. I know that, as a member of the Lord's Church, I should be a light to the world. I am afraid that perhaps I have caused others to fall by my unwillingness to love others unconditionally.

"Loving others unconditionally. I think it would help my judgmental attitude if I learned to truly love others. I will study that topic tomorrow for my scripture study."

After this very successful session of scripture study you kneel in prayer and ask your Father in Heaven to help you to put these things you have learned to work in your life. You rise feeling renewed, refreshed and ready to live better.

The Lessons of Life

When we develop a habit of consistent, prayerful scripture study, we strengthen ourselves and our families. President Spencer W. Kimball explained one way we are strengthened, saying,

We learn the lessons of life more readily and surely if we see the results of wickedness and righteousness in the lives of others. To know the patriarchs and prophets of ages past and their faithfulness under stress and temptation and persecution strengthens the resolves of youth. To come to know Job well and intimately is to learn to keep faith through the greatest of adversities. To know well the strength of Joseph in the luxury of ancient Egypt when he was tempted by a voluptuous woman and to see this clean young man resist all the powers of darkness should fortify the intimate reader against such sin. To see the forbearance and fortitude of Paul when he was giving his life to his ministry is to give courage to those who feel they have been injured and tried. ("What I Hope You Will Teach My Grandchildren and All Others of the Youth of Zion," Address to seminary and institute personnel, Brigham Young University, 11 July 1966, p. 6.)

We can strengthen ourselves by following the righteous examples of those who have gone before, and thus avoid the dangerous rocks that obstruct our way to eternal life. President Brigham Young said, "It is your privilege and duty to live so as to be able to understand the things of God. There are the Old and New Testaments, the Book of Mormon, and the book of Doctrine and Covenants, . . . and they are of great worth to a person wandering in darkness. They are like a lighthouse in the ocean, or a finger-post which points out the road we should travel. Where do they point? To the Fountain of light." (*Discourses of Brigham Young*, p. 127.)

Our daughter Jeanie called from Texas one morning in a state of excitement. She said, "Mom, you remember the question I was troubled with yesterday? This morning in our family scripture study, just reading directly through the Book of Mormon with the children, this passage jumped out at me. It is the answer I was looking for. Isn't that splendid that the answer came just in our regular reading!" How grateful we both were that she and her family were opening themselves to that inspiration on a regular basis.

President Kimball gave us this challenge and warning: "The Lord is not trifling with us when he gives us [the scriptures], for 'unto whomsoever much is given, of him shall be much required.' (Luke 12:48.) Access to these things means responsibility for them. We must study the scriptures according to the Lord's commandment (see 3 Nephi 23:1-5); and we must let them govern our lives and the lives of our children. So

I ask all to begin now to study the scriptures in earnest, if you have not already done so." ("How Rare a Possession—The Scriptures!" *Ensign*, September 1976, p. 5.)

Many heeded President Kimball's invitation, and feasting on the scriptures has blessed their lives. Today we have better study aids and helps than ever before, with personal computers, videos, CDs and tapes readily available. But we don't need to wait to acquire those enhancements. Let's use *today* what is available, and add these ideas and resources to help us in a conscientious study of the holy word. You and your family will be blessed more than you can now comprehend for daily scripture study. Let's all receive these precious blessings.

21

You Can Receive the Blessings of the Temple

The Purpose of Temples

The holy temple has been a hallmark of the Lord's covenant people throughout history. It signifies the connection between earth and heaven; between mortals on earth, and their Heavenly Father; between time and eternity.

When Nephi and his people settled in the promised land, one of the first things they did was build a temple. In 2 Nephi 5:16 we read, "And I, Nephi, did build a temple; and I did construct it after the manner of the temple of Solomon save it were not built of so many precious things; for they were not to be found upon the land, wherefore, it could not be built like unto Solomon's temple. But the manner of the construction was like unto the temple of Solomon; and the workmanship thereof was exceedingly fine." Even though they did not have the resources to build their temple of the same precious materials with which Solomon built his temple, they made sure that what they built was the best they could do, and as Nephi says, "the workmanship . . . was exceedingly fine."

The divine injunction to do temple work was reestablished with the Restoration of the gospel. In the early days of this dispensation the Saints labored with scanty numbers and resources to build magnificent temples at Kirtland and Nauvoo. Pioneers, exiled to the west, built the beautiful temples that still stand today at Salt Lake, St. George, Manti, and Logan. Today, we are still a temple-building people. Sacred temples dot the earth, and in them the children of God receive eternal blessings.

President Ezra Taft Benson said, "The blessings of the house of the Lord are eternal. They are of the highest importance to us because it is in the temples that we obtain God's greatest blessings pertaining to eternal life. Temples are really the gateways to heaven." (*The Teachings of Ezra Taft Benson*, p. 255.)

Why do we build these temples? Elder W. Grant Bangerter said, "As we study the scriptures, we learn that the doctrine of the temple requires the following of the Latter-day Saints:

"First, the building of temples.

"Second, going to the temple for our blessings.

"Third, returning to perform the ordinances for deceased relatives.

"Fourth, doing the work for others as well.

"Fifth, frequent attendance for personal spiritual benefit." (CR, *Ensign*, May 1982, p. 71.)

Let's look at each of these elements.

The Building of Temples

The Doctrine and Covenants affirms that God's people are always commanded to build temples. "Therefore, verily I say unto you, that your anointings, and your washings, and your baptisms for the dead, and your solemn assemblies, . . . for the glory, honor, and endowment of all her municipals, are ordained by the ordinance of my holy house, which my people are always commanded to build unto my holy name." (D&C 124:39.)

Elder Mark E. Petersen explained that the restoration of the gospel and the restoration of temple building came at the same time:

> As the gospel was restored in these last days, temple building and temple ordinances also were restored through the Prophet Joseph Smith. The Latter-day Saints were taught by their Prophet that celestial glory could be theirs in the eternal world, but only through "obeying the celestial law, and the whole law, too."
>
> Speaking to his people on April 8, 1844, the Prophet Joseph said that the temple ordinances as he was giving them were so important that "without [them] we cannot obtain celestial thrones. But there must be a holy place prepared for that purpose." (*History of the Church of Jesus Christ of Latter-day Saints*, 6:318-20.)
>
> Without temples, therefore, the blessings could not be given. The answer consequently was that the Saints should build temples, and this the Lord commanded them to do. ("Why We Build Temples," *Temples of the Church of Jesus Christ of Latter-day Saints*, p. 60.)

Today we are greatly blessed to have temples in many parts of the world for the blessing and sanctification of the Saints. President Benson expressed gratitude for the multitude of Latter-day temples, saying, "I thank the Lord for the temples and for the sacred ordinances performed therein and the sweet spirit which is always prevalent in the house of the Lord. I love the temples of God and thank the Lord that we are building more and more of them." (*The Teachings of Ezra Taft Benson*, p. 255.)

Going to the Temples for Our Blessings

One of the first instructions given by President Howard W. Hunter upon being sustained as prophet was to heighten the importance of the temple in our lives. He said, "I invite the Latter-day Saints to look to the temple of the Lord as the great symbol of your membership. It is the deepest desire of my heart to have every member of the Church worthy to enter the temple. It would please the Lord if every adult member would be worthy of—and carry—a current temple recommend. The things that we do and not do to be worthy of a temple recommend are the very things that ensure we will be happy as individuals and as families.

"Let us be a temple-attending people. Attend the temple as frequently as personal circumstances allow." (CR, *Ensign*, November 1994, p. 8.)

What the prophet is asking is that each of us go to the temple and receive the ordinances performed there, in order to gain our exaltation. In the temples we make covenants that govern how we live our lives. President Gordon B. Hinckley said, "Surely these temples are unique among all buildings. They are houses of instruction. They are places of covenants and promises. At their altars we kneel before God our Creator and are given promise of his everlasting blessings." ("Why These Temples?" *Temples of the Church of Jesus Christ of Latter-day Saints*, p. 8.)

In these sacred houses of instruction we are trained in the higher education of the gospel, and receive the ordinances that pertain to the dispensation of the fulness of times in which we live. In the Doctrine and Covenants we read, "And verily I say unto you, let this house be built unto my name, that I may reveal mine ordinances therein unto my people; For I deign to reveal unto my church things which have been kept hid from before the foundation of the world, things that pertain to the dispensation of the fulness of times." (D&C 124:40-41.)

This instruction is necessary so that we can learn what is required of us to return to our Father in Heaven after we have passed the tests of this life. There we make covenants and receive promises of everlasting blessings.

President Ezra Taft Benson also pointed to the temple as a place of instruction when he said, "This temple will be a constant, visible symbol that God has not left man to grope in darkness. It is a place of revelation. Though we live in a fallen world—a wicked world—holy places are set apart and consecrated so that worthy men and women can learn the order of heaven and obey God's will. . . . One of the Brethren has referred to the temple as the 'university of the Lord.'" (*The Teachings of Ezra Taft Benson*, p. 252.)

Before we are instructed in the temples, we prepare ourselves so that we are worthy to have the companionship of the Holy Ghost, because it is through the power of the Spirit that we will comprehend some of the magnificent teachings of the temple.

President Benson taught that in the temple we learn through the power of the Holy Ghost: "Everything we learn in the holy places, the temples, is based on the scriptures. These teachings are what the scriptures refer to as the 'mysteries of godliness' (see 1 Timothy 3:16; D&C 19:10). They are to be comprehended by the power of the Holy Ghost, for the Lord has given this promise to His faithful and obedient servants: 'Thou mayest know the mysteries and peaceable things' (D&C 42:61)." (*The Teachings of Ezra Taft Benson*, p. 245.)

Ideally, our young people will be married in the temple for time and all eternity. President Benson said, "Thank the Lord we have a temple in this land where our marriages may be sealed! All the young people should qualify and plan to be married in the house of God." (*The Teachings of Ezra Taft Benson*, p. 260.)

President Gordon B. Hinckley asks,

Was there ever a man who truly loved a woman, or a woman who truly loved a man, who did not pray that their relationship might continue beyond the grave? Has a child ever been buried by parents who did not long for the assurance that their loved one would again be theirs in a world to come? Can anyone believing in eternal life doubt that the God of heaven would grant his sons and daughters that most precious attribute of life, the love that finds its most meaningful expression in family relationships? No, reason demands that the family relationship shall continue after death. The human heart longs for it. The God of heaven has revealed a way whereby it may be secured. The sacred ordinances of the house of the Lord provide for it." ("Temples of the Church of Jesus Christ of Latter-day Saints," p. 4.)

There are many instances in which a family goes later, after the birth of children, to be sealed in the temple. Whether this is the result of conversion later in life or a period of inactivity, all should strive to make their family relationships eternal.

If you as the father of your family haven't taken your family to the temple yet, we suggest that you prepare yourself and your family to enter the temple and receive your eternal blessings.

Think of becoming a "forever family"—imagine being sealed to your wife for time and all eternity—to have her as your wife in the next life—to have your children sealed to you and your wife for eternity—to continue in the bonds of love forever!

President Ezra Taft Benson told a moving story of a ward who helped several families prepare themselves for temple blessings:

I received a telephone call from a bishop in Ogden who said to me, "Elder Benson, do you think you could spend one night for our good ward?" I told him I would like to. I told him that "there are only some four thousand wards in the Church" and that "yours must be one of the best." He said, "We have five wonderful men in our ward, and we have been working with them for about two years. They all have families and have just received the Melchizedek Priesthood and were ordained elders." He said, "We want to bring them to Salt Lake and have you meet us in one of the sealing rooms of the temple and perform the sealings of wives to husbands and children to parents." I was happy to comply with his request and I spent one of the happiest evenings of my life in a sealing room in the Salt Lake Temple. All of these parents had children with them. One couple had nine children, all under eighteen years of age. I think I shall never forget that mother. She was so filled with emotion she could hardly control herself. Finally when the work was all done and the people were leaving the sealing room, she apologized to me and said, "You will have to forgive me for the way I have acted tonight, but I have waited nineteen years for this moment." She further said, "All during those nineteen years, I have prayed to God night and morning that the time would come when my husband would be counted worthy to receive the Melchizedek Priesthood and be worthy to bring me and the children to the house of the Lord." She said, "Tonight my prayers have been answered."

I do not suppose it is possible for us to realize her joy, but I daresay that in this temple district this very day, there are mothers and wives in a similar condition hoping and praying the time will soon come when their husbands will be able to receive the holy priesthood and bring them to the house of the Lord and there experience the richest blessings known to men and women in this world. (*The Teachings of Ezra Taft Benson*, pp. 258-259.)

We have been present at the sealing of a number of families. What a thrill it is to accompany these families to the temple and witness the joy of their sealing to each other. The mother and father are joined for time and all eternity. The children are also sealed to the parents for eternity. The Lord's covenants with them are stated. Tears flow. The spirit is strong. What fulfillment radiates in the temple!

It is never too late. We went to the temple with a dear sister who was sealed to her departed spouse on their sixty-first wedding anniversary. She was in her eighties, and died a very happy woman within a year. Another dear brother was sealed to his wife after more than twenty-five years of marriage. It was a most touching time for them both. Our dear aunt participated with us in the Jordan River temple in her hundredth year of life at the sealing of ancestors for whom she had done the research!

Many saints have sacrificed a great deal in order to go to the temple. The following story typifies this fact:

Brother and Sister Paloma knew that the gospel of Jesus Christ was true. The Mormon missionaries had come to their small home on a Pacific Island. They had listened to the beautiful truths and were soon baptized and confirmed members of the Church. They tried with all their hearts to live righteously.

The Paloma family longed to go to the temple to be sealed together for all eternity. The Hawaii Temple was the closest one to them, but they never seemed to have enough money for the trip. There were twelve children to feed, clothe, and educate. The parents taught their children the importance of eternal marriage. With joy and longing they watched their firstborn son and his bride leave the island to be married in the temple at Hawaii.

"Someday, Mother, we will find a way," Brother Paloma told his wife.

But the years brought more sacrifice as some of the children were called on missions. Each time one of the children was ready to marry, the family managed to raise enough money for the couple to travel to Hawaii. Gratefully and tearfully Brother and Sister Paloma would send their children to be married in the temple.

Grandchildren added to their joy and also to their longing to be united as a family forever.

Soon the Paloma's youngest child, Marthe, and Ken, her husband-to-be, were ready to marry in the temple. Soon twelve sons and daughters would all have been married in the temple.

"Now, Mama, surely we will find a way," Papa said.

Then letters began to arrive saying, "Papa, Mama, it is your time now! Come with Marthe and Ken." Each of the children sent a letter containing money to make their parents' journey possible.

Gathered from many places, all the sons and daughters of the Palomas came to the temple in Hawaii to be sealed to their parents. Brother and Sister Paloma saw their last beloved child married and had an unforgettable temple wedding ceremony of their own. They knelt at the altar of God, surrounded by twelve sons and daughters, and by the power of the priesthood they were sealed as a family for time and all eternity. The long awaited dream had come true. No words could describe it, but Mama was heard to say, "Today, we saw a glimpse into eternity." (*Walk in His Ways*, Basic Manual for Children Part A, 1987, pp. 50-51.)

This family prepared their children for temple marriage. How can we teach our children to hold sacred the goal of temple marriage? First, we set the example. President Ezra Taft Benson said, "The temple will be an ever-present reminder that God intended the family to be eternal. How fitting it will be for mothers and fathers to point to this temple and say, 'That is the place where your mother (or father) and I were married for eternity.' By so doing, they will instill within the minds and hearts of their children, while very young, the ideal of temple marriage." (*The Teachings of Ezra Taft Benson*, p. 258.)

When our family was young, as we drove to southern Utah to visit Grandma and Grandpa, we might go out of our way to see the Manti Temple where we were married. On family trips we have arranged to take them to visit temples in the locality. We would take our family to see the visitor center, watch the films, and hear the guides bear testimony to temple work.

When our daughter Ruth was about two years old we went to Temple Square. With the other children, Ruth enjoyed the displays, the movies, the beautiful grounds, and the sight of the lighted temple. Everything seemed just right for her. However, on the way home she started to cry. She seemed inconsolable. She wouldn't tell us what was wrong, and finally cried herself to sleep. In the night Arda Jean heard her crying again. She went to her, took her up in her arms, and asked again why she was crying. Ruth sobbed, "I went to the temple, but I didn't get married!"

In the quiet of the night Arda Jean explained the beautiful principle of temple marriage. She told her that she was too young to be married in the temple now, but the day would come when she would fall in love with a wonderful man, and we would all go to the temple to witness her marriage. Ruth felt good about the explanation and fell sound asleep.

When Ruth was born her Aunt Marie had presented her with a little white handkerchief done up with bows and stitches to fashion a bonnet, just right for her tiny head to wear the day she was given a father's blessing in the Church. The poem that accompanied it instructed us to put it away and, after clipping the stitches, use it again as a hanky to take with her to the temple for her wedding.

Years later, after she met her "handsome prince," we had the crowning experience of our lives when all eight of our children and all eight of their partners assembled in the Salt Lake Temple for Ruth's wedding. The little hanky dried her eyes as our hearts spilled over with the wonder of that precious day, with the magnitude and breadth of the eternal promises exchanged, and the souls on both sides of the veil who gathered rejoicing. It was what we had worked for all our lives. Ruth's mom thought, as she hugged each member of the eternal family, "It doesn't get any better than this."

President Howard W. Hunter encouraged us to teach children the importance of temple ordinances and marriage: "Let us share with our children the spiritual feelings we have in the temple. And let us teach them more earnestly and more comfortably the things we can appropriately say about the purposes of the House of the Lord." (CR, *Ensign*, November 1994, p. 88.) And again: "Keep a picture of a temple in your home that your children may see it. Teach them about the purposes of the house of the Lord. Have them plan from their earliest years to go there and to remain worthy of that blessing." (p. 8.)

May we teach our children in weekly family home evening the blessings that will come to them when they are married in the temple for time and all eternity. May this be as emotional an issue with each of our children as it was with little Ruth. When they feel that strongly about temple marriage, they will be married in the temple and honor their temple covenants.

Ordinances For Deceased Relatives and Other Dead

As part of the restoration of the gospel in the dispensation of the fulness of times, it was prophesied that the Prophet Elijah would return to the earth to "plant in the hearts of the children the promises made to the fathers, and the hearts of the children shall turn to their fathers." (D&C 2:2.)

What does it mean to turn the hearts of the children to their fathers? The Doctrine and Covenants explains that "the Prophet Elijah was to plant in the hearts of the children the promises made to their fathers, [f]oreshadowing the great work to be done in the temples of the Lord in the dispensation of the fulness of times, for the redemption of the dead, and the sealing of the children to their parents, lest the whole earth be smitten with a curse and utterly wasted at his coming." (D&C 138:47-48.)

When we form these links of love and redemption we fulfill the commandment of the Lord. For this purpose we as individuals and as a Church in these latter-days have made great commitments of time, money, and effort to genealogical research. Why do we do this for those who have died? Elder David B. Haight answers, "Because we love them. Because they are entitled to the same blessings that we enjoy. Because this is a major part of the heavenly plan for this, the dispensation of the fulness of times, for the blessing of all people." (CR, *Ensign*, May 1991, p. 75.)

When we do the temple work for those who have passed away, we do a work for them that they cannot do for themselves. We become "saviors on Mount Zion." (See Obadiah 1:21, also *Teachings of the Prophet Joseph Smith*, p. 330.)

President George Q. Cannon encouraged us to "rise up" and prepare our genealogical work so that our ancestors can receive the blessings of the temple: "It is your duty now to rise up, all of you, and trace your genealogies and begin to exercise the powers which belong to saviors of men, and when you do this in earnest, you will begin to comprehend how widespread, how numerous your ancestors are, for whom temple work has to be performed, in order that they may be brought into the fold; and when you get stopped, the Lord will reveal further information to you; and in this way the work of salvation and redemption will be accomplished." (*Gospel Truth*, p. 365.)

The Lord will help us as we seek out our ancestors and perform their temple work. All who engage in this great work bear testimony that they are guided and aided by those beyond the veil in accomplishing the necessary research.

When one of our daughters was eighteen she wanted something important to do for the summer. She thought about the possibilities and decided to go to the Family History Library and do research on the family genealogy. She came to her mother and asked for some family group sheets from which to start. Arda Jean showed her some early American families, some of which went only a few generations back.

She got on the bus for the trip downtown and looked over the material. "How do I begin?" she thought. But it was intriguing, and she was excited to try. At the library, she followed instructions, and began looking up names. At first all she could find was what she already had on the pedigree chart. She found no new information. She remembers sitting at the desk and thinking, "This is a blank. I can't find anything beyond what we already have. I can't even find this ancestor's birth certificate." It seemed overwhelming. She silently said a prayer for help as she sat at the table.

A card catalogue in the library listed books of genealogy that had been compiled. She thought of looking up the surname of the woman she was searching for, but doubts overcame her enthusiasm. She thought, "As though I'm going to find a book sitting on the shelf that says, "The History of Hannah Rogers."

Nevertheless, she went to the card catalogue and looked up the name. She didn't find the name of her ancestor, but she did find a book about people with the surname "Rogers." This was hopeful.

"But surely that won't be my 'Rogers'," she thought. She went anyway and located the book on the shelf. It was a thick book with name after name listed. Could she ever hope to find anything in in that large volume?

At first she thumbed through the pages, but when she started reading actual names, she saw that they were listed by years. More excited, she found the approximate time period when the elusive ancestor lived, and as she went down the page she was startled to see the name of her actual ancestor staring up at her!

With great elation she looked through the genealogy that was given and discovered that this woman had ancestors who came to America on the "Mayflower." She came home from her first day with several new generations, and enough enthusiasm to last the rest of the summer. As she proceeded with the search she was able to find a continuation of names back into the middle ages.

Our ancestors depend upon us to perform their work in the temple. We should remember, however, as President Benson explains, we need our ancestors as much for our own salvation as they need us for theirs:

> It is not sufficient for a husband and wife to be sealed in the temple to guarantee their exaltation—if they are faithful—they must also be eternally linked with their progenitors and see that the work is done for those ancestors. "They without us," said the Apostle Paul, "cannot be made perfect—neither can we without our dead be made perfect" (D&C 128:15). Our members must therefore understand that they have an individual responsibility to see that they are linked to their progenitors—or, as sacred scripture designates, our "fathers." This is the meaning of section 2, verse 2, in the Doctrine and Covenants when Moroni declared that Elijah "shall plant in the hearts of the children the promises made to the fathers, and the hearts of the children shall turn to their fathers." (*The Teachings of Ezra Taft Benson*, pp. 248-249.)

In the holy temples we can forge these links that will bind us into eternal family units, providing the opportunity of salvation to us and our kindred dead.

Frequent Temple Attendance for Personal Spiritual Benefit

President Howard W. Hunter said, "We again emphasize the personal blessings of temple worship and the sanctity and safety that are provided within those hallowed walls. It is the house of the Lord, a place of revelation and of peace. As we attend the temple, we learn more richly and deeply the purpose of life and the significance of the atoning sacrifice of the Lord Jesus Christ. Let us make the temple, with temple worship and temple covenants and temple marriage, our ultimate earthly goal and the supreme mortal experience." (CR, *Ensign*, November 1994, pp. 87-88.)

Once we have been to the temple and received our own personal blessings, we need to return often to refresh our memories of the sacred ceremonies performed therein. President Benson said,

> I make it a practice, whenever I perform a marriage, to suggest to the young couple that they return to the temple as soon as they can and go through the temple again as husband and wife. It isn't possible for them to understand fully the meaning of the holy endowment or the sealings with one trip through the temple, but as they repeat their visits to the temple, the beauty, the significance, and the importance of it all will be emphasized upon them. I have later had letters from some of these young couples expressing appreciation because that item was emphasized particularly. As they repeat their visits to the temple, their love for each other tends to increase and their marriage tends to be strengthened. (*The Teachings of Ezra Taft Benson*, p. 258.)

Many of us live within a short distance of the temple. For this we should be humbly grateful. For those who live farther away, it is still worth the effort to attend the temple as often as possible.

Of his own temple attendance, President Benson said, "I am grateful for the weekly temple sessions that Sister Benson and I enjoy together. The temple is the house of the Lord. Our attendance there blesses the dead and also blesses us, for it is a house of revelation." (*The Teachings of Ezra Taft Benson*, p. 255.)

When he said this in 1986, he and his wife attended a temple session weekly. As busy as he was with all the duties of the President of the Church he still took time to attend the temple on a regular basis. Shouldn't we all attend the temple regularly?

In the Doctrine and Covenants the Lord tells us of the blessings that come to us when we attend the temple: "For behold, I have accepted this house, and my name shall be here; and *I will manifest myself to my people in mercy in this house.*

"Yea, *I will appear unto my servants, and speak unto them with mine own voice*, if my people will keep my commandments, and do not pollute this holy house.

"Yea the *hearts of thousands and tens of thousands shall greatly rejoice* in consequence of the blessings which shall be poured out, and the endowment with which my servants have been endowed in this house." (D&C 110:7-9, emphasis added.)

We know that the Lord walks the halls of His temples. What a sacred privilege it is for us to walk those same halls! Surely we "greatly rejoice" because of the privilege of attending the temple.

President Gordon B. Hinckley issued a challenge and a promise to members of the Church to make themselves worthy of a temple recommend, and to attend more often, stating: "Every man or woman who goes to the temple in a spirit of sincerity and faith leaves the house of the Lord a better man or woman. . . . If every man in this church who has been ordained to the Melchizedek Priesthood were to qualify himself to hold a temple recommend, and then were to go to the house of the Lord and renew his covenants in solemnity before God and witnesses, we would be a better people. There would be little or no infidelity among us. Divorce would almost entirely disappear. So much of heartache and heartbreak would be avoided. There would be a greater measure of peace and love and happiness in our homes. . . . And I am confident the Lord would smile with greater favor upon us." (CR, *Ensign*, November 1995, p. 53.)

Certainly these promised blessings hit at the heart of today's needs. If we will, in humility, go to the temple with a specific purpose, something we feel the need of special help in solving, we can gain answers to the difficult questions in our lives. Elder John A. Widtsoe tells this instance of a problem being solved during temple attendance: "The temple is peculiarly a place of revelation. Many experiences have proved it. Perhaps the most impressive is this: For several years, under a Federal grant with my staff of workers we had gathered thousands of data in the field of soil moisture; but I could not extract any general law running through them. I gave up at last. My wife and I went to the temple that day to forget the failure. In the third endowment room, out of the unseen, came the solution, which has long since gone into print." (*In A Sunlit Land*, p. 177.)

I love to meditate in the temple. Sometimes when I have a problem I go to the temple praying for an answer to my problem. I always get an answer before I leave. What a blessing the temple has been in my life. I never leave the temple without feeling like I want to strive harder to keep all the commandments and build the kingdom of God.

Elder A. Theodore Tuttle also spoke of the blessings of temple attendance when he said, "A temple recommend is one of the highest accolades we may receive. To use it regularly permits us to participate in the choicest gifts within the keeping of the Church. Those who attend feel a special spirit there. Peace comes. I know that their service there assists a departed one to gain exaltation. And I know that they in turn qualify for blessings from the other side of the veil. And I know that blessings will follow you home from the temple." (CR, *Ensign,* May 1982, p. 66.)

Elder Tuttle says that blessings would follow us home from the temple. What are some of these blessings?

The Lord in the Doctrine and Covenants tells us that in the last days "my disciples shall stand in holy places, and shall not be moved; but among the wicked, men shall lift up their voices and curse God and die." (D&C 45:32.) In the temple we gain the spiritual strength we need to "not be moved" by the wickedness of the last days.

President Benson spoke of this blessing of spiritual strength when he said,

> Let us make the temple a sacred home away from our eternal home. This temple will be a standing witness that the power of God can stay the powers of evil in our midst. Many parents, in and out of the Church, are concerned about protection against a cascading avalanche of wickedness which threatens to engulf Christian principles. I find myself in complete accord with a statement made by President Harold B. Lee during World War II. Said he: "We talk about security in this day, and yet we fail to understand that . . . we have standing the holy temple wherein we may find the symbols by which power might be generated that will save this nation from destruction" (CR April 1942, p. 87).
>
> Yes, there is a power associated with the ordinances of heaven— even the power of godliness—which can and will thwart the forces of evil if we will be worthy of those sacred blessings. This community will be protected, our families will be protected, our children will be safeguarded as we live the gospel, visit the temple, and live close to the Lord. (*The Teachings of Ezra Taft Benson,* p. 256.)

We do live in perilous times, and we need the spiritual power that is generated by temple attendance if we are to save ourselves and our families from the "cascading avalanche of wickedness" that exists in these latter days.

President Benson further spoke of the perils of these days when he said,

The Prophet Joseph Smith declared that the heavenly messenger Moroni, "informed me of great judgments which were coming upon the earth, with great desolations by famine, sword, and pestilence; and that these grievous judgments would come on the earth in this generation" (Joseph Smith-History 1:45).

We live in a time when those days are imminent. Temples have been provided by a benevolent Father to protect us from these tribulations. Hear the promise given by President George Q. Cannon of the First Presidency: "When other temples are complete, there will be an increase in power bestowed on the people of God, and they will, thereby, be better fitted to go forth and cope with the powers of darkness and with the evils that exist in the world and to establish the Zion of God never more to be thrown down" (*Journal of Discourses*, 14:126). (*The Teachings of Ezra Taft Benson*, p. 245.)

When we regularly and worthily attend the temple, we are better able to cope with the trials of each day, in the difficult yet marvelous time in which we live. While speaking at the laying of the cornerstone for the Jordan River Utah Temple President Benson said, "The Saints in this temple district will be better able to meet any temporal tribulation because of this temple. Faith will increase as a result of the divine power associated with the ordinances of heaven and the assurance of eternal associations." (*The Teachings of Ezra Taft Benson*, p. 245.)

Elder John A. Widtsoe beautifully stated the power generated by temple worship when he said, "We can increase in knowledge and enlarge our capacity, and in that way receive greater gifts from God. I would therefore urge upon you that we teach those who go into the temples to do so with a strong desire to have God's will revealed to them, for comfort, peace, and success in our daily lives." ("Temple Worship," *The Utah Genealogical and Historical Magazine*, April 1921, pp. 63-64, as quoted in Relief Society Personal Study Guide, 1989, pp. 97-98.)

If we are worthy to go to the temple and have a temple recommend, we will grow spiritually by attending the temple on a regular basis. This is one of the best ways to get close to our Father in Heaven and protect ourselves from the evils of our day.

The covenants we make in the temple will help us to remain steadfast in the gospel. Elder S. Dilworth Young spoke of the strength early members of the Church gained from their temple covenants:

One day in the upper room of a house in Nauvoo the Prophet Joseph gathered half a dozen men and their wives. After preparing the proper clothing beforehand, he gave them the covenant of the endowment. Each one there made his personal covenant with God. Then the commandment was given that this should be done only in holy places. They now knew why they were to build the Nauvoo Temple as commanded. So they worked with all their might to build it. In my opinion, after the death of the Prophet, the thing that sustained the Saints as they came west with all the hardships, terrible hunger, thirst, sorrow and death was the covenant they had made with the Lord. They were promised that if they kept it they would attain the celestial kingdom. They knew that was so. So they went forth to their bitter struggle with fairly light hearts and assurances that they would be able to weather it through. (*Covenants and Commandments*, BYU Speeches of the Year [Provo, 3 Aug 1971], p. 6.)

The trials that we face are as difficult as those faced by the pioneering members of the Church. We also need strength gained by making sacred covenants in the temple so that we can have the assurance that we, too, will be able to "weather it through."

In this day when "the love of many [is waxing] cold" (Matthew 24:12), we are promised an increase of love in our homes from attendance at the house of the Lord: "When you attend the temple and perform the ordinances that pertain to the house of the Lord, certain blessings will come to you: You will receive the spirit of Elijah, which will turn your hearts to your spouse, to your children, and to your forebears. You will love your family with a deeper love than you have loved before. You will be endowed with power from on high as the Lord has promised." (*The Teachings of Ezra Taft Benson*, p. 254.)

Consider the blessings of deeper love for your family, coupled with the endowment of power from on high. In the trials of the latter days, these precious blessings will give us the vigor and stamina to win.

One time when I was in the temple doing ordinance work a temple worker confided, "I enjoy this work so much. I don't even want to go home at night." I could feel the Spirit radiate from him—a truly enjoyable experience. I feel the same way. I love feeling the sweetness of the spirit in the temple. Everyone is so kind and polite. The beauty of the temple ceremony draws me closer to the Lord.

Elder Lance B. Wickman of the Seventy told the words of a patriarch and temple sealer: "The joy I receive is more than just being in the temple. *The temple is in me!* And when I leave the temple, its peace goes with me." (CR, *Ensign*, November 1994, p. 83.)

Elder Franklin D. Richards noted the blessings that came into the life of a sister ordinance worker:

> I have witnessed the joy and satisfaction that come to those who serve in the temple. I recall on one occasion a sister coming through the temple door, her face bright with anticipation and her step quickened. She was a temple worker who had been back home for a visit. She grasped my hand and said, "It's so good to be back. I love my service in the temple, and know I cannot be happy, really happy, away from it. It brings me a joy and satisfaction that is found in no other place. I feel a sense of accomplishment in doing something of eternal value. It's a little like the work of the Savior, who did for mankind what they could not do for themselves. This work brings peace to my soul—yes, the peace that passeth understanding." (CR, *Ensign*, November 1986, p. 71.)

Be Worthy to Enter the Temple

In order to gain the blessings of temple attendance, we must make the effort to be worthy to attend the temple. When we attend the temple worthily, the Holy Spirit can comfort, inspire, and bless us, as President David O. McKay said in the dedicatory prayer of the Los Angeles Temple:

> May all who seek this holy temple come with clean hands and pure hearts that thy holy spirit may ever be present to comfort, to inspire, and to bless. If any with gloomy forebodings or heavy hearts enter, may they depart with their burdens lightened and their faith increased; if any have envy or bitterness in their hearts, may such feelings be replaced by self-searching and forgiveness. May all who come within these sacred walls feel a peaceful, hallowed influence. Cause, O Lord, that even people who pass the grounds or view the temple from afar, may lift their eyes from the groveling things of sordid life and look up to thee and thy providence." (*Improvement Era*, April 1956, p. 227.)

President Marion G. Romney explained that even our feelings should be right when we attend the temple:

God grant that we may be worthy to stand in his presence when we come here. To come unworthily into this temple and receive our endowments will not prove to be a blessing to us. Every soul when he comes here should be at peace in his own heart; his feelings should be at peace toward every other person in the world. He should have no hard feelings toward anyone. There should be no feelings of competition, no feelings of jealousy, nothing but the Spirit of the Living God and love toward our fellow men and toward each other, for here in his house we literally stand in the presence of the Lord. God grant that we may do so worthily." ("The House of the Lord," at dedication of Oakland Temple, *Improvement Era*, February 1965, p. 120.)

We should teach our children to keep themselves worthy, and make the goal of temple covenants be the guiding factor in their lives. President Howard W. Hunter pled with us to "prepare every missionary to go to the temple worthily and to make that experience an even greater highlight than receiving the mission call. Let us plan for and teach and plead with our children to marry in the house of the Lord. Let us reaffirm more vigorously than we ever have in the past that it does matter where you marry and by what authority you are pronounced man and wife." (CR, *Ensign*, November 1994, p. 88.)

Temple attendance will prepare us for eternal life. Elder F. Enzio Busche called the temple a "university" to teach eternal truths:

It has become my conviction that the temple is the only "university" for men to prepare spiritually for their graduation to eternal life. The temple is the place where the Lord wants us to make a sincere evaluation of our mortal lives. He wants us to know the consequences of the fact that this life is a probationary time. . . .

My dear brothers and sisters, I know of no better place where we can grow in the understanding of the principles of honesty than in the house of the Lord. I know of no better place to learn to grow in the dimensions of becoming our own judge than in the house of the Lord. We have reason to rejoice because the understanding that this life is a time for men to prepare to meet God has come to us while we still have time to consider the consequences of this message. We are still alive, and our probationary state is not yet over. Temples have been erected as houses of the Lord. They are standing ready to serve as instruments to our own gradual awakening to the full dimensions of truth on our inevitable road to eternity. (CR, *Ensign*, May 1989, pp. 71-73.)

President Hunter said, "All of our efforts in proclaiming the gospel, perfecting the Saints, and redeeming the dead lead to the holy temple. This is because the temple ordinances are absolutely crucial; we cannot return to God's presence without them. I encourage everyone to worthily attend the temple or to work toward the day when you can enter that holy house to receive your ordinances and covenants.

"May you let the meaning and beauty and peace of the temple come into your everyday life more directly in order that the millennial day may come, that promised time when 'they shall beat their swords into plowshares, and their spears into pruninghooks: nation shall not lift up sword against nation, neither shall they learn war any more . . . [but shall] walk in the light of the Lord' (Isaiah 2:4-5). (CR, *Ensign*, November 1994, p. 88.)

We are on the earth and in the Church during the dispensation of the fulness of times for a specific purpose. For Latter-day Saints that includes helping prepare the world for the coming of the Savior. President Hunter directed our efforts toward this end. We still have time on our side. We can make deep commitments, attend the temple regularly, and learn the gospel in a deeper sense. Let's humbly make, understand, and keep our temple covenants. Let's prepare ourselves for sanctification. "Wherefore, stand ye in holy places, and be not moved, until the day of the Lord come; for behold, it cometh quickly, saith the Lord. Amen." (D&C 87:8.)

22

You Can Receive Sanctification

Enter Thou into the Joy of the Lord

In this mortal world of afflictions and distress, it is sometimes easy to lose sight of the fact that the purpose of this life is to find joy. Even though life may be demanding, it should not be discouraging. Nephi told us, "Men are that they might have joy." (2 Nephi 2:25.) Joseph Smith added his affirmation: "Happiness is the object and design of our existence." (*Teachings of the Prophet Joseph Smith*, p. 255.)

The Savior's words of compensation to the faithful steward were: "Enter thou into the joy of thy lord." (Matt 29:21. Compare Alma 16:17; D&C 51:19, 70:18.) This reward is for a well-lived life. If we love the Lord and are striving to live to the best of our ability, entering into His joy is more than a possibility, it is a promise.

The triumphal hope of the faithful Latter-day Saint is to achieve Zion in this life, and hereafter return to Heavenly Father's presence and inherit the Celestial Kingdom. Patriarchal blessings have phrases like, "I seal you up to a glorious resurrection, and eternal life in the Kingdom of God." We know this scripturally, and as a doctrine, but do we, individual struggling members of the Church, actually *expect* to receive this reward? Do we think we are going to "make it"? Or are we still somehow feeling that it is beyond our reach, that it is for the apostles and prophets, but not for mere members?

We should expect to achieve the Celestial Kingdom. It is the hope in Christ which burns in the bosom of all true believers. It is the promise of our Savior. Furthermore, we should expect to receive the blessings of sanctification. We don't have to be superheroes. If we are doing what is required for a temple recommend, if we are being honest with ourselves and the Lord, if we take His work and our covenants seriously, we will make it. Elder Bruce R. McConkie said, "Everyone in the Church who is on the straight and narrow path, who is striving and struggling and desiring to do what is right, though is far from perfect in this life; if he passes out of this life while he's on the straight and narrow, he's going to go on to eternal reward in his Father's kingdom." ("The Probationary Test of Mortality," Fireside at Salt Lake Institute of Religion, January 10, 1982.)

Use of the Term "Sanctification"

Sanctification is a basic principle of the gospel, but not well understood. By its usage in the scriptures, we find a number of meanings, all connected.

1. *New birth.* In one sense sanctification is synonymous with being "born again," the purging of dross from our sinful selves by the Holy Ghost. The declaration by the Savior to the Nephites, and to us, was: "Now this is the commandment: Repent, all ye ends of the earth, and come unto me and be baptized in my name, that ye may be sanctified by the reception of the Holy Ghost, that ye may stand spotless before me at the last day." (3 Nephi 27:20.)

Baptism signifies that we accept His infinite sacrifice in our own life, and take upon us His name to bear with honor before the world. It is symbolic of His death, burial, and resurrection into a newness of life, as well as a symbolic washing of our past transgressions. Through our repentance and His forgiveness we likewise come forth as a new creature determined to live as He did, being cleansed and fit to receive the Holy Ghost. Sanctification consists of accepting the marvelous plan of redemption in our minds and in our hearts, and implementing it in our actions in every aspect of our lives. Dross and impurities are burned away by the Holy Ghost, and we stand spotless before our Savior Jesus Christ, himself a "lamb without blemish and without spot." It is indeed a new birth, a new life free from the fetters of baseness and mediocrity, and it assures us of the glory we desire in the eternal world to come.

2. *Becoming purified.* In another application, sanctification refers to the gradual, day by day process of purifying our lives by following the prompting of the Holy Ghost to apply our efforts to a particular fault or

weakness until we have mastered it. The Book of Mormon speaks of those who were sanctified: "Nevertheless they did fast and pray oft, and did wax stronger and stronger in their humility, and firmer and firmer in the faith of Christ, unto the filling their souls with joy and consolation, yea, even to the purifying and the sanctification of their hearts, which sanctification cometh because of their yielding their hearts unto God." (Helaman 3:35.)

In this step by step renewal and purification we activate the power of Jesus Christ's atonement. We receive a new cleansing each time we partake of the sacrament. We are prepared by this new remission of our sins for the Holy Ghost to enter our hearts and testify to us the truths taught by the speakers in our sacrament meetings. Our past mistakes are wiped clean and we are pure as we receive His Spirit to be with us. This is a strengthening process. We are changed inside and made stronger for the next trials and challenges which await us.

A parable may be made wherein using the gospel principles to change your life is like wearing a miner's hat. The Holy Ghost is the light which keeps scanning the way in front of you. The light shines on one rock, one aspect of your life. Your assignment is to remove that rock or blemish from your life. You may have been unaware of it before, but now the light dispels the darkness and shows you what to work on, and how. The more rocks you remove, the fewer you stumble over.

An example is contention. You may not even notice its effects in your life. When the light shines on it, gradually you abhor it and do anything possible to avoid it. The same is true with swearing, faultfinding, watching movies with bad content, and so on. If you act on the light and remove the stumbling block, you receive more light, then can go forward with the process of purification or sanctification. As you remove contaminants from your life, you not only become clean, you become better able to recognize others of them and also remove them from your life. Your faith, coupled with the power of Jesus Christ through the Holy Ghost, makes it possible.

Elder McConkie confirms that sanctification happens gradually. "Except in miraculous and unusual circumstances, as with Alma (Mosiah 27), spiritual rebirth is a process. It does not occur instantaneously. It comes to pass by degrees. Repentant persons become alive to one spiritual reality after another, until they are wholly alive in Christ and are qualified to dwell in his presence forever. Similarly, conversion is a process and sanctification is a process. They increase in the hearts of the obedient in process of time as they more fully keep the commandments and seek the Lord." (*Doctrinal New Testament Commentary*, vol. 3, p. 401.)

3. *A mighty change of heart.* The term sanctification also refers to the mighty change of heart which occurs when we accept the Atonement. It comes through the Lord's grace. On the day the Church was organized, Joseph Smith received a revelation that restated the need for faith in the Lord Jesus Christ, and repentance in order to gain salvation (D&C 20:29), and further told us that we can be sanctified through the Savior's grace: "We know that justification through the grace of our Lord and Savior Jesus Christ is just and true; And we know also, that sanctification through the grace of our Lord and Savior Jesus Christ is just and true, to all those who love and serve God with all their mights, minds, and strength." (D&C 20:30-31.)

Justification is a process of legality, making us innocent before God our Father. After our faith and repentance, the Holy Ghost lifts us to a guiltless state before God, through the atonement of Jesus Christ. When we reach this state we are no longer under the weight of sin, but ready for receiving sanctification by the blood of Christ (see Moses 6:59-60).

In this condition, we are ready for the enabling power of Jesus Christ to make a mighty change of heart, as Alma talked about: "Have ye spiritually been born of God? Have ye received his image in your countenance? Have ye experienced this mighty change in your hearts?" (Alma 5:14.) Alma speaks of "singing the song of redeeming love" as a counterpart to the mighty change of heart.

Fallen man cannot achieve this condition on his own. He must apply the redeeming blood of Jesus Christ in his life, and be acted upon by the Holy Ghost in order to overcome sin, purify his heart, and become sanctified. Elder Bruce R. McConkie wrote,

> Baptism of the Spirit is the way and the means whereby sanctification is made available. Thus, Jesus commands all the "ends of the earth" to be baptized in water "that ye may be sanctified by the reception of the Holy Ghost, that ye may stand spotless before me at the last day." (3 Nephi 27:20.) Truly, the Holy Ghost is a sanctifier, and the extent to which men receive and enjoy the gift of the Holy Ghost is the extent to which they are sanctified. In the lives of most of us, sanctification is an ongoing process, and we obtain that glorious status by degrees as we overcome the world and become saints

in deed as well as in name. (*A New Witness for the Articles of Faith*, p. 266.)

We receive the right to the Holy Ghost when we are confirmed members of the Church. Beyond that, Elder Glenn L. Pace explains, going to the temple gives us additional power through the Holy Ghost:

> When we go to the temple, we receive the endowment and more power through the Holy Ghost is given to us, if we remain true to these covenants, that we "may grow up in [God], and receive a fulness of the Holy Ghost, . . . and be prepared to obtain every needful thing." (D&C 109:15.)
>
> Members who go to the temple have access to a fulness of the Holy Ghost that is not available to those who have only received the gift of the Holy Ghost. This is a very real blessing. For example, those who have received their endowments can reflect on the beautiful blessings given at the time they were washed and anointed in the initiatory work. In effect their body, mind, and soul were dedicated to righteous purposes. I would counsel all to listen carefully to those blessings the next time they perform initiatory work. Great power is given in that part of the endowment.
>
> . . . Is there a greater power that we can receive in the temple than to conquer our own flesh to the point that our very desires or dispositions are to do only good? It is part of receiving a fullness of the Holy Ghost. As we remain true to our covenants, the sanctification, the purification, and the refining are taking place day in and day out, during temple sessions and between temple visits. That process is an endowment of righteous power, a power to purge ourselves of even the desire to do evil. (*Spiritual Revival*, pp. 128-129.)

4. *Personal revelation.* Sanctification will be accompanied by personal revelation through the Holy Ghost. The Nephites who experienced the mighty change of heart found that they were receiving personal revelation, also through the power of the Holy Spirit. They said, "through the infinite goodness of God, and the manifestations of his Spirit, [we] have great views of that which is to come; and were it expedient, we could prophesy of all things." (Mosiah 5:3.)

The Prophet Joseph Smith affirmed this also: "No man can receive the Holy Ghost without receiving revelations. The Holy Ghost is a revelator." (*Teachings of the Prophet Joseph Smith*, p. 328.)

Are we seeking this gift in our lives? Do we know that we are entitled, as members of the Church, to receive revelation for ourselves and our families? The Holy Ghost will give us revelation in regard to our personal problems. He will give us guidance in regard to our families, our church duties, and our businesses. He will help us in our relationships with spouse, children, and friends. He will comfort us in time of need. He will send peace to our souls, gladness to our hearts, and joy to our whole being. He will lead us back to Heavenly Father.

President Joseph F. Smith said,

> The spirit of inspiration, the gift of revelation does not belong to one man solely; . . . It is not confined to the presiding authorities of the Church, it belongs to every individual member of the Church; and it is the right and privilege of every man, every woman, and every child who has reached the years of accountability, to enjoy the spirit of revelation, and to be possessed of the spirit of inspiration in the discharge of their duties as members of the Church. It is the privilege of every individual member of the Church to have revelation for his own guidance, for the direction of his life and conduct. (*Conference Report*, April 1912, p. 5.)

5. *The Second Comforter.* In another usage, sanctification refers to an event, a manifestation of the power and presence of God termed "having one's calling and election made sure." It is the reward for staying on the strait and narrow path, for struggling through the other purifying processes and achieving them, for enduring to the end, and conquering by faith. Sanctification in this sense is the glory, the prize, the winner's crown, the destination of our journey through life. Some receive it in this life, like Moses, the brother of Jared, and Joseph Smith. Many Latter-day Saints have received this witness, and some have testified of it.

The Prophet Joseph Smith taught the principle, calling it "the Second Comforter":

> After a person has faith in Christ, repents of his sins, and is baptized for the remission of his sins and receives the Holy Ghost, (by the laying on of hands), which is the first Comforter, then let him continue to humble himself before God, hungering and thirsting after righteousness, and living by every word of God, and the Lord will soon say unto him, Son, thou shalt be exalted.
> When the Lord has thoroughly proved him, and finds that the man is determined to serve Him at all hazards, then the man will find his

calling and his election made sure, then it will be his privilege to receive the other Comforter, which the Lord hath promised the Saints . . . when any man obtains this last Comforter, he will have the personage of Jesus Christ to attend him, or appear unto him from time to time, and even He will manifest the Father unto him, and they will take up their abode with him, and the visions of the heavens will be opened unto him, and the Lord will teach him face to face, and he may have a perfect knowledge of the mysteries of the Kingdom of God; and this is the state and place the ancient Saints arrived at when they had such glorious visions—Isaiah, Ezekiel, John upon the Isle of Patmos, St. Paul in the three heavens, and all the Saints who held communion with the general assembly and Church of the Firstborn. (*Teachings of the Prophet Joseph Smith*, p. 150.)

Sanctification in This World

We can enter into the joy of the Lord while still in this world if we do what is required: "Learn that he who doeth the works of righteousness shall receive his reward, even peace in this world, and eternal life in the world to come." (D&C 59:23.)

Eternal life will be a continuation of the condition of faithfulness we achieve in this lifetime. The reward "enter thou in to the joy of thy lord" is not merely for the eternal worlds to come, but also in the day by day experiences of this life. The reason for learning the gospel and obeying the commandments is to make this happen—the gospel principles are tools, enablers which produce the desired result. It is an upward spiral to joy, an act of becoming. A motto I heard once was, "Learn to do by doing." By doing, we become better able to do. The process lifts and strengthens us, enables us to do more and do it better, which produces joy. The performance of the actions of going to Church, partaking of the sacrament, hearing and teaching spiritual lessons, and participating in personal and family prayer makes our lives better—happier, more capable, more peaceful, more secure. We were never meant to fail. The gospel makes it happen.

The joy of the Lord was a reward in this life to King Benjamin's people who filled the requirements: "And it came to pass that after they had spoken these words the Spirit of the Lord came upon them, and they were filled with joy, having received a remission of their sins, and having peace of conscience, because of the exceeding faith which they had in Jesus Christ who should come, according to the words which king Benjamin had spoken unto them." (Mosiah 4:3.)

Mormon describes the joyous condition of the members of the church after the coming of Christ to this continent: "The people were all converted unto the Lord, upon all the face of the land, both Nephites and Lamanites, and there were no contentions and disputations among them, and every man did deal justly one with another. And they had all things common among them; therefore there were not rich and poor, bond and free, but they were all made free, and partakers of the heavenly gift. And there were great and marvelous works wrought by the disciples of Jesus . . . And the Lord did prosper them exceedingly in the land . . . the love of God . . . did dwell in the hearts of the people . . . and surely there could not be a happier people among all the people who had been created by the hand of God . . . And how blessed were they! For the Lord did bless them in all their doings." (4 Nephi 1:2-18.)

In contrast to this is the account of the people of Israel under Moses, who had the opportunity to be blessed in the same manner. The Lord brought them forth from physical bondage, and planned to relieve them of spiritual bondage but they were unwilling to give up their sins, remaining hardhearted and unrepentant: "Now this [the gospel] Moses plainly taught to the children of Israel in the wilderness, and sought diligently to sanctify his people that they might behold the face of God;

"But they hardened their hearts and could not endure his presence; therefore, the Lord in his wrath, for his anger was kindled against them, swore that they should not enter into his rest while in the wilderness, which rest is the fulness of his glory.

"Therefore, he took Moses out of their midst, and the Holy Priesthood also." (D&C:84:23-25.)

The Israelites not only wandered forty years in the wilderness, they lost the privileges of the Priesthood, the great and marvelous blessings of obedience, and the leadership of Moses. We are at the same crossroads in our day. If we accept the offered reward, we may be blessed exceedingly as were the people of Benjamin or those after the time of Christ. If we remain hardhearted, collectively we will lose our hope of Zion; individually we lose our promise of peace in this world and eternal life in the world to come.

Zion, a Oneness With God

Sanctification includes bringing our will into consensus with the will of God. "Therefore, sanctify yourselves that your minds become single to God, and the days will come that you shall see him; for he will unveil his face unto you, and it shall be in his own time, and in his own way, and according to his own will." (D&C 88:68.)

What does it mean to have one's mind single to God? President Brigham Young said, "When the will, passions, and feelings of a person are perfectly submissive to God and His requirements, that person is sanctified. It is for my will to be swallowed up in the will of God, that will lead me into all good, and crown me ultimately with immortality and eternal lives." (*Journal of Discourses*, vol. 2, p. 123.)

Christ was the perfect example of this: "Yea, even so he shall be led, crucified, and slain, the flesh becoming subject even unto death, the will of the Son being swallowed up in the will of the Father." (Mosiah 15:7.)

When the Lord's people subject themselves to the will of God, and become one with Him, they achieve a condition called Zion, or the pure in heart. President Spencer W. Kimball writes,

> For many years we have been taught that one important end result of our labors, hopes, and aspirations in this work is the building of a Latter-day Zion, a Zion characterized by love, harmony, and peace —a Zion in which the Lord's children are as one. . . .
>
> Unfortunately we live in a world that largely rejects the values of Zion. Babylon has not and never will comprehend Zion. . . .
>
> Zion can be built up only among those who are pure in heart, not a people torn by covetousness or greed, but a pure and selfless people. Not a people who are pure in appearance, rather a people who are pure in heart. Zion is to be in the world and not of the world, not dulled by a sense of carnal security, nor paralyzed by materialism. No, Zion is not things of the lower, but of the higher order, things that exalt the mind and sanctify the heart.
>
> . . . As I understand these matters, Zion can be established only by those who are pure in heart, and who labor for Zion, for "the laborer in Zion shall labor for Zion; for if they labor for money they shall perish." (2 Nephi 26:31.) (*The Teachings of Spencer W. Kimball*, pp. 362-63.)

Unity with the will of God is approached when there is no more disposition to evil, but instead a love which seeks the good of fellowmen as equal to oneself, a guileless approach to relationships with others, a perfect honesty with self, others, and deity, plus a pure love for God the Father and His Son Jesus Christ. Submission to His will impels people to concentrate on others rather than seeking one's own perfection. Lifting others and serving their needs tend to become the channel through which purification flows. People in every nation who love and serve each other are the leaven Jesus spoke of which raises the whole loaf (Matthew 13:33). When these Zion people come together and live in one society, they become amazingly effective, even in the eyes of the rest of the world (see D&C 97:18-21). In its essence, becoming pure in heart is the process of yielding one's will to the will of God, of recognizing His omniscience combined with His pure love for His children, and accepting His will as being what is best in life. In this attitude, people are able to seek the best for each other as well as themselves; they are able to love purely and freely; and they bend their efforts in service, learning, and teaching in the Kingdom of God. In the process, their own purification and perfection is happening, better than if they are actively pursuing it.

Sanctification Through Love and Service

Christ told us that the two great commandments are to love God and love others. Love is the great center of the entire gospel. God loved us, so He sent His Son to redeem us. Christ loved us, so He was willing to endure the pains of His sacrifice for us. We must likewise give our whole hearts to God and obey Him because of our great love for Him, and for our Brother who gave His all for us. In doing this, our hearts are drawn out toward our brothers and sisters, and we care for them, care about them, and serve them. Remember King Benjamin's admonition that service to our fellow men is really service to God? (See Mosiah 2:17.) And we do this to glorify God, who told us His work and glory is to bring about the salvation of man (see Moses 1:39).

The Book of Mormon tells us that part of enduring to the end includes love for our fellow men: "Ye must press forward with a steadfastness in Christ, having a perfect brightness of hope, and a love of God and of all men." (2 Nephi 31:20.)

At baptism we covenant to keep all of God's commandments, including the commandment to love and serve one another. When Alma's people desired to be baptized, he asked them if they were willing to serve one another:

> And now, as ye are desirous to come into the fold of God, and to be called his people, and are willing to bear one another's burdens, that they may be light;

Yea, and are willing to mourn with those that mourn; yea, and comfort those that stand in need of comfort, and to stand as witnesses of God at all times and in all things, and in all places that ye may be in, even until death, that ye may be redeemed of God, and be numbered with those of the first resurrection, that ye may have eternal life—

Now I say unto you, if this be the desire of your hearts, what have you against being baptized in the name of the Lord, as a witness before him that ye have entered into a covenant with him, that ye will serve him and keep his commandments, that he may pour out his Spirit more abundantly upon you? (Mosiah 18:8-10.)

It is our privilege as well as our duty as members of the Church to be charitable and care for one another. King Benjamin said it this way: "For the sake of retaining a remission of your sins from day to day, that ye may walk guiltless before God—I would that ye should impart of your substance to the poor, every man according to that which he hath, such as feeding the hungry, clothing the naked, visiting the sick and administering to their relief, both spiritually and temporally, according to their wants." (Mosiah 4:26.)

If we choose to mock the poor we are committing a grave sin: "Whoso mocketh the poor reproacheth his Maker." (Proverbs 17:5.) Rather, as disciples of Christ, we are to give love and concern, and the actual care they need. "And remember in all things the poor and the needy, the sick and the afflicted, for he that doeth not these things, the same is not my disciple." (D&C 52:40.)

Elder Glenn L. Pace says, "the greatest sanctification takes place with person-to-person help. Hence, the greatest compassionate service each of us can give may be in our own neighborhoods and communities. Wherever we live in the world, there is pain and sorrow all around us. We need to take more initiative as individuals in deciding how we can best be of service." (*Spiritual Revival*, p. 91.)

Do we remember those whom Jesus called the "least of these"? We hope that we will live together in love, so that someday Christ will say to us,

Come, ye blessed of my Father, inherit the kingdom prepared for you from the foundation of the world:

For I was an hungred, and ye gave me meat: I was thirsty, and ye gave me drink: I was a stranger, and ye took me in:

Naked, and ye clothed me: I was sick, and ye visited me: I was in prison, and ye came unto me.

Then shall the righteous answer him, saying, Lord, when saw we thee an hungred, and fed thee? or thirsty, and gave thee drink?

When saw we thee a stranger, and took thee in? or naked, and clothed thee?

Or when saw we thee sick, or in prison, and came unto thee?

And the King shall answer and say unto them, Verily I say unto you, Inasmuch as ye have done it unto one of the least of these my brethren, ye have done it unto me. (Matthew 25:34-40.)

We who have taken upon us the name and service of Jesus Christ will find it a blessed privilege to "succor the weak, lift up the hands which hang down, and strengthen the feeble knees." (D&C 81:5.) There is a story from the pioneer era that illustrates this point. In a time when food was scarce, one of Brother Joseph Millett's children came to him and told him that Brother Newton Hall's family was out of bread. He took some of his flour and put it in a sack to send to the Halls. Just then Brother Hall came to his house. Brother Millett asked him if he had any flour, to which he replied that they had none. Brother Millett then gave him the sack of flour, telling him that he was just about to send it to him, because his children had learned that the family was out of bread.

Brother Hall began to cry and told Brother Millett that he had tried several places to see if he could borrow some flour, but had not found any. He then went to a grove a trees and prayed, and the Lord told him to go to Brother Millett. "Well, Brother Hall," replied Brother Millett, "you needn't bring this back. If the Lord sent you for it, you don't owe me for it."

Later he recorded in his journal, "You can't tell how good it made me feel to know that the Lord knew that there was such a person as Joseph Millett." (Joseph Millett Jr. Record Book, microfilm of manuscript [Salt Lake City: Church Historical Department], pp. 88-89. Quoted in *Visions of Zion* by Alexander B. Morrison, pp. 115-116.)

When a person lifts another, he becomes nearer to God in the process. It is a double benefit, uplifting both the receiver and the giver. When gospel principles are in action, acts such as these "leaven the loaf" of society. They characterize the Zion people we seek to become.

Remember that God knows you and me by name. He knows our circumstances and the desires of our hearts. There are opportunities around each of us to help those in need. If we look, we will see those that are obvious. If we listen to the still, small voice, He will give us impressions of where unseen desperate needs can be met. When we have compassion for those around us by helping them in their hour of need, it has a sanctifying effect on our own souls. Elder Glenn L. Pace said, "when we get emotionally and spiritually involved in helping a person who is in pain, compassion enters our heart. It hurts, but the process lifts some of the pain from another. We get from the experience a finite look into the Savior's pain as he performed the infinite atonement. Through the power of the Holy Ghost, a sanctification takes place within our souls, and we become more like our Savior. We gain a better understanding of what he meant when he said, 'Inasmuch as ye have done it unto one of the least of these my brethren, ye have done it unto me.' (Matthew 25:40.)" (*Spiritual Revival*, p. 30.)

The Book of Mormon exhorts us to "give, if we have, to those who stand in need." Who are the "haves" and who the "have nots"? You may consider yourself to be a "have-not" but consider this: if we compare the average in the United States with the average in South America, the average in the United States is truly rich. If we compare the average in South America with the average in, say, Ethiopia, we begin to get the picture. Let's be liberal with the goods with which the Lord has endowed us in helping those in need. After all, as President Kimball said, "What honor is there in being the richest man in the cemetery?" (*The Teachings of Spencer W. Kimball*, p. 353.)

By living the great law of consecration we insure not only temporal salvation but spiritual sanctification. President Kimball writes, "As givers gain control of their desires and properly see others' needs in light of their own wants, then the powers of the gospel are released in their lives. They learn that by living the great law of consecration they insure not only temporal salvation but also spiritual sanctification." (*The Teachings of Spencer W. Kimball*, p. 365.)

Needs are not always for goods. Often the need is for something spiritual: love, interest, strength, comfort, direction, support, kindness, sympathy, or caring. James reminds us that "pure religion" includes our visiting and caring for the fatherless and widows. (James 1:27.)

One of the best ways to serve others is to do missionary work, making available to them the joy and hope that an understanding of the gospel brings. This not only helps the recipient, but as Elder William R. Bradford explained, doing missionary work helps us to be perfected by serving Christ:

. . . Come unto Christ and be perfected in Him. This is done by serving Him with all of our heart, might, mind, and strength. If we do this, we receive a remission of our sins and become holy and without spot and may return to our Heavenly Father and dwell again with Him, to live the kind of life He lives.

The Savior stands with His hands extended, offering us glorious blessings if we will serve Him. As we study what He means by this service we come to understand that it is fundamentally the service of teaching the truths of his gospel to those who do not know it. . . .

This is a marvelous plan. It is a process of sanctification. When a missionary is placed in a mission environment of order and discipline where all that is done is in harmony with the Spirit, the missionary experiences a great transformation. The heavens open. Powers are showered out. Mysteries are revealed. Habits are improved. Sanctification begins. Through this process the missionary becomes a vessel of light that can shine forth the gospel of Jesus Christ in a world in darkness. (CR, *Ensign*, November 1981, pp. 49, 51.)

Elder Bradford spoke these words inviting young men and women to serve missions, but the principle of sanctification through service is the same for all of us. Glorious blessings are offered to all who serve Christ, those who teach the gospel and those who receive it. The blessings of Heaven attend the missionary effort in both directions. Arda Jean remembers, "We may wonder how far the effect of our work will reach. How beautiful it was while I was on a mission to the Northwestern states, to meet a couple who had accepted the gospel when my father was a missionary in Chicago many years before. Far from the place of their baptism, and forty years later, they recognized me as the daughter of "their special elder." The husband was now on the High Council, and they were both continuing to give service, receive joy, and bless the lives of others. The work of the Lord goes out like ripples in the water from each life refined by His message. How satisfying it was to be where these ripples came together, and hear the words of love and gratitude expressed later."

It is important that we both learn for ourselves and teach to others the saving gospel principles. Attention to the eternal aspect of this life may be difficult, but is essential. President Kimball said, "If we spend our mortal days in accumulating secular knowledge to the exclusion of the spiritual then we are in a dead-end street, for this is the time for man to prepare to meet God; this is the time for faith to be built, for baptism to be effected, for the Holy Ghost to be received, for the ordinances to be performed." (*The Teachings of Spencer W. Kimball*, p. 390.)

The Oath and Covenant of the Priesthood

The saving ordinances of the gospel are performed through the power of the Holy Priesthood, administered by worthy men ordained to this office and calling through authority. When this priesthood is received, the holder covenants with his Eternal Father with a solemn oath that he will accept this power and authority as an integral part of his life, honor it, use it only in righteousness, and magnify it by doing the will of the Father. In turn, his Eternal Father covenants with him with an eternal oath that He will honor in Heaven the works performed through this Priesthood on the earth, and that the bearer is entitled to receive all that the Father hath on condition of his faithfulness.

President Ezra Taft Benson described the oath and covenant of the priesthood thus, in an area conference in England in 1976:

> When a priesthood holder takes upon himself the Melchizedek Priesthood, he does so by oath and covenant. . . . The covenant of the Melchizedek Priesthood is that a priesthood holder will magnify his calling in the priesthood, will give diligent heed to the commandments of God, and will live by every word which proceeds "from the mouth of God" (see D&C 84:33-44). The oath of the Melchizedek Priesthood is an irrevocable promise by God to faithful priesthood holders. "All that my Father hath shall be given unto them" (see D&C 84:38). This oath by Deity, coupled with the covenant by faithful priesthood holders, is referred to as the oath and covenant of the priesthood. (*Teachings of Ezra Taft Benson*, p. 223.)

President Joseph Fielding Smith spoke of this covenant: "And so Christ is the great prototype where priesthood is concerned, as he is with reference to baptism and all other things. And so, even as the Father swears with an oath that his Son shall inherit all things through the priesthood, so he swears with an oath that all of us who magnify our callings in that same priesthood shall receive all that the Father hath." (CR, *Ensign*, December 1970, p. 27.)

The Holy Priesthood is for service only. To magnify it means to use it in faithful service in the Lord's kingdom, as directed through authority in that Priesthood. President Marion G. Romney spoke of the "transcendent blessings the Father promises the receiver of the Melchizedek Priesthood by an oath and covenant," and then stated: "Ordination to the priesthood is a prerequisite to receiving [these blessings], but does not guarantee them. For a man actually to obtain them, he must faithfully discharge the obligation which is placed upon him when he receives the priesthood; that is, he must magnify his calling."

He continued: "It is of utmost importance that we keep clearly in mind what the magnifying of our callings in the priesthood requires of us. I am persuaded that it requires at least the following three things:

"1. That we obtain a knowledge of the gospel.

"2. That we comply in our personal living with the standards of the gospel.

"3. That we give dedicated service."

And further, "The nature of this service is spelled out in detail in the revelations and by the living prophets. The burden of it the Lord has laid upon his priesthood. It can be done properly only by men who are magnifying their priesthood; who know the gospel, conform their lives to its standards, and who enthusiastically give dedicated service." (CR, *Ensign*, June 1962, pp. 416-417.)

The saving ordinances of the gospel, bestowed by the power of the priesthood, are in force in this life and in the life to come. They are performed by faithful priesthood holders in behalf of worthy members of the Lord's Church. All members receive the benefit of these ordinances, and no priesthood holder performs ordinances in his own behalf, except in administration of the Sacrament. The priesthood is for service only, and for the orderly accomplishment of the work of saving souls. Those who keep their priesthood covenants will receive eternal life.

The Reward of the Sanctified

What are the blessings available to us if we are obedient? "But as it is written, Eye hath not seen, nor ear heard, neither have entered into the heart of man, the things which God hath prepared for them that love him.

"But God hath revealed them unto us by his Spirit: for the Spirit searcheth all things, yea, the deep things of God." (1 Corinthians 2:9-10.)

The rewards are so great that we have never even imagined them! If we can open our hearts in trust and faith to our Heavenly Father, He will reveal to us more, better, grander vistas than we have ever known or could conceive. The refiner's fire removes our impurities and makes us better than we knew we could be. We are raised to a higher level of consciousness, of caring, and of compassion; we are lifted to a higher plain of intellect, interest, and interaction; we are elevated to a greater capacity for courage, creativity, and comprehension. Listen to the Lord, Himself, describe some of it in language we can understand:

"For thus saith the Lord—I, the Lord, am merciful and gracious unto those who fear me, and delight to honor those who serve me in righteousness and in truth unto the end.

"Great shall be their reward and eternal shall be their glory.

"And to them will I reveal all mysteries, yea, all the hidden mysteries of my kingdom from days of old, and for ages to come, will I make known unto them the good pleasure of my will concerning all things pertaining to my kingdom.

"Yea, even the wonders of eternity shall they know, and things to come will I show them, even the things of many generations.

"And their wisdom shall be great, and their understanding reach to heaven; and before them the wisdom of the wise shall perish, and the understanding of the prudent shall come to naught.

"For by my Spirit will I enlighten them, and by my power will I make known unto them the secrets of my will—yea, even those things which eye has not seen, nor ear heard, nor yet entered into the heart of man." (D&C 76:5-10.)

The Lord has prepared it, and He wants us to receive it. The plan of eternity is in operation, our Savior Jesus Christ has done His part, the Eternal God of Heaven waits with open arms for us to make the choices that will bring us home to Him. We can do it.

How is It to be Done

Whether we receive sanctification in this life or the next, we should go forward with hope and rejoicing. We are in the Lord's cause. We have the principles of faith and repentance. We have the Lord's word and the gift of the Holy Ghost to guide us. We have every reason to expect success.

Elder Bruce R. McConkie urged us to start where we are, and go forward with faith: "Work on the projects ahead, and when you have taken one step in the acquiring of faith, it will give you the assurance in your soul that you can go forward and take the next step, and by degrees your power or influence will increase until eventually, in this world or in the next, you will say to the Mt. Zerins in your life, 'Be thou removed.' You will say to whatever encumbers your course of eternal progress, 'Depart,' and it will be so." ("Lord, Increase our Faith," Speech given at Brigham Young University, October 31, 1967.)

The Church of Jesus Christ of Latter-day Saints is a vehicle for salvation. Its stated purpose is to spread the gospel, perfect the saints, and redeem the dead. If we are in the Church, following its precepts and associating in its activities, maintaining ourselves in a steady course, we shall achieve the desired end. Elder McConkie encourages us again: "As members of the Church, if we chart a course leading to eternal life; if we begin the processes of spiritual rebirth, and are going in the right direction; if we chart a course of sanctifying our souls, and degree by degree are going in that direction; and if we chart a course of becoming perfect, and step by step and phase by phase, are perfecting our souls by overcoming the world, then it is absolutely guaranteed—there is no question whatever about it—we shall gain eternal life. Even though we have spiritual rebirth ahead of us, perfection ahead of us, the full degree of sanctification ahead of us, if we chart a course and follow it to the best of our ability in this life, then when we go out of this life we'll continue in exactly that same course. We'll no longer be subject to the passions and the appetites of the flesh. We will have passed successfully the tests of this mortal probation and in due course we'll get the fulness of our Father's kingdom—and that means eternal life in his everlasting presence." ("Jesus Christ and Him Crucified," Address at Brigham Young University, September 5, 1976.)

23

You Can Endure to the End

The Prophet Nephi lived a remarkable life and saw many miracles because of his faith. When he was concluding his writings in the Book of Mormon, he asked whether baptism, the entrance to the "strait and narrow path," is all that is required of us to obtain eternal life:

> And now, my beloved brethren, after ye have gotten into this strait and narrow path, I would ask if all is done? Behold, I say unto you, Nay; for ye have not come thus far save it were by the word of Christ with unshaken faith in him, relying wholly upon the merits of him who is mighty to save.
>
> Wherefore, ye must press forward with a steadfastness in Christ, having a perfect brightness of hope, and a love of God and of all men. Wherefore, if ye shall press forward, feasting upon the word of Christ, and *endure to the end*, behold, thus saith the Father: Ye shall have eternal life. (2 Nephi 31:19-20, emphasis added.)

In this final message to us, Nephi tells us that what is required is that we "endure to the end." President Joseph Fielding Smith also explained that after we have complied with the first principles and ordinances of the gospel, we still have to endure to the end in order to gain salvation:

> *We must endure to the end*; we must keep the commandments after baptism; we must work out our salvation with fear and trembling before the Lord; we must so live as to acquire the attributes of godliness and become the kind of people who can enjoy the glory and wonders of the celestial kingdom. ("The Plan of Salvation," *Ensign*, November 1971, p. 5, emphasis added.)

The scriptures contain numerous promises to us that if we are faithful to the end, we shall be saved in the Kingdom of God. Here are some of these promises:

> But he that shall *endure unto the end*, the same shall be saved. (Matthew 24:13, emphasis added.)

> Behold, I am the law, and the light. Look unto me, and *endure to the end*, and ye shall live; for unto him that *endureth to the end* will I give eternal life. (3 Nephi 15:9, emphasis added.)

> If thou wilt do good, yea, and *hold out faithful to the end*, thou shalt be saved in the kingdom of God, which is the greatest of all the gifts of God; for there is no gift greater than the gift of salvation. (D&C 6:13, emphasis added.)

> And we know that all men must repent and believe on the name of Jesus Christ, and worship the Father in his name, and *endure in faith on his name to the end*, or they cannot be saved in the kingdom of God. (D&C 20:29, emphasis added.)

What Does It Mean to Endure to the End?

When we say "endure to the end" we could have reference to two occurrences. The first is obvious: the end of our mortal lives. The second is the end of the world as we know it, or the Second Coming of Christ. Living as we do in the Saturday night of time and expecting the advent of the Millennial reign of Jesus Christ, we could make reference to that as being the end to which we should endure. In either case, the personal principle is the same. We are to remain faithful and active throughout our mortal probation, until we have overcome our test and proved ourselves worthy.

Nephi gives an explanation of how to endure to the end when he tells us, "Unless a man shall endure to the end, *in following the example of the Son of the living God*, he cannot be saved." (2 Nephi 31:16, emphasis added.) How do we follow Christ's example? We know that Christ was obedient to His Father in all things: "For I came down from heaven, not to do mine own will, but the will of him that sent me." (John 6:38.) We also must be obedient to our Father in Heaven.

What are some of the things our Father expects of us? Elder Hartman Rector, Jr. made this summary:

Then after baptism by the water and the Spirit, it appears that all the Father requires of us is that we endure to the end. What does that mean? I believe it means basically three things.

One: We must continue to repent for the rest of our lives because we will still make mistakes, and we must go home clean or we can't dwell with the Father and the Son (see D&C 84:74).

Two: we must continue to forgive others. If we do not forgive others, we cannot obtain forgiveness ourselves (see D&C 64:9-10). And three: Yes, we must be nice. If we're not nice, I don't think we're going to make it. In other words, we must have charity, which is really love plus sacrifice. We must serve our fellowmen, women, and children, and if we do all else but we do not serve the poor, the needy, the down-trodden, the oppressed, the sick and afflicted, both temporally and spiritually, according to their wants, we cannot retain a remission of our sins from day to day. Without serving others, we cannot "walk guiltless before God" (Mosiah 4:26). (CR, *Ensign*, November 1994, p. 26.)

When we are thus preoccupied with love of God and love of our fellowmen, we find that study of the scriptures, Church activity, sustaining those who serve by presiding over us, forgiving those who may offend, observing the sabbath, being moral and honest, and keeping other commandments are tools, enablers by which we are strengthened and able to give the service we desire to give. There are important reasons for every commandment our Father has given, and the bottom line is to raise us up, and help us lift others. He loves all of us, and so should we. Let us never be too busy to be caring and helpful to our brothers and sisters.

In spite of the frequent admonition in the scriptures that we have to endure to the end to be saved, some seem to feel that they have done enough, and that they can just "coast" through their later years. To these people President Joseph Fielding Smith said,

All who have received law and who have known the truth in a degree will be judged according to the truth that they have known, and if they have not lived up to that which they have known, or which they have been taught or had the privilege of receiving, then they cannot enter into the celestial kingdom. . . .

If you are slipping, if you are careless and indifferent and you violate the covenants you made when you went through the temple

and you continue to do that, remember the Lord has said repeatedly that it is he who endures to the end who shall be saved. And if that is what you have been doing, that leaves you out. You will not gain salvation. . . .

"Oh," someone says, "the Lord is just and merciful. He is a merciful God and when man repents, God will give him these privileges. The Lord will reinstate him after he is dead when he repents." Every man has to repent eventually and every knee has to bow, even those going into the telestial kingdom. . . .

"And no unclean thing can enter into his kingdom; therefore nothing entereth into his rest save it be those who have washed their garments in my blood, because of their faith, and the repentance of all their sins, and their faithfulness unto the end." (3 Nephi 27:14-19.)

Now, every knee must bow, the Lord has said, and every tongue confess that Jesus is the Christ; but that does not mean the bowing or bending of the knee and confessing Jesus as the Son of God is going to put people in the celestial kingdom. (*Doctrines of Salvation*, 2:192-194, emphasis included.)

This may seem like a harsh doctrine, but, as the Prophet Joseph Smith said, "Reflect for a moment . . . and enquire whether you would consider yourselves worthy [of] a seat at the marriage feast with Paul and others like him, if you had been unfaithful? Had you not fought the good fight, and kept the faith, could you expect to receive?" (*Teachings of the Prophet Joseph Smith*, p. 64.)

In D&C 14:7 we read, "And, if you keep my commandments and endure to the end you shall have eternal life, which gift is the greatest of all the gifts of God." Enduring to the end means remaining faithful until the end of our mortal lives. We will never come to a time in our lives when faithful observance of the commandments is no longer required of us.

Belle S. Spafford, former general president of Relief Society, spoke of the need to endure to the end. She attended a Relief Society meeting in a nursing home, and told this of the visit.

During the meeting, the sisters had expressed the hope that they might endure to the end. Yet, in private conversations, these same sisters showed signs of weakness. One admitted that at her advanced age she no longer attended sacrament meeting nor felt the need to partake of the sacrament. Another no longer paid tithing, excusing herself by saying that she did not think the Lord expected it of her. A third sister had begun drinking tea, something she had never done previously. A fourth sister no longer asked for administration by the priesthood saying that she had lost faith in it. Sister Spafford then added, "Attendance at sacrament meeting, partaking of the sacrament, renewing one's covenants, the payment of tithing, observance of the Word of Wisdom, love of family, Priesthood administration—all basic laws of the gospel—had been abandoned by one or the other of these sisters with a feeling of justification; yet each had earnestly prayed that she might endure to the end. . . .

"Let us avoid the tendency to justify disobedience to God's commandments because of untoward personal circumstances just as we would avoid a plague. . . .

"Regardless of the adversities of life and the difficulties encountered in striving faithfully to endure, success can be achieved. . . . This, we can and must do if we would enjoy the blessings promised by the Lord to those who endure to the end." ("Those Who Endureth to the End," *Relief Society Magazine*, November 1967, pp. 805-9, as quoted in Relief Society Courses of Study, 1984, p. 31.)

To endure properly we cannot rationalize away the keeping of the commandments. We must keep them fully to the end of our lives.

We Need Not Be Perfect In This Life To Be Saved

Lest we be discouraged, let us understand that keeping the commandments faithfully does not mean that we are or will be perfect in this life. Elder Bruce R. McConkie gave us great encouragement when he said,

This is true gospel verity—that everyone in the Church who is on the straight and narrow path, who is striving and struggling and desiring to do what is right, though is far from perfect in this life; if he passes out of this life while he's on the straight and narrow, he's going to go on to eternal reward in his Father's kingdom.

We don't need to get a . . . feeling that you have to be perfect to be saved. You don't. There's only been one perfect person, and that's the Lord Jesus, but in order to be saved in the Kingdom of God and in order to pass the test of mortality, what you have to do is get on the straight and narrow path—thus charting a course leading to eternal life—and then, being on that path, pass out of this life in full fellowship. I'm not saying that you don't have to keep the commandments. *I'm saying you don't have to be perfect to be saved.* If you did, no one would be saved. The way it operates is this[:] you get on the path that's named the "straight and narrow." You do it by entering the gate of repentance and baptism. The straight and narrow path leads from the gate of repentance and baptism, a very great distance, to a reward that's called eternal life. If you're on that path and pressing forward, and you die, you'll never get off that path. There is no such thing as falling off the straight and narrow path in the life to come, and the reason is that this life is the time that is given to men to prepare for eternity. Now is the time and the day of your salvation, so if you're working zealously in this life—though you haven't fully overcome the world and you haven't done all you hoped you might do—you're still going to be saved. You don't have to do what Jacob said, "Go beyond the mark," You don't have to live a life that's truer than true. You don't have to have an excessive zeal that becomes fanatical and becomes unbalancing. What you have to do is stay in the mainstream of the Church and live as upright and decent people live in the Church—keeping the commandments, paying your tithing, serving in the organizations of the Church, loving the Lord, staying on the straight and narrow path. If you're on that path when death comes—because this is the time and the day appointed, this the probationary estate—you'll never fall off from it, and, for all practical purposes, your calling and election is made sure. ("The Probationary Test of Mortality," Address given at LDS Institute, University of Utah, January 10, 1982, p. 9, emphasis added.)

What a comforting doctrine this is! The Lord does not require us to achieve perfection in this life, simply to be on the road that *leads* to perfection.

President Heber J. Grant said, "I do not believe that any man lives up to his ideals, but if we are striving, if we are working, if we are trying, to the best of our ability, to improve day by day, then we are in the line of our duty. If we are seeking to remedy our own defects, if we are so living that we can ask God for light, for knowledge, for intelligence, and above all, for His Spirit, that we may overcome weaknesses, then, I can tell you, we are in the straight and narrow path that leads to life eternal." (*Gospel Standards*, pp. 184-85.)

Enduring to the end may sound like a "nose to the grindstone" experience, unless we realize that those same commandments that will lead us to eternal life will *also* make our earthly lives better. The Lord does not reserve all the blessings for the next world. In Mosiah 2:41 we are assured of the blessings that we will receive in *this* life if we keep the commandments: "I would desire that ye should consider on the blessed and happy state of those that keep the commandments of God. For behold, they are blessed in all things, both temporal and spiritual; and if they hold out faithful to the end they are received into heaven, that thereby they may dwell with God in a state of never-ending happiness."

Examples of Those Who Have Endured to the End

Let's look at the examples of some of those who have endured faithful to the end. Nephi was a man who endured great trials, but also received great blessings. Near the end of his life he engraved these words on the golden plates: "And I know that the Lord God will consecrate my prayers for the gain of my people. And the words which I have written in weakness will be made strong unto them; for it persuadeth them to do good; it maketh known unto them of their fathers; and it speaketh of Jesus, and persuadeth them to believe in him, and *to endure to the end*, which is life eternal. (2 Nephi 33:4, emphasis added.)

Nephi knew what it was to endure to the end, and he died firm in his faith that those who are "reconciled unto Christ, and enter into the narrow gate, and walk in the strait path which leads to life, and continue in the path until the end of the day of probation" would be "saved in his kingdom at that great and last day." (2 Nephi 33:9, 12.)

Enos was another Book of Mormon prophet who died firm in the faith, trusting that because he endured in faith to the end, he would inherit eternal life. He left us this touching final testimony:

And it came to pass that I began to be old. . . .

And I saw that I must soon go down to my grave, having been wrought upon by the power of God that I must preach and prophesy unto this people, and declare the word according to the truth which is in Christ. *And I have declared it in all my days*, and have rejoiced in it above that of the world.

And I soon go to the place of my rest, which is with my Redeemer; for I know that in him I shall rest. And I rejoice in the day when my mortal shall put on immortality, and shall stand before him; then shall I see his face with pleasure, and he will say unto me: Come

unto me, ye blessed, there is a place prepared for you in the
mansions of my Father. Amen. (Enos 1:25-27, emphasis added.)

How beautiful it would be to face the end of one's mortal probation
and anticipate seeing the Lord's face "with pleasure," knowing that one's
life has pleased Him!

The Prophet Joseph Smith talked of the Apostle Paul as one who
endured to the end and would inherit eternal life:

> That those who keep the commandments of the Lord and *walk in
> His statutes to the end*, are the only individuals permitted to sit at this
> glorious feast, is evident from the following items in Paul's last letter
> to Timothy, which was written just previous to his death,—he says:
> "I have fought a good fight, I have finished my course, I have kept
> the faith: henceforth there is laid up for me a crown of righteousness,
> which the Lord, the righteous Judge, shall give me at that day: and
> not to me only, but unto all them also that love His appearing." No
> one who believes the account, will doubt for a moment this assertion
> of Paul which was made, as he knew, just before he was to take his
> leave of this world. Though he once, according to his own word,
> persecuted the Church of God and wasted it, yet after embracing the
> faith, his labors were unceasing to spread the glorious news: and like
> a faithful soldier, when called to give his life in the cause which he
> had espoused, he laid it down, as he says, with an assurance of an
> eternal crown. . . . No one, we presume, will doubt the faithfulness
> of Paul to the end. None will say that he did not keep the faith, that
> he did not fight the good fight, that he did not preach and persuade
> to the last. And what was he to receive? A crown of righteousness.
> (*Teachings of the Prophet Joseph Smith*, pp. 63-64, emphasis added.)

Paul suffered many trials and afflictions in his lifetime. However he
was faithful to the end and received a crown of righteousness. The same
is true of Joseph Smith.

In our day there are many who endure faithfully, and die firm in the
hope of a glorious resurrection. This privilege is not reserved for
prophets or the heroes or heroines of scripture. President Thomas S.
Monson told this story of a faithful member of the Church who endured
to the end:

> The branch president of the Kingston [Canada] Branch of the
> Church, . . . Gustav Wacker was from the old country. He spoke

English with a thick accent. He never owned or drove a car. He plied the trade of a barber. The highlight of his day would be when he had the privilege of cutting the hair of a missionary. Never would there be a charge. Indeed, he would reach deep into his pockets and give the missionaries all of his tips for the day. If it were raining, as it often does in Kingston, President Wacker would call a taxi and send the missionaries to their apartment by taxi, while he himself, at day's end, would lock the small shop and walk home—in the driving rain.

I first met Gustav Wacker when I noticed that his tithing paid was far in excess of that expected from his potential income. My efforts to explain that the Lord required no more than ten percent as tithing fell on attentive but unconvinced ears. He simply responded that he loved to pay all he could to the Lord. It amounted to about half his income. His dear wife felt exactly as he did. Their unique manner of tithing payment continued throughout their earning lives.

Gustav and Margarete Wacker established a home that was a heaven. They were not blessed with children but mothered and fathered their many Church visitors. A sophisticated and learned leader from Ottawa told me, "I like to visit President Wacker. I come away refreshed in spirit and determined to ever live close to the Lord."

Did our Heavenly Father honor such abiding faith? The branch prospered. The membership outgrew the rented Slovakian Hall and moved into a modern and lovely chapel of their own. President and Sister Wacker had their prayers answered by serving a proselyting mission to their native Germany and later a temple mission to the beautiful temple in Washington, D.C. Then, just three months ago, his mission in mortality concluded, Gustav Wacker passed away peacefully while being held in the loving arms of his eternal companion. Only one label appears fitting for such an obedient and faithful servant: "Who honors God, God honors." (See 1 Sam. 2:30.) (CR, *Ensign*, November 1983, p. 20.)

I'd like to tell the story of another Latter-day Saint, a valiant sister in the Gospel. She was born in a small pioneer community. When she was a child, while helping a neighbor she fell from a ladder and injured her leg, causing her to be lame in that leg for the rest of her life.

At the age of thirty-three she was courted by a widower with seven children. They were married, and she gave birth to four children, while mothering her husband's children as well. She was always in poor health, and there were times when she was confined to her bed for long periods of time. From there she carried on the work of raising her children—preparing food for dinner, or ironing on a board stretched over her lap.

She insisted on strict obedience to the commandments from each of her children. Her children remember that it was easier just to tell her when they had done something wrong, because she would keep asking questions until the whole truth had come out. She instilled in them a love of the Gospel and a desire to serve the Lord.

Just before their 21st wedding anniversary, her husband died of cancer, leaving her with three teenage children at home, one son in the mission field, a mountain of medical bills to pay, and a farm to run. Her oldest son returned home for the funeral and said that he would stay home to help the family pay off the debt. She insisted that he return to his mission, trusting that the Lord would bless them. They were blessed. While many at that time had great difficulty making a living by farming, she and her children supported all three sons as they served missions.

As she grew older, her hearing failed, yet she could always be found attending her church meetings, even though she was unable to hear what was being said. Her grandchildren remember spending the night at her house and hearing her pray aloud, pleading for the blessings of the Lord in behalf of her children and grandchildren.

She passed away at the age of 89, and her life stands as a testimony that, despite difficult trials, she remained faithful to the end. She spent her life building the kingdom of God, and we trust that this promise will be fulfilled for her: "Blessed are they who shall seek to bring forth my Zion at that day, for . . . if they endure unto the end they shall be lifted up at the last day, and shall be saved in the everlasting kingdom of the Lamb." (1 Nephi 13:37.) This brave woman is my mother, Lula Payne Christensen.

The Lord Will Sustain Us In Our Trials

The Lord has promised us that we will never have more trials than we can bear. Elder Robert E. Wells said, "Sometimes we go many years with no problems, and then they seem to come all at once, and the burdens seem to be more than we can bear. But through it all, we have two main strengths to rely on: (1) We knew before we came that it would be like this, yet we wanted to come because the blessings of remaining faithful to the end would earn us eternal exaltation. (2) We will never be tempted beyond our ability to resist." ("How Well Can You Fly It When Everything Goes Wrong?" *New Era*, June 1978, p. 5.)

It will also help us if we remember that all our trials will eventually be for our good. President Brigham Young explained how our trials advance our quest for exaltation:

> Every trial and experience you have passed through is necessary for your salvation. . . .
> Every vicissitude we pass through is necessary for experience and example, and for preparation to enjoy that reward which is for the faithful. . . .
> Joseph [Smith] could not have been perfected, though he had lived a thousand years, if he had received no persecution. If he had lived a thousand years, and led this people, and preached the Gospel without persecution, he would not have been perfected as well as he was at the age of thirty-nine years." (*Discourses of Brigham Young*, pp. 348, 351.)

The Prophet Joseph Smith was perfected and refined by his sufferings. His afflictions were particularly great while he was in the Liberty Jail. As he felt the weight of these sufferings bearing down upon him, he cried out to God, and received this reply: "My son, peace be unto thy soul; thine adversity and thine afflictions shall be but a small moment;

"And then, if thou endure it well, God shall exalt thee on high; thou shalt triumph over all thy foes." (D&C 121:7-8.)

We, also, can take courage from the Lord's reply. We can trust that the Lord will strengthen us, and that we can eventually triumph over all our foes, too.

In the Doctrine and Covenants the Lord says, "Be faithful and diligent in keeping the commandments of God, and I will encircle thee in the arms of my love." (D&C 6:20.) Our daughter and her husband explain that in their hour of deepest trial, the sudden death of a toddler son, the Lord took them in His arms and cradled them, as He promises the obedient. All of us touched by the anguish of this event wonder how it could have been endured without the hope offered by Jesus Christ, and promise of life hereafter. And yet, this was a time of heightened spiritual sensitivity; the young grieving parents were granted personal revelation, manifestations of eternal truths, and foreknowledge of things to come. The agony was not without compensation, and they wait in grief and faith for understanding which will only come in another realm.

If we submit cheerfully and with patience to our trials, the Lord will "consecrate [our] afflictions for [our] gain." (2 Nephi 2:2.) No pain that we suffer, no trial that we experience is wasted. Sister Ardeth Greene Kapp, former General President of the Young Women, writes:

> In view of this challenging time for which we have been reserved, we can expect some pain, discouragement, disappointments, trials, and temptations. When we choose to follow the Savior, we can expect some suffering, some loneliness, and some injustice. But in times such as this, it is well to remember the words of Elder Orson F. Whitney: "No pain that we suffer, no trial that we experience is wasted. It ministers to our education, to the development of such qualities as patience, faith, fortitude and humility. All that we suffer and all that we endure, especially when we endure it patiently, builds up our characters, purifies our hearts, expands our souls, and makes us more tender and charitable, more worthy to be called the children of God. It is through sorrow and suffering, toil and tribulation, that we gain the education that we come here to acquire and which will make us more like our Father and Mother in Heaven." (*The Joy of the Journey*, p. 139.)

Job suffered more than most of us will ever suffer, and yet he remained faithful. He lost all his property. His children all perished in an accident. His body was covered with boils. His friends and his wife accused him of bringing these punishments upon himself. Still, Job did not lose faith in the Lord, and testified, "I know that my redeemer liveth, and that he shall stand at the latter day upon the earth: And though after my skin worms destroy this body, yet in my flesh shall I see God." (Job 19:25-26.)

James, in his epistle, spoke of Job and the importance of enduring to the end when he said, "Take, my brethren, the prophets, who have spoken in the name of the Lord, for an example of suffering affliction, and of patience.

"Behold, we count them happy which endure. Ye have heard of the patience of Job, and have seen the end of the Lord; that the Lord is very pitiful, and of tender mercy." (James 5:11.)

We must not allow our trials to destroy our faith, or cause us to turn against the Lord or His Church. We must believe in His promises that He will help us overcome all of our trials. In the Doctrine and Covenants He gives us a promise that He will sustain us in all our adversity: "Be patient in afflictions, for thou shalt have many; but endure them, for, lo, I am with thee, even unto the end of thy days." (D&C 24:8.)

Enduring valiantly brings great blessings, while those who succumb to their trials taste the bitterness of failure, and never gain the blessings the Lord has in store for the faithful.

President Howard W. Hunter assured us:

Despair, doom, and discouragement are not acceptable views of life for a Latter-day Saint. . . . There have always been some difficulties in mortal life, and there always will be. But knowing what we know, and living as we are supposed to live, there really is no place, no excuse, for pessimism and despair. . . . I reassure you that things have been worse, and they will always get better. They always do— especially when we live and love the gospel of Jesus Christ. . . . Every individual person has a particular set of challenges which sometimes seem to be earmarked for us individually. . . . I acknowledge that I have faced a few. . . . When these experiences humble us and refine us and teach us and bless us, they can be powerful instruments in the hands of God to make us better people, to make us more grateful, more loving, and more considerate of other people in their own times of difficulty." ("An Anchor to the Souls of Men," *Ensign*, October 1993, pp. 70-73.)

In her fine book, *The Joy of the Journey*, Sister Kapp talks about how the Lord is always with us:

As we move forward on our individual paths with our common goals through our valleys and our mountains, we can expect to be refined through the furnace of affliction. (1 Nephi 20:10.) Let us remember the promise of the Lord: "I will go before your face. I will be on your right hand and on your left, and my Spirit shall be in your hearts, and mine angels round about you, to bear you up." (D&C 84:88.) A well-known story, titled "Footprints," seems to convey the message we're talking about:

"One night I had a dream. I dreamed I was walking along the beach with the Lord, and across the sky flashed scenes from my life. For each scene I noticed two sets of footprints in the sand. One belonged to me and the other to the Lord.

"When the last scene of my life flashed before me, I looked back at the footprints in the sand. I noticed that many times along the path one set of footprints. I also noticed that it happened at the very lowest and saddest times in my life. This really bothered me, and I questioned the Lord about it.

"Lord, you said that once I decided to follow you, you would walk with me all the way, but I have noticed that during the most troublesome times in my life, there is only one set of footprints. I don't understand why in times when I needed you most, you should leave me."

"The Lord replied, 'My precious, precious child. I love you and would never, never leave you during your times of trial and suffering. When you saw only one set of footprints, it was then that I carried you.'" (p. 173.)

As we seek to remain faithful to the end, our lives will be blessed and we will gain a firm testimony that all the blessings the Lord has promised us will be fulfilled. Elder Melvin J. Ballard had this glorious experience that gave him powerful motivation to endure to the end:

I found myself one evening in the dreams of the night in that sacred building, the temple. After a season of prayer and rejoicing I was informed that I should have the privilege of entering into one of those rooms, to meet a glorious Personage, and, as I entered the room I saw, seated on a raised platform, the most glorious Being my eyes have ever beheld or that I ever conceived existed in all the eternal worlds. As I approached to be introduced, he arose and stepped towards me with extended arms, and he smiled as he softly spoke my name. If I shall live to be a million years old, I shall never forget that smile. He took me into His arms and kissed me, pressed me to his bosom, and blessed me, until the marrow of my bones seemed to melt! When he had finished, I fell at his feet, and, as I bathed them with my tears and kisses, I saw the prints of the nails in the feet of the Redeemer of the world. The feeling that I had in the presence of him who hath all things in his hands, to have his love, his affection, and his blessing was such that if I ever can receive that of which I had but a foretaste, I would give all that I am, all that I ever hope to be, to feel what I then felt!

. . . I see Jesus not now upon the cross. I do not see his brow pierced with thorns nor his hands torn with the nails, but I see him smiling, with extended arms, saying to us all: "Come unto me!" (*Sermons and Missionary Services of Melvin J. Ballard*, pp. 156-157.)

Can you imagine the wonderful experience of being enfolded in the arms of the Savior? What glorious love would fill your heart! Let's live with the same desire expressed by Elder Ballard—that we would give all that we are or ever hope to be, to feel what he felt when he had this experience in the Savior's presence.

Let us be like Enos, Job, Gustav Wacker, and Lula Christensen. Let us live so that at the end of our lives we can say with Paul, "I have fought a good fight, I have finished my course, I have kept the faith: Henceforth there is laid up for me a crown of righteousness, which the Lord, the righteous judge, shall give me at that day." (2 Timothy 4:7-8.)

Determination Brings Success

The intent of this book and its companion volume has been to discover the principles that guide us in our personal quest for exaltation. Along the road we have discussed the gospel tools that help us have a better life, which are also the means to achieve that final and greatest goal, exaltation in the celestial kingdom of God.

We have learned the importance of governing our thoughts, inasmuch as they decide our actions and what we ultimately become. We have discussed specific and powerful ways to control thoughts, ways to expel evil from our minds, how to choose right over wrong, and how to draw power from heavenly sources.

We have unmasked Satan, the father of lies, so that we can arm ourselves in the fight to overcome evil.

We have reviewed the basic principles of the gospel, the "gate by which ye should enter" the road leading to eternal life. Faith, repentance, baptism, and the gift of the Holy Ghost are the basic principles that put us upon that road.

We have also explored many of the elements that produce purity of heart—prayer, love of God and love of fellowmen, service in the Lord's work, daily scripture study, forgiving others, and overcoming pride and anger.

As we move onward with our eyes on our eternal destination, we develop spirituality, endeavor to purify our hearts, understand the significance of the temple experience, and learn of sanctification. We determine that we will endure to the end.

It is that determination we would like now to examine.

Carry On

Webster's dictionary defines the word "determined" as "having one's mind made up; decided; resolved; . . . resolute; unwavering." (*Webster's New World Dictionary of the American Language*, p. 384.)

Developing this attitude of determination will give us the fortitude necessary to keep ourselves on the road that we are striving to walk. Certainly it is not an easy road. Difficulties come into every life, and walking the "strait and narrow path" will not prevent adversity from entering our lives. We are to carry on with determination no matter what befalls us. Elder Marvin J. Ashton pointed out that the Savior encountered greater affliction than all of us, and yet carried on: "Jesus is the Christ. He is our redeemer, our Lord and Savior and friend. We constantly give thanks through deeds and prayer for his unmatched example of carrying on under circumstances that caused him to bleed from every pore and anguish in the misunderstanding and misconduct of his associates. *Joy and happiness come through determination and the practice of carrying on under all conditions.* May God help us to so do and reap the rewards in this present day." (CR, *Ensign*, November 1989, p. 37, emphasis added.)

We should determine ahead that we will carry on through the gravel and glory of life, committing ourselves to follow Jesus Christ. He led the way by giving us an example of a perfect life. He still leads the way by daily guidance. Feeling the elation of meeting challenges and the relief of overcoming difficulties are some of the rewards of determination. His course also helps us avoid many struggles and disappointments.

We are strengthened and directed by using gospel tools such as praying, reading the scriptures and other good books daily, attending our meetings, helping the less fortunate, magnifying our callings in the Church, being good mothers and fathers and raising righteous children, and living by the Spirit. Our determination to endure to the end is also thus strengthened.

Sister Ardeth G. Kapp, Young Women's General President, spoke of the importance of hope as we strive to carry on:

> I hear your messages, young women. I hear you with my ears and with my heart. I want to reach out to you and share with you what I have learned over the years about *hope*. I would give it to you if I could, but I've learned that it only comes from your own upward

climb. You see, this brief time away from our heavenly home and parents is a time when we are given our agency for the purpose of being tried and tested in every way (see 2 Nephi 2:24-28). You should expect some "down" days and some hard tests. Learn from them. Grow from them. Be stronger because of them. Whenever I face things that I don't understand, I repeat in my mind the words of a song I learned years ago when I wondered if my prayers were being heard and I needed hope to carry on:

> In the furnace God may prove thee,
> Thence to bring thee forth more bright,
> But can never cease to love thee;
> Thou art precious in his sight.
> God is with thee, God is with thee;
> Thou shalt triumph in his might.
> (*Hymns*, 1985, no. 43.)
> (CR, *Ensign*, November 1986, pp. 87-88.)

God has a plan for each of us. We should strive to pass the test which God has laid out for us without complaining, because He arranged the tests to fit the needs and abilities of each of us personally. Our trials are designed to strengthen us in the way we need, like a personal fitness coach. Father in Heaven knows us personally. He loves us personally, and he wants us to succeed, to "pass the test."

We agonized with our son and his dear wife as she went through the painful physical and emotional devastation of fighting cancer. Her faith was a light not only to us, but to the doctors and nurses who cared for her. We were touched when she said, "The Lord knows I belong to Him. If He takes me home, I will be glad to go. If he leaves me here to finish bringing up my family, I will like that even better. I am in His arms." Her little son, staying at our home while Mom was in the hospital, prayed with like faith: "Bless my mom that she may be healed from this affliction." Then, almost an addendum, "And bless the rest of us, that we will be able to handle this." The rest of us echoed that prayer very fervently, as well. The family is not yet finished with this test, and we still pray both prayers. We have learned much about adversity, about helping, about enduring, and about love.

Be assured, your Father in Heaven does love you. He wants to help you, to comfort you, and to put His loving arms around you. He knows that you have hard times. He aches for you, but He knows the reason hard times come. Even though there will be heavy loads, if you are determined and put your trust in God, you will become stronger and you will keep advancing.

And remember, there are lots of warm, sunny days as well. Take the joy where you find it, and glory in it!

Determination Defeats Temptation

One kind of determination that will help us remain faithful in all circumstances is to decide in our minds before the temptation occurs what we will do when tempted. When we do this, we avoid a lot of pressure when the moment arrives.

Making these decisions ahead of time is like living in the farm home I grew up in. My mother grew a huge garden, and she cultivated all kinds of good things to eat. It was hard work to plant, water, weed, hoe, water, weed, and harvest these good things. It was work again to prepare these good foods for storage: pick, clean and prepare the produce, carry up the bottles and scrub them, fill them with the fresh food, and process it in the pressure cooker over a wood and coal fire. But in the winter, there were shelves filled with beets, beans, peas, corn, peaches, pears, applesauce, gooseberries, rhubarb punch, pickles, tomatoes. There were cellars filled with fresh apples, potatoes, carrots, squash, cabbage—now, with some fried chicken out of the henhouse, could you make a Sunday dinner from that pantry? Oh, yes!

Deciding before you get into the circumstance is like filling those shelves, crocks, and cellars with all that food. When winter came, when guests came, when the kids came home from school, when troubles came, there was plenty. Determination had already taken care of the situation. Likewise, it may require a lot of effort to determine ahead of time what we will do, but when temptation comes, when need arises, we have plenty of strength on reserve, power in storage, to see us safely through.

President Spencer W. Kimball said:

I have mentioned at this pulpit before some determinations made early in my life, which decisions were such a help to me because I did not have to remake those decisions perpetually. We can push some things away from us once and have done with them . . . without having to brood and redecide a hundred times what it is we will do and what we will not do.

Indecision and discouragement are climates in which the adversary loves to function, for he can inflict so many casualties among mankind in those settings. My young brothers, if you have not done so yet, decide to decide! . . .

When I was young, I made up my mind unalterably that I would never taste tea, coffee, tobacco, or liquor. I found that this rigid determination saved me many times throughout my varied experiences. There were many occasions when I could have sipped or touched or sampled, but the unalterable determination firmly established gave me good reason and good strength to resist.

The time to decide on a mission is long before it becomes a matter of choosing between a mission and an athletic scholarship. The time to decide on temple marriage is before one has become attached to a boy friend or girl friend who does not share that objective. The time to decide on a policy of strict honesty is before the store clerk gives you too much change. The time to decide against using drugs is before a friend you like teases you for being afraid or pious. The time to decide that we will settle for nothing less than an opportunity to live eternally with our Father is now, so that every choice we make will be affected by our determination to let nothing interfere with attaining that ultimate goal. (*The Teachings of Spencer W. Kimball*, p. 164.)

If you have not yet fully committed yourself to the Lord, we challenge you to decide to decide right now. At this moment, make a permanent, irreversible decision to serve the Lord and keep His commandments the rest of your life, so that you may live eternally with your Father in Heaven.

Now, having made this decision, don't you feel good inside? We promise you that this commitment will make your life more joyful and make your burdens easier to bear. We know this from the scriptures, the words of the living prophets, and personal experience.

Peter Vidmar, Olympic gymnastics champion and member of the Church, writes of an experience where his early commitment to do what is right helped him in a difficult, very public situation:

Let's not settle for mediocrity. Let's always try our best. Let us decide now what type of person we want to be, and when a difficult situation comes along we will be prepared to pass the test.

I feel very blessed that at a young age I was taught the importance of keeping the Word of Wisdom. I committed myself to keeping that commandment. I remember a very prestigious competition in Germany, when I won the vaulting event. As I stood on the victory stand, I received a gold medal, flowers, and gifts. I couldn't have been more pleased.

Before walking off the stand, I noticed another individual coming forward with a silver cup, and I thought, "How great! Another prize!" But as the presenter moved closer with this cup, I noticed it was full of wine.

Turning to my German friend and competitor, I asked what it was for, and he explained that tradition calls for the champion to drink out of the cup and to pass it to the next athlete.

I told him, "Well, I don't drink."

He responded with: "Then just take a little sip and hand it to the next person."

Then I explained, "No, it's against my religion, and I can't even take a sip."

My friend proceeded to explain to the officials in German that I wouldn't drink it, but for some reason they insisted I take the cup.

So I took the cup and held it high in the air for the crowd to see. And then, without taking a sip, I handed it down to the next person. I admit that amidst the laughter of the crowd I felt a bit embarrassed, but I felt proud that it was easy to say no. I believe that if we make proper decisions before we are faced with a temptation, we will find it much easier to resist that temptation. (CR, *Ensign*, May 1985, p. 40.)

By making up our minds as to what we will do before the temptation presents itself, we secure ourselves against failing. Another way of safe-guarding ourselves against temptation is to make a commitment in our minds that when a temptation comes we will pray until it leaves. If we pray, God will send us the strength to overcome.

"There hath no temptation taken you but such as is common to man: but God is faithful, who will not suffer you to be tempted above that ye are able; but will with the temptation also make a way to escape, that ye may be able to bear it." (1 Corinthians 10:13.)

God will make a way for us to escape temptation. If we put our faith in Him, stand determined, and pray for strength, we can withstand the temptations that come in our lives.

President Spencer W. Kimball said, "The difference between the good man and the bad man is not that one had the temptations and the other was spared them. It is that one kept himself fortified, and resisted temptation, and the other placed himself in compromising places and conditions and rationalized the situations." (*The Miracle of Forgiveness*, pp. 231-32.)

When we place ourselves in compromising situations and rationalize our presence there, we are giving Satan an open invitation to tempt us. Satan is a dirty fighter. He doesn't keep any rules. He may, sooner or later, get us with a low blow. The risk is too great. We must keep ourselves reinforced and stand firm against Satan's temptations at all times.

The time to decide on the route we will take is before we are at the fork in the road. President N. Eldon Tanner said, "Temptations come to all, but long before we are faced with them, we . . . must have determined what our course will be. It is too late if we wait until the moment of temptation before making our decision." (CR, *Ensign*, December 1971, p. 34.)

Keeping an eternal perspective on our lives will help us to be determined to do what is right at all times. If we remember that our most important goal is eternal life, it will make some decisions easier that could, if made wrongly, lead us down the wrong paths.

Peter Vidmar also spoke of the importance of perspective, saying:

> I would like to emphasize keeping a proper perspective on our goals. Let us never lose sight of the gospel in pursuing our temporal ambitions. We didn't come to this world to become Olympic champions, or great doctors, lawyers, or businessmen, or to become rich and famous. We came here to prove ourselves worthy of returning back to the presence of our Heavenly Father. We came here to set and reach the highest goal possible.
>
> I know how hard I worked to compete in the Olympics. At times I trained as much as six hours a day, six days a week. It sometimes seemed it took all of my energy and resources. I think I'm beginning to realize how serious my commitment to the Lord's work must be if I am to receive God's greatest gift. Indeed, it will take all of my talent, energy, and resources—my heart, might, mind, and strength —to earn and receive eternal life.
>
> Just imagine what it's like to be an Olympic champion! Imagine the feeling of having that medal placed around your neck as you stand on the victory platform. It's a feeling I can't describe. But let's realize one more thing. We can all have an experience infinitely greater than that. If we prove worthy, we will return to our Heavenly Father's presence. (CR, *Ensign*, May 1985, p. 40.)

As Brother Vidmar says, passing the test, proving worthy, is the most important thing we can do in this life. "We will prove them herewith, to see if they will do all things whatsoever the Lord their God shall command them." (Abraham 3:25.) If we remember that *this* is the purpose of our lives on earth, we will be more likely to spend our lives working with determination toward goals that will result in our exaltation.

"Plant Your Feet Firmly on the Path to the Celestial Kingdom"

There are difficulties in this life. There are problems and heartaches. However, never forget that each trial successfully overcome makes us stronger.

Sister Ardeth G. Kapp made this encouraging and inspiring statement: "With daily prayer, scripture study, and our feet firmly planted on the road to the celestial kingdom, we have a 'perfect brightness of hope' (2 Nephi 31:20). There will be some steep climbs ahead, but our Lord and Savior Jesus Christ has covenanted and promised to climb with each of us every step of the way. Think of it! Young women, covenant this day, this very day, if you haven't already, to plant your feet firmly on the path to the celestial kingdom. Lift up your heart, lift up your heart, and let your soul rejoice, and never, never, never give up." (CR, *Ensign*, November 1986, pp. 88-89.)

When I was a young man my father was called to the other side of the veil to help his father do missionary work. The last words I heard my father speak were, speaking to my mother, "I am turning the reins over to you."

My mother carried on beautifully. Under her motherly leadership we three boys went on missions, and all four of her children were married in the temple. We have all remained active in the Church, and are rearing our families to do the same.

Elder Marvin J. Ashton recounts the last earthly moments of Elder Bruce R. McConkie:

> Just before our esteemed, honored Apostle and special friend of Aaronic Priesthood and their leaders worldwide, Elder Bruce R. McConkie, passed away nearly four and one-half years ago, with his sweetheart and eternal companion, Amelia, at his bedside, some very significant words were shared. As Sister McConkie held his hand during his final earthly minutes, she asked, "Bruce, do you have a

message for me?" Though weak and expiring, he responded in a firm voice his last words, "Carry on."

Here was one of God's choicest servants, who had studied, pondered, and written as extensively on the life and mission of Jesus Christ as anyone else in his time, using these two powerful words for direction and encouragement. Sister McConkie has since shared with me the great importance and strength of "carry on" as time has passed. Elder McConkie knew as a special witness the importance of, "Then said Jesus to those Jews which believed on him, If ye continue in my word, then are ye my disciples indeed;

"And ye shall know the truth, and the truth shall make you free." (John 8:31-32.) Salvation and exaltation are here emphasized as being based primarily upon commitment and enduring.

Enduring, or carrying on, is not just a matter of tolerating circumstances and hanging in there, but of pressing forward. I know that's what most of us find difficult—to endure joyfully. (CR, *Ensign*, November 1989, p. 36.)

A full commitment to the gospel will enable us to endure to the end. This means a determination to serve God with all our heart, might, mind, and strength, showing our love to Him by keeping His commandments and building His kingdom here on earth. It includes praying to Him morning and night, asking for strength to keep his commandments, and asking for inspiration and revelation to solve our daily problems. Such a course will entitle us to the constant companionship of the Holy Ghost, that we may be protected and guided, cleansed and purified, and made ready to live with our Father in Heaven.

Many times as I have read the Book of Mormon, my eyes have watered because the Spirit was so strong bearing testimony of its truthfulness. Father in Heaven has been extremely kind and generous to me. He has given me a loving, sweet, faithful wife whom I love with all my heart, and wonderful children. I feel blessed beyond measure. I am grateful that I feel His Spirit in my life daily, encouraging, leading, and comforting me, and giving me peace of mind.

I have a testimony that God lives, that Jesus is the Christ, the Son of God, the Savior of the world. Joseph Smith is a true prophet. Through him, the Kingdom of God was restored upon the earth, even The Church of Jesus Christ of Latter-day Saints. A true prophet leads this Church on the earth today. The Spirit has revealed this to me.

It is my hope that this book will help you to develop a stronger personal testimony of the gospel, make important changes in your life, and come to taste the sweetness that I have found in relying on the Lord and conforming my life more closely to His will. I know that these principles are true. They will help you fulfill your mission on this earth and look forward with hope to return to live with your Father in Heaven. With the help of the Lord, you can do it!

Works Cited

Ballard, Melvin J. *Sermons and Missionary Services of Melvin J. Ballard.* Compiled by Bryant S. Hinckley. Salt Lake City: Deseret Book Co., 1949.

———. *Three Degrees of Glory.* A discourse given September 22, 1922, in the Ogden Tabernacle. Salt Lake City: Magazine Printing & Publishing, 1975.

Bangerter, W. Grant. "Enjoy It." *Brigham Young University 1982-83 Devotional and Fireside Speeches.* Provo: Brigham Young University Press.

Benson, Ezra Taft. *Come Unto Christ.* Salt Lake City: Deseret Book Co., 1983.

———. *The Teachings of Ezra Taft Benson.* Salt Lake City: Bookcraft, 1988.

———. "The Law of Chastity." *Brigham Young University 1987-88 Devotional and Fireside Speeches.* Provo: Brigham Young University Press.

Brockbank, Bernard P. "Love Versus Contention." Address at Brigham Young University, January 14, 1969. Provo: Brigham Young University.

Cannon, George Q. *Gospel Truth.* Edited by Jerreld L. Newquist. Salt Lake City: Deseret Book Co., Classics in Mormon Literature Series, 1987.

Clark, James R., compiler. *Messages of the First Presidency.* 6 vols. Salt Lake City: Bookcraft, Inc., 1975.

Cook, Gene R. *Living by the Power of Faith.* Salt Lake City: Deseret Book Co., 1991.

Covey, Stephen R. *Spiritual Roots of Human Relations.* Salt Lake City: Deseret Book Co., 1970.

Craven, Rulon G. *Faith For A Better Life.* Salt Lake City: Bookcraft, Inc., 1991.

———. *The Pursuit of Perfection.* Salt Lake City: Bookcraft, Inc., 1988.

Grant, Heber J. *Gospel Standards.* Salt Lake City: An Improvement Era Publication, 1943.

History of the Church of Jesus Christ of Latter-day Saints. 7 vols. 2nd ed. revised. Salt Lake City: Deseret Book Co., 1980.

Holy Scriptures, The, Inspired Version. Translated by Joseph Smith Jr. Reorganized Church of Jesus Christ of Latter-day Saints. Independence, Missouri: Herald Publishing House. Tenth printing, 1964.

Hunter, Howard W. "Fear Not, Little Flock." *Brigham Young University 1988-89 Devotional Speeches of the Year*. Provo: Brigham Young University Press, 1989.

Hymns of the Church of Jesus Christ of Latter-day Saints. Salt Lake City: The Church of Jesus Christ of Latter-day Saints, 1985.

Journal of Discourses. 26 vols. Liverpool and London, 1867; Photo Lithographic Reprint, Salt Lake City, 1966.

Kapp, Ardeth Greene. *The Joy of the Journey*. Salt Lake City: Deseret Book Co., 1992.

Kimball, Spencer W. *Faith Precedes the Miracle*. Salt Lake City: Deseret Book Co., 1978.

———. *The Miracle of Forgiveness*. Salt Lake City: Bookcraft, Inc., 1969.

———. *The Teachings of Spencer W. Kimball*. Edited by Edward L. Kimball. Salt Lake City: Bookcraft, Inc., 1982.

———. "What I Hope You Will Teach My Grandchildren And All Others of the Youth of Zion." Address to Seminary and Institute Personnel, Brigham Young University, July 11, 1966. Provo: Brigham Young University Press.

Lee, Harold B. *Stand Ye in Holy Places*. Salt Lake City: Deseret Book Co., 1974.

Ludlow, Daniel H., ed. *Latter-day Prophets Speak*. Salt Lake City: Bookcraft, Inc., 1948. Collector's edition printing 1988.

Maxwell, Neal A. *Meek and Lowly*. Salt Lake City: Deseret Book Co., 1989.

———. *Notwithstanding My Weakness*. Salt Lake City: Deseret Book., 1981.

———. *That My Family Should Partake*. Salt Lake City: Deseret Book Co., 1974.

McConkie, Bruce R. *A New Witness for the Articles of Faith*. Salt Lake City: Deseret Book Co., 1985.

———. *Doctrinal New Testament Commentary*. 3 vols. Salt Lake City: Bookcraft, 1992.

———. *Mormon Doctrine*. Salt Lake City: Bookcraft, Inc., 1966.

———. *The Millennial Messiah*. Salt Lake City: Deseret Book Co., 1987.

————. *The Promised Messiah*. Salt Lake City: Deseret Book Co., 1978.

————. "Jesus Christ and Him Crucified." Address at Brigham Young University, September 5, 1976. Provo: Brigham Young University Press.

————. "Lord, Increase Our Faith." Address at Brigham Young University, October 31, 1967. Provo: Brigham Young University Press.

————. "The Probationary Test of Mortality." Address given at LDS Institute, University of Utah, Jan. 10, 1982. Salt Lake City: University Institute of Religion.

McConkie, Joseph Fielding and Robert L. Millett. *The Holy Ghost*. Salt Lake City: Bookcraft, Inc., 1989.

McKay, David O. *Gospel Ideals*. Salt Lake City: The Improvement Era, 1953.

————. *Pathways to Happiness*. Compiled by Llewelyn R. McKay. Salt Lake City: Bookcraft, Inc., 1963.

————. *Secrets of a Happy Life*. Compiled by Llewelyn R. McKay. Salt Lake City: Bookcraft, 1967.

Morrison, Alexander B. *Visions of Zion*. Salt Lake City: Deseret Book Co., 1993.

Oaks, Dallin H. *Pure in Heart*. Salt Lake City: Bookcraft, 1988.

Pace, George W. *Our Search to Know the Lord*. Salt Lake City: Deseret Book Co., 1988.

Pace, Glenn L. *Spiritual Plateaus*. Salt Lake City: Deseret Book Co., 1991.

————. *Spiritual Revival*. Salt Lake City: Deseret Book Co., 1993.

Packer, Boyd K. *Teach Ye Diligently*. Salt Lake City: Deseret Book Co., 1975.

————. *That All May Be Edified*. Salt Lake City: Bookcraft, Inc., 1989.

Petersen, Mark E. *Why the Religious Life*. Salt Lake City: Deseret Book Co., 1966.

Peterson, H. Burke. *A Glimpse of Glory*. Salt Lake City: Bookcraft, Inc., 1986.

Pratt, Parley Parker. *Key to the Science of Theology*. 5th ed. Salt Lake City: George Q. Cannon & Sons Co. Publishers, 1891.

Roberts, B. H. *A Comprehensive History of the Church of Jesus Christ of Latter-day Saints, Vol. 1*. Published by the Church. Salt Lake City, Deseret News Press, 1930.

————. *The Gospel*. Published with *Man's Relationship to Deity*. Salt Lake City: Cannon & Sons, 1901.

Romney, Marion G. *Look to God and Live*. Compiled by George J. Romney. Salt Lake City: Deseret Book Co., 1973.

Sill, Sterling W. *What Doth it Profit*. Salt Lake City: Bookcraft, Inc., 1965.

Smith, George Albert. *Sharing the Gospel with Others*. Salt Lake City: Deseret Book Co., 1950.

Smith, Henry A. *Matthew Cowley: Man of Faith*. Salt Lake City: Bookcraft, Inc., 1954.

Smith, Hyrum M., and Sjodahl, Janne M. *Doctrine and Covenants Commentary*. Revised ed. Salt Lake City: Deseret Book Co., 1954.

Smith, Joseph. *Teachings of the Prophet Joseph Smith*. Selected by Joseph Fielding Smith. Salt Lake City: Deseret Book Co., 1976.

Smith, Joseph F. *Gospel Doctrine*. Salt Lake City: Deseret Book Co., Classics in Mormon Literature Series, 1989.

Smith, Joseph Fielding. *Doctrines of Salvation*. 3 vols. Compiled by Bruce R. McConkie. Salt Lake City: Bookcraft, Inc., 1954.

Snow, Lorenzo. *The Teachings of Lorenzo Snow*. Compiled by Clyde J. Williams. Salt Lake City: Bookcraft, Inc., 1984.

Stuy, Brian H., compiler. *Collected Discourses Delivered by President Wilford Woodruff*, et. al. 5 vols. 2nd ed. B. H. S. Publishing, 1993.

Talmage, James E. *Jesus The Christ*. Salt Lake City: Deseret Book Co., 1945.

———. *The Articles of Faith*. Salt Lake City: The Church of Jesus Christ of Latter-day Saints, reprinted 1977.

Temples of the Church of Jesus Christ of Latter-day Saints. Salt Lake City: The Ensign, 1981.

Webster's Third New International Dictionary. 3 vols. Chicago: Encyclopedia Britannica, Inc., 1981.

Widtsoe, John A. *A Rational Theology*. 7th ed. Salt Lake City: Deseret Book Co., 1966.

———. *In a Sunlit Land: The Autobiography of John A. Widtsoe*. Salt Lake City: Published by Milton R. Hunter, G. Homer Durham, Deseret News Press, 1953.

———. *Joseph Smith, Seeker After Truth, Prophet of God*. Salt Lake City: Bookcraft, Inc., 1991.

Woodruff, Wilford. *Leaves from My Journal*. 4th ed. Salt Lake City: The Deseret News, 1909.

Young, Brigham. *Discourses of Brigham Young*. Compiled by John A. Widtsoe. Salt Lake City: Deseret Book Co., 1978.

Young, S. Dilworth. "Covenants and Commandments." Address at Brigham Young University, August 3, 1971. Provo: Brigham Young University Press.

Other Sources Cited:

Conference Reports. Salt Lake City: The Church of Jesus Christ of Latter-day Saints. Month and year cited in text.

Deacons Course A and Course B Manual. Salt Lake City: The Church of Jesus Christ of Latter-day Saints, 1984.

"Duties and Blessings of the Priesthood." Basic Manual for Priesthood Holders, part A. Salt Lake City: The Church of Jesus Christ of Latter-day Saints, 1980.

Ensign. Salt Lake City: The Church of Jesus Christ of Latter-day Saints. Month and year cited in text. Conference Reports designated CR.

LDS Church News, News of the Church of Jesus Christ of Latter-day Saints. Salt Lake City: Deseret News. Articles cited in text.

Relief Society Courses of Study 1979-80; 1984; 1985; 1989. Salt Lake City: The Church of Jesus Christ of Latter-day Saints.

Standard Works, Scriptures of The Church of Jesus Christ of Latter-day Saints: Holy Bible, King James Version; The Book of Mormon, Another Testament of Jesus Christ; The Doctrine and Covenants; The Pearl of Great Price; Salt Lake City: 1981.

The Friend. Salt Lake City: The Church of Jesus Christ of Latter-day Saints. Month and year cited in text.

The Improvement Era. Salt Lake City: The Church of Jesus Christ of Latter-day Saints. Month and year cited in text.

"The Latter-day Saint Woman." Basic Manual for Women, Part B, Salt Lake City: The Church of Jesus Christ of Latter-day Saints, 1979.

The Life and Teachings of Jesus and His Apostles. Prepared by the Church Educational System. Salt Lake City: The Church of Jesus Christ of Latter-day Saints, 1979.

The New Era. Salt Lake City: The Church of Jesus Christ of Latter-day Saints. Month and year cited in text.

The Relief Society Magazine. Salt Lake City: General Board of Relief Society of The Church of Jesus Christ of Latter-day Saints. Month and year cited in text.

"Walk In His Ways." Basic Manual for Children, Parts A & B. Salt Lake City: The Church of Jesus Christ of Latter-day Saints, 1987.

Index